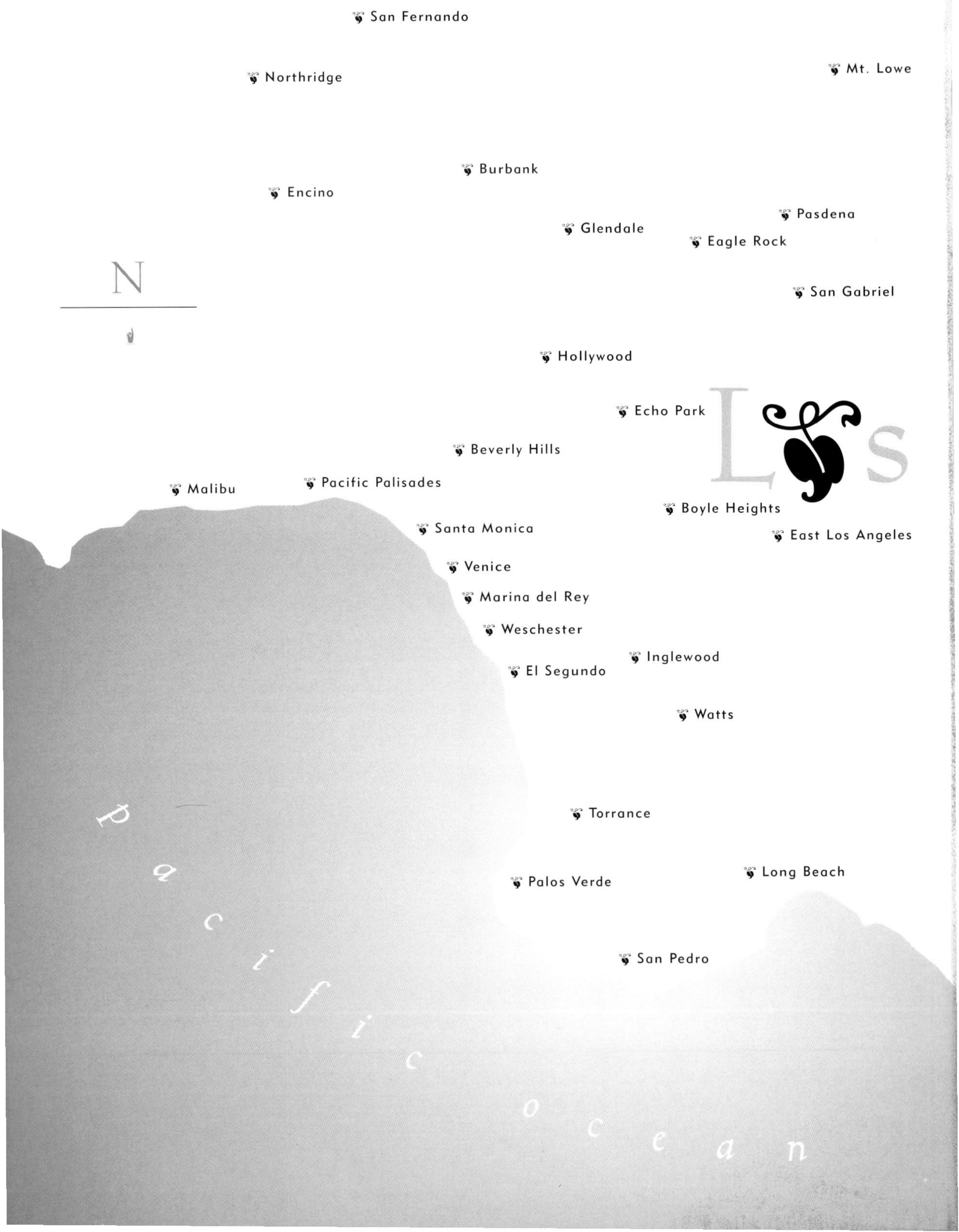

San Fernando

Northridge

Mt. Lowe

Burbank

Encino

Pasdena

Glendale

Eagle Rock

N

San Gabriel

Hollywood

Echo Park

L☙s

Beverly Hills

Malibu

Pacific Palisades

Boyle Heights

Santa Monica

East Los Angeles

Venice

Marina del Rey

Weschester

Inglewood

El Segundo

Watts

Torrance

Pacific

Palos Verde

Long Beach

San Pedro

ocean

The End of the Rainbow

Angeles:

Lys

Angeles: The End of the Rainbow

MERRY OVNICK

photographs by Carol Monteverde

BALCONY PRESS

LOS ANGELES

10 9 8 7 6 5 4 3 2

Published in the United States of America, 1994
No part of this book may be reproduced in any manner without written permission except in the case
of brief quotations embodied in critical articles and reviews.
For information, address Balcony Press, 2690 Locksley Place, Los Angeles, California 90039.

LOS ANGELES: *The End of the Rainbow* © 1994 Merry Ovnick and Carol Monteverde

Library of Congress Catalog Card Number: 94-079219
ISBN 0-9643119-0-9

TABLE OF CONTENTS

PREFACE

"Los Angeles did not acquire an image so much as it projected an image which produced a city."
— Carey McWilliams

THIS IS A HISTORY OF A CITY'S ATTRACTION to newcomers as evidenced in its domestic architecture. It is our thesis that a study of existing houses can inform the inquisitive observer of their builders' values, dreams, and concepts of place. The houses of Los Angeles architecturally depict the historical development of lifestyle, attitudes, and land use. They have physically shaped the urban image which selectively enticed successive waves of immigrants. Residential architecture is the medium through which this book explores settlers' accommodations to the region's unique features; the exotic imagery associated with Los Angeles; the casual lifestyle endemic to Southern California; the promotional myths woven and rewoven into the conceptual fabric of the city; the pattern of economic development, characterized by booms in pioneer endeavors with attendant opportunities for daring newcomers; and, finally, the nature of Los Angeles and its residents, the Angelenos. This book traces the development of projected images of the city, and the houses which both reflected and created those images over time.

The historical literature on Los Angeles is rich for the 18th and 19th-centuries, and, to a somewhat lesser extent, for the first two decades of the 20th century. Scholars and participants have studied and synthesized the material, criticized each other's work and reevaluated the past as new diaries and archeological discoveries have come to light. Fascination for the early film industry and for pioneering efforts in oil and aircraft has yielded a considerable literature of its own. The controversial issue of L.A.'s acquisition of Owens Valley water has also produced several detailed studies. However, no one has yet attempted a comprehensive history of Los Angeles for the period since World War I. There are special interest studies of narrow topics such as the Zoot Suit Riots of 1943 or the ministry of Aimee Semple McPherson. There are a number of popular histories, but they slight the historical continuum in favor of colorful, largely apocryphal anecdotes. Biographies of living or well-remembered figures are marked by controversies. Without an established body of historical literature for the period since World War I, there was little choice but to research the raw data of economic reports by banks and the Chamber of Commerce, newspaper events and advertisements, demographic material, and military reports on wartime activities. This information then had to be sifted and weighed to reach conclusions as to the origins and contemporary significance of social trends, and the prevailing cultural tone of the '20s and '30s, war, post-war, and recent periods. I hope these efforts, in search of the relationships between the cultural and economic history of Los Angeles and vernacular expressions in domestic architecture will encourage others to further investigation.

This book was the result of a long gestation. Both Carol and I were born in Los Angeles. We grew up looking at the city and its structures: seeing them — but not really seeing them. Others helped us begin to perceive the visual joys of L.A.'s man-made features — the delightful details, the eclectic ensembles — and to sense the spectrum of ideas and dreams of generations of Angelenos pinned to earth in architectural form.

In the '70s and '80s I taught a course on The Cultural Heritage of Los Angeles at Los Angeles Valley College, followed in the '90s by a course in Los Angeles History at California State University, Northridge. Each of the students enrolled in these courses contributed a different perspective, a fresh insight, to interpreting the meaning of Los Angeles. I am grateful to them all and to the passersby, pharmacy clerks, waitresses, and elevator co-occupants who joined in conversations about L.A., its buildings, and their feelings about them.

Professor Robert Winter of Occidental College, in lectures, preservationist causes, and conversations, has, with irrepressible ebullience, charm, and humor, stimulated an appreciation for L.A.'s lesser and greater architectural monuments among countless Angelenos, myself included. The book he co-authored with Professor David Gebhard of the University of California, Santa Barbara in 1977 updated in 1994 as, "Los Angeles: An Architectural Guide" — compendious guides to noteworthy buildings, arranged geographically, have accompanied and informed us in adventurous forays into unfamiliar neighborhoods.

We are deeply indebted to the residents of the houses we have pictured in the pages that follow. They graciously gave permission to trespass, when camera angles required doing so. We have honored any requests that addresses not be revealed. The care and individualization that distinguish all the homes and apartment houses we have illustrated are not only expressions of their occupants' pride but gifts to the public eye. ♪

Merry Ovnick

PART ONE

FOUNDATIONS

PART ONE

FOUNDATIONS

I

MYSTICAL ESSENCE / TANGIBLE ARCHITECTURE

architecture

sums

up

the

civilization

it

enshrines

— LEWIS MUMFORD[1]

ARCHEOLOGISTS OF THE FUTURE will surely be perplexed by a city where houses resemble caves or mushrooms, Tudor manors, Cape Cod cottages, Cinderella castles, Spanish haciendas, or Mayan temples. The diversity of images captured in the domestic architecture of Los Angeles reflects the succession of visions of a new life that have drawn its population.

Los Angeles was formed by periodic waves of immigration from distant places. Even now, the majority of its residents were born elsewhere (75% according to the 1990 census).[2] It is not the typical product of the American westward movement: a location settled by an expanding population from over the next ridge or from the next county eastward. Atypically, it was populated by settlers from half a continent away who, in the pre-Columbian ages, in the colonial era, in the 1870s, 1880s, 1920s, 1940s and since, have pulled up roots themselves, left the familiar, the secure, the conventional behind, and headed for this particular spot on the southwestern rim of the nation. Why? What was there about Los Angeles that drew people across forbidding geographical and cultural distances?

Traditional social historians analyze demographic relocations on the basis of concrete, quantifiable elements such as droughts, unemployment, or revolution in the source location, coupled with an economic expansion and available land at the destination. But another factor underlies demographic dynamics: the image of the new and better homeland in the mind of the immigrant, an image the new settler trusts as fact. Rumor, advertisement, movie scenery, and brief tourist treks, are the data prospective settlers filtered through the realities of life at home to conjure up new lives in Los Angeles, lives about as real as if they had stepped off of the movie screen. Fixed images sufficient to inspire breaking home ties and making the hostile journey to the coast were, and are, moving forces of history demanding study.

To determine how each succeeding wave of incipient Angelenos felt about their destination, about the sort of lives they expected to find there, the most visible and lasting record they have left for us is the homes they built. A house makes a statement about the beliefs, pretensions and aspirations of its occupants. It does so whether the house is the creation of a well-known architect or designed by a builder or owner from pattern books or individual whims, and even where a house is one among monotonous rows in a tract. Each represents its owner. An architect's design becomes fact only when the architect's philosophy or the specifics of the design are consonant with the owner's preferences. Likewise, to be marketable, the design features incorporated by a tract developer must be attuned to the tastes of prospective buyers. People

1. Detail of Berg residence, 1926-27

moving into a dwelling and remaining for any length of time must find it at least tolerable, or they would alter or disguise it, even in small ways on limited budgets. In this sense, the homes that remain from each period of Los Angeles' past form a standing historical outline of the major illusions that drew or suited its population, that reveal the kind of people who found such images appealing, and trace the shifts in the dreams over time.

To ward against the possibility that selective preservation of atypical houses could skew our findings, we looked for confirming evidence from other data sources for each era. For example, the fact that wooden versions of the Italianate style predominate among the few surviving examples of 1870s houses could be dismissed as a local, low-cost version of a national trend popular a decade and more earlier in the East. But the evidence of 1870s tourist literature and local social advancement, both relied on establishing Los Angeles as a New Italy; the cheap building material was apologetically referred to by one booster as an earthquake preparedness measure. Such signs of self-consciousness confirm these houses as purposeful vehicles for establishing cultural status in society.

Our first criterion for selecting examples for each era was their relationship to the image that drew the subsequent wave of settlers: houses that corresponded with the descriptions of tourist literature and advertising, or houses that were recognized in their day by Angelenos as icons of the meaning of Los Angeles. Other categories include houses that introduced and legitimized new styles or freedom from conventions, or houses of a type so numerous that they typified the place. Finally, of course, only where examples of such houses survived to the present could they serve as our indicators of the past.

Many unique L.A. houses belong in any strictly architectural catalogue of the area. The reader is referred to David Gebhard and Robert Winter's "Los Angeles, An Architectural Guide", Paul Gleye's "The Architecture of Los Angeles", and "The City Observed"; "Los Angeles, A Guide to Its Architecture and Landscapes" by Charles Moore, Peter Becker and Regula Campbell.[3] Our goal, instead has been to examine a cross-section representative of the ideals of each era's settlers that contributed to forming the Los Angeles we know today.

One example of our selection criteria is that in 1910 streetcar baron, Henry Huntington had an elaborate Italian Renaissance mansion built in San Marino with terraces and porticos extending into luxurious botanical gardens featuring sub-tropical specimens and roses. The house and its gardens appeared in national publications, local tourist pamphlets and even souvenir postcards. At the same time, the laborers who laid Huntington's streetcar tracks lived in hovels in rail camps outside of town or behind fences where few Angelenos or visitors saw them. Huntington's house survives gloriously as a museum and library; the hovels are gone. We show the house not only because it has been an icon and tourist attraction from the beginning but also because the outdoor terraces of Huntington's mansion were widely taken up in vernacular housing. Year-round roses were one of the local wonders featured in tourist copy, package tours, and the annual New Year's Rose Parade.

Small tract developers and multi-family housing investors acknowledged the sales appeal of the sub-tropical garden imagery by planting signature palms in each yard and organizing even the smallest rental units as bungalow courts in garden settings. The lasting popularity and financial viability of bungalow courts with gardens proved that even at the low end of the housing market, the attractive vision of the good life in Los Angeles demanded garden homes, even if they must be tiny. We could not photograph the rail labor camps, which have disappeared, but would not have included them since they were reported to be ill-tended by their occupants, never replicated by independent home-seekers and thus do not represent part of the drawing vision. They were merely a temporary shelter for workers until they might move on to something they could invest with pride and care, a single-family structure in a garden.

To summarize, then, it is the central thesis of this book that the major factors motivating the settlement of Los Angeles can be defined, illustrated, and traced in the visual record of domestic architecture, when confirmed by supplementary historical evidence. Six sub-themes run through the story told by this visual text.

1.   **The rare climate and geography of the Los Angeles basin have been key determinants in image-formation.**

The natural features of the Los Angeles region distinguished it from surrounding areas and served as its fundamental attraction from prehistoric times to today. Since its climate and natural features are so elemental to its image conception, a description is in order.

Los Angeles lies in a cornucopia-shaped basin opening on the Pacific Ocean, its temperate climate maintained by the warm ocean currents which sweep southward along its beaches. To the east, it is protected from the arid Mojave Desert by two mountain ranges. They are watersheds which feed the natural water supply of the city, historically represented by the Los Angeles and San Gabriel Rivers. Large surrounding valleys, such as the San Fernando Valley, which also collect water to feed the two rivers, have been drawn into the social, economic, and political unit that is now Los Angeles.

Mystical Essence / Tangible Architecture

The region enjoys a 'Mediterranean' climate, that is, year-round warmth, dry summers, rain only in the three winter months, and a twelve-month growing season. As a consequence of a mean precipitation of 14.5 inches[4] coupled with a generally low humidity level, thunder and lightening are rare. The varied topography of the 464 square miles of Los Angeles County allows for a variety of agricultural subclimes: fertile alluvial plains open to the moist sea breezes, inland valleys and passes inviting dry desert wind, and smaller glens which are protected from both; valleys where night frost might occur, foothills that are frost-free, ocean-facing hillsides that get more rain than leeward slopes. These fine, varied agricultural and living conditions contrast with those in most of the Eastern United States and serve as important attractions to newcomers and leading factors in the development of Los Angeles culture.

2 .   Los Angeles is a city formed by periodic waves of
        long-distance immigration.

The Los Angeles basin is physically isolated from the rest of the continent by a forbidding expanse of desert and by ridge after ridge of mountains. Even by sea, Nature did not bless the place with a safe harbor. Thus its geography decreed that Los Angeles would not be formed along the demographic pattern of gradual expansion from a contiguous region. There was no nearby population base. Settlers came from considerable distances and dissimilar environments. Their transplantation occurred in dramatic surges interspersed with lulls, as we can see in a generalized way from census figures.

The period of Spanish rule was one of slow growth: from 44 colonists in 1781 to 141 residents in 1790, to 315 in 1800, to 650 in 1820. In the Mexican era the region was credited with a population of only 1,675 (in 1836), with little change by the first American census here in 1850 which showed 1,610 in the newly delineated County of Los Angeles.

Then came a wave of newcomers: by 1860 the County had 11,333 residents. Ten years later there were 15,309 in the County, 8,504 of them within the political subdivision of the City of Los Angeles. A dramatic influx between 1870 and 1890 quintupled the City figures to 50,395. The next decade saw it double again to 102,459. By 1910 that population had tripled, to 319,198. In the next twenty years the City figure reached 1,238,048. Growth lagged during the Depression decade. In 1940 the City recorded 1,504,277, the County 2,785,643. Due to suburban spread, it is the County figures that show the most dramatic increase since 1940. By 1950 the County contained 4,151,687 people; by 1960, 6,038,771; by 1990 the County population was set at 8,863,164, while the City totaled 3,485,398.[5] A series of disasters in the 1990s arrested the influx, but rebuilding proceeds rapidly and population is predicted to continue increasing.

3 .   **Immigrants to Los Angeles have been lured by a dream of a life that would be different.**

Because of the seemingly inhospitable stretches west of the Mississippi and the more forbidding Mojave Desert, foreign sovereignty in the early days, and transportational limitations, a move to Los Angeles required a permanent severing of the ties to home that had comforted so many pioneers elsewhere. The distance and the difficulties mandated a different set of motives for the Los Angeles settler. He would choose Los Angeles over more congenially located destinations only because he believed it offered something different than any closer alternative: a way of life, an environment, or an opportunity he believed would be distinctly superior to those at home. It was a vision of an ideal life, not a wish to continue the familiar, that brought settlers to Los Angeles. The vision had to be potent to induce settlers to sever connections with roots and the

2. Neighborhood of mixed styles, 1920s

familiar, often an irrevocable commitment. Their expectations did not always turn into realities. As precipitating motives for the move, what mattered was the intensity of the dreams and the determination with which they were pursued.

4 .   **Immigrant selectivity has affected the city's developing style.**

The plethora of architectural styles, the lack of conventionality, indicates not only vivid images but a selectivity of immigrants. Their susceptibility, especially in the days of difficult transportation conditions, to visions of a new life distinguished them from those who were content at home. These were people who were willing to take a chance, to gamble their futures on a dream. They included the misfits, the "black sheep." They were likely to be more imaginative, seeking outlets for their creative expression. They were often those least comfortable in the behavioral codes demanded by the community at home. They were impulsive. Or, considering the propaganda of land-sales promoters, advertisers, and motion pictures, the settlers of Los Angeles may have included a disproportionate share of the gullible. Certainly they were not tradition-bound. Seeking something very different from their backgrounds marked them as dissatisfied and searching for something other than what they had.

In a number of ways besides architecture we can see signs of this dissatisfied searching. Los Angeles has often been lampooned as an incubator of zany cults and mystic philosophies, demagoguery and swindles, kitsch, the avant-garde, and one fashion or amusement after another. The truth is that people who have crossed a continent believing they can transform dreams into reality are not people who are easily gratified. They are uprooted, and they must seek or create for themselves a form of security, or continue on the edge, searching for their receding mirage. Domestic architecture, in the social record it provides, reveals the value Angelenos have placed on free expression, on fun and leisure, on pretense and escapism.[5] Sometimes it also shows a search for security, for a cultural heritage, for a sense of identity with past ages in this new place.

First, there are homes in which dreams were literally expressed: the Taj Mahal, the fairytale castle, the Hansel and Gretel cottage fit for a sugary

witch, and the Mission-styled repository of Spanish Colonial romantic legends,
to name a few.

Second, home buyers and builders exposed their insecurities in the
nostalgic recreation of the familiar, of the roots left behind, or at least roots one
pretended were real: the Easterner who built a steeply gabled house for a climate
without snow, the New Englander whose L.A. house sported a Captain's Walk
without a sea view, the Southerner whose success was proclaimed with a
mansion in the old-plantation manner.

A third category belongs to those immigrants whose personal
confidence found an outlet in an experimental joy in newness, startling
departures from convention. Their homes celebrate the freedom to express their
new sense of place in untried terms (or do they expose the insecurity of a
braggart craving attention?).

5 .   The perceived essence of L.A. is layered: each era of building
         modifies the flavor of the whole and directs the tastes of the future.
      The houses we have chosen as illustrations record three major elements
in the cultural history of a unique city: the images of Los Angeles which

attracted newcomers; the transformation of those images over the course of time; and the nature of the individuals who responded.

The pooled image composed of one generation's homes became the physical reality and the touted reputation that selectively attracted the next. In the 1830s and '40s, for example, the Los Angeles life was expressed in low-profile Hispanic adobes. It was an outdoorsy, hospitable life at a relaxed pace. Most Easterners of the period were repelled by the dirt-floored, mud-walled houses and the culture compatible with them. But the image the simple houses exuded proved irresistible to a few adventurers from New England, Kentucky, and Europe, the impact of formed image on succeeding immigration. Only those to whom the already created appearance appealed would uproot themselves and head for the place.

If they had directly adopted the housing style they found there — signaling an unreserved desire to merge with life as they found it, our story would be quickly told: we would find one, unchanging face of Los Angeles, one image to decipher; we would find a homogeneous population selectively matched to the attraction of that single image. Los Angeles is much more complicated than that. The English-speaking newcomers to early nineteenth-century L.A. admired what they found, but insisted on incorporating comforts to which they were accustomed. To the adobe houses they built for themselves, they added interior stairways, wooden floors, glass windows, and formal gardens. Their dreams of a good life, like the homes they built, were a compromise between their experiences back east and their expectations of Los Angeles.

By the time they finished adding the comforts and trimmings demanded by their past to the L.A. they had discovered, the city had been transformed. Later dreamers' images of the town would be based on this new physical atmosphere. In effect, as starting point, each wave of newcomers had to accept the previous settlers' definition of the good life. But at the same time, immigrants brought their own cultural baggage with them. This process of layering dreams, one generation's forming the basis for the next generation's, has created Los Angeles as we know it.

6 . **Recurrent themes unite the architectural expressions of L.A.'s past.**

The layered nature of the L.A. dream is predicated on settlers' fondness for what they perceive to be reality. Each immigrant comes to L.A. liking the kind of place it is (or seems to be), and then, subtly or profoundly, modifies it. The Los Angeles region has been portrayed as distinctly different from most places. These differences were what drew people. Each wave of immigrants had to deal with these same features in its turn. The Healthy Outdoors, Exotic Tropicana, and The Romantic Spanish Past are images which contrast with regions of origin, and are central to the L.A. dream. Even as each underwent periodic revision. The Healthy Outdoors theme was a promotional claim for tourists in the 1870s. A naive public believed exaggerations of miraculous medical cures. The theme reappeared in the 1910s in the progressives' back-to-nature and self-improvement credos. Its 1950s guise was one of swim-suits and suntans. Architecture expressed the Outdoors Living refrain with verandas in the 1870s, sleeping porches for the progressives, and sliding glass walls and backyard swimming pools for the 1950s.

The same themes have resurfaced over and over in the Los Angeles image, each time somewhat altered, as new generations arrived, rediscovered the old themes, redefined them to fit their own values, and then re-expressed them in a new idiom. In fact, it is the redefinition of themes which permits us to measure the impact of changing times on the nature of the immigrants, and on the stylistic directions the city's buildings took and continue to take. By looking at how themes have altered as they were recycled, we can measure the essence of the city and its people, one era against another.

We look at visions of ideals made tangible in wood and stucco. Each house reveals an individual's idea of what Los Angeles meant to him. The city's stock of domestic architecture traces the ideas that drew the populace, the kind of people susceptible to projected images, and the layered effects of time and elaboration on the imagery. For a city built of dreamstuff, it is fitting that it bears an other-worldly name, The City of the Angels. 🐝

CHAPTER

II

SIMPLY PARADISE: THE INDIANS, TO 1769

The gods smiled

on the Gabrielinos.

And their unabashedly

temporary houses

reflect their relaxed

appreciation of a simple,

unhurried,

easy life in paradise .

THE INDIANS OF THE LOS ANGELES BASIN (termed *Gabrielinos* and *Fernandeños* by the Franciscans, after the missions established for their conversion) made no written record of their history or feelings. By the 1860s they had become culturally extinct.[1] Descriptions prepared by Franciscan padres, Spanish soldiers, renowned natural scientists, and a Scottish settler who married into an extended Gabrielino family provide us with some information.[2] ILLUSTRATION 4 represents a modern replica of the typical Gabrielino home. What can it tell us about the people and their image of Los Angeles?

First, the materials of which the wickiup, or *jacal* (the more accurate Spanish term; pronounced "hah-kahl") was constructed were willow poles and tule grass. These were abundantly accessible to the sites chosen for their villages or *rancherías*—always near an adequate, year-round water source.

The technique of construction was simple. Willow poles were pounded into the earth in a circle and tied together at the top to form a dome. Horizontal poles were tied on at intervals around the circumference to form a framework. The skeleton was then covered with a tule-grass thatch or with mats of platted grass. A doorway and a central smoke hole were left open in what was, basically, an inverted basket.

If a jacal became vermin-infested or overly sooty or if its thatch deteriorated, it could be vacated, burned down, and replaced in one day. Such a method of spring house-cleaning is counter to the idea of permanency and the sense of security which normally attaches to lasting architecture. Could this impermanence hint at cultural insecurities? Not in Southern California. Our concepts of the cozy, snug cottage and a sturdy, lasting structure were defined in climates where the elements of nature are hostile and man must seek a refuge from them. The Indians of Los Angeles lived in a virtual paradise. Their houses did not have to serve the same functions as European homes.

The functions of the jacal were social, occasional shelter, and food storage. The need for privacy, for a retreat from public observation and comment, would be sufficiently served by the thatched basket-house.

The need for shelter was intermittent. The Gabrielinos wore very little in the way of clothing. They were acclimated to the weather and usually slept, cooked, and ate out of doors. But the jacal provided shelter from the discomforts of the occasional rain, wind, and frost. The dome shape, coupled with the vertical pattern of overlapped layers of thatch, is an excellent design for shedding the light to moderate rains encountered in Los Angeles. Today the average annual rainfall is 14.5 inches, but it may have been less before manmade reservoirs and watered lawns, with their evaporative contributions.[3]

4. Gabrielino jacal

As for wind protection, the doorways were built to face down-wind. In some parts of the Los Angeles basin, such as the rancheria sites in San Fernando, the seasonal Santa Ana winds of fall and spring can be very strong. The Santa Anas are foehn winds from east of the Sierra Nevada which are drawn into the basin by seasonal low-pressure fronts. They funnel into the basin through gaps in the surrounding hills bringing gusty blows to the areas below. A solid structure would be severely buffeted by such winds but the jacal reduced wind-resistance by permitting some filtering. Besides, it was anchored into the ground with flexible willow poles. A fire in the middle for warmth and cooking, woven grass mats and animal-hide blankets to wrap the occupants, and the partial wind protection afforded by the structure provided adequate comfort on the windiest days.

Frosty nights, the bane of citrus farmers in a later period, are more prevalent in valley bottoms than on hillside slopes. In hilly Los Angeles, rancherias were most often located in the valley bottoms, near water. On chilly nights the Gabrielinos slept indoors on platted grass mats around warm fires. The mats protected the sleepers from the damp earth.

The earliest Spanish

5. Paiute summer encampment, Great Basin region

observers were disdainful of the California Indians because they had produced so little evidence of cultural advancement and because they seemed so extremely lazy. Their homes were certainly not as impressive as the magnificent temples and palaces the Spaniards had seen in Mexico and Peru. There were no stone friezes or murals adorning these simple shelters. There was, in fact, no attempt at decoration at all. The reason for the lack reflects the attitude of the Gabrielinos toward not only their jacales, but toward their lives and their locality.

California's Indians, politically organized no further than as small villages of 100 to 1000 in population, are categorized instead by linguistic variations. Those of the Los Angeles basin spoke a dialect of the Shoshonean language family. The Mojave Desert and the Great Basin (Utah-Nevada) were also Shoshonean linguistically. Evidence points to these Shoshone peoples moving into Southern California around 500 BC, eventually settling a wedge-shaped territory 100 miles north to south along the coast, widening to a 600-mile spread near the present eastern border of California. This wedge of intrusion pushed aside the Hokan-speaking residents whose descendants retained the Santa Barbara area to the north (Chumash Indians) and the San Diego area to the south (Yumans). Nomadic Shoshone-speaking Indians of the Nevada desert were still constructing brush shelters for protection from the intense sun and rain in the 19th-century. ILLUSTRATION 5 shows one of these shelters photographed in the 1890s. They were crude piles of brush barely large enough for one man to crawl into. They show no sense of design in technical perfection. The Shoshone peoples of Los Angeles, along with their coastal neighbors north and south, lived sedentary lives. Their dietary staple was the abundantly available acorn, processed into a mush. For this easy life they had refined their nomadic ancestral house style into a symmetrical form with an aesthetically pleasing, uniform texture of thatch which met all the requirements of California living.

From perhaps 500 AD to the demise of the Indians in the 19th-century, the house-style remained basically unchanged, as far as archeologists can determine: there was no need to change it. As for embellishment, the jacal was a temporary, disposable structure, used on a weather-related irregular basis. The Gabrielinos were renowned for their fine baskets, adorned with designs based on highly stylized animals and natural phenomena. Their arrow and spear points were technically refined. Drilled shell necklaces were elaborate. Wood-plank boats designed for the open sea were decorated with inlaid shell patterns. Other than work of an occasional nature such as seasonal acorn harvests and periodic small game hunts, men, particularly, were free to enjoy leisure. The women spent hours each day treating acorns. But this was not incompatible with gossiping, child-tending, and interruptions dictated by whim.

Food was plentiful, the climate was mostly benevolent. Living in a land where all the needs of life were so easily met, the Gabrielinos had no reason for a strong sense of material acquisitiveness, nor for a priest and temple cult to placate feared gods. The gods smiled on the Gabrielinos. And their unabashedly temporary houses reflect their relaxed appreciation of a simple, unhurried, easy life in paradise.

The postscript to the Gabrielino Garden of Eden was a tragic one of cultural conflict. The frontier-pacification system employed by the Spanish was a dual church-state project. Missions for the Los Angeles area were established at San Gabriel in 1771 and San Fernando in 1797 to "civilize" and Christianize the natives. Regimented into a work force scheduled around religious rituals, the Indian found his activities regulated around the clock. The emphasis was on continual attentiveness to channeled productivity and the replacement of self-direction with obedience to authority. Escape was thwarted by each mission's military contingent and by the fear of punishment, if not in this life, in the next. The Indians' sense of harmony with nature and of the importance of leisure were destroyed. By the time the missions were dismantled in the 1830s, their Indian charges had been removed from the wilds by two and three generations: they could not return to that now unfamiliar life. And the missions' secularization left most without any economic stake with which to establish themselves in majority society. Their non-materialistic cultural heritage, coupled with degradation of the spirit, encouraged gambling, alcoholism, and vagrancy. They were easily exploited as a cheap source of labor. Finally, in the 1860s, an epidemic of smallpox (a disease to which the Indian had no genetic resistance) destroyed the last visible survivors of the Gabrielino people who, in a population of 4,000 to 5,000 had roamed the basin for a thousand years before the white man came.✠❧

EL PUEBLO
DE NUESTRA SEÑORA
LA REINA
DE LOS ANGELES

EL PUEBLO
DE NUESTRA SEÑORA
LA REINA
DE LOS ANGELES

CHAPTER

III

SPANISH PUEBLO, 1781–1821

Over this island of California

rules a queen,

Calafia, statuesque

in proportions,

more beautiful than

all the rest,

eager to perform great deeds

"EL PUEBLO de Nuestra Señora la Reina de Los Angeles" — the Town of Our Lady, Queen of the Angels: a beautiful Spanish name.[1] With the name comes an aura of Spanish Romance based on a (supposed) Spanish Heritage, of noble dons, kindly padres, and lovely senoritas in lace mantillas serenaded by guitar-strumming swains, of a gracious time of leisure and fiestas, sunshine and plenty. Generations of dreamers have identified with the figures of these romantic myths — but the myths were artificially constructed to sell books and, on a larger scale, to sell a city — "the best advertised city in the world."[2]

Who were the real Spanish Angelenos, and why were they here? They lived on the edge of civilization in adobe huts with dirt floors. Flies buzzed in and out through the open doors and windows. Chickens scratched in the dirt lanes. On Sunday afternoons Angelenos sat on the edges of their flat roofs or leaned on their window sills to watch the bullfights in the plaza. When a rider succeeded in tagging the bull, the barricades were taken down and the relieved animal loped away to graze on the hillsides around the little settlement. In the neighboring valleys a few families had been granted land for ranching. Remote from their neighbors, they too, lived in tiny rectangular houses, confining, dark, and unadorned, but conforming with the European sense of four-walled security. Their time was The Age of Enlightenment, historians tell us. However, they were not enlightened: they were both illiterate and uninformed. From 1781 to 1821, the years of Spanish administration of the city, the events of the rest of the world had very little to do with Los Angeles.

A more glamorous image of California had once existed. In the 16th-century, the Spanish soldiers of fortune, the conquistadores, whiled away idle hours reading chivalric romances. One of the least restrained of these fantasies provided California with its name:

"Know ye that on the right hand of the Indies there is an island called California, very near the Terrestrial Paradise and inhabited by black women without a single man among them... They are robust of body, strong and passionate in heart, and of great valor... Their arms are all of gold, as is the harness of the wild beasts which, after taming, they ride. In all the island there is no other metal... Over this island of California rules a queen, Calafía, statuesque in proportions, more beautiful than all the rest, in the flower of her womanhood, eager to perform great deeds..."[3]

In 1519, an armed expedition of Spanish adventurers under Hernan Cortez penetrated the New World. They found in Mexico an advanced civilization with an intricate political structure, magnificent architecture, and fabulous wealth. Within two years they had conquered the Aztecs. A treasure began to pour into the Spanish treasury and the pockets of the lucky adventurers. The search for more treasure lands was on.

Word-of-mouth information from Indian sources had led Spanish cartographers to believe that California was an island, that the Gulf of California, which separates mainland Mexico from the peninsula of Baja California, was a through passage, perhaps the long-sought shorter route through the Americas which the English called the Northwest Passage and the Spaniards the Straits of Anián.

The exploration of the coastlines of Baja (lower, now a part of Mexico) and Alta (upper, now the 31st state of the United States) California was undertaken in response to a hunger for wealth, adventure, and a new route to the Orient. While individual expectations may not have been quite so exaggerated, this was the basic motivation of the 16th-century adventurer. That the yet-unexplored California should be named after the novel's Terrestrial Paradise indicated its illusory image right from the start.

In 1542-43, two ships under the command of Juan Rodríguez Cabrillo carefully explored the California coastline and offshore islands. Not only did these explorers find no statuesque Amazons, nor a short-cut route to the Orient, they found nothing of interest to them at all: no signs of gold or jewels to take as booty, no advanced political systems to overthrow. In fact, all they found were near-naked Stone Age primitives who lived in brush huts and ate acorn mush with insect condiments, raw fish, and berries (a balanced diet, but distasteful to the Europeans' bread-and-meat palates). Even the climate, though pleasant, was too familiar to Mediterranean-bred men to be of interest. The golden image of California proved a bitter disappointment to the Spaniards who relegated the land to neglect. It was too remote from the busy scene of development and exploitation in New Spain for settlement. From 1543 to 1769 — over two hundred years — the only interest the Spanish exhibited in California was the idea of using it as a supply depot for the galleons trading between New Spain and the Orient whose return voyages followed the Japan Current clockwise across the North Pacific and down the California coast. Even that idea was not pursued after 1602. California's image was so poor that it had no attraction for settlers. The Indians remained in undisturbed possession of Los Angeles. When California was finally colonized by the Spanish, it was not its magnetic charms that drew Spanish settlers. The first Spaniards came because they were sent.

By the 1760s Spain's power in world affairs was eroding. The northern fringes of New Spain were threatened by the expansion and consolidation of the thirteen English colonies on the mainland and the British presence in the

Caribbean. English sea power menaced Spain's communication routes to its New World empire. At the same time, Russian expansion eastward had been accompanied by fur-hunting activities in the North Pacific and exploration ever further southward along the coast of North America. By sea and land, New Spain was vulnerable on its northwestern coast, in California. The Spanish monarch's representative (*visitador-general*) in New Spain, José de Galvez, perceived these threats to the frontiers in conjunction with ambitions of his own. He determined to carry out a bold exercise in garrisoning the California portion of New Spain's far reaches as a buffer zone to protect the Mexican heartland. This plan was a refined version of the Spanish mode of conquest and domination, which was closely patterned after that of Imperial Rome.

The Romans' policy had called for a string of garrisoned fortifications at communicable distances from each other to pacify the frontier and to hold off barbarian attacks. The enticement to soldiers and the incentive not to desert was the gem in the Roman system: when a frontier soldier retired he was given a piece of land near his post, where he likely had married a local woman, fathered children, and established roots. Family ties to local society helped inculcate Latin civilization in conquered regions. Rome's plan was expensive, in terms of both soldiers' pay and provisions; the Spanish plan was similar but cost very little.

Putting to use the religious fervor of 18th-century Spain and Spain's treaty commitment to convert the native populations over which it ruled, the frontier policy for California called for a string of Catholic missionary establishments, at first sited strategically, eventually to be filled in until they were one day's distance from each other on a connecting road, *el Camino Real*. An order of the regular clergy would set up the missions both to convert the natives to Christianity and to transform them from barbarians into civilized Spanish citizens (that is, by European definition, "civilized"). The Indians would receive religious instruction. They would also be taught the agricultural and industrial skills associated with the European life. In the process of learning these practical skills, food and basic manufactured goods needed to maintain a garrisoned frontier would be produced, thus insuring a self-sufficiency the Romans would have envied. By the Law of the Indies, a ten-year time limit was projected for this dual transformation into Christians and productive Spanish citizens. At that time the material assets and lands of the missions were to be distributed among these new Spanish subjects of Indian blood, who would then have a stake in preserving local security.

To assist the missionary effort and to protect it against native uprisings and foreign aggression, during its infancy, *presidios* (forts) would be erected at selected strategic points. A small garrison would be maintained at each presidio, and a detail of five or six soldiers would be attached to each mission. Upon retirement, a soldier might be rewarded for his years of loyal service with a grant of land on the frontier he had served, again after the Roman example.

The initial phase of this government project of frontier settlement began in 1769 under the leadership of Gaspar de Portolá and Fray Junípero Serra.[4] It included three classes of people, first, the padres whose dwellings were the missions. The second category of government-detailed agents was military officers, who would serve only a limited term in California. To this educated group of officers, California was merely a temporary assignment on a remote frontier.

The third category was made up of the enlisted men and what we would term the non-commissioned officers. Common soldiers sent to California were sometimes assigned there as punishment for previous infractions. To these, a remote frontier with none of the comforts or distractions of civilization had to be viewed as a "bad duty lot." To recruit more volunteers than punishment could provide, and to lift morale, enticements were offered: the lure of attaining status in the new community, and the possibility of becoming a landowner in the only way open to the common soldier in the Spanish New World.

In a new, open land, however, with no social superiors except the few temporary officer families, a soldier could be a social lion in his community. Spanish land grants were not deeds of possession, as we think of them, but concessions for use.[5] A house could be built, a kitchen garden cultivated, and cattle pastured on the unfenced hills and valleys for miles around on the sparsely populated land. As for laborers, the grantee could use the labor of the natives residing on his parcel, as long as, following the Spanish colonial pattern of the estate, or *encomienda*, he provided for their spiritual and physical needs.

José María Verdugo was one of the first to realize such dreams in Los Angeles. He had come on the 1769 expedition as one of the "leather-jackets" or common soldiers. For years after the 1771 founding of the San Gabriel Mission he served as corporal of its guard detachment. In 1784 he applied to his commanding officer and governor of California, Pedro Fages, for a land grant, on the basis of his dedicated service, his health, and the fact that he had accumulated some cattle. He was rewarded with the Rancho San Rafael — some 36,000 acres in what is now Glendale and Burbank. Since he was still on active duty he sent his brother to build a house and develop the rancho. In 1797 his age and the state of his health permitted him to retire there to raise his family of six children. Although Spanish land grants were not deeds of permanent ownership, lack of contest and later Mexican confirmation made them so for all practical purposes. Don Verdugo, once a common soldier, lived the life of a landed gentleman, in unchallenged possession of a huge estate and many cattle, until his death in 1831.

The carefully constructed plan for securing the frontier, which had brought men like Verdugo to Los Angeles, did not work as well in practice as expected. The missionaries complained because the soldiers often failed to lead exemplary lives. And the soldiers, they said, misused Indian labor. The military establishment repeatedly levied crippling requisitions for food and equipment on the missions rather than pressuring Mexico City for supplies. As for the missions themselves, the planned dual transformation of the Indians was never fully accomplished. The few soldiers, the few priests, and their dependent Indians together did not provide a secure frontier buffer state.[6]

A third institution was added to the system, the *pueblo*, or town, which the Spanish hoped would solve the problems. Civilian *pobladores*, or settlers, were to be recruited in Mexico to form civilian towns close enough to the California missions to receive spiritual benefits, but far enough away to avoid hampering the missions' efforts among the Indians.

The pobladores were to form an agricultural community whose excess produce would provide for the needs of the military. They would also serve, in times of threat, as a civilian militia. Three such pueblos were established: San José (1777), El Pueblo de Nuestra Señora la Reina de Los Angeles (1781), and Villa de Branciforte (1797). The last, near present the Santa Cruz, failed and was abandoned.

Los Angeles had been chosen as a pueblo site because it was in a well-watered, fertile plain some nine miles from a mission, and twice that distance from the ocean. The town was clearly meant to serve as a local breadbasket rather than as a profitable trading center. It was settled by forty-four persons, comprising eleven families, who had been recruited on government orders from northwestern Mexico, mostly from Sonora and Sinaloa. All were illiterate. The simple life for which they came to Los Angeles did not require literacy. No school was established until 1817, and it only lasted a year.[7]

This small group of settlers was of mixed racial background: two *españoles* (Spaniards), one *mestizo* (Spanish-Indian mix), two *negros*, two *mulatos* (Spanish-Negro mix), and three *indios* (Indians). All the wives were either indias or mulatas.[8] Spain itself was a land of racial mixture — the early Celts had been diluted by incursions of Gauls, Franks, Romans, Vandals, and Visigoths. The eighth-century Moorish Conquest had brought Africans, Arabs and Jews. The

Spanish nationalism which had triumphed in the Reconquista in 1492 was an identity neither by place nor by race, but a sense of nationhood based on a shared belief in Catholicism. Citizenship and marriage were unrestricted along racial lines, but dictated absolutely by the requirement that the parties be good Catholics. Social discrimination in Spanish America gave preference to white skin and Spanish ancestry. The social class recruited for the pueblo of Los Angeles was not the discriminating stratum of society. Fitness for labor was the selection that did apply. The instructions issued for the recruitment of the settlers stipulated:

"The head or father of each family must be a man of the soil,... healthy, robust, and without known vice or defect that would make him prejudicial to the [Indian population].... Among the said families must be included a mason, a carpenter who knows how to make yokes, ploughs, solid wooden wheels, and [carts], and a blacksmith, who will do if he knows how to make ploughshares, pick-axes, and crowbars."[9]

We have seen what standards they were expected to meet. We know who the settlers were. What were their hopes for their lives in the Town of Our Lady, Queen of the Angels? These recruits were volunteers, as were many of the common soldiers who eventually settled around Los Angeles. What motivated their decisions to join the colonizing expedition?

They must have been people with nothing to lose by leaving, no future inheritance waiting or land to risk. They were to be provided with the basic farming implements, so they may not have owned even the basic tools for survival in an agricultural society. The opportunity to start over in a new land where only hard work would be required to obtain land and a home must have seemed a near miracle to such people. As land-owning (and founding) citizens of a new pueblo in a new place, they would be able to be more important members of their community. It was a dream worth pursuing. Even so, the government had to provide additional incentives. The original instructions had called for twenty-four families. Recruits were to be furnished with tools, rations (to be progressively reduced over five years), and tax-exemption for five years. After five years of diligent labor on individually-assigned plots, community-owned plots, and public works projects, the settlers were promised cattle brands and titles to town lots and farm lots. Even with these enticements and an extension of time, only eleven families could be found to leave for Los Angeles.

The homes built by those who actually arrived were as unpretentious as the builders' origins: one-room, dirt-floored adobes built for immediate occupancy, to the standards of minimal adequacy. But in this land there was

6. Outbuilding ca. 1797

room for expansion. As prosperity and families grew, the houses of the pueblo grew: room after room was built on to the end of the structure, sometimes creating 'L' or 'U' shapes.

The material, *adobe* (bricks made of sun-dried mud and straw), was a material widely familiar in Spain and throughout Spanish America. The knowledgeable padres had selected it as the preferred building material for the earlier missions. This was the material most readily accessible to the pueblo site, the large alluvial basin of Los Angeles where trees were not numerous and not of timber quality. Sometimes, when suitable rocks were abundant to the site, houses were built of stone (ILLUSTRATION 6), but adobe predominated.

To support the weight of the upper layers, adobe brick walls must be very thick, commonly one and a half to two feet, forming good insulation. They also result in windows with very deep wells. Light and fresh air enter, but the summer sun's direct rays rarely penetrate. The old adobes were cool retreats on hot days. Because timber was hard to come by, dried bullock hides were hung in the doorways as substitutes for wooden doors, a practice still common in 1829. A shortage of iron for civilian purposes led to the substitution of leather thongs for nails. Window glass was not available, as none was manufactured in California. The settlers had little enough to trade for more essential goods from

New Spain and glass was not a priority while foreign trade was forbidden by law. Without glass, windows were, by necessity, open. The few small windows and the doorway, all left open, provided a breeze-through that prevented the dwellings from seeming confined.[10]

The smallness of the earliest homes in Los Angeles was partly a response to the climate. The infrequency of really nasty weather encouraged outdoor living. Eating, cottage crafts and chores, and most of the cooking took place outdoors, as it did for the Indians. A small brick stove indoors was a luxury feature of better homes, but as the smoke and cooking odors were un-pleasant in the small rooms, most often the cooking and baking were done in the open air under a ramada, a tule or cane shelter over an outdoor stove (ILLUSTRATION 7).

The earliest settler and soldier families were interested only in minimal construction of the bare basics. Their rectangular one-room shelters were topped with flat roofs made of cane (*carrizo*) or tule, covered with sticky black brea (*asphaltum*) found in natural seeps nearby (now Hancock Park, the site of the George C. Page Museum). In hot weather the brea melted and trickled down the adobe walls.

Direct rain contact wears away adobe walls. The labor-rich missions could indulge in fired clay tile roofs with overhanging porticos to shield the walls from the rain. Furthermore, they could oversee the processing of seashells and lime deposits into a lime stucco with which to surface the exterior walls. There is no record of any tile-roofed

7. Hugo Reid Adobe, restored to 1839

8. Los Angeles from
Fort Hill, 1853

houses in the pueblo before the Mexican era. And, desirable as plaster was as a retardant of the adobe's melting process, most houses were the dull brown color of dried mud. With so little annual rain, a flat roof and unsheltered walls were feasible. The artist's hillside view of Los Angeles in ILLUSTRATION 8 shows us the town in 1853, after years of expansion since its Spanish beginnings. Flat roofs still predominate.

ILLUSTRATION 6 shows a small stone out-building for the de la Osa Adobe on Rancho Los Encinos in the San Fernando Valley. It is thought to have been used earlier as the home of the first Spanish concessionaire in the valley, Francisco Reyes, who took up residence at the site in 1797. If not, his domicile would have been similar. Reyes was an ex-soldier who settled in Los Angeles. He had served as *alcalde* (mayor-judge) of the town from 1793 to 1795. Then he took up ranching in the nearby San Fernando Valley, using resident Indians as laborers. In 1797, when the padres decided the location for the San Fernando

Spanish Pueblo

Mission should be Reyes' homesite, his use of the place and its natives was terminated. He took up a new claim on the other side of the same valley, where he lived at the location of this stone cottage.

Life in a ranch-house like this one, or in the adobe town houses of similar size in the pueblo proper would be, in today's view, a squalid existence. Lacking embellishment, meeting only the minimum requirements for European living patterns, only an accident of fate coupling Iberian roots with California's claimants making them adaptable to resources and climate, these dwellings nevertheless represent the dreams of their inhabitants, built in adobe.

The pobladores and soldiers who built the adobes came north expecting a life of toil and sweat. They may have been inspired by thoughts of a society where they could enjoy a rough equality with others. They could expect to make a living and to have their children grow up to lead lives like their own. Even for soldiers, hopes for land grants were not immediate, by any definition. Long service was expected: Juan José Dominguez served thirty years in the military to qualify for the grant he received in the San Pedro area in 1784, Jose Maria Verdugo was granted the San Rafael Rancho in 1784 but he was required to remain at his post for another fourteen years before he could take up ranching.

During the Spanish years Los Angeles existed as a far-away frontier settlement, little noticed by the rest of the world. There were not many in the years following the town's founding, who would find such a remote place attractive enough to lure them from Mexico. The rate of population growth confirms this. From the 44 pobladores and a few guards of 1781, the populace had grown to 141 persons by the census of 1790, mainly due to a high birthrate and the addition of a few retired soldiers. There were 28 households. By 1800 there were 70 households, totaling 315 persons. Again, births and retirements account for more than new arrivals. In 1820, near the end of forty years as a Spanish pueblo, Los Angeles and the outlying ranchos numbered 650 people.[11]

Foreigners were not permitted to settle in Spanish California. However, as with Mexicans, not many would have wanted to do so. At the time of Mexico's independence there was only one foreign resident of Los Angeles. Joseph Chapman, a crewman of a pirate ship captured in a marauding foray in Monterey, was permitted to remain. He claimed he had been forced into piracy, which, if true, could explain why he would prefer life in Los Angeles over the life he had escaped.

None of the residents of Los Angeles, even those who ended their lives holding ranchos of thousands of acres, came with visions of riches. Spanish mercantilist policy forbade trade between colonists and ships of other nations.

The agricultural produce of California was in little demand elsewhere and was insufficiently profitable for regular shipping. With nothing to be gained from overproduction, settlers were not likely to work beyond providing for their needs and for the limited market of the military posts. There was considerable leisure time available for social activities and the crude and earthy sports of frontiersmen: bear-and-bull baiting, impromptu horseraces, and cockfights. No incentive for embellishing this life existed, nor is any embellishment evident in the homes. An aura of contentment enhanced the homes in the eyes of their inhabitants. Besides, since so much of daily life was carried on out of doors, the concept of home would likely not be confined to the small dwellings, but would include the open, sunny space outside. For these settlers, their simple life was far improved over what they had experienced at home.

The social structure did not remain static. A three-way social difference began to emerge in the town: Indians at the bottom performed the menial labor, pobladores farmed or provided services such as tailoring or blacksmithing, and soldiers' families assumed the superior social rank. Within a generation the shortage of women led to marriages between colonists' daughters and soldiers. Colonists' sons (less dashing, perhaps, than military men) settled for marrying Indian women. They were likely to live in the same style as their settler neighbors, since military pay was often far in arrears, but they seem to have felt and acted superior due to the centurion habit of command. At any rate, by the second generation the military class had stratified, socializing and marrying exclusively among themselves. Since they were the recipients of the few Spanish land grants of thousands of acres, while the pobladores had only their town lots and farm plots to bequeath to sons, a difference in potential wealth, as represented by land and laborers, was created. Families such as the Picos, Sepulvedas and Verdugos came to be related by marriage, enjoyed social pre-eminence, and had access to political favors (such as land grants for their sons in the Mexican period). They were to become the wealthy *rancheros* (ranchers) in the countryside around Los Angeles. However, their maternal grandparents were often pobladores, whose other grandchildren were small farmers and simple artisans in town, making it obvious that stratification of the new society was by no means absolute or complete. In the provincial capital of Monterey and the other presidio towns, the presence of civil officials and military officers with their families, and of occasional visitors from foreign nations and Mexico City, created a true social hierarchy, providing incentives for the building of more elaborate houses to demonstrate refinement, style and wealth. In contrast, Los Angeles, was just a remote farm town. 🌱

IV

FROM
MEXICAN PUEBLO
TO
BILINGUAL COWTOWN

The image which engendered

romantic dreams

in later waves of settlers was the elegant

cultural synthesis of the fine

corridored adobes,

twined with yellow roses

MEXICO WON ITS INDEPENDENCE from Spain in 1821. Monterey heard the news a year later because California's distance from Mexico City was so great and its importance so slight. The change of government only remotely concerned most *Californios* (Californians), who were accustomed to official neglect. Life in the Pueblo of Los Angeles, changed little over the forty years of its existence, went on as before. Within two years, however, new policies of foreign trade and land grants would bring a transformation. The sleepy village of mud huts would evolve into a busy social center surrounded by enormous cattle ranches. Within twenty years Los Angeles would draw newcomers from the United States and Europe, as well as from Mexico, with a fantastic vision: an enterprising young fellow of humble origins, so it went, could become a feudal baron, the master of tens of thousands of acres and a large manor house, the possessor of more cattle than he could count, the husband of a vivacious young lady, more overtly sexual than a proper New Englander dared imagine. He would be accepted there as a grandee in the top echelon of society. The dream drew many and came true for some, mirrored in the manor houses of the Mexican era.

Spanish policy forbade trade with foreign ships. In the two decades prior to Mexico's independence, though, smuggling by British and New England trading ships became common. Revolutionary ferment in Mexico after 1810 left Californios without any supply source for many of those years, so the English-speaking smugglers were welcomed. The frontier economy was primarily one of agricultural self-sufficiency and barter. Manufactured items such as needles, yard goods, iron items and shoes, as well as exotic imports such as sugar and chocolate, were obtained by trading cattle hides and sacks of rendered tallow.

The new government in Mexico wisely decided to permit this already-flourishing foreign trade, but subjected it to customs collection. The legalization of trade and the traders' demand for hides and tallow (raw material for New England industries) stimulated consumerism among the Californios. Cattle-ranching was suddenly profitable and landownership more desirable. The ability to buy fineries was proportional to the size of one's cattle herd, which, in turn, was limited only by the size of land holdings.

The hide and tallow trade introduced the Californios to new luxuries. Yankee merchant companies developed a three-way trade between the United States, the Orient, and California, bringing porcelain, silk shawls, and lace mantillas from the Orient, and men's boots, ladies' slippers, brooches and knives from Boston. In trade rooms aboard ships, later in shops built ashore, these wares were spread out to tempt Californio families. Such luxuries were within reach of cattle-ranching landowners. They were not necessities, but a taste for

9. Tomás Sanchez Adobe, 1867

them was created by the exposure and it grew as acquaintances displayed their purchases. The appearance of houses around Los Angeles began to change. Families with the largest cattle herds set tables with blue and white willow-ware porcelain, poured Madeira wines, installed glass window panes (ILLUSTRATION 9), entertained in formal parlors set with horsehair sofas and carved sideboards, and married off their daughters in satin gowns made by New England dressmakers.

The demand for land outside the settlements had been small during the years of Spanish rule. Grants of land-use had been awarded for long military and public service. In those days a ranchero had subsisted by infrequent sales of beef and hides, if and when he could find a townsman or a presidio commissary to buy his products. Mostly, ranching had provided for the ranchero's family alone, so they ate beef and produce from their kitchen garden. He might have grown small crops of grapes and grains, harvested by Indian laborers and processed for a fee at a mission mill. He welcomed foreign traders willing to exchange the newly introduced luxuries for the cattle by-products he had previously been unable to sell.

Soldiers and the grown sons of influential families petitioned for land grants. To meet the demand, the Mexican Colonization Act of 1824 permitted confirmation of direct titles to old Spanish grants and provided secure titles for new land grants, which could be obtained on petition by any Mexican citizen, provided one had sufficient influence and was Catholic, a requirement for citizenship. Grants were limited to eleven square league (a league is about 4,438 acres). New ranchos soon proliferated. From a total of five formal grants in the Spanish era, ranchos within today's Los Angeles County borders multiplied to fifty-nine by the end of the Mexican period in 1848.[1] The demand for land close to population centers was the major pressure leading to the disbandment, or secularization, of the missions in the 1830s. One after another, each of the twenty-one missions was broken up; its livestock dispersed, frequently to neighboring ranchos; its Indian charges dispossessed to become the experienced laborers for rancheros; and its lands, made available after inventory, for grants to families with good political connections. San Gabriel Mission was disbanded in 1833; San Fernando Mission in 1834.

By the late 1820s Los Angeles was a different place, for any of the few who came there. The little town twenty miles inland from the nearest port on a sparsely populated stretch of coastline was so remote that few would hear of it. Communication proved the selective factor to immigration. News of changes in the pueblo reached Mexico by reports and observations of those who passed through on government business. The news reached three kinds of foreigners: fur-trappers, sailors and sea-captains, and merchants or traders.

A man of affairs in Mexico, learning of land availability and the hide and tallow market opportunities in Los Angeles, could envision a life comfortably familiar yet with a good chance for enhancement. The language and culture would be his own, though on the cruder level typical of a frontier outpost. In such a provincial setting he could expect to impress the locals with his more refined manners, his superior education, and his knowledge of the current news and fashions in Mexico City. A man with political influence who could develop the right contacts in Monterey would not find it hard to come by a large spread of land in an area in or near the Los Angeles basin. Such influence was particularly fruitful under the governorship of Pió Pico (1845-1847). Ygnacio Coronel, a retired Mexican military hero who arrived in Los Angeles in 1834, is a good example of the many newcomers from Mexico whose numbers peaked in the mid-1830s. His wider experience in the world, coupled with his educational advantage, won him instant respect in the pueblo. In a short time he was a successful rancher and social leader. His dream and his reality coalesced in Los Angeles.[2]

American and European trappers, traders, and seamen also saw in Los Angeles a potential for dramatic economic advancement. The dream of riches, as a reason to relocate was different for each, depending on background and resources. Fur trappers were, by nature, unwashed social outcasts, and by profession wanderers not prone to settling in one place for long. Those who were willing to settle down and meet social expectations, along with the underpaid, hard-worked seamen who succeeded in jumping ship, were welcomed for their marketable skills in the new era of economic growth. One with carpenter skills able to make finer furniture than the pueblo's maker of rough wooden carts and plank tables could easily find rancheros willing to pay handsomely.

A person who came to Los Angeles as a merchant-representative of a Boston firm in the hide and tallow trade, or one who had the cash, credit, or connections to obtain a consignment of trade goods and become an independent merchant, could expect a more dramatic boost in fortunes than an artisan. His sophistication was more likely to win him social acceptance in the leading circles. The isolation of Angelenos from the wider world had left them ignorant of fair pricing, so savvy traders could charge inflated figures, becoming rapidly wealthy in the process.

If profits for both working-class and educated Yankees were so well assured, we might assume a heavy influx of Americans between the 1820s and 1840s, corresponding with houses in familiar American styles. We would be wrong. The first wood-frame building did not appear in Los Angeles until the 1850s.[3] The population of Los Angeles in 1836 was 1,675 (Indians were not counted), of whom only 40 were listed as foreign-born. Bancroft estimated 1,800 in 1840, of whom 1,100 were townsfolk and 700 lived in the surrounding countryside. Of the total he believed 40 to 50 were foreigners.[4]

Europeans and Americans viewed Los Angeles across formidable cultural barriers. To develop the great economic opportunities of the area demanded adaptation to an alien way of life. That price was too high for most. Those who came and stayed and were the most successful were those who were willing to acculturate. They came first because they dreamed of riches, and second, because they found the contrast between the Los Angeles way of life and their own to their liking. Social and cultural differences, then as in later periods, was one drawing point. Those who assimilated would build homes that were outsiders' versions of admired local traditions. Their own roots gave them a source of inspiration for some improvements to the local idiom, but their visions of life in Los Angeles were formed in imitative admiration.

What were the cultural features that distinguished Californios from their foreign observers and set the tone of life in Los Angeles? Their institutions, racial characteristics, values, social relationships, and standards of living were sufficiently different to provoke caustic criticism by some American travelers who wrote descriptions, guidebooks, and diaries in this period. Others, more open-minded, saw in this little Mexican town a paradise, a beautiful sunny land where a genial people lived a good life at an easy pace.[5]

Most Eastern Americans found the governmental structure in California unacceptable. Customs rates as high as 50%, bribery, and justice that was more personal than it was law-bound, irritated even those who were part of the system.[6] An educational system was likewise lacking: a first-year acquaintance with letters and sums had always been adequate for the simple business dealings of pastoral California. There was little sense of urgency about formal schooling on the part of parents or officialdom. However, New Englanders' dedication to universal education was the acclaimed soul-song of Ralph Waldo Emerson in this same era. Californios' disinterest in learning required an adjustment in thinking for relocating Yankees.[7] Although the padres complained of poor church attendance by Angelenos, in American eyes the religion of the place was a major strike against it. Anti-Catholicism was not only widespread in the United States but close to hysteria at this time. Conversion to Catholicism for land-owning or citizenship provoked a battle of conscience for most Protestants.[8]

The relationship between American attitudes and American dealings with Indians and Blacks could not easily accommodate cordiality with dark skins and Indian features among the Californios. The Hispanic acceptance of miscegenation, as long as both parties were Christian, and the racially-mixed Angelenos, together resulted in a potpourri that was particularly discomfiting to many Americans.[9]

Yankees and Californios defined honor and dignity differently. Certain traits of Spanish cultural heritage predominated, even so remote from centers of Spanish influence as Mexican Los Angeles in the 1822-1848 period. Stemming from a seven-century stress on military values in the Iberian Reconquista, courage, dignity, and a high sense of personal honor were essential male character traits. The dignidad of the Hispanic frontiersman differed from the dignity of the New Englander in being independent of social or civic status. It was based on a sense of personal self-worth or self-respect. West Coast dignity was rooted in a gravely sober sense of personal honor and pride. The concomitant self-assurance extended to an esteem for others' dignity, and was evidenced by relationships of formality and courtesy. One consequence was that written contracts were virtually unknown before Yankee influence became dominant. A man's word was bound by his sense of personal honor.[10]

For Californios to appear penurious or greedy was undignified. To haggle with a neighbor over a property line or a few calves at branding time was unseemly. An example of the prevailing attitude was that the Mexican land grants had no strictly surveyed boundaries. If there were an issue over use of a spring between one rancho and the next, an arbitrator was called in. If land or cattle hides were to be bought or sold, there was no need for written contracts — one's word was enough. In Los Angeles there was plenty of land and the cattle were numerous. Dignity was more important than material things which were so bountifully provided by nature.[11]

As for the attitude toward spending, the new trade in luxuries supplied a surplus in addition to a life that already seemed plentiful. If a daughter wanted ribbons or lace and there were hides (or credit) to pay for them, why not? Life had not been hard enough to nurture a cultural emphasis on thrift and saving for rainy days.

Spanish-speaking Californians had a different opinion of work, as well. There had never been a reason for working beyond what would provide *bastante* (enough). Even when the boom in hide and tallow came along, the nature of the business and the social structure served to reinforce the traditional Hispanic non-acquisitive attitude toward property. Cattle multiplied naturally. Pasture land was not fenced. In the proper season *rodeos* (round-ups) were conducted. Indian *vaqueros* (cowboys) did the bulk of the work, although the ranchero and his sons participated in the excitement. Periodic slaughters were staffed likewise, followed by the skinning and fat-stripping, both done by Indian laborers. There was little other work for a ranchero to do. The Bostonian puritanical certainty that idleness equated with sin was missing from the Hispanic view of priorities. But then, Bostonians did not live in paradise. As one traveler from the East put it,

"[Californians'] aversion to Industry, evidently arose...from the fact of their [sic] being no apparent necessity to labor, or, in other words, from the unparalleled facilities...which here exist for acquiring a competency, and even a superfluity, by the easy process of doing nothing."[12]

Days were free to spend with the family, or visiting at a leisurely pace, or at all-day *meriendas* (picnics) with a score of merry-makers, or paying week-long calls on relatives. Hospitality was freely extended to Anglo visitors. Travelers who stopped to ask a night's lodging at even the poorest abode were given the best the house had to offer in food and beds, and yet, to their amazement, the hosts would refuse remuneration with the frequent answer, "No, God will pay."[13]

As for the women, foreign men found a real contrast in customs and mores. In the United States in this period, women wore bonnets to keep their skin as white as possible; they encased themselves in rigid whalebone corsets; and they wore such a series of skirts and crinolines that no hint of human form existed from waist to ankles. They resembled fragile china dolls more than real live women. Men with polite backgrounds admitted to knowing no other kinds of women. In California, the daughters of the leading families, though chaperoned, were lively participants in mixed society. They often went barefoot and wore skirts to mid-calf. Their arms and heads were bare. They were rosy-cheeked, tan, and healthy: the prototypical California Girls. Edwin Bryant, describing a lady he met, spoke of them all when he wrote:

"The dark lustrous eye, the long black and glossy hair, the natural ease, grace, and vivacity of manners and conversation, characteristic of Spanish ladies, were fully displayed by her..."[14]

In Southern California even leading citizens lived in homes made of adobe with packed earth floors. To outsiders from a land of wood, stone, or brick houses, invariably wooden-floored, adobe homes seemed filthy. The table habits of Angelenos of every class, though polite, were marked by a lack of utensils. Furniture in all but the most affluent homes in the 1820s consisted of rough plank tables, simple benches, beds of stretched rawhide strips across rude wooden frames or just pallets on the floor, sometimes a wooden or leather-covered chest for a few belongings. There are no records of fireplaces. A few coals on a piece of tile in the center of the room for chilly nights were a far cry from the Easterner's essential hearth. The Atlantic seaboard was two centuries removed from such crude simplicity.

To the Yankee, these rough surroundings could appear squalid, the women shocking. Attitudes about property, spending, gambling, work, and generosity went contrary to a New Englander's upbringing. To some they seemed wicked, to others they indicated foolishness and gullibility. But there were those who came to know the Californios well, who found them refreshing alternatives to their own overly materialistic, competitive neighbors back home. In the Mexican period, a number of Yankee and European fur trappers, seamen, and merchants chose to reframe their lives in Angeleno terms. The merchants got rich: the contrast between the Yankee practices of salesmanship, contracts, compounding interest and ledger accounting and the Californio concepts of conducting business with honor, dignity and minimal education worked in the merchants' favor.

In addition to helping us understand the appeal of Californio culture to a selected group of distant newcomers during the Mexican period, this brief analysis of Californio culture, which is drawn from the observations of American visitors published in the East, serves three goals. First, it presaged the submersion of the Hispanic way of life in the flood of Anglo newcomers following the Gold Rush. Second, it provides a foundation for evaluating the myth that took root in the 1880s and hardened into conviction in the 1920s and '30s, the myth of a romantic Spanish past. Third, Yankee accounts of Mexican California published in the eastern United States are an early instance of a literature depicting a contrast between readers' environments and Los Angeles prospects. Such literature would continue to serve as the leading stimulus to migration to Los Angeles from these early 19th-century accounts through generations of booster publications to the present day. Such descriptions specifically selected people who wanted to live differently than they were.

In the Spanish era, before a way to wealth in hides and tallow trading had sailed into the bay at San Pedro, adobe houses were built by recruited settlers for minimal living, in familiar style and materials (ILLUSTRATIONS 6 and 8). The only elaborate buildings were institutional, the missions, built under the direction of the architecturally self-trained, but broadly educated and often European-born padres. The houses of those who came to stay in Mexico's Los Angeles are of two types. On the one hand, there are the one-story, flat-roofed houses which represent the old traditions on a grander scale. For the improvements to the old simple model in line with new prosperity, owners turned to the missions and to the haciendas of Mexico for inspiration. On the other hand, some houses followed the basic appearance of traditional Los Angeles adobes, but accommodated foreign tastes for symmetry, second stories, interior staircases, and plank floors. Such blending of the best of source and destination cultures are what their owner-builders selected for their lives.

One-story adobes, now several rooms, continued as the major style. The structure was arranged in a string of rooms one room wide, usually connected to each other by interior doorways. Houses in town often fronted directly on the street, so that entrance by the exterior doorway into one chamber, and going through the other rooms might cause internal traffic

10. De la Osa Adobe, 1849

problems and would certainly infringe on privacy. The ranchos, like the missions' *convento* (living quarter) buildings, usually had extended eaves supported by posts along the entire length of the building, forming a covered corridor. Each room then had an exterior door opening onto the front or rear corridor or onto both (ILLUSTRATION 10).

Along with rising wealth and more imported furniture, rooms grew larger. Windows, which had been few and small in the homes of the early pobladores, were now placed in each room. Through the 1830s, windows were usually unglazed. They were just holes, sometimes protected by wooden grilles and interior shutters.[15] The growing disparity in wealth, the lack of trust for the swelling labor force of Indians maintained on each rancho, and the devotion of at least one room to office functions for the conduct of ranching or trading business made security measures desirable.

Ranchos were situated in the gently rolling countryside radiating out from the pueblo. The ranchero could choose a house site on a low hill from which he could look over the operation of thousands of acres of his ranch. It was also important to be near a spring, creek, or high water table for easy well-digging. The sides of most of the era's ranchos, as a result, were open to a long, unobstructed sweep of prevailing breezes. The thick adobe walls provided thermal insulation and the covered corridors kept them from dissolving in the winter rain. The covered corridors also shaded the walls from solar heat. Windows and doors could be opened to admit air currents. A well-planned house was carefully oriented on an axis best suited to the direction of afternoon airflow. The doors and windows on the southeast side of the de la Osa Adobe, Los Encinos (ILLUSTRATION 10) catch the breeze which comes from that direction on most afternoons in the Encino area. In the pueblo proper, white-washing or plastering was the exception rather than the rule. Travelers described the dun-colored houses, in contrast to the more cosmopolitan town of Monterey, where the townsfolk apparently took more pride in their homes' appearance. Lime plaster was uniformly applied to the missions, and it was likewise used by the well-to-do rancheros who had Indian laborers to produce and apply it. It served as added protection from overheating sunshine and the melting power of the rains.[16]

In the Mexican period, floors of fired clay tile marked an improvement over the earlier packed-earth flooring. The Andres Pico Adobe (ca. 1839, may have been built earlier as a mission out-building) near the San Fernando Mission, had tiles in its original room. Second-hand tiles were abundant only after the abandonment of the missions. Roof tile was likewise rare. One early historian

51

stated that only five houses in Los Angeles had tile roofs in the Mexican era. The art of making tiles was associated with the missions, and it declined with the dispersal of their skilled craftsmen. Well into the American years, the town's roofs were flat, covered with tule or carrizo, over which brea was spread, sometimes mixed with horsehair, rocks, or other binders.

A century later in the 1920s, romantic nostalgia created a market for Spanish Colonial Revival houses with uneven plaster, exposed patches of brick, plank doors, and arches to express the ambiance of an Arcadian age. In the 1822-1848 period, an uneven wall of mud or lime plaster was hardly intended by the plasterer. If here and there a chunk of plaster had fallen away it indicated poor maintenance rather than quaintness. Homeowners may have preferred smooth doors, but could get only the rough-hewn versions of which their Indian workers were capable. And there are no arches known to domestic structures in Spanish or Mexican California. Houses were simple because the owner/designers' imaginations and the laborers' skill with construction materials were limited.

The tastes and comments of outsiders influenced Californios who were improving their material way of life. Foreign standards of housing began to

11. Rancho los Cerritos, 1844

appear in Los Angeles early in the 1830s. The Los Cerritos Adobe, built by Jonathan Temple in 1844 (ILLUSTRATION 11), serves as a prime example of the harmonious blending of native traditions and imported features. Temple came to Los Angeles in 1827 from Reading, Massachusetts, by way of Hawaii. He became a Mexican citizen (a prerequisite to landowning or marriage) and, in 1830, married Rafaela Cota of Santa Barbara. He engaged in the merchandising business in Los Angeles at great profit, so that by 1852 he was the richest man on the Los Angeles County tax assessor's records.[17]

In 1843 Temple bought Los Cerritos Rancho to develop his own source of hides and tallow. The house, completed the next year, had a two-story living quarter, about 100 feet long. To support an upper story, he imported redwood *vigas* (beams) from Northern California. The lack of timber for vigas in the local area had restricted most houses to single stories. There is some indication, though, that one other two-story house may have existed on the Plaza as early as the 1820s.[18] Temple's vigas, like those of the missions, were hand-hewn, squared beams which rested on wooden corbels bonded into the wall.

12. Rancho los Cerritos, 1844

Extending from the living quarters were two wings, each about 140 feet long, housing the workshops necessary for a large working ranch, such as a smithy, dairy room, and storage rooms. The open end of the 'U' was closed off with a gated adobe wall to form a courtyard (ILLUSTRATION 12). The grand entrance was an aristocratic flourish that signified a dream come true in a rustic setting.

The view in ILLUSTRATION 11 was originally the back of the house. Its covered corridor was the family gathering place, facing a fenced, two-acre formal Italian garden. This was a foreigner's vision of the ideal life, and at the time was a unique expression of a personal vision. But, observing the house unobstructed by such a garden today, we can see two other style characteristics which were grafted to the adobe tradition by foreigners. One was the insistence on the symmetrical (or at least evenly-spaced) arrangement of doors and windows. The typical home prior to the foreign influx was a haphazard structure, with windows and doors set wherever whim, breeze, and function dictated. The neo-classicism which was represented in Georgian, Federal, and Greek Revival architecture for a century and a half east of the Mississippi had thus arrived to impose regularity on California architecture. Another feature of Los Cerritos is its two-tiered

From Mexican Pueblo to Bilingual Cowtown

veranda. It is possible to see kinship with the French Colonial (Caribbean) influenced Southern plantations. The two features together are the keynotes of what came to be called the Monterey Style, in deference to the trend begun in Northern California by T. O. Larkin's house in 1835.

The ready access to imported elements was not monopolized by foreign settlers. A desire for glass-paned windows, paneled interior doors, and lace curtains was brought by settlers like Temple who were used to them and considered them indispensable. Their appearance in such newcomers' homes then set styles followed by native men of means. The glass windows pictured in ILLUSTRATION 9 from the Sanchez Adobe were the style in Los Angeles by the 1840s for those who could afford to import the glass, the frames and the sashes from around the Horn. To install them in existing buildings required some remodeling. In the Temple house, fired bricks for both the foundation and the paving of the rear corridor were also imported from the Atlantic seaboard.

The red tile roof is not original. Los Cerritos, like most adobes, foreign-built or not, had a flat roof covered with brea, later a shingled roof. By the 1860s, the development of coast-wise shipping and the redwood industry in the northern part of the state had made shingle roofs fashionable.

Wood plank floors, shipped from Northern California, were a feature throughout the central portion of Los Cerritos. Temple did not introduce these to the area, but his house typifies the preferences of foreign settlers. As early as 1832 the house of Nathaniel Pryor, a former fur trapper who had come to L.A. in 1828, was described as having glass windows and a partial plank floor.[19] Scotsman, Hugo Reid, ordered planks custom cut in the San Bernardino Mountains for his 1837 house near San Gabriel. The difficulty and expense of obtaining cut planks put them out of reach of all but the wealthiest residents. The first sawmill in California dated from 1844, the first in Southern California from 1846.[20]

The interior stairway inside the central entrance of the Temple home was a rare feature in the 1840s. Most ranch houses which followed the two-story Monterey style settled for an external stairway at each end of the second-story veranda, possibly because of inexperience at engineering an interior stairwell.[21] The arrangement of interior living space was an expression of Eastern traditions altered for Western hospitality. In the Temple house, a formal parlor, a separate dining room, and two bedrooms occupied the long central section of the house. The entire upstairs was given over to a series of bedrooms. Indian workers did not live in the building, and the other employees bunked in the lateral wings. The Temple family consisted of three persons. Entertaining the large families of

54

13. El Palacio ca. 1842

friends and relatives in the California style necessitated the large number of rooms.

Though Los Cerritos is (with the inclusion of the non-authentic tile roof) the style we think of as typical of the rancho period ideal, it must be kept in mind that very few homes of this quality and scale were built. Though the Lugo family, the del Valle family, and, later, Pió Pico, constructed two-story homes with similar features, few Angelenos had the combination of wealth and foreign-influenced taste to build such houses. Temple's grand adobe illustrates the process of cultural synthesis, one of the paths of acculturation open to foreign settlers in Mexican Los Angeles. In an effort to integrate into the culture he admired, Temple converted to Catholicism, became fluent in Spanish and married into the Cota family. Temple maintained the New England fervor for hard work and ambitions of financial success and a penchant for displaying such marks of wealth as Italian gardens and formal parlors. His home exhibited a blending of the values of the Californio culture into which he had integrated, and the imported comforts, technology and status markers suitable to a rich Yankee.

The happy blend of cultures represented by Los Cerritos was not the only route to acculturation. Don Abel Stearns, also of Massachusetts, also a merchant and ranchero, likewise became a Mexican citizen and married into a prominent California family. Stearns arrived in 1828, settling permanently in Los Angeles in 1833. On the current site of the Hollywood Freeway depression in downtown Los Angeles he constructed the finest and largest house in the pueblo. Nicknamed "El Palacio", the palace (ILLUSTRATION 13), it was only a larger version of the typical pueblo house: one-storied, flat-roofed, with one room added to the next until it covered the equivalent of a city block. Here was a foreign entrepreneur fitting in with the natives but on a larger scale. By 1842, wealthy and prominent, he purchased Los Alamitos Rancho in what is now Long Beach. He remodeled the 1806 adobe ranch house as a summer home and ranch headquarters, adding glass windows, hard floors, and other comforts foreigners preferred. However, for the strictly utilitarian functions of a bunk house and ranch headquarters, he abandoned thoughts of cultural synthesis and built what

14. Hugo Reid Adobe

15. Detail from Rancho los Cerritos

he knew to be practical — a long wooden wing in the vernacular board-and-batten style of American farm buildings of his time. In town, the Palacio portrayed Stearns as a Yankee who had given up his native culture to become Californio. When it came to the practical matter of running his business, his working buildings revealed that he remained a Yankee.

Scotsman Hugo Reid arrived in 1834. He defied the conventions of the merchant and ranchero set by marrying an Indian widow from the San Gabriel Mission. It was at that point that he constructed his first house. It was built of adobe and had two stories plus an attic. He faced it with clapboards so that, externally, it stood apart from its neighbors, representing an alien cultural intrusion. The house confirmed his initial reputation as a maverick. His second home (ILLUSTRATION 14), built in 1839, was a typical three-room, one-story adobe with earthen floor and unglazed windows. It marked an unreserved acculturation without reference to Reid's heritage.

In studying the historical record formed by Los Angeles houses that remain from past eras, the goal is either to identify those houses that influenced a succeeding wave of newcomers as symbols of their own dreams, or to find architectural expressions of the dream that somehow represented a whole period of settlement. Temple's house did both. To 20th-century romantics, the few grand homes of the rancho period, of which Los Cerritos is the finest surviving example, symbolized the hospitable, leisurely life of an idealized era. Later newcomers sought to replicate its features and capture its ambiance for their own lives. It was not the change-resisting nostalgia of Reid's first house, nor Stearns' direct adoption of local culture in his townhouse, nor Stearns' Yankee bunkhouse that caught the fancy of later generations. The image which engendered romantic dreams in later waves of settlers was the elegant cultural synthesis of the fine corridored adobes, twined with yellow roses like Temple's Los Cerritos.

The rancheros' Arcadian era did not last long. The Mexican-American War broke out in Texas in the spring of 1846, reaching Los Angeles in August. After a flurry of resistance, the defeated Californios signed an armistice at Cahuenga Pass in January, 1847. The Treaty of Guadalupe Hidalgo made California an official part of the United States in February, 1848. In 1850 she became the 31st state in the Union.

16. Banning Mansion, 1864

17. L.J. Rose house, 1862

The transformation from Mexican pueblo to American town cannot be better illustrated than by contrasting Los Encinos Adobe, 1849 (ILLUSTRATIONS 10) and Los Cerritos Adobe, 1844, (ILLUSTRATIONS 11 and 12) with the Banning Mansion, 1862-64 (ILLUSTRATION 16) and the L. J. Rose House, 1862 (ILLUSTRATION 17). Newcomers in the 1830s and '40s had tried to fit into the existing Hispanic society. Newcomers in the 1850s and '60s rejected the lifestyle they found. In the flush of Manifest Destiny the victor's culture was imposed on the conquered land in the physical form of architecture. New arrivals from the East no longer built adobe houses.

The 1848 treaty granted automatic U.S. citizenship to all former Mexican citizens who chose to stay in California. Everyday living patterns changed more slowly. Spanish continued to be the primary language into the 1860s. An event with even more dramatic consequences was the discovery of gold in January 1848 near Sacramento. If any group ever subjected themselves to incredible hardships on the strength of dreams, it was the 49'ers from all over the world who made up the Gold Rush. At first, Los Angeles was only remotely peripheral to the discovery. From 1848 through the 1850s Los Angeles attracted few newcomers. The population estimate for 1840 of 1,100 townspeople swelled to 1,610 by 1850 and 4,366 by 1860.[22] The difference over the ten years between 1840 and 1850 could scarcely account for a stable population with a reasonable birth rate. Not only were newcomers bypassing L.A., Angelenos were heading north.

In the 1848 season a few Angeleno prospectors, such as Antonio Coronel, struck it rich. But as winter closed in on the diggings, racial violence escalated. War-related racism, the language barrier, and economic competition combined to focus the violence on Spanish-speaking miners. Most of the native Californian gold-seekers went home and did not return. The Southern California cattle ranchers did not need to return north to find gold — they discovered it on the hoof at home.

By overland routes alone, the migration of Americans to the gold fields in 1849 has been estimated at 22,500, and it doubled in 1850[23]. A food shortage

From Mexican Pueblo to Bilingual Cowtown

quickly developed, driving up prices. Cattle, which had been slaughtered for hides and tallow, never bringing more than $4 each, now sold for beef at $25 a head. Driven overland to cattle buyers in the north at a transporting cost of two to four dollars, cattle brought prices from $35 to as high as $75 a head. Tens of thousands of cattle were driven north.[24] Old rancheros, including the small ones, raked in the money, and, as had always been the custom, spent it as quickly. The old aristocrats spent heavily on external appearances: silver-trimmed saddles, fine clothes, carriages, and horse racing. In 1852, Pió Pico lost to Jose Andres Sepulveda in a horse race with the stake at $25,000 in gold, 1000 horses, 1000 cattle, and 500 sheep.[25]

A Californio ranchero newly wealthy from the unexpected cattle bonanza was apt to acquire a house and furnishings patterned after the dons he had envied: an adobe in the two-storied Monterey style or with a walled courtyard. This was the good life as he understood it; now it was within his reach. Such men were not newcomers to Los Angeles, but they were new to the spending power they now enjoyed. Still-standing examples of homes built with new wealth on old-wealth patterns are the Olivas Adobe in Ventura and the Palomares Adobe in Pomona.

Like gold in the north such wealth was too good to last. By 1855 hundreds of thousands of competing cattle had been brought to northern California from the Midwest and Texas, better beef than the inbred, stringy California stock. The development of sheep as a meat source significantly reduced beef demand by 1860. In 1856 a drought in Southern California caused cattle losses and sales at give-away prices. The chance to get rich from cattle-raising and move into the lifestyle of the aristocrat was passing.[26]

Los Angeles became the destination of a second kind of dreamer during and after the northern Gold Rush. Among the flood of argonauts were large numbers from gold-producing regions such as Mexico's state of Sonora, Peru, and Chile.[27] The technological advantage enjoyed by these Spanish-speaking 49'ers aroused resentment among the competing Anglo-American miners. In the summer of 1850, discriminatory taxes, vigilante attacks on Hispanic miners, and constant harrassment drove as many as 10,000 Hispanics from Calaveras, Mariposa and Tuolumne counties.[28]

The presence of large quantities of gold and the unsettled state of society drew predators. The crime rate mounted in the mining counties and vigilante mobs blamed the crimes on Hispanics. Mob action against all Spanish-speaking residents of the mining regions in 1853 led to a significant exodus of Hispanics from the mining counties. Los Angeles was a Spanish-speaking, adobe town similar to hometowns in Sonora, a welcome refuge for the expelled miners. Los Angeles was not a destination of choice for this group, but by default. Some may have regarded L.A. as temporary, planning to return to the mines. Others brought their families and stayed, finding work as vaqueros on the cattle drives north. If they viewed the town as home, it was still second-best to the golden visions that had drawn them to California. Those who settled and built homes did so not only with economic limitations on style, but with limitations imposed by imaginations lingering elsewhere. A settlement known as Sonoratown grew up in the 1850s north of the Plaza, a knot of small adobe hovels, dirt-floored, glassless windows, flat roofs, as small, crude, and lacking in pleasing proportion or ornament as the houses built by the simple Spanish colonists of 70 years earlier, packed close together without the benefit of space for the outdoor living enjoyed by the earlier settlers. These were homes for the defeated. They have not been preserved for us to photograph. But they, like other accretions to the visual image, drew a new sort of immigrant after them.

The imbalance of men to women, along with the lawlessness bred by the Gold Rush, created opportunities for professional gamblers, gunmen, prostitutes, cattle-rustlers, and con men in California.[29] The slums of Sonoratown and "Nigger Alley" in Los Angeles were havens where criminals from the north could spend gold, sell cattle of suspicious origins, and find sympathy among fellow outcasts. In 1854, with a population of less than 3,000, Los Angeles was said to average a homicide a day.[30] Outlaws are usually nomads who do not leave records in the form of houses. But they left Los Angeles with a very bad image — an image that retarded its settlement by families. Los Angeles continued to suffer from a negative reputation from 1848 to 1868. Clouded land titles, the decline of a cheap labor supply, and a series of natural disasters added to the disadvantages.

The inability of would-be settlers to buy land anywhere in coastal California stemmed from the haphazard boundary definitions of the Mexican land grants and the oral sales contracts by which they had changed hands. Grants of many square leagues with unspecified boundaries, grants whose perimeters were marked by rock outcroppings or oak trees (since cut down), grants which had never been recorded, overlapping grants: all these meant that an ex-miner looking for farmland and a new home for his family could not know what land was unowned and available. It also meant that an American, following the western tradition of squatting on any land that seemed unused, could not be legally evicted by the grant-holder, because the latter lacked clear proof of ownership and boundaries. To resolve the problems Congress passed the Land

Act of 1851, setting up a commission to hear claims in California. The burden of proof was placed on the grant-claimant, who had two years in which to present evidence or forfeit claim. The commission, with a brief exception, met in San Francisco. None of the appointed commissioners understood Spanish.

Every Los Angeles area ranchero had to travel to San Francisco, paying for lodgings and travel expenses for himself and any acquaintances who could vouch for his family' long tenure on the claimed property. He also had to pay for the necessary lawyers and court interpreters. Court processes were prone to delay. Hotel bills escalated. Unable to tend to ranching business (or squatters) back home, and chronically short of hard cash, the old rancheros found themselves borrowing heavily on the collateral of their cattle and land. Unfamiliar with the mathematics of compounding, they agreed to interest compounded monthly, usually at 4 to 7%. Expenses, loan repayment, and the newly introduced property taxes had to be paid by selling land or further borrowing. Until the titles were cleared, the land could not be sold except to speculators willing to buy land of uncertain title for next to nothing. Most of the 813 land claims heard by the Commission were appealed through the courts, some to the U.S. Supreme Court. Historian Walton Bean estimated the average time from claim submittal to winning proof of ownership at seventeen years. By that time, the rancheros' debts were so high that little would be left after the land was sold, attached by creditors, or auctioned to clear tax liens. American farmers, who had typified Westward settlement for two and a half centuries, were prevented from settling in the Los Angeles area by the long-disputed land issue. When deeds were finally cleared, land in large undivided expanses was in the hands of the speculators. Even the City of Los Angeles, which had optimistically authorized a survey in 1849 and laid out its streets accordingly, with an eye to selling town lots for the good of the public treasury, found its claim to its 1781 Spanish grant tied up until 1866.[31]

The decline of cattle prices, following the introduction of better beef from out of state, and the effect of title issues on either the sale or the improvement of agricultural land, were probably enough in themselves to kill off the cattle-ranching economy of Southern California. But the smallpox epidemic of 1862-63 exterminated the last of the local Indians and nearly depopulated Sonoratown. They had been the sources of cheap ranch hands, and they were gone.[32]

Finally, the weather struck the ranchers. A year of drought climaxed in October, 1859, when temperatures soared to 110°. Then, in December, the rains came. On December 4, twelve inches fell in one day. The San Gabriel River overflowed. The Los Angeles River changed its course. The cattle suffered:

"Lean and weakened from the ravaging drought through which they had just passed, the poor cattle, now exposed to the elements of cold rain and wind, fell in vast numbers in their tracks."[33]

On December 24, 1861, a rainstorm began that lasted 30 days, flooding many areas, including the downtown business district. Then, from the spring of 1862 through the 1864 season, little more than four inches of rain fell. Vegetation dried up and cattle died by the thousands. Abel Stearns alone lost 30,000 head. Los Angeles appeared to be finished: its major industry was dead, its land was worthless and unbuyable.[34] Only a gambling spirit with a dream so tenacious it could hold on through the crises would venture to look to Los Angeles as a new homein this period. Such men might have been called fools by their contemporaries. If luck was with them, later historians have called them men of vision. Without them, the town might have remained the bilingual cowtown of the 1850s and '60s. More than a century later, their fine houses remain, painstakingly preserved, as monuments to their successes, while those of their contemporaries have long since been demolished or remodeled beyond recognition. History has long favored heroes. The housing record does as well, in dynamic urban centers such as Los Angeles. In the 1930s a new rail terminal displaced the Chinese sector and to create a tourist-oriented Chinatown the last delapidated vestiges of Sonoratown were demolished.

Phineas Banning was a man of vision. He came to Los Angeles from Delaware in 1851. He was only 21, but he had been supporting himself since the age of 12. His home (ILLUSTRATION 16), completed in 1864, was located at the edge of the mud flats in San Pedro Bay, the nearest port to Los Angeles, 20 miles away. Here was a man in his early 30s, building a 30-room house with a carriage entrance and an enormous ballroom in the midst of flooding, droughts, the Civil War, and local economic instability. The house alone tells us he was either a rich eccentric or an astute and ambitious businessman. He was the latter. The style of the house is another clue to the owner/designer. It was built of redwood by ships'carpenters in the Greek Revival style, which had been the mode among wealthy Easterners in the 1830s. Banning was a self-made man. As a store clerk in his teens in Philadelphia, houses like this must have impressed powerfully. No longer the style in the East by the 1860s, the Greek Revival cornices, pediment, pillars, wide architraves, side-lights framing doors and windows, and the white paint and green shutters proclaimed that a boyhood dream had come true.

Two other details of the house relate it functionally to the builder's life. The cupola provided a view of the entire San Pedro-Wilmington Bay, the source

From Mexican Pueblo to Bilingual Cowtown

of his wealth. From a start as a shipping clerk there he had entered business for himself: first with a freight line between the bay and L.A.; then a stage line; then a lightering service (transhipping from cargo vessels to shallow-water wharves); his own piers and warehouses; freight lines to Salt Lake City and Yuma; the establishment of the town of Wilmington on the old Dominguez Rancho he had purchased; and finally the profitable construction, paid for by a Los Angeles bond issue, of Southern California's first railroad, between his bay-area monopoly and the city.

The upper porch arrangement was designed for the oratorical talents of a politician. Banning's early lobbying had won for San Pedro first, the status of a U.S. Port of Entry, which aided his own businesses; second, construction of a Coast Guard lighthouse; and third, federally-funded harbor improvements. Active in Republican Party politics, Banning's vigorous efforts on behalf of both the Union and his own pocket were rewarded in 1862 when Fort Drum was established in Banning's front yard in Wilmington. He provided the land; he won the construction contract; he held the 7,000-man post's provisioning contract; and his monopoly of transportation in Wilmington gave him all the armed services' shipping business from the Pacific to Arizona and New Mexico. After the Civil War he served two terms in the State Senate where he promoted a bill for his own railroad. From his upper porch he promoted patriotism and his projects to generously wined and dined Angelenos at Union rallies and Fourth of July picnics.[35]

Banning's house, stylistically, was not part of any local tradition, nor was it designed to capture the benefits of a balmy climate. It was strictly an importation. It was a Wilmington, Delaware, boy's dream come true. That boy stopped off in Los Angeles en route to the Gold Rush and stayed, because he saw opportunity in the transportation business. His ambition was to get rich and he did so, ruthlessly. It was not Los Angeles' charms that lured him or the many others who came in this period. They came for the unparalleled opportunities for exploitation by those willing to take chances.

There was not room in transportation for many to prosper. A more certain future in horticulture beckoned in the 1850s, providing land and water could be obtained. One of the foreigners who had settled in Los Angeles in the Mexican period of easy land availability was Luis Vignes (Jean Louis Vignes), a Frenchman who came about 1831. Purchasing 100 acres where Union Station now stands, Vignes planted grapes from San Gabriel Mission stock. He built an adobe winery. By the late 1830s he was shipping his wines, improved by cuttings imported from France, statewide. After he sold his expanded operation to two nephews, the Sainsevain brothers, the firm set up offices in both San Francisco and New York. By 1857, New York connoisseurs ranked Los Angeles wines with French products.[36]

The export of Los Angeles wines publicized the possibilities of viticulture here. The potential of oranges was less well known because they were not successfully shipped to Eastern markets until 1877. William Wolfskill is credited with the introduction of commercial citrus growing. The Kentucky fur-trapper had come to the Mexican pueblo in 1831, first supporting himself by carpentry. After becoming a citizen he received a land grant in 1836 on which, besides growing grapes for wine, he experimented with oranges until he had successfully improved the sour, seedy mission strain into a marketable product. By 1857 Wolfskill had several thousand orange trees in production and was selling oranges profitably throughout the Far West and Mexico. His experiments with other fruits — walnuts, peaches, pears, apples, quince, plums, limes, apricots, olives, figs and table grapes — had become lucrative as well. All of these products drew attention to the horticultural potential of Los Angeles.

18. Leonis Adobe, restored to 1879

Leonard J. Rose, a German farmer in Iowa, heard of the fruited Garden of Eden from his brother-in-law. Rose, like Banning, was an indefatigable pursuer of his dreams. He gathered a party of ten families, 35 hired hands, one guide, and a large number of livestock and headed for Los Angeles. The party was attacked by Mojave Indians at the Colorado River. Nine of the party were killed or wounded. With lifetime savings gone, livestock reduced to too few to pull all the wagons, and without food, the survivors straggled back on foot across the deserts of Arizona and New Mexico to Albuquerque. But the mental picture of orchards like Wolfskill's was strong enough to keep Rose going. After two years in the hotel business in Albuquerque he had earned enough money to try again. Once in Los Angeles, he bought 160 acres from Wolfskill. Within a few years his farm, christened Sunnyslope, was a 2000-acre showplace of oranges, grapes and other fresh fruits, and he was experimenting with new varieties perfected for local growing conditions.[37]

Rose's home (ILLUSTRATION 17) was constructed in 1862 in San Gabriel. It could be a pleasant Iowa farmhouse of the 1850s. Like the cottages illustrated in the 1856 builder's pattern book, Village and Farm Cottages, it has a fan-bracketed colonnade, a steeply-pitched roof appropriate to Midwestern winters, gabled dormers, and full-length porch windows. The louvered shutters reminiscent of the Deep South, may have been a concession to fresh air circulation. Primarily, though, this was a sprightly Iowa farmhouse, a dream unaltered from its Iowa inception, made real by the exotic horticulture possible only in Southern California.[38]

Only a few determined men like Rose and Wolfskill could succeed in agriculture here because specialty crops like theirs required irrigation. To sink wells or construct dams and canals required a large initial capital investment. Rose arrived in 1860 with $14,000 to spend. Wolfskill and Vignes had developed their enterprises over many years by reinvesting profits. Also, unless a secure land title could be obtained no one would want to risk investing in water systems.

The Leonis Adobe (ILLUSTRATION 18) representsanother way to agricultural success without the necessity of a large cash outlay. Miguel Leonis was a Basque with a past that smacked of smuggling. He came to Los Angeles at mid-century to work as a sheepherder. The Gold Rush demand for meat made sheep-raising a boom industry along with cattle. The number of sheep skyrocketed. By one means and another, not all of them scrupulous, Leonis quickly acquired large flocks of sheep and 1100 acres in Calabasas, seizing outlying lands by force to form an enormous domain. Leonis could not have known that the secession of the Southern states and the unmet demand for cotton in the North would cause a wool boom. But this good luck, coupled with a driving ambition, brought Leonis his successes.[39]

A small adobe on his property was remodelled, probably sometime in the late 1860s. The transformed and enlarged adobe was not stylistically related to his origin in the French Pyrenees. He took great efforts to hide any trace of the adobe core. The wooden exterior, in board and batten, is the American farmhouse vernacular. The scroll-bracketed colonnades and cutout porch balcony railing are Gothic Revival details. Under its cloak of American carpentry and Monterey verandas, the house gives a hint of its true identity: its deep interior window wells betray thick adobe walls (ILLUSTRATION 19). The form of the front portion of the house is Monterey, as in ILLUSTRATION 11, harking back to the rancho era. Leonis left no records that explain the effect he was trying to achieve but his house has something to tell us. Here is a building that rejects both its own past (by disguising the adobe walls) and its owner's past (no trace of French influence), but incorporates the only two architectural manifestations of rural prosperity that Los Angeles had known to that date: the Monterey style developed by the rich bi-cultural rancheros of the Mexican period, and the carpenter Gothic brought by the new American arrivals who were taking over the leadership of Los Angeles society. This house is as bilingual as the countryside in which it was built.[40] ❧

19. Detail of
Leonis Adobe

PART THREE

SOLD!
TO THE MAN
IN THE
FRONT ROW!

SELLING A CITY

SOLD!
TO THE MAN
IN THE
FRONT ROW!
SELLING A CITY

V

1870s PROMOTIONALISM:
THE RAILROAD, AGRICULTURE, AND HEALTH

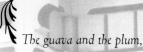

The guava and the plum,

the olive and the squash,

are found

in Los Angeles County

in the most loving

companionship side by side

UNTIL 1867-68 ONLY THE PIECEMEAL DESCRIPTIONS of Los Angeles by travelers, traders, and brothers-in-law occasionally broke through its general reputation as just another rough frontier town. But in 1867 calculated imagery was disseminated for commercial gain: the new art of advertising was applied to the City of the Angels. From that time on, the outsider's image of Los Angeles would be a designed image. The truth about Los Angeles became less important.

Beginning in the late 1860s, land speculators advertised the area to attract subdivision buyers. In the 1870s the railroads began touting the attractions of the L.A. basin in order to boost passenger traffic, the freight business, and the sale of railroad-owned land. Speculators and railroads were joined by a developing business community hoping to spur the growth of a community of consumers. These three overlapping interests marshaled a number of selling points with which they hoped to selectively attract those settlers who would be a source of profit to their particular business enterprises. Their selling points became the basic sources of the Los Angeles image in the 1867-1884 period, not because all of them were new features at this time, but because this was when they were first brought to the attention of the general American public. To sell Los Angeles to prospective settlers, nineteenth-century advertisers chose to emphasize the different-and-better aspects of climate, agricultural potential, opportunities for easy wealth, health, vacationland beauty, and romance.

Some of these concepts, notably health benefits and romantic beauty, originated in the 1870s as sales claims. Others were already popularly associated with Los Angeles, but were given new significance and wider acceptance. The demonstrated subtropical agricultural potential of earlier innovators such as Vignes, Wolfskill, and Rose was the foundation on which land salesmen planted dreams of even more exotic and profitable crops in the 1870s. Once widely accepted as a part of the essence of Los Angeles, a unique quality becomes ingrained in the myth. It is built on or altered by succeeding generations to fit evolving concepts of the good life, but it never disappears altogether. Perhaps that may be laid to the human reluctance to admit that one has acted on a misjudgment. Even after tea and pineapple crops failed, tropical fertility remained part of L.A.'s essence. If rural Midwesterners learned to be skeptical and stayed away, the urban Easterner still accepted this part of the dream, on a flower-garden scale, and the tourist still believes it on the strength of New Year's Day Rose Parades in Pasadena.

The uncomplicated local economy in the middle of the nineteenth-century reveals the selective nature of the city's appeal. The ad campaigns of the

1870s were mounted in three stages, the first directed at farmers, the second at health-seekers, the third at tourists. The distribution area and tone of each campaign were clearly directed to attract settlers of predetermined class, occupation, and character. A decade of settlement by pre-selected cultural categories would clearly shape the kind of city to which the next wave of newcomers would be drawn.

By the time ownership disputes on the old ranchos were finally resolved, many of the owners were desperate to sell. Land speculators who had amassed large spreads by buying up land options and extending loans prepared to reap the windfall. The challenge was where to find high-paying customers for ranch lands. Floods, droughts, labor shortage, and outside competition had ruined the cattle industry. Transportation to Southern California entailed hardships. Fortunately for the sellers, the end of the Civil War in 1865 stimulated capital investments and a new mobility. Young men already severed from familiar pursuits by military service, Southern families whose security had been destroyed by the course of the war, and budding capitalists with war contract gains to invest became the domestic targets of the advertisements. Abroad, Europeans with industrial capital or inheritances looking for investment possibilities served as prospective customers.

Some land sales occurred without soliciting, to customers in search of good buys. In 1869 Isaac Lankershim, a stockman and grain grower from Napa County and San Francisco, riding through the San Fernando Valley, noticed the prolific growth of wild grain there. Negotiations with the owners, Pió and Andres Pico, led to the purchase of 59,500 acres for $115,000 — less than $2.00 an acre — by Lankershim's syndicate of San Francisco investors later joined by New Yorker Isaac Van Nuys. The syndicate, known as the San Fernando Homestead Association, first put the land to use grazing sheep, later for wheat farming.[1] Buying huge expanses of land at sacrifice prices, moneyed interests like Van Nuys and Lankershim could afford newly-invented farm machinery and stock-breeding experiments. Merino sheep for breeding, new varieties of seed wheat, steam threshing outfits, and irrigation works were within their means.[2]

Investors like these who chanced on the scene were rare. To sell ranch lands when titles cleared in the 1860s, subdivision into smaller plots affordable to a wider public stimulated by advertising was more likely to result in sales. In 1867 and 1868 owners began to employ land agents and popular speakers to hawk the fertility, money-making opportunities, and climate advantages of the subdivided parcels. In handbooks, brochures, open letters, and personal speaking

SELLING A CITY

tours these early brokers exaggerated magnificently. They claimed high profits, easy shipping facilities, as many as four grain crops per year, certain futures in exotic products like silk-worms and tea, and personal witness to enormous vegetables. Most of these claims proved untrue, but advertising was in its infancy and audiences were naive. The pitchmen found takers. In 1868 Abel Stearns, once the grandest of the old pueblo dons, found himself in the same desperate position as many of his old compadres. Liens for delinquent taxes, overdue debts, and heavy mortgage obligations had been compounded by the drought and flood losses of the '60s. To salvage what he could, he permitted an investment syndicate to buy for subdivision a 7/8 interest in his remaining ranch lands. 177,796 acres were marked off into plots of 20 to 160 acres and within a few months 12,000 acres had been sold on credit terms at $10.00 per acre. The Picos' San Fernando Valley had been sold, undivided, at less than $2.00 per acre.[3]

By 1869 the heated optimism of farmers from the old Northwest, the South, and from Europe (Germany, France, Great Britain, the Netherlands, and Scandinavia) had been stoked by advertising circulars, causing a rush to Los Angeles. In the years from 1866 to 1869-70, Los Angeles County's population nearly doubled.[4] Farmers who were part of this first subdivision boom were family men who brought with them everything they owned. They had exciting visions of sudden enrichment from exotic crops with which they had neither personal experience nor the benefit of trustworthy instructions. Most small farmers planted income crops of familiar corn, barley, or wheat on part of their purchased plots, orchards or vineyards on ten or twenty acres, and a house with a garden to complete the new setting. Their hopes for a bright future rested with the exotic fruits, but vines and orchards required an initial investment, plus a waiting period of three to five years before a marketable yield could be expected.[5]

While the 1868-69 wave of newcomers was waiting impatiently for their seedlings to bear fruit and wealth, Los Angeles excitement began to abate. The first transcontinental railroad, connecting Sacramento with Omaha by the Ogden route, was completed in 1869. Eastern attention refocused on Northern California. A nationwide depression reached serious proportions by 1873. In the hiatus between the immigration wave of 1868-69 and the next one that began in the mid-'70s, advertisers found new promotable features and a new and powerful ally.

The year after the Central Pacific Railroad celebrated the completion of the first transcontinental line, its four directors organized the Southern Pacific Railroad. In 1871 the Southern Pacific was chartered by the state to extend southward through Los Angeles, then eastward across the desert to the Colorado River, where it was to connect with a southern transcontinental line. As on the Big Four's earlier routes, the state promised enormous land subsidies for each mile of track laid, making the rail company the state's leading real estate promoter.[6] To optimize the extension of its transportation monopoly in Southern California,[7] the Big Four's railroad applied pressure to extract valuable concessions from towns through which it planned to pass; it engaged in an unprecedented advertising campaign to inflate the resale value of the land it was to acquire; it promoted the production and marketing of crops to increase rail shipping; and it sold the world a multiple image of Southern California designed to draw health-seekers and tourists (translate: ticket-buying passengers) and settlers (that is, buyers of railroad land and shippers of railroad freight).[8] Late in 1872, the Southern Pacific Railroad became the Number One booster of Los Angeles, after the Los Angeles voters approved the concessions the transportation monopoly had demanded: a prime terminal site, an existing short rail line to San Pedro, and a bond issue.[9]

The carefully nurtured vision of Southern California began with inflated claims of the fertility of the land for farming.[10]

"Almost everything grown on earth can be raised in Los Angeles County. The pomegranate flourishes side by side with the potato, the banana with the tomato, the orange, lime and apricot with the peach, pear and apple. The yield of the grape is so prolific that a statement of the fact excites the astonishment and even incredulity of any one who is only acquainted with the meager yield of the European vineyards. The guava and the plum, the olive and the squash, are found in Los Angeles County in the most loving companionship side by side."[11]

The next step was to persuade Eastern farmers that the fertility and climate made farming here easier; more profitable; and, to quell worries about higher land prices, cheaper over the long run. "...in the southern parts of the State it is the custom to make fences of sticks of willow, sycamore, or cotton-wood, cut to the length of eight feet, and stuck into the ground in December. These strike root at once, and grow so rapidly that in the second year the farmer cuts his fire-wood from these living fences. Where Nature has done so much man gains a quick reward for his efforts. Our costliest and rarest greenhouse flowers grow here out-of-doors all winter, almost without care. In the vineyards are planted by the acre the grapes which at home are found only in the hothouses of the wealthy. The soil is so fertile... that the ground is better after it has yielded two crops than at the first ploughing. [T]he climate... permits children to play out-of-doors without overcoats...for at least 330 days in the year.... I do not exaggerate when I say that what a farmer in Iowa, Minnesota, or Kansas must pay out in two years for fuel to keep him and his family warm in winter, and for the shelter of his cattle from cold, would pay his way to California, and, if he chose well, almost buy him a farm."[12]

Exaggerated claims of fertile land and easy agricultural fortunes to be made in agriculture did not originate with the railroad-subsidized writers. The rancho subdividers and independent real estate agents had made similar claims, but the railroad developed advertising on a grand and institutionlized scale. Real estate agents and railroad men were joined by other businessmen who found the flurry of new settlers enriching. Lawyers, nurserymen, lumber dealers, and drygoods merchants wanted to continue the rising volume of business. In 1872 they formed the nucleus of support for voter acceptance of the Southern Pacific's terms for extending rail service to Los Angeles. They were the initiators of a Los Angeles Board of Trade in 1873, an early chamber of commerce. It published a pamphlet full of inflated claims in 1874. And one of its leaders, lawyer William McPherson, put out a high-pressure guidebook, Homes in Los Angeles City and County, and Description Thereof..., in 1873. In addition to assurances that pumpkins grew to 125 pounds and watermelons ranged from 45 to 75 pounds, he listed the annual profits to be expected for each crop, for example, $2,700 per acre for oranges, $1,164 for almonds.[13]

Even the apparently disinterested raconteur described a farmer's paradise. Ludwig Salvator's 1876 travel observations, published in Germany in 1878 and 1885, swore to a yearly income of $150 to $500 per acre in a land where the weather was perfect all but 20 to 30 days of the year, farming was not a taxing occupation, and "The farmer, furthermore, can have his house surrounded every month of the year with splendid fruit and glorious flowers."[14]

Who took the bait? What sort of people saw a pot of gold in a 60-acre patch of farmland near Los Angeles? The advertising was disseminated most heavily in the Midwest and the old Northwest, from Kansas and Missouri to Minnesota, and eastward to New York, with activity around New Orleans and in Texas added after the Southern Pacific's 1883 link-up to the South. Frequent comparisons to the work loads, fuel and shelter requirements, and yield per acre of farmers in those areas were clearly meant to persuade rural rather than urban people. Real estate promoters might not see beyond the mere sale of land. But railroad promoters wanted land-buyers who would also produce cash crops to fill boxcars. Civic leaders did not want to precipitate an influx of failures who would become a class of indigents. So selective advertising was aimed at established farmers, not just any farmers, but those with a nest egg. First there would be a down payment on the land parcel, then the purchase of seedlings or vines for ten or twenty acres, the seed for the rest. There would be expenses to bring in an irrigation system. And, immediately, the new Angelenos would need a house.

A prospective land purchaser arrived in Los Angeles after a long journey by wagon, ship, or rail car. He was taken by a salesman to the rural development that sounded good in the salesman's pitch or pamphlet. Within a matter of days the newcomer's family found themselves on an undeveloped plot, miles from the commercial center of Los Angeles. Building a house was a high-priority matter. Maybe it was because of this rush that the outlying rural development houses of the 1868-1885 period were so plain, identical to farm houses being built in the Middle West. There was a temporary quality about them as if the owners were waiting until their crops began to yield quantities of cash which would pay for additions or replacements. This settler built a board-and-batten or clapboard house, narrow, vertical, without time-consuming trimmings. It had the Easterner's steep roof and rear lean-to extension. Walls, frame, and shingle roofs were of redwood. It was likely to go unpainted and just weather to an innocuous gray. When painted, an 1876 observer reported, these houses were most often "gray or grayish-yellow in color."[15]

The dream-dealers might have been selling a pastoral picture to farmers who hated cold winters. But the picture was so clearly drawn that it shaped the region's population profile and its economic development. It was intended to appeal to persons with community spirit and a dedication to productive labor. Just such persons responded.

In the 1872 edition of his promotional book, publicist Charles Nordhoff called for colony settlement. Pasadena was settled in that way. In an Indianapolis parlor in the winter of 1872-73, enthusiastic discussions of Los Angeles' attractions resulted in the establishment of the California Colony of Indiana. Pooled resources financed a land-scouting foray and an arrangement to purchase 4,000 acres of the former San Pascual Rancho for the cooperative. The original group of investors fell apart before the capital could be raised, so a new organization, the San Gabriel Orange Grove Association, was incorporated to make the purchase. Stock was sold to more outsiders than to the original Hoosiers, but the nickname, Indiana Colony, remained for many years interchangeable with the name Pasadena. Subdivided into individual plots of 15 to 180 acres, the land was planted to oranges. The stockholder-farmers cooperated in building irrigation works, a church, a library society, and a school. By 1881 Pasadena oranges were winning prizes at state fairs. A settled community with all the neighborly ties of a Midwestern farm town had taken root in Southern California.[16]

The corporate nature of the San Gabriel Orange Grove Association selectively attracted would-be farmers of higher-than-average leadership, business acumen, and neighborliness. The home pictured in ILLUSTRATION 20 was built by one of the original company directors of the Association, W. T. Clapp of Massachusetts. He arrived in 1873 with his wife and two children and completed this house in 1874. It is not a minimal, utilitarian farmhouse but a modest example of the Greek Revival style popular in Clapp's native state twenty and more years before. It has sculptured brackets and columns and a carved cornice

20. Clapp house, 1874

of stylized dentils. These are strictly ornamental features. The form of the house is pleasingly proportioned with a sober symmetrical arrangement of doors and shuttered windows. It was clearly not a makeshift shelter, but a carefully planned house for a person who envisioned a life of propriety, responsibility and community position. Indeed, what we know of its builder bears out these visual clues. Mr. Clapp was Treasurer of the Association from its inception. When his daughter, Miss Jennie Clapp, was hired as the community's school teacher, Mr. Clapp offered the use of one room of his house for a temporary schoolroom until a schoolhouse could be built. Mr. Clapp, a Congregationalist back home, taught Sunday school for the interdenominational congregation that met during the first year of the Colony's existence. When a Presbyterian Church was formally established, Mr. and Mrs. Clapp were among the twenty-two founding members, Mr. Clapp also serving as the church treasurer.[17]

In the 1882 edition of his book, Charles Nordhoff again recommended settlement by colonies as preferable to settlement on an individual family basis. Now he could point to the prosperity of communities such as Pasadena. A settlement of neat, respectable homes like the Clapp house, set among orange groves, became a visual selling point. The cooperative construction of irrigation canals, ditches, and dikes was more efficient and less costly, Nordhoff advised, so that "where water is thus secured the price of land at once rises, often from two dollars and a half an acre to thirty or fifty dollars."[18]

The railroad land office liked colony settlements: more land could be sold in large lots and the success rate in production of freightable goods was higher. Private developers liked them, too. A fold-out map of the "Abel Stearns' Ranchos" subdivision in the advertisement section of one 1873 guidebook lists prices for tracts from 20 to 240 acres and announces in capital letters, "TERMS TO COLONIES EXTRA FAVORABLE."[19]

Pamphlets discouraged dreamers who were not hard-working, "Many of the prime natural conditions lessen labor [here], at least many classes of it, and this is a most important fact in the economy of life; still, it does not follow that apples of gold are to be plucked out of pictures of silver, at merely nominal prices, however multitudinously they may exist. No charm has yet been found abiding here, by which the way to them...other than labor, can be reliably pointed out."[20] The respondents, Midwestern church-social regulars committed to self-discipline, planned settlements with all the benefits of civilized society in a countryside of picture-postcard-perfect farms.

The Southern Pacific started building rail lines in Los Angeles in 1873. At first it constructed or absorbed lines radiating from the city. Cross-country travelers came by train to San Francisco and then took steamships to San Pedro, or came south by a combination of stagecoach and short rail stretches. In 1876 the final connection was made linking San Francisco to Los Angeles by rail. It was not until 1883 that the Southern Pacific's Sunset Route completed a direct transcontinental railroad to Los Angeles from New Orleans. In the ten years from 1873 to 1883 the leading goal of railroad advertising was the sale of the railroad's undeveloped lands. To this end the company offered three ticket options: colony groups could obtain discounted rates; purchasers of one-way tickets to California could book passage on emigrant cars equipped at no extra charge with reclining seats convertible for sleeping; and, once in San Francisco, the price of land-seekers' tickets for in-state routes were applicable to the purchase of any railroad land.[21] Until 1883 the railroad publicists actively discouraged everyone but farmers:

"To professional men, to clerks, to book-keepers, to salesmen, to all who mean to or want to live by their wits, or by in-door labor, California offers less opportunity than almost any State in the Union. It is overrun with such people, and they are more helpless there, and more exposed to suffering, want, and degradation, than in any other of the older states."[22]

Once the Sunset line was completed from Los Angeles through Texas to New Orleans, the railroad changed its tune. Land-seekers could not fill enough passenger seats on both the Ogden and New Orleans routes. The track touters began to round out another facet of the projected L.A. image: the healthiness of the climate. Climate, of course, was the major factor in the agricultural optimism the Big Four had been stimulating for years. Since about 1870, travelers' accounts had reported curative properties of L.A. sunshine. The Mediterranean climate of low rainfall, abundant sun, and a fairly constant temperature range was a feature of Southern California's coastal plains and valleys unique to few places in the world. The ad men discovered a new pitch.

"The enchanted isles of the dreams of our free and careless youthful imagination have here their actual earthly reality; the paradise, as far as climate can make it, is in this favored region. Here diseases and death may be kept at bay and life enjoyed to the end of the term of man's natural existence." —P. C. Remondino, M.D., 1892.[23]

In times past, the medical profession commonly prescribed a change of scene as a remedy for many ills. Doctors' recommendations of fresh air and a vigorous life had sent Richard Henry Dana to California back in the 1830s. His travel account, testifying to restored health, may have been the first promotion of the health resources of California. Easier travel in 1869, the year the transcontinental railroad opened, brought a rush of invalids. "Oh! what a lot of coughing suffering mortals are coming here!" exclaimed the Indiana Colony's land purchaser, D.M. Berry in 1873. He himself discovered relief from asthma in Pasadena and recognized the commercial possibilities. He wrote to the Colony leader in Indianapolis, "Send along...some... enlightened man to build a Sanitarium next the mountains. It would be filled in a day and every visitor would be an advertiser of our fruit to all sections of the country."[24]

Railroad writers, guide books, pamphlets, travel accounts, and popular-level studies by doctors and climatologists proclaimed the health benefits of the Southern California climate — tuberculosis, dyspepsia, and aging were arrested here; malaria and rheumatism never occurred, and testimonials of complete cures from almost any ailment were rife. Truthfully, the weather is more conducive to exercise; there is a relationship between sunshine and vitamin D; and the year-round availability of fresh fruits and vegetables was at the time unique to this climate. But, as with the claims of farming opportunities, the true potential was exaggerated and florid copy was the rule:

"One may meet in every county of this part of the State people who, having tender throats or lungs, came thither from the East or Europe, and have made a complete recovery. I know myself, not dozens but hundreds of instances, of men and women who would have perished in the more Eastern part of the United States... who, after a winter in California, found themselves capable of enduring fatigue and exposure with enjoyment..."[25]

Claims such as these led so many sickly souls to head west that the Los Angeles newspapers bemoaned a shortage of facilities for housing or caring for them. Hotels and resorts sprang up to meet the demand. The Sierra Madre Villa in the San Gabriel Valley, built in 1875, was a world-renowned destination by 1880. It provided tallyho tours for its guests to take in the ocean airs, mineral springs, and the ubiquitous orange grove at an easy pace designed for weakly Easterners. The influx of health-seekers stimulated by the new ease of transportation and advertising brought not only the ailing. It brought their families and it attracted others who saw their fortunes in meeting invalids' needs: hotel staffs and tour operators, sellers of patent medicines and doctors. Commercial enterprises flourished.[26] While the land-sales campaigns had developed a scattered settlement of partially self-sufficient newcomers, health promotion brought people who would stay in or near towns, eat in restaurants or hotels, and buy ready-made clothing. An 1883 newspaper ad by B.F. Coulter's department store marked the advent of invalid consumerism:

"Invalids and all others who wish to protect their systems, should buy

78

the Los Angeles Woolen Mills' Flannels and Underwear."[27]

 If perhaps eight to twelve percent of the region's population were invalids in the last quarter of the nineteenth century, multiplied by family members for each, there would surely be an impact on housing.[28] Many health-seekers came as transients, the architectural effects being on hotel styles rather than on single-family residential forms. But those who came and stayed tended to have educated, urban, middle or upper-middle class backgrounds. The health worries that sent them searching so far for a cure, not to mention the prevalence of symptoms as conversation topics in a town posing as a health resort, meant a preoccupation with L.A.'s supposedly curative properties: fresh air, sunshine,

21. Romain Grand house, ca. 1877

pleasantly cool nights. The pamphlets had disparaged the malarial vapors, stifling summer nights, ice-bound winter days, and stuffy interiors of other states. The stress on out-of-doors living contributed sleeping porches, larger windows, and cross-ventilation to Los Angeles architecture. The need to "take the airs" encouraged the relocation of a number of indoor activities to porches or gardens. Reading, parlor games, conversations, meals, and sometimes sleeping moved outdoors. The veranda or porch of Eastern houses was extended to two full sides or even three in California houses. Health and tourist pamphleteers preferred the fancier term, "piazza" to "porch" or "veranda." "[T]he climate... makes the piazza or neighboring shade-tree pleasanter than a room, in winter as well as summer...," wrote one.[29] Piazzas were not limited to those who had come for health. The orange-planting colonies also built houses allowing full enjoyment of the out-of-doors. "Their piazzas command attractive views; the perfume of rose and heliotrope hangs round them; and specimens of all the fruits are brought forth for our tasting, both with a lavish hospitality and an honest pride in their perfection."[30] ILLUSTRATION 21 shows such a piazza for a brick house built about 1877 in the suburb of Boyle Heights.

Another contribution of the new wave of urban middle-class believers was a more up-to-date consciousness of current Eastern fashions in architecture. In the decades before the Civil War it had become fashionable for young men from wealthy American families to be sent to Italy and France for the Grand Tour. This display of wealth and cultural polish was echoed in American architecture: prosperous families commissioned homes in the Italian Villa style or, after the massive renovation of Paris in the 1850s and '60s, in the Neo-Baroque grandeur favored by France's Second Empire. By the 1870s the middle class had appropriated the main features of these styles, modified by reduced means. The Italian Villa style was evoked in the smaller-sized, less boldly ornamented, more symmetrically secure Italianate style. Instead of the stone or plastered masonry employed in the Italian Villa, the vernacular Italianate most often appeared in wood, the building material rendered inexpensive and labor-saving by newly devised construction methods.

Italianate houses of the 1870s and early '80s were marked by wooden replicas of classical forms: projecting cornices supported by scroll-shaped corbels; sculptured bay windows; Corinthian columns and colonettes; apertures framed in replica voussoirs and keystone, and quoins at building corners. Likewise, the Neo-Baroque elegance taught at the Ecole des Beaux Arts and demanded by the rich private and public patrons in Napoleon III's Paris and by late 19th-century plutocrats in America was scaled down to the vernacular style labeled Second Empire. It also converted the expensive ornamentation and durable materials into factory-produced trimmings and cheap wood-frame construction. Its most prominent feature was the mansard roof, pierced with gabled windows and supported, like the Italianate, by a bracketed cornice. It also featured classical structural elements such as quoins and paneled frieze boards; windows with curved heads or "eyebrows"; decorative iron work including cresting on the roof and lacy balustrades; and verandas and bays supported by delicately spindled

22. Detail of Romain
Grand house

columns. The urban health-seekers and the trades-
men who served them brought both styles with them.

The house pictured in ILLUSTRATIONS 21 and
22 is usually described as Italianate. It was built by
Romain R. Grand, a French blacksmith who had
come to Los Angeles in 1871. The structural support
and the unfinished appearance of the flat roof have
convinced historians that the house was intended to
have an upper story which, for some reason, was
never completed. If the house were crowned with a
mansard roof, it would make a good example of the
Second Empire style. Modishly ornate, with the wrap-
around piazza demanded by health-conscious
Angelenos, this house of the late 1870s is far removed
from the severely simple farmers' houses of a few
years earlier.[31] The use of brick was not uncommon.
Two local brickyards had opened for business in the
early 1850s, but cost restricted the use of bricks for
the most part to commercial and public buildings. Wood was more common.
Since the 1850s, the redwood forests along the coast north of San Francisco had
been harvested and the lumber brought by sea to the port at San Pedro.
Banning's house had been built of redwood. Fir and pine from the Northwest,
along with redwood, were readily available to Los Angeles builders via the
harbor.

A new type of construction, balloon-frame, had become standard by the
1850s. The traditional heavy timber frame, joined by spikes, which had limited
house width to the length of available logs, became obsolete. In balloon-frame
construction, the walls themselves, built of two-by-four studs held together by
wire nails, were the supporting structure of the building. Standardized studs and
nails could be mass-produced. Houses could be built quickly and cheaply.
Balloon-frame construction put large houses within the reach of the middle class.
The use of wood for a revival of Italian and French masonry or stone models was
inauthentic, of course. In the East, stucco-covered masonry was preferred for
these styles. But in Los Angeles, by this date, wood was the common material,
easily available and requiring less labor. One foreign observer found his own
explanation for Angelenos' preference, "Earthquakes occur fairly frequently,
usually in August; this is probably why many rich families prefer to live in
wooden houses."[32]

23. Cornice detail, Mt.
Pleasant house, 1876

The prosaic fact was that wood was less expensive. ILLUSTRATION 23 shows a detail of an Italianate house in wood. Notice that the quoins, which were corner-supporting blocks of marble in the Italian Renaissance buildings from which the style derived, are here merely ornaments made of wood. The view also provides a good look at the brackets which were the trademark of the style. It was particularly fitting that this fashionable house, built in 1876, should be in wood: its owner, William Hayes Perry, had made his wealth in the lumber business. Perry came to Los Angeles in 1854 as a cabinet-maker. By 1873, the rush of newcomers had encouraged him to shift from cabinetry and furniture to "dealing in lumber, moldings, doors, sash, blinds, builders' hardware and finishing supplies of all kinds." By the turn of the century he was selling 30 to 80 million feet of lumber per year. Perry's booming business, based on the numbers of newcomers stimulated by railroad hucksterism, enabled him to employ the city's leading architects, Kysor and Mathews, to build his $9,000 mansion. It sat on a knoll he called "Mt. Pleasant," in such a way that the scenery and the garden setting could both be appreciated to their best advantage. Ludwig Salvator, the Austrian Archduke from Tuscany, repaid Perry's hospitality in his description of the view, "Viewed from a distance, Los Angeles is entrancing from every angle. Perhaps the best view, however, is that from Mr. Perry's house with its charming garden in the foreground, or from the west end, with the magnificent Sierra looming up in the background."[33]

The style chosen for the house announced not only the owner's affluence but his cultural pretensions on a direct note: he had sent his eldest daughter to Milan for operatic training. His choice of an Italian flavor for his house underscored the former cabinetmaker's successes.

The climate of Southern California fostered a third avenue for advertisement: the picturesque scenery and sunny days in which tourism flourished. Tourism took third place in the early boosters' priorities because land sales, freight build-up and a permanent increase in consumerism depended on settlers, rather than visitors. But the incidental realization that exposure could turn tourists into settlers gradually turned the railroad, developers, and civic leaders toward the tourist business.

Former State Senator Charles Maclay, with the financial assistance of

24. Lucky Baldwin's guest
cottage, 1881

the Southern Pacific Railroad, whose interests he had loyally pursued in the legislature, purchased 57,000 acres of the San Fernando Valley in 1873 at $2.35 per acre before the rail company had divulged its plan to run a line through the tract. Maclay platted out the town of San Fernando. The Southern Pacific laid track from Los Angeles to the town site, driving up the parcels' value. Maclay marketed twenty-five foot town lots for $10 to $50 each. To benefit Maclay, the Southern Pacific ran free excursion trains out on the new line. The passengers were treated to a free barbecue, sales pitch, and land auction by the developers. The railroad added further incentive to purchasers by extending them half-fare passes good for one year, plus half-rates on the shipment of lumber for home-building. In 1874 the excursions to San Fernando were a popular entertainment for Angelenos and a "must" on the visitor's agenda.[34]

Private developers without railroad backing also combined tourism with land sales. The lovely Queen Anne gingerbread house pictured in Illustration 24 had one purpose: to attract tourists who could be converted to land purchasers. E. J. "Lucky" Baldwin had netted five and a half million dollars from

25. Detail of Lucky
Baldwin's guest cottage

a Comstock gold and silver venture in 1875. One of his investments was the purchase of the Santa Anita Rancho, once the home of Hugo Reid and his wife. Sparing no expense, he created a splendid garden, surrounded by demonstration fruit orchards and vineyards. The small lake beside Reid's old adobe was turned into a heavily planted lagoon, later used as the set for Tarzan movies. Brooks, waterfalls, lily ponds, and bridges, along with exotic plants from the Orient, Australia, South America, and many other places made up an exquisite display of landscaping artistry.

Next to the lagoon, architect A. A. Bennett built a lacy guest house and carriage barn. Baldwin himself lived in the refurbished Reid adobe, where all the cooking and eating took place. The guest cottage contained only bedrooms, a parlor, an office, and a bathroom. The style and decoration were chosen for a single purpose: to create a spectacular impression which, coupled with the floral display and produce demonstration, would sell land at inflated prices. Baldwin is supposed to have admired the English exhibit in the new Queen Anne mode at the 1876 Centennial Exposition in Philadelphia. But this house, particularly the detail in ILLUSTRATION 25, is more accurately termed Carpenter Gothic, or Stick Gothic. Popularized by pattern books since the 1830s, Stick Gothic was here given a touch of the imported Queen Anne by adding a belltower.[35] Baldwin's architect did his best to create a show place. Every imaginable corner and edge dripped with gingerbread. Of such trim one woman later reminisced, "...sharp gables edged with paper lace, something like the perforated paper in the boxes of perfumed toilet soap, — perhaps meant to remind [one] of icicles."[36]

In the 1880s thousands of sight-seers came out in coaching parties to see Baldwin's gardens; prospective major customers came by invitation to stay in the guest house. The rampantly adorned cottage awed and delighted visitors and sold real estate.

The lures of Maclay's San Fernando and Baldwin's Arcadia developments were the fun of a train ride or tallyho outing; free food and free entertainment; and the spectacle of exotic flowers and scenery. Many fun-seekers went, had a good time, and bought no land at all. But their party-going spirit alerted promoters to the potential of tourism and established another of the enduring themes in the world's definition of Los Angeles. Los Angeles was a place for fun and frolics, especially outdoor fun.

In 1883, when the Southern Pacific made the Los Angeles-New Orleans link-up, its own publicists began to push sight-seeing, for the sake of passenger ticket sales. Their widely-read publicity agent, Major Ben Truman, published Tourists' Illustrated Guide to the Celebrated Summer and Winter Resorts of California Adjacent to and upon the Lines of the Central and Southern Pacific Railroads that year. The section on Los Angeles is found in the chapter entitled, "Famous Winter Resorts of California."

"But the winters of Los Angeles — ah! While all is rude, and cold, and leafless, and flowerless, and changeable in all the States east of the Sierra, in Los Angeles wind and weather are almost perfection; and heaven and earth seemingly conspire, in sunshine and blue sky, in leaf and blossom, and golden fruit, to make this period the very crown of the year. From the plaza, down the long hazy sweep of the main thoroughfare of the city, all is wrapped in verdure and bloom. The bright pepper and acacia and eucalyptus trees stand full against the darkness of the orange and the lemon... The grass in the gardens, on each hand, is like the 'freshly-broken emeralds' that Dante saw; hyacinths and tuberoses are springing up, and every slope is inhabited by modest members of the flowery kingdom; while the ivy and honey-suckles, that climb over the porches of pleasant domestic altars, glitter with fresh tips of constant growth; and everywhere there are roses — such roses... — freighting the very atmosphere with their incomparable odors and aromatic sweets."[37]

Bees humming in the heliotrope, roses and bougainvillea climbing over the piazzas, the sublime fragrance of the orange blossoms became part of every promoter's description, often compounded by the presence in the scene of tender honeymooning couples. The contrast between the sunny gardens of Los Angeles and the blizzards in the East appealed to the entire reading public.

Another tourist appeal which would hereafter enjoy periodic revivals in the Los Angeles image was the resemblance to Italy. Writers played on the same snob-appeal that had earlier popularized Italianate architecture nationwide when they referred to the "Mediterranean" climate of Southern California. Occasional poetic comparisons between Southern California and Italy were formalized early in 1875 when the developers of Artesia began publishing a monthly newspaper, partly subsidized by the Los Angeles business community. It was named The New Italy, and it glowingly reported the similarities in climate, flowers, and healthfulness between the two regions. Comparisons of Mt. Baldy to Mont Blanc, descriptions of local scenes in terms of "the American Nice," as "charming as any Italian village," lemon groves superior to those on the Italian

Lake Guarda, were slipped into the booster literature more and more frequently beginning in 1883. The full potential of writers' comparisons of the tourist highlights of Europe with California's was not developed until the 1890s when the literature insisted that Los Angeles was actually preferable. In the 1880s the idea that the two were much alike beckoned the status-seeker.[38]

Even without the snob appeal of the Italian connection, the variety of scenery within a single rail-direct region was attractive to travelers on a budget. The backdrop of snowy mountains to the sunlit town, the ocean with its cresting waves, the delicately scented groves, the myriad picnic sites, the gardens of exotic plants, the cosmopolitan quality of theaters and restaurants were brought out in the guidebooks and pamphlets. These sights were alluringly different from familiar scenes. Descriptions of travelers' enjoyment invariably indicated a leisurely, unscheduled, relaxing pace, making L.A. seem the ideal place for a get-away-from-it-all vacation. Wealthy families responded to the beauty and variety, often spending the entire winter in hotel suites or vacation cottages in the area.

The crowning tourist touch was the Spanish Past. One of the key attractions for the American in Europe was the ruins, or "antiquities." Old castles, cathedrals, and classical ruins were key features of the Grand Tours taken by the rich. Since the early years of the nineteenth-century, the Picturesque style of painting had been popular in England. The crumbling castle walls and warm sunset lighting of Turner's early paintings were part of a major genre of Romantic art. The elements of time-mellowed sadness, of nostalgia for an irretrievable past, a quaint sentimentality: these aspects of Picturesque art appealed to the sympathies and yearnings of the rising middle-class, pressured by materialistic ambitions and concerns. Artists who elicited deep emotions in their romantic portrayal of landscapes, were hard-put to provide picturesque scenes of America which could be imbued with nostalgia and a long-gone human past, until they discovered the missions in the 1870s and began exhibiting paintings of their charming ruins.[39]

But it was a popular writer, rather than any artist, who fastened on Southern California the myth of an idyllic Spanish past. A New England writer of romances who came to California as a tourist discovered that the missions were charming and popularized them accordingly. Helen Hunt Jackson wrote an account of her California travels in 1883, the same year railroad publicity concentrated on sight seeing. Jackson's enthusiasm centered on the decaying mission ruins. In describing Los Angeles of the 1880s, Mrs. Jackson pictured the Californios, whom she called "Spanish" (so much more elegant sounding than "Mexican"), as a beautiful fallen people living in fond but not bitter memories of a halcyon age.

The same adobe houses which formed the slum of Sonoratown in the 1850s, not improved by thirty years' wear, she described as quaint and charming. "The City of the Angels is a prosperous city now. It has business thoroughfares, blocks of fine stone buildings, hotels, shops, banks, and is growing daily …. But it has not yet shaken off its past. A certain indefinable, delicious aroma from the old, ignorant, picturesque times lingers still, not only in byways and corners, but in the very centres of its newest activities."[40]

Other authors of 1883 also wrote of quaint Mexican characters, the soft Spanish language, the strange foods, the "piquantly foreign" flavor of the place. The San Gabriel Mission, after years of American disinterest, acquired the patina of antiquity, "…six green old bronze bells hang in as many niches together. The fern-like shadows of a line of pepper trees print themselves in the sunshine against the time-stained white wall. No more than the church now remains, the great agricultural establishments connected with these missions having been swept away years before…"[41]

In 1884 Helen Hunt Jackson expanded her brief observations of Mexican Americans and Indians in the Los Angeles scene into a best-selling novel, "Ramona." The tender romance of Ramona and Alessandro offered American readers a bittersweet vision of a Southern California lifestyle much finer than their own, a "half-barbaric, half elegant, wholly generous and free-handed life," "a picturesque life, with more of sentiment and gayety [sic] in it, more also that was truly dramatic, more romance, than will ever be seen again on those sunny shores. The aroma of it all lingers there still…"[42]

Readers rushed west to savor the aroma while it still lingered. Tourists flocked to sites reputed to have been Ramona's home, Ramona's wedding place, to see persons claiming to have known Ramona. The book was a romantic hit still popular in paperback today, over a century later. It has been through 135 editions, in many languages.[43] Its readers then were sure they knew all about life in Southern California in its glorious past, a genteel life in shady, flower-decked haciendas; kindly padres, beautiful señoritas, strumming guitars and waiting lovers, and an inevitable cultural demise. "Ramona" became part of the flavor of Los Angeles, a new place, but old in fictional romantic memories.

The picture, formed by nearly twenty years of ballyhoo, was too fantastic to appeal to those who were restrained by cynicism or tradition or stodginess. The projected image was all the more convincing precisely because the pre-selected groups of settlers were so inexperienced at detecting the staged illusion. ❧

VI

1880s BOOM: VICTORIANA EXOTICIZED

We have built Homes

for men who were

little known until they

were occupying their homes,

and then public attention

was drawn to them simply

because their

house was so striking

"WHAT INTERESTS THE PHILOSOPHER is the inquiry, What sort of a community will ultimately result from this union of the Invalid and the Speculator?" — Charles Dudley Warner 1889[1]

The Boom came in 1886. Here again, the railroad was the catalyst. The statewide transportation monopoly maintained by the Southern Pacific had kept freight and passenger rates at the maximum the market would bear. It was with high expectations, then, that Californians watched the approach of a rival railroad, the Atchison, Topeka and Santa Fe, as it laid tracks westward. In spite of all the obstructions the Southern Pacific resorted to, the Santa Fe reached the state border in 1883. The Southern Pacific closed a deal with its competitor allowing joint use of tracks and price fixing of rates. In September 1885, the first Santa Fe entered Los Angeles. After the Santa Fe had completed its own tracks to Southern California cities, discord arose between the two giants over shares and conduct of the business. A rate war began: the cost of a passenger ticket from Missouri to Los Angeles fell from $125 to $95 and kept dropping. The rivalry climaxed in March 1887 when rates reached a low of $1.00 on March 6. Prices were soon stabilized, but for over a year the price of a ticket from Kansas City to Los Angeles remained under $25 on both lines.[2]

Suddenly the fabled land of sunshine, fruit, flowers, and opportunities was within the reach of middle-class families in the Ohio and Mississippi Valleys. A human flood hit Los Angeles beginning in 1886 and cresting in 1887. Not every kind of person came, of course, only those with enough money and job security to afford the time off, tickets for the whole family perhaps, and hotel accommodations; only those with imaginations susceptible to the extravagant booster literature; primarily townspeople who worked nine-to-five hours and had cash to spend, rather than country folk.

The prices of city lots began going up sharply in 1886. The health-seekers who had been settling for a decade included an increasing number of wealthy families who came only for the mild winters. They had built expensive winter cottages with extensive gardens. The orange growers were by now comfortably settled amid flourishing groves. The tourists of 1886 watched from the train window as the miles of desert dissolved into a paradise. Everything was green and, because it was so new, everything was picture-perfect. Even those who had been to Los Angeles at some time in the past were amazed at the change. "Everywhere in the wide circle around the visitor, wreathed in a blaze of flowers, rose houses such as he had never before seen in any farming country, and new places were brightening on almost every plain and slope and hill where but lately all was open cattle-range..."[3]

Many who had only come for a vacations returned East just long enough to liquidate their assets so they could return to buy a lot and build a home in Los Angeles. Impulsiveness was thus added to the composite character of the city. The quickening property sales spurred prices and the smell of profits to be made in real estate brought "schemers and promoters of all kinds with a little money which they were anxious to increase at the expense of some one else... and capitalists of high and low degree, who had heard that the country was prosperous...," as one critic called them.[4]

Until mid-year, 1886, newcomers bought property just because they saw the place and "fell at once into blind, unreasoning love with it."[5] Rising prices and the arrival of more and more speculative boomers changed the tone. Property was purchased just as a speculative investment to be resold as prices went up. As profits became the subject of hotel-lobby boasts, the turnover of property, each time for a higher price, grew more rapid, until some lots sold and resold several times in a day, real estate offices stayed open late into the night, and there was not time to record a sale before a resale took place. Pushing the pace to a frenzy were the professional boomers. Purchasing a parcel of land on credit, a speculator would plat out a new town or a city tract. He would invest little: a small down payment, white stakes which were set out in the fields or orange groves to indicate the different town lots to be sold, a speaker's platform, a brass band of uneven quality, and the cost of printing up handbills or running a newspaper ad:

"GRAND CREDIT AUCTION SALE!
-at-
South Pasadena!
On Wednesday, December 22, 1886, at 11:45 a.m.,
THE MALABAR TRACT!
(old Leavitt Homestead)
128 Lots in Splendid Location
Terms, one-third cash, balance on time. Special train leaves
Los Angeles and San Gabriel Valley Railroad depot at 10:15 a.m.   for the
tract itself on day of sale and returns after sale. Tickets, at specially reduced
rates, can be obtained at our office day before sale and at railroad depot on
day of sale. Free lunch on grounds. Band in attendance. SPECIAL
INVITATION TO THE LADIES for whom lunch, with hot tea and coffee,
will be served in house on tract....
Russell, Cox & Brandt Real Estate Agents 43 1/2 S. Spring St."[6]

SELLING A CITY

Carriage rides, reduced rate train excursions, free lunches, and the certainty of making money by buying and then selling, then buying again, assured large crowds for the opening of a new tract. But to stimulate prices and the buying fever even more, specialized techniques in salesmanship were

26. Land auction,
Monrovia, 1886

employed. Bands led the way, Pied-Piper style, to close-in tracts or serenaded the arriving coaches at distant sites, with stirring march music. An auctioneer, professional or former fiery minister of the Gospel, gestured and pounded and shouted as the crowd's impatience grew.

"Your very own home, ladies and gentlemen — right over there where the cool Sierra breezes mingle daily with the Pacific's gentle zephyrs; right there with green lawns and palm trees and bird-of-paradise plants; right there with a swing for the children and a fountain for those delightful song birds who flock here year around to serenade your evenings; right there with a view of snowy mountains and orange groves from your own piazza; right there within convenient distance of a modern, up to the minute street car line which will be built to the city business district! Do I hear a bid from that man in the front row? — You, Sir!" And when the bidding started, "plants" in the audience started the bidding high or made the first pretended purchase at a high price to get the crowd going.

When the town of Azusa was opened, $280,000 in lots were sold the first day, and as a sideliner commented, "Not one in ten of the purchasers had seen the town site, not one in a hundred expected to occupy the land purchased."[7] In the San Gabriel Valley alone, 36 new towns were laid out in the speculative mania. Some of them, to beat the competition, added extra gimmicks: a resort hotel, street lights, donation of land to persuade a church-affiliated college to locate there, or paved sidewalks thrown in with any purchase. Many promised street car lines that never materialized. The developer of Monrovia built not only a hotel, but speculation houses scattered one to a block throughout the tract. The town already looked better than the staked orchards had. Purchasers who would build immediately were given discounts on the purchase of their sites. Lots that had sold for $150 in mid-1886 could be resold in 1887 for $5,000 to $8,000.[8]

> "Burch & Boals'
> CARTER GROVE TRACT
> Every lot covered with choice deciduous fruit trees. Only two
> blocks from street cars. Not far from schools and churches, being near the
> University. A choice locality, very healthy and easy of access. Good
> neighborhood, either to buy for home or on speculation. Call at 56 N. Spring
> St. at 10 a.m. or 3 p.m. and get a free ride out and see them."[9]

The fact that the prospective home sites were obstructed by rows of orchard trees was praised as if it were a great advantage, and each tract, playing on familiar themes, claimed a healthier or more pleasant climate than that of nearby competitors. No one knows for sure how many arrived. The 1880 census had listed 33,381 in the whole county. Orange County was still a part of Los Angeles County until 1889. By the 1890 census, although significantly reduced in size by the creation of the new county out of its southern portion, the rump Los Angeles County counted 101,454. An estimated 20,000 in the City of Los Angeles grew to some 80,000 in the two years the Boom lasted. In the period from August to December 1887 the Los Angeles post office handled the mail for 200,000 transients.[10] When a town of 20,000 is called upon to serve the needs of 200,000 tourists, there are golden opportunities in the hotel business, the building trades (rental units as well as new houses, hotels, and real estate offices), hack services, and other fields. Solid businessmen who did not engage in the trading mania established comfortable business foundations during the rush.

The Boom, of course, ran out of steam eventually. The developers had purchased on credit, usually for one-third or one-fourth down. Counting on selling enough lots at inflating prices to meet the payments, the customers also bought on credit terms for more money than many of them had, intending to resell before payments became due. By January 1888 the supply of gullible Easterners with enough money and gambling spirit to head for California was running dry and a month of flooding rains disrupted trains intermittently and put a damper on the claims of sunny weather. The whole boom had depended on a steady supply of newcomers to make new down payments with which previous purchasers could meet credit payments. When the supply declined, defaults occurred, banks tightened credit, and the Boom slowed to a complete halt by summer, 1888. The Los Angeles Times editorialized, "The wild speculative craze has subsided, and we are very glad of it... the gambling era having drawn to a close, the era of development has fairly set in."[11]

The Boom contributed a number of permanent improvements to Los Angeles. Eleven miles of street railway track in 1880 had grown to more than 80 miles by 1889. Piped water systems, sewers, and street lights had been contracted and paid for at the peak, and they were completed. There had been no paved streets in Los Angeles before the Boom. By the end of 1890 there were some 87 miles of paved streets and 78 miles of concrete sidewalks. Colleges had been founded, some, such as the California Institute of Technology and Occidental College, flourish to this day. By 1890, after the auctioneers and speculators had left, the census recorded 50,395 for the City of Los Angeles itself, nearly a five-fold increase since 1880.[12]

When no buyers could be found for resale, many investors found their assets tied up in land parcels on which, by necessity, they settled. There were inconveniences for a while: purchasers of lots in Pasadena orange groves found no neighbors but trees and weathering white stakes; the sidewalks in front extended in either direction only to their property lines; and there were tight budgets for a while. But the permanent population had expanded, and business opportunities with it. An estimated 100 new homes per month were erected in 1886. In January 1888 alone, 260 new houses were under construction. Los Angeles was acquiring a new look.[13]

The leading choice of urban middle-class families in the 1880s was the Queen Anne style. As popularly applied in the United States, the term described turreted castles in wood, dynamically asymmetrical, with a verticality that made the houses seem imposing. The form was broken up into numerous surfaces, each of which became a display board for decorative surface treatment. With a

The 1880s Boom: Victoriana Exoticized

27. Hale House, ca.
1885-1887

silhouette composed of a melange of gables, towers, high chimneys, and dormers, the Queen Anne mode was both a romantic haven from reality and a pronouncement of material success.[14]

The rising American middle class during the Industrial Age had succumbed to an exuberant faith in the American success myth on the Horatio Alger pattern.[15] A leading tenet of this faith, ascribed to by everyone from the store clerk to the millionaire, was that with luck, pluck, and virtue, anyone could acquire greater riches and status, which were equated with happiness. The more ornate one's external display in dress, carriage, and house, the more one was admired in this highly materialistic age. On the other hand, the combination of driving ambition, cutthroat competition, and comparative display encouraged a countervailing romantic escapism. The Queen Anne style was a means of expressing the materialistic values and the romantic imagination of urban, upwardly-mobile Americans.

The Boomtime spate of new houses in Los Angeles was built for a particular segment of this group: the more impulsive proclaimers of the American success story, the gamblers, the vacation-happy. These were the people who really believed the flamboyant ads, the health claims, the romance, the picturesqueness. The boom-respondents were here to have a good time and to show off their affluence to themselves and their less-traveled neighbors back home. Their homes here would not be restrained, dignified, or austere; they would be as giddy, as holiday-spirited, as surprising as the people who had flocked here in the 1880s. Thus, in Los Angeles, the Queen Anne style became even more effusive and exotic than was customary elsewhere. Foreign elements were incorporated to enhance the sense of exoticism. Moorish, Baroque, and Chinese elements were indiscriminately blended. There was often a confusing mixture with the Eastlake style. (This term is based on an incorrect understanding of Charles Eastlake's furniture patterns, characterized in architecture by pierced patterns on flat surface ornaments, an eschewal of curved surfaces, and a fondness for lathe-turned posts and newels like table-legs.) In terms of form, at its local extreme, Queen Anne-Eclectic houses had as many different shapes, often quite unrelated, as could be stuck together, and as many

28. Ferdinand Heim
house, ca. 1887

29. Sanders house, 1887

different protuberances skyward as possible. As for surface texture, the Queen Anne vernacular had all the attention-drawing decorative diversity the owner could afford. This immodesty was the popular choice of the newly arrived Angeleno. The machine age had made the wooden lace and spindles cheap. Wood was inexpensive on the Pacific coast and factories making art glass and wrought ironwork were soon doing a thriving business. Even a person of middling means could aspire to a showy house.

ILLUSTRATION 27 shows not so much a house as a way of thinking. Built in 1885-1887 for an estimated cost of $3,500, it would have been within the means of the upper middle-class. Ornamental chimneys, a turret with elaborate finial, gables and wrought iron top a structure that engages the roving eye for some time without finding any real coherence. Neo-classical elements of a triangular pediment trimmed with dentils on a house decorated with carved roses and curlicues; windows of differing sizes; a turret on one side, a cut-away corner and upper balcony on the other; unmatched railings and pillars on the two floors; decorative elements in the pierced Eastlake manner on the one hand, carved relief work with non-repetitive designs on the other; fish-scale surface on one floor, horizontal siding on the next. Climaxing this plethora of attention-drawing fancies was the exterior color scheme — six shades of green, three shades of red, and three of yellow![16] The preferred colors for the carpenter Gothic houses of the 1840s-1860s period had been gray, drab, or fawn. Those were modest houses for modest people. The 1887 owner of this house was not modest. He clearly wanted an outrageous, even garish house. He was proudly displaying material successes and his stylishness (by which he meant as many elements of the style as he could afford). Succeeding generations were embarrassed by the gaudiness and painted such houses an all-over white. Yet, with all its wild array of colors and shapes, this house expresses a contagious exhilaration, a joyful optimism, a spontaneity that we might envy.

These homes were not built for Old Money. A local brewer could build a wooden Queen Anne castle with a crested tower such as the one in ILLUSTRATION 28. This house was part of an 1886 development known as Angelino Heights, whose

Daring Originals

promoters made good on a promise to run a cable-car line out to the tract from the civic center. A warehouse operator across the street caught the romantic nostalgia for the medieval in the shape of the cyma corbels in the gable, shingled to express the Queen Anne delight in decoratively textured surfaces (ILLUSTRATION 29).[17]

Most Victorian houses were not designed by well-known architects. Pattern books published drawings of finished houses, with floor plans and details. Building contractors or draftsmen or what have been called "Low Art architectural practitioners" commonly built the homes of white-collar workers and small businessmen.[18] The client looked through the pattern books and a combination of a turret on one page, a verandah on another, and a bay window on another was agreed upon and plans drawn up. In the case of the house in ILLUSTRATION 30, the floor plan and general form are very similar to some of the Eastlake cottages in a popular pattern book published in 1882, Cheap Dwellings, by architect John C. Pelton, Jr.. The squares of art glass around the windows were recommended by Pelton. But this one-and-a-half story house, built in 1886 for Daniel Innes, a City Councilman, real estate agent, and merchant, was less ostentatious in its decoration than Pelton's houses. Such restrained design was closer to Eastlake's own principles than the "Eastlake" houses Pelton was inspiring in San Francisco.[19] Even though success in real estate usually rewards assertiveness rather than reticence, Mr. Innes must have been uncommonly self-restrained or self-assured. For some reason he did not shout his importance in bright colors. While his neighbors painted their houses various shades of red, green, peach, and yellow, the original color of Innes' house was a uniform slate blue.[20]

30. Innes house, 1886

Verticality of form in Victorian houses was sought as early as 1850 as "an expression of strength and truthfulness." The twelve-foot ceilings were intended to keep the rooms cooler and to provide a feeling of airy spaciousness.[21] But even large rooms, if they are taller than they are wide, seem confining and rigid. The moral expectations of the 1870s and 1880s were likewise confining and rigid. As a California lifestyle defined itself, the tall narrow rooms would disappear. Clothing houses in an elaborately textured sheathing was a feature of the display function housing provided for successful Americans. The house in ILLUSTRATIONS 31 and 32 must have taxed the ingenuity of the builder to create so many different surfaces and to fill each space so richly. The pierced squares on the barge boards are the Eastlake signature. The spiraled porch columns contribute a Baroque truth. The overall effect is testimony to the material success of its owner, a transplanted Iowa hardware merchant. The rose-covered cottages which had figured so conspicuously in the tourist literature were perhaps responsible for the choice of a rose motif (ILLUSTRATION 33) for the relief carvings decorating the Hale House (ILLUSTRATION 27). Pattern-book writers boasted of their ability to incorporate multiple historical decorative motifs into their designs. The pattern of the porch-top latticework shown in ILLUSTRATION 34 is Chinese-influenced. The same pattern was employed on the Eastlake house in ILLUSTRATION 30, where its rectangularity forms a pleasing harmony with the form of the house itself.

One of the architects who arrived with the Boom was J. Cather Newsom. As the author of a number of pattern books and an architect popular with middle-class clients, Newsom's fame rested on his ability to create buildings that he called "picturesque," "striking and commanding," "artistic," and "commanding attention," but adapted to "Families Having Good Taste and Moderate Means." His brother and sometime partner, Samuel Newsom, in the introduction to one of his own pattern books, appealed directly to the upwardly mobile, "We have built Homes for men who were little known until they were occupying their homes, and then public attention was drawn to them simply because their house was so striking and well carried out."

The Newsoms were products of the nineteenth-century, caught up in the thrill of an age in which Progress seemed certain and their own upward advance limitless. They believed in expressing their excitement and their achievements in ornamentation. "[T]he degree of ornamentation," J. Cather Newsom explained, "will be governed, more or less, by the size of the builder's purse, though nowadays beauty in this form is becoming happily less and less of a luxury."[22]

About 1888 dairyman Charles Sessions employed Newsom to build the house in ILLUSTRATION 35. The twelve-room house, undergoing restoration at the time this photograph was taken, was intended by the architect as a "Californian" house. The conscious adoption of exotic foreign elements and accommodations to the climate mark a transition to the post-boom years, when slower growth allowed a more thoughtful inquiry into exactly what the Los Angeles essence was

Daring Originals

31. Aaron Phillips house,
1887

and how it might be expressed. Originally, the downstairs wing on the right was not enclosed; it was a wrap-around piazza for northern and eastern exposures. Aesthetically, this house is much more pleasing than the usual conglomerations from assorted pages of pattern books. The lines of the various gables and the tower flow together to form a unified roofline. The circular form of the upper porch is echoed by the fractured circles of the entry and the woodwork pattern in the upper pediments. The Chinese touches of porch-guarding lions (normally facing each other) and the circular, moon-gate openings are overshadowed by the architect's conscious attempt at "Moorish" imagery. The lacy screenwork, especially the harem spool-and-spindle effect upstairs, were meant to open up the living space to the outside. The full scope of the designer's imagination is revealed in the exterior detail of the stairwell, ILLUSTRATION 36. The oriel serves as the landing for the interior stairway. The cut-out side of the house forms a keyhole arch, which is Islamic, "Moorish" in Newsom's terminology. The end point of the Islamic arch forms the apex of an overhanging Gothic arch for the side window. The cyma bracket which supports the window-well was repeated on the upper-story sides of the house, perhaps to provide shade for windows or perhaps to provide continuity of line from gable ends to the balcony level. In spite of its mixed images, the house is an unusually unified work for the Queen Anne style. At the same time, it is a madly romantic and joyous expression of affluence and exoticism in Los Angeles in the 1880s.[23]

The excited imagination which brought the crowds to The City of Angels and which inspired their houses was not limited to proprietors of dairies, breweries, and warehouses. The store clerk, the tallyho driver, and the waiter in the restaurant also built homes in the Queen Anne style. ILLUSTRATION 37 shows one of the small plan-book cottages which sprang up on the edge of Boyle Heights in 1887 and 1888. The historical borrowings include the Tudor half-timbering on the gable end and the chinoiserie effect of the porch lattice. Even on a small house, about 35 by 45 feet in plan, there is room for an arched piazza. Unrestrained romanticism and display were just as characteristic at this level. ❧

32. Detail of Aaron Phillips house, 1887

33. Detail of
Hale house, ca. 1885-1887

34. Detail of
Sanders house, 1887

35. Sessions house, 1888

36. Detail of
Sessions house,
1888

37. Pattern book residence, ca. 1887

DEFINING
AN
IDENTITY
1890s · 1920

DEFINING
AN
IDENTITY
1890s ⁄ 1920

CHAPTER

VII

THE 1890s: A SEARCH FOR MEANING

Southern California

in general needs

more people of the

right kind.

It needs people

with money,

with energy,

with enterprise

and with industry.

WHEN THE BOOM FADED, no banks failed. Conservative lending policies, a willingness to extend due dates for payments, and the number of speculators who abandoned property without reclaiming down payments combined to stabilize the economy. However, L.A.'s businesses had been predicated on a high growth rate, and when newcomers stopped arriving business leveled off distressingly. Concerned entrepreneurs met and formally inaugurated a new Chamber of Commerce to "canvass the resources" of the county and develop them, to stimulate immigration, and to establish manufacturing, the last owing to a conviction by the members "that no permanent prosperity could ever be achieved without that interest was cultivated."[1]

In December 1888 the new body began its campaign to reinvigorate its domain with a series of pamphlets which marked a new era of intensified city-selling: simpler images were recycled into professionally-packaged products.[2] The difference between the salesmanship of the 1880s and that of the 1890s (more accurately, from late 1888 to the early 1900s) was a more businesslike approach with more insistent selling techniques, more artificially-created attractions, and a more selective appeal to persons of substantial means. As we shall see, each field of advertisement had, as well, an incidental side-effect on the public's perception of L.A..

The 1890s versions of the old health claims were less specious but more professionally couched. The Chamber's first pamphlet included two chapters on the subject: "Los Angeles, The Healthiest City in the World," a testimonial including specific case histories by an army surgeon, and "What Will the Climate Cure?," a local physician's clinical observations.[3]

The effort to lure invalids declined by 1905. Medical advances led more doctors to attempt cures themselves rather than sending their patients off to California. Competitive health resorts arose in Arizona and Colorado. The City Fathers turned to soliciting a more contributive element, wealthy investors and healthy settlers. Health claims were relegated to brief mentions in the back pages of the tourist brochures. It became fashionable for wealthy Easterners to maintain winter cottages in Pasadena, San Gabriel or Santa Monica. The attention given in the society pages of New York, Philadelphia, and Chicago newspapers to their departures and returns made it a mark of social distinction to go to Southern California. An estimated 20,000 people came to winter came each year during the final decade of the century.[4]

In the 1890s agricultural land selling, based on a highly structured model of success, was redirected to the capital investor alert to modern

A Search for Meaning

marketing methods. In 1877 William Wolfskill's son had rail-shipped a carload of paper-packed oranges in ice to St. Louis. His high profits pointed to new markets via the railroad, subsequently assured by the introduction of refrigerated cars. Nationwide citrus marketing would benefit both the growers and the railroads.[5]

At the height of the boom, orange groves had been sold for subdivision. However, as developers defaulted on their loans and cottony cushion scale disease attacked the citrus orchards, the post-boom purchasers were able to buy at much lower prices. They were not so often small farmers as "gentleman farmers" who could afford the risks. They bought up parcel after parcel to form large citrus-growing corporations. Their participation in businessmen's organizations led to advertising innovations. From 1890 on, the Los Angeles Chamber of Commerce mounted exhibits of the region's agricultural products at fairs, maintained a permanent display in the city, and in partnership with the Santa Fe Railroad, sponsored exhibits in distant cities. Beginning in 1889 the Chamber and the railroads had joined to send "California on Wheels," a car outfitted as a moving display of the state's products, annually through every town of importance in the mid-West. In two years an estimated one million visitors saw the exhibit. By 1891 the Chamber boasted that it had published four pamphlets with a combined circulation of 165,000, four bulletins with a circulation of 50,000, and 100,000 "other pieces" promoting the agricultural future of the county.[6]

Caught between high rail-freight charges and the machinations of distributors, orange growers began organizing cooperative marketing ventures as early as 1885. In 1893, the Southern California Fruit Exchange was formed. By 1895 the Exchange was packing, shipping, and marketing 32% of California's oranges. One of its marketing devices was the labels on the orange crates. The members of the Exchange were advised as to the best sales images. "Ramona Memories" with a picture of a lovely señorita and mission arches; pictures of long avenues flanked by palms and eucalyptus; flower-decked gardens; orange groves in the moonlight beyond a shadowy mission espadaña; winsome beauties offering baskets of oranges. Growers and their marketing cooperative were selling oranges, but they were also creating an image of California that was shipped nationwide.

After the Exchange spread statewide in 1905 under the Sunkist trademark, it joined with the Southern Pacific Railroad in a nationwide sales campaign based on the slogan, "Oranges for Health — California for Wealth." They chose Iowa for a saturation campaign and deluged the state with special

DEFINING AN IDENTITY

trains, grocers' displays, and orange poetry contests in the schools. Orange sales rose 17.7% nationwide, 50% in Iowa. Heavy advertising had proved its merits; it became the norm from 1907 on. Until the 1950s, citrus advertising portrayed orange groves as a dominant feature of the Los Angeles landscape.[7]

The business of selling Los Angeles to new settlers who would become consumers faced a hurdle after the dust had settled from the boom. Small farmers in the depression-ridden decade of the 1890s found agriculture too risky and the competition with large growers too great to tackle. To stimulate a resumption of immigration, business leaders had to find some new field of employment which could support new residents. They targeted capital investors, particularly industrial concerns. An 1897 souvenir book, in a chapter called, "What the City and Country Needs," explained the situation:

"The primary need of Los Angeles city is, I should say, more manufactories, which would give employment and afford means of sustenance to...large numbers.... Southern California in general needs more people of the right kind. It needs people with money, with energy, with enterprise and with industry. There are opportunities for the safe and reasonably profitable investment of capital."[8]

However, commercial interests' early attempts to attract such capital were thwarted. Limited raw materials, labor pool, markets, cheap transportation, and cheap fuel led industrialists to reject Los Angeles for more favorably situated towns such as Chicago and Cleveland.[9] Chamber of Commerce pamphlets from 1888 to 1911 attempted to downplay these problems. They stressed the attractive physical setting for business relocation. Los Angeles did present a modern, clean look about its business district. Most of the buildings dated from 1886 or later; streetcar systems were new; and streets were wide. Some brochures discussed working-class salaries, banking stability, and the potential for West Coast marketing.[10]

The boost in manufacturing finally occurred around 1894. Two years earlier E. L. Doheny and C. A. Canfield had struck oil in a residential neighborhood near the L.A. civic center. By 1894 local oil production was large enough to support burgeoning industry. By 1901, when both railroads converted to oil-burning locomotives, the oil business itself was a major industry here. In 1900 $3 million worth of oil (over 4 million barrels) was being produced per year.[11] Cheap oil supplies spurred industrial investment. At the dawn of the new century, businessmen with capital began relocating to Los Angeles and starting new enterprises there. Harrison Gray Otis, owner of the <u>Los Angeles Times</u> and a founding member of the Chamber of Commerce, in a 1910 article floridly

A Search for Meaning

entitled, "Los Angeles, the Ardent Hebe of the Sensuous South; A Sketch," claimed that Los Angeles had a more advantageous business climate than any other city in America.[12]

The most fertile field for promotion in the 1890s was tourism and the sale of a unique life style. The wives of the business proprietors to whom Otis and the Chamber were addressing their assurances would be captivated by this 1898 claim.

"Los Angeles is a residence city of marvelous beauty. On every hand it requires but a few steps from business activity to carry one into the bowery repose of the tropical gardens which every citizen seems to take so much pride in keeping up about his home..."[13]

These rising middle-class housewives enjoyed a new leisure because of labor-saving devices and their ability to hire household help, but they found themselves pressured by a fervent and competitive desire to display material prosperity. Inexperienced in their new social milieu, they needed guidance in how to project the proper image without committing gaffes. New periodicals came to their rescue. Magazines such as the Ladies' Home Journal, established in 1883, told them everything they needed to know in order that they, their families, and their homes should appear to their best advantages before the critical outside world: how to decorate their parlors, what architectural styles they should aspire to, how to dress, how to bring up their children, what leisure activities they should pursue. During the decade of the '80s, under such guidance and peer pressure, ladies became intensely interested, even competitively interested, in cultivating flower gardens. Women's magazines, as they still do today, contained articles on new varieties of roses, on Mrs. So-and-so's prize-winning garden, on how to plan a garden for successive blooms.

Since the 1870s Los Angeles had presented an image of a garden wonderland. L. J. Rose's Sunnyslope, Lucky Baldwin's Santa Anita, and the gardens of the Sierra Madre Villa were major tourist destinations. Magazine and brochure pictures of such gardens, of roses in winter, of gardens overflowing with flowers Midwesterners found impossible to grow, and the presence of imported exotics they had never seen fascinated backyard gardeners. The travelers who came with the 1886-1888 boom and stayed were heavily representative of the flower-loving middle class. They were quick to plant ornamental gardens and lawns around the new homes they built. They were thrilled with the climatic invitation to lavish attention on plants that were rare or nonexistent in their home states. By the early '90s the front yards of houses all over Los Angeles, from small cottages to grand mansions, were showplaces. By

DEFINING AN IDENTITY

1894 there were forty-five nurseries in Los Angeles County stocked with plants imported from China, Japan, India, the Mediterranean, and South America.[14]

Self-conscious of their gardens as showplaces, wealthy Easterners with winter homes in the area maintained gardening staffs. Between the middle-class housewife's efforts and gardeners' exertions, the private yard played a major role in the expansion of the Los Angeles image in the 1890s and 1900s. Formerly a rustic delight of aromatic flowers run rampant over roofs and fences, it had become a purposely created Garden of Eden. The business community in Pasadena capitalized on the image with a Rose Parade in 1890. Carriages covered with roses in January produced such positive publicity that the parade is an annual fixture to this day.[15]

The commercial possibilities of flowers were fully realized in Hollywood. Mrs. Daeida Wilcox Beveridge, a former temperance crusader from Hicksville, Ohio, had come to Los Angeles in 1883 with her first husband, a Kansas real estate promoter. In the course of the 1886-1888 boom their fortune rose and fell, leaving them in possession of considerable land in the Cahuenga Valley, which Mrs. Wilcox Beveridge named Hollywood. Through the '90s the settlement showed little growth. It was a small country town in a lemon and vegetable growing area. In this same period in New York, Paul de Longpre, a French artist popular for his paintings of flowers, was admiring the flowery heaven pictured in the Los Angeles tourist literature. Troubled by the expense of the hothouse blooms he used as models, he succumbed to its charms in 1899 and headed west. His own charm and marketing potential led Mrs. Wilcox Beveridge to give him three 65-foot lots on Cahuenga Avenue if he would build a fine house, studio, and flower gardens there. Mrs. Beveridge was so smitten with the idea that she had her own house moved from the site to accommodate the flower-painter and she later added an adjoining lot valued at $3,000 in exchange for three paintings.

As soon as de Longpre's flowers were blooming, Hollywood became one of the leading tourist attractions around Los Angeles. Thousands of visitors came each year to stroll in the floral wonderland, stop by the famous artist's studio, and perhaps buy a painting. Newspaper writers were always given a personal welcome by the artist himself and treated to French cuisine and guided garden tours, resulting in free newspaper publicity worldwide. A tallyho service, eventually replaced by a street railway, brought the tourists in. Hotels and restaurants sprang up to serve them. By 1907 Hollywood had a population of 3,415 and Mrs. Beveridge's property prices rose because of the heavy demand. People wanted to settle where they had enjoyed such charming scenery.[16]

A Search for Meaning

De Longpre's flower gardens and the Rose Parade were not the only commercialized attractions on the "must see" list of 1890s tourists. There were tours of the ostrich farms for 25 cents. Ostriches, raised for the feathers which adorned ladies' hats, were rare, amusing, and uniquely subtropical.[17] The beaches were developed into tourist resorts and praised as "matchlessly lovable and peerlessly lovely," and much better than any seaside resort on the Atlantic coast. Santa Monica attracted thousands each summer weekend who came by the trainload from every part of Los Angeles to stroll on the boardwalks, sit under beach umbrellas fully dressed with bustles and high-button shoes or three-piece black suits and bowler hats, to socialize with other awe-struck Midwesterners.[18] Santa Catalina Island was another must-see item on the vacationer's agenda — "a park in the Pacific, a mountain range at sea," with cottages, hotels, curio shops, a golf course, superlative fishing and hunting, mountain coach tours, beaches, shell collecting, and glass-bottom boat rides — all available by a daily steamer ride, year-round, twenty-two miles from Los Angeles. Mt. Lowe, with its "Great Incline" and cliff-hanging rail rides was even more thrilling.[19]

By the nineteen-oughts, vacationers were no longer trusted to find enjoyment here on their own. The natural advantages had been capitalized, institutionalized, taken over and packaged as commercial enterprises and advertised nationwide as desired destinations for every reader. Thrills, variety, and a pressured search for fun had become part of what Los Angeles was all about. Thus a number of familiar facets of the Los Angeles image had been commercially exploited by civic and private boosters to attract tourists and investors. Behind all the boisterous confusion of sensory delights described in the brochures are two consistent themes: the newness of the man-made environment (that is, no tradition-bound image); and the exotic subtropical nature of the environment.

Behind their exotic palm trees, pampas grass, and flowers, the houses built from about 1890 to the early 1900s reflect the profusion of imagery in an incoherent choice of styles, all pre-packaged and in the latest style, with no other relationship to the unique Los Angeles setting. In a few, one senses an early groping for an architectural language to express the essence of this new place but most were non-localized three-dimensional calling cards for owners expressing pride in their financial success. The general tone of the homes in this period differed from those of the 1880s. They were more massive and imposing. The delicacy of the decorative flourishes of the '80s turned heavy-handed and emphatic.

The 1890 house in ILLUSTRATION 38 was an early and conscious effort to

DEFINING AN IDENTITY

38. "A California House", 1890

40. Detail of Mooers house, 1894

39. Detail of Mooers house, 1894

design a "California" house for the unique living conditions here. J. Cather Newsom, as was his custom, searched in his books and came up with a combination of several styles which he felt met the challenge. The facades are plainer, less luxuriously surfaced than the earlier Newsom houses we have illustrated. The eclectic jumble of Moorish references, a Moon Gate, a classical pediment, piazzas, and a Second Empire mansard tower, is an admission of some confusion as to what "California" meant. But the garden setting clearly projected a single subtropical image. The wide lawns and open space are highlighted by an original planting of pampas grass, poinsettias, ginger torches, and other imported ornamentals.

The bird-of-paradise plant, a dramatic rarity to 1890s newcomers, was no less dramatic than the riot of frills and furbelows and the wealth of wood-carving combined in ILLUSTRATION 39, surmounted by the voluptuously exaggerated balcony arabesque in ILLUSTRATION 40. Taken altogether, these details defy the constraints of traditions. The details of the tower (ILLUSTRATION 41) extend eclecticism to new heights, speaking of Asian mysticism in the mixed modes of cusped arches à la Constantinople, topped by the chatri — the stylized Bodhi tree symbol of Buddhism.[20] The 1894 house, designed by architects

A S e a r c h f o r M e a n i n g

41. Detail of Mooers house, 1894

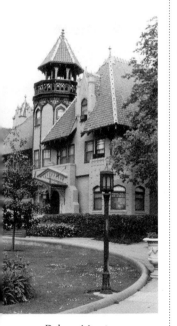

42. Doheny Mansion, 1899-1900

Bradbeer and Ferris and built as a speculative venture of the contractor, was acquired in 1898 by a drifter-prospector named Frederick Mitchell Mooers, who had struck gold in the Mojave Desert in 1895. His own life story was as incredible as his house.[21]

The flamboyance and eclecticism so vividly displayed in the Mooers house was not uncommon in 1890s Los Angeles. A group of architects exhibiting photographs of their wares in 1896 boasted, "California has not, in the opinion of the writer, as yet developed a characteristic architecture of its own;...The Colonial, the Queen Anne, Moorish [and other derivative styles] have all been represented; but the tendency of the day seems to be towards a utilization of such features of each style of architecture as are best calculated to produce a picturesque effect, and at the same time enjoy to the fullest extent the advantages of sunshine and view."[22]

The tourist literature of the 1890s and 1900s employed views of private homes as major sights to be seen. These booklets and fold-outs reveal that homes as picturesquely eclectic as the Mooers house were not so unusual as we might suppose from the few that have survived. One after another are characterized by onion domes, bulbous towers, strange masses of discordant shapes, and delirious dashes of ornamentation.

The confusion over what Los Angeles held in store might be expressed by composite imagery, or an owner could demand a house that portrayed their own historical model of grandeur. They could build a French Gothic castle, an Elizabethan manor, or an American Colonial mansion, none historically accurate, but, rather, indicative of their limited understanding of the prominent features of those styles and flavored by the personal fantasies associated with such settings. The French chateau could be realized on the grand scale such as that shown in ILLUSTRATION 42 by noted architects, Eisen and Hunt in 1899-1900.[23] Architects Merithew and Haley built the more modestly scaled French chateau in wood seen in ILLUSTRATIONS 43 and 44 in 1896.[24]

The acres of gardens surrounding the mansion in ILLUSTRATION 42 included Southern California's first glass conservatory, where the owner, oil magnate E. L. Doheny, collected rare palms, cycads, and orchids. The subtropical garden setting was too much a part of the meaning of Los Angeles to be

43. French chateau in wood, 1896

44. Detail of French chateau in wood, 1896

subverted into gardens appropriate to a pre-selected house style.[25] Thus we see a half-timbered Tudor manor-house guarded by a splendid pair of palm trees (ILLUSTRATION 45). The claim to the stylistic label, "English-German Medieval Chateau", applied to this house, is verified by details such as the hinges on the front door (ILLUSTRATION 46).[26]

"American-Colonial" was the label for the rooming-house seen in ILLUSTRATION 47, but America's founding fathers would never recognize it as such. True, its symmetry and classic pediment were featured in their Age of Reason. But the neo-Baroque beaux-arts appliquéd garlands and wreaths, the florid Corinthian columns, and the demi-hexagonal towers were the flourishes of a less reasonable age than the 18th century. Originally all-white, the frosted wedding-cake look with claims to an American Colonial heritage was popular nationwide from the 1890s through the 1910s.

The multi-faceted imagery projected by boosters in the 1890s emphasized the exotic, subtropical nature of the region. It also revealed the lack of fixed local traditions which encouraged newcomers to bring any currently popular or outrageously far-fetched style into this landscape.

El Miradero (a Spanish term for scenic viewpoint, usually referring to a high place overlooking an extensive plain), built in 1903-04 for real estate developer L. C. Brand, is an attempt to find an architectural style appropriate to the subtropical image (ILLUSTRATION 48). Brand was a real estate man who had come to L.A. in 1886 to take advantage of boom conditions. He left town shortly after the economy collapsed, returning in 1895 with new capital and new ambitions. Various enterprises succeeded, most notably the practice of buying up large land tracts of undeveloped land, while secretly participating in capitalization of major improvements which, once announced, drove up the price of the real estate he planned to sell. In the newly-developed community which followed, Brand would have arranged to monopolize the key services such as banks, newspapers, mortgage companies, and utilities. After the town was well-established and the value of these endeavors had grown, he could sell them at high prices. He did this first in conjunction with an interurban rail line to develop the town of Glendale (1900-1910). In 1904, when disputed water rights

A Search for Meaning

had lowered the value of land in the agricultural San Fernando Valley to a record low, he was one of a group of business barons who bought up 20,000 acres with the secret knowledge of a forthcoming water system for Los Angeles to be built from the Owens River 238-miles to the underground recesses of the Valley. The coming of water, and his development of urban infrastructure for the town of San Fernando, were proof again of Brand's shrewd business dealings.[27]

The vision of a subtropical wonderland where ruthless business acumen could build real-life dreams, was to be expressed in Brand's home. But the Missouri boy's knowledge of subtropical foreign places on which to model his palace was limited. The most exotic buildings he had ever seen were the exhibit halls at the World's Colombian Exposition in Chicago in 1893. The East Indian pavilion, as he recalled it in memory, was his model. His brother-in-law, Nathaniel Dryden, served as architect, completing a building variously labeled Saracenic or

46. Detail of Barmore house, 1905

Moorish. From a distance the cusped, or scalloped, arches (ILLUSTRATION 49), domes and minaret-finials might seem to mix images of the Moorish Alhambra and the even more imaginative Taj Majal, but in Brand's view it was as deliciously exotic as his palm-lined drive and no less suitable for a Southern California Ali Baba.

At heart, though, Brand and his architect were products of the Victorian Age and when it came to decorative details too small to be remembered from the Exposition, it was their Victorian tastes that prevailed. What we might

47. American Colonial rooming house, ca. 1905

believe was a peacock design in leaded glass over the front entry (ILLUSTRATION 50) was better known as a fan pattern in use in houses nationwide in the 1880s. The interior woodwork was very similar to that in the Newsoms' 1880s houses. For Brand, however, the house and the views from its windows were the glorious realizations of an ambitious man's dreams: the south-facing windows overlooked the town of Glendale; the west windows took in the San Fernando Valley.

Some residents consciously sought for a genuine expression of L.A.'s unique identity, a style which would be steeped in local meaning. Their homes echoed two of the current promotional refrains: Los Angeles as the New Italy,

48. El Miradero, 1902-1904

49. Detail of El Miradero

50. Detail of El Miradero

and Los Angeles of the Old Mission Days. Both of these tourist-pamphlet designations underwent a commercialization process: from tenuously suggested sales approaches to slick persuasions, to institutionalized attractions, to popular acceptance as definitions of the genuine Los Angeles, to architectural expression in local residences.

A well-traveled lady in an 1895 magazine article, "Memories of 'Our Italy'," explained Southern California to her less-experienced readers,

"It was an Italy without the trying features of that exquisite land... It is difficult in Italy to escape from the sight of beggars, from squalor and poverty.... The odors of the loathsome surroundings of some of Italy's choicest spots enter your nostrils at the same time that the beauty of the scene penetrates your brain. While you see all that nature can do in California, you are at the same time in the midst of our own countrymen, the most delightful people in the world, and made more so by the sunshine which mellows and enriches nature..."[28]

Instead of yearning for European travel, the provincial parvenu was taught to favor a California vacation. The commercialization of the Italian image began as early as 1890. Pasadena's Rose Parade, so successful at drawing attention to the floral delights of its winter season, concluded with chariot races.[29] The ultimate crystallization of the Los-Angeles-as-Italy theme was the brainchild of Abbot Kinney. A wealthy New Jerseyan of colonial stock, high political connections, and tobacco wealth, Kinney had a background of European education and travel, adventures in the Middle East, and a penchant for altruistic causes. Chronic insomnia brought him to Los Angeles in 1880. He took up citrus growing and he devoted time and family wealth to such diverse causes as Indian welfare, forestry, parks, libraries, and anti-feminism. In 1893 he visited the Columbian Exposition in Chicago. Whether the concept of a planned community built in a unified architectural style around waterways and park spaces stemmed from this exposure or from an idealistic concept of his youth, is unclear. At any rate, when a land development partnership in Ocean Park

A Search for Meaning

dissolved, leaving Kinney holding 160 acres of marshlands and sand dunes south of Ocean Park, he conceived a romantic vision of converting this waste into a new Venice, canals and all. The community of Venice-of-America, as Kinney christened it, like other communities distant from the city center, required streetcar linkage to the city. Kinney successfully finagled a car line direct to the Venice beachfront in 1903 as part of the Pacific Electric system Henry Huntington was putting together. Not only did his plans call for draining the land and building waterways as a residential subdivision, patterned on its Italian namesake, Kinney determined to launch an American cultural renaissance from his replica Venice.[30]

East coast resort communities were studied, Venetian architecture was researched. Architects Norman F. Marsh and C. H. Russell worked with Kinney to plan a community centered around a salt-water lagoon, the Grand Canal, and six tributary canals(ILLUSTRATION 51). Linking these internal waterways to the beach was the short stretch of Windward Avenue, lined with three hotels (with therapeutic salt water baths), curio shops, and eateries. Windward Avenue led onto the Venice Pier, with a pavilion for uplifting cultural exhibitions and an auditorium seating 3,400. Kinney's dreams of a cultural rebirth were to be realized through the Venice Assembly, a program of lectures, poetry readings, orchestral and dramatic programs. The grand public and commercial structures were wood and stucco likenesses of Venetian architecture. The Piazza San Marco's colonnades were recreated the length of Windward Avenue; hotels and a bathhouse on the Lagoon were architecturally dressed in a combination of Byzantine and Italian Renaissance costumes.

The new community opened with fireworks, musical entertainments and patriotic speeches for 40,000 spectators for three days of Fourth of July festivities in 1905. Visitors were poled about the canals by singing gondoliers. Realtors sold 355 house lots in two hours.[31] But Venice-of-America did not spark the American Renaissance. Kinney soon found that the seats in his Auditorium were empty; the Venice Assembly lost money from the start. Kinney was a shrewd businessman who understood the value of giving the public what it wanted. By the following year he had abandoned his notions of cultural uplift and built a honky-tonk midway. He constructed a miniature railroad to take residents and visitors over the arched Rialto-style bridges to the homesites and back to a turn-around by the Lagoon — all for a nickel. Venice had become a residential amusement park. In the decade of the 1910s, thousands of people flocked to Venice each weekend to enjoy its beauty contests, barnstorming, auto races, boxing matches, wintering circuses, and three roller coasters.

51. The Lagoon at Venice-of-America, ca. 1905

52. Venetian villa, ca. 1905-1907

DEFINING AN IDENTITY

53. Huntington Mansion, 1910

54. Wrigley Mansion, 1906-1914

When 1890s publicists likened Southern California to Italy they had intended to appear sophisticated. In the first glow of Kinney's development, Venice residents could take pride in their cultural awareness when they built homes in a Venetian architectural blend of Italian Renaissance and Byzantium. ILLUSTRATION 52 is one of the few private dwellings built in styles related to the Venice-of-America theme. The unexpected transformation of the Italian image from cosmopolitan to tawdry made it unacceptable as a housing style for most ordinary folks — the kind who came by streecar to eat the cotton candy. For them, Italy, or Venice, had come to mean a midway and roller coaster haven. For Angelenos to whom Italy meant, instead, the memories of European travels, Mediterranean styles were still acceptable residential expressions of dreams about the life to be lived in "Our Italy." The mansions in ILLUSTRATIONS 53 and 54 display Italian Renaissance elements to entirely different effects than those in Venice-of-America.

By the 1890s the New York Vanderbilts and others of their set were choosing Beaux-Arts Classicism as the style for their city mansions. Architects Richard Morris Hunt, and McKim, Mead and White were in heavy demand to build Fifth Avenue palaces reminiscent of European baroque models like the Grand Trianon at Versailles. By the turn of the century Beaux-Arts was the preferred style for banks, libraries, city halls, and museums nationwide.[32] The monumental scale required by the style did not lend itself to small or medium-sized homes. As domestic architecture it was reserved for the mansions of the very rich. Rotundas, pillared porticos or double-columned facades, classical statuary, and urn balustrades were common features. The French Ecole des Beaux-Arts' combination of classical elements, baroque ornamentation, and a fondness for all-white purity gives the style its sculptured sense of elegance, authority, and intricacy.

Henry Huntington, the nephew and groomed successor to railroadman Collis P. Huntington, could afford to build a Beaux-Arts house on the scale appropriate to the style (ILLUSTRATION 53). Henry and Collis' widow, Arabella, were the principal heirs to his 150 million dollar fortune in 1900. Henry sold his interests in the Southern Pacific, moved to Los Angeles and began building his

55. El Alisal, mission wing,
1897-1910

own empire in street railways and land development. In 1913 he reconsolidated his uncle's fortune by marrying the widow. They moved into the mansion, which had been built in the midst of Southern California's most splendid botanical gardens. Architects Myron Hunt and Elmer Grey combined the standard Beaux-Arts features of paired columns, tiers of urn-shaped balustrades, and free-standing sculpture, adding Italian Renaissance villa features of tiled terrace, double dentils, and clay tile roof. The tiling and the low spread of the building, which differentiate it from Manhattan Beaux-Arts mansions, harmonize well with the setting: it stands on a gentle mound of green velvet lawns rising from acres of perfectly manicured gardens, against a backdrop of purple mountains. It was the best of Italy, bettered.

Both Huntingtons were accustomed to wealth and had the confidence to prefer subdued elegance to excessive display. By 1910, such a sense of security was not confined to the Huntington level. The home in ILLUSTRATION 54, built 1906-1914 by George W. Stimson under the direction of his son, architect G. Lawrence Stimson, was likewise a dignified Italianate Beaux-Arts. There are the multiple applications of balustrades, the tripled Italianate corbels, and the keystoned arches. The tiled terrace and the Italian pergolas connect the house with the wide lawns. The house is roofed in green tile, harking back to the villas of Palladio's day. The imitation of Italian themes in Los Angeles remained, but in everyday life as distinct from weekend amusements, it was limited to the wealthy.

The other pre-boom image to blossom architecturally in the 1890s was the romanticized Mission era as embodied in the writings of Helen Hunt Jackson and various railroad publicists. It was packaged in 1894 as an annual carnival called La Fiesta de Los Angeles. Four days were devoted to costumed frolics, dons and doñas, fans and lace mantillas, guitars, parades and firework displays.[33] The old Spanish flavor could thus be paraded as one of the exotic touches to the L.A. image. In that sense it would appeal to those who preferred the shallow romance, the fiction of "Ramona," to the historical reality of the former Mexican pueblo.

But what might have been no more than the Angelenos' passing fancy

DEFINING AN IDENTITY

for a mythical past deepened into a reverent passion for the old Spanish way of life, thanks to an odd young Harvard man named Charles Fletcher Lummis. In 1884 this rather unstable but very passionate Bohemian undertook to walk from Ohio to Los Angeles, writing a colorfully rambling account of his travels in the form of letters for the <u>Los Angeles Times</u> which, by prearrangement, hired him as an editor when he finally arrived. En route, he fell in love with his nostalgic concept of the Indian and Spanish cultures of the Southwest. Once in Los Angeles, he reconstucted, from his acquaintance with old families such as the del

56. Detail of El Alisal

Valles, a life without the materialistic values, the artificial prudery and puffery he saw in his own culture. He idealized the old Californios' gracious hospitality, warm vivacity, self-respecting dignity, slower pace, and frontier simplicity. It became the mission of his life to educate Americans to the superiority of the Spanish heritage of the Southwest, his goal an American cultural transformation, a blending of Hispanic values and romanticized history into a modern American reality.[34]

In 1895, Lummis took over the editorship of a tourist advertising folio called "Land of Sunshine." Under his direction, important writers and artists developed themes of cultural significance to the West featuring local and Southwestern history. The attractive monthly, with Art Nouveau illustrations, painted the Southwestern corner of the United States in warm colors, graceful, leisurely lines, and nostalgic Spanish charm. The ruins of the missions were the durable remnants of the charm of which Lummis and his friends wrote. Missions soon became glyphs representing the entire myth of a romantic Spanish heritage. The writers who wrote for "Land of Sunshine", or "Out West," as it was renamed in 1902, were joined by others who published independently in the same genre. Tourist brochures from the mid-nineties to the First World War never failed to include a mission scene or two.[35]

57. Detail of El Alisal

In addition to the magazine and his own ten books on the region, Lummis made himself a caricatured illustration of the old Spanish lifestyle he admired by dressing flamboyantly in corduroy suits cut in the old Mexican way, sombreros, embroidered shirts, and wide, red sashes. From 1897 to his death in 1928 he worked at building "El Alisal," his house and stage (ILLUSTRATIONS 55, 56, and 57), blending into it symbols of every one of his enthusiasms — the missions, the Pueblo cultures of the Southwest, the arts of pre-Columbian Peru

A Search for Meaning

58. Pomeroy Powers house, 1904

59. Detail of Pomeroy Powers house

60. Erasmus Wilson house, ca. 1895-1897

and Mexico, his friendships, and eventually a place for his own ashes.

It was Lummis who, believing the California missions to be grand symbols of a golden age, formed the Landmarks Club, an organization to rescue them. The missions had been deteriorating for years. Tourist pamphleteers had found their decrepitude colorful, ever since Mrs. Jackson and the picturesque painters had called them to public attention. By the mid-'90s ridges of melted adobe outlines were all that remained of some. The San Fernando Mission served as a pig farm. Lummis took up the preservation of these ruins as a personal crusade. "They are monuments and beacons of Heroism and Faith and Zeal and Art. Let us save them...for Humanity."[36]

Lummis' campaign brought together private contributors, the Santa Fe Railroad, architects, and a widespread public interest in mission preservation. In 1916 the Landmarks Club, to raise money for work on the San Fernando Mission, held a candlelight ceremony, selling candles, each bearing the donor's name, for a dramatic and solemn processional: over 6,000 were sold.[37]

Unlike the Italian image whose vulgarization had removed it from the residential realm, the old Mission days appealed to a growing American desire for a simpler, less harried life style, a desire which was conscious and widely discussed by the turn of the century. Lummis and his writer friends presented readers with a higher quality of life in terms of human values, a finer age, more rugged but more leisurely and less materialistic.

To capture in architecture the admiration for Hispanic culture elicited by romantic writers, the first and simplest method was to copy the missions themselves. The resulting Mission Revival style is an indigenous California architecture. The homes we have shown to this point represent imported concepts grafted onto the L.A. scene. The Mission style sprang from the native soil, well-watered by romantic notions, but native none the less.[38]

DEFINING AN IDENTITY

61. Multi-family dwelling, remodeled 1913

The new versions of "Spanish" influence began to show up in Los Angeles residential architecture in the 1890s in a number of otherwise nondescript, typically bulbous piles, monstrosities with tile roofs, their vernadas supported by heavy pillars, reminiscent of the missions' convento cloisters.[39] The State of California took a hand in popularizing the Mission style. It held a competition for the design of the California Building for the 1893 Columbian exposition, specifying the "Mission-Moorish" style as appropriately "Californian."[40] The houses, resort hotels, and railroad stations that followed are represented by the homes in ILLUSTRATIONS 58 to 61. The most prominent feature of each is the espadaña, the curved and recurved pediment over the front entry.

Most of the Franciscan missions were crude, severely simple buildings. Spanish colonial churches in Mexico showed a number of baroque characteristics such as polychrome domes, twisted columns, and elaborate decorative surface sculpture. In the 18th century, colonial artists had overthrown the formal restraints of baroque and developed exuberantly individualistic ornamentation. But the California padres, restricted to crude-cut stone and adobe, inexperienced workmen, and a rustic setting, had produced plain and stolid frontier churches.[41] It is instructive that in the search for a style which could be appropriated to residential structures in the 1890s, the most curvaciously baroque mission, San Luis Rey (ILLUSTRATION 62), was consciously chosen as the architectural model.[42]

In ILLUSTRATION 58 we can see the characteristics that comprise the Mission Revival style: the scalloped gable, the irregular balance of a large and a small "bell"-tower, the tile roof, and the cloister arches. A quatrefoil or circular window piercing the espadaña was more typical than this latticed diamond, but the quatrefoil appliqués on the lower level provide the same effect. The purposely uneven texture of the stuccoed surface obvious in ILLUSTRATION 59 was one of the characteristics which lent a sense of antiquity.[43]

The more refined version of the style seen in ILLUSTRATION 60 retains the baroque espadaña insignia and the tiled roof. However, the balconet at the ballroom window, the reproportioned tower which assumes near-equal importance with the scalloped gable, and its tri-part columned window evokes Tuscany rather than provincial California. The elaborate decorative treatment is also a departure from true Mission style. Instead of ornamentation taking over the structure, as it does in the Mooers house (ILLUSTRATION 40), a thin line along the scalloped edge and the wider line around the arched window merely accentuate the structural lines.[44]

The multi-family dwelling in ILLUSTRATION 61 brings the Mission Revival style down from the mansion level of the previous illustration to the common level. The tiled roofs and the espadaña skyline, with screened diamond aperture, mark the everyday version of the style.[45] The romantic Spanish past had been accepted at every level. Numerous examples remain today to remind us of its popularity from the 1890s to the 1910s.

Of the Mission style houses still standing in Los Angeles today, there are few so lyrically expressive as Lummis' own (ILLUSTRATION 55), complete with bell and vine-covered walls. This is the dining wing of the house Lummis built himself, mostly between 1897 and 1910. In his own house he captured both the image of the Mission and the major ideas of the Arts and Crafts movement we will look at next: the beauty of natural materials, the virtues of hand-crafting, and the concept of house and man in harmony with nature. ❧

120

62. Mission San Luis Rey de Francia, 1811-1815

C H A P T E R

VIII

FACING WEST

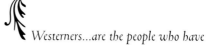

Westerners...are the people who have

Moved because they could Do Better....

For it must always

be remembered that the typical

Westerner is an Easterner graduated....

[He] has made his choice

as an intelligent being.[1]

—CHARLES F. LUMMIS, 1902

THE SEARCH FOR AN ARCHITECTURAL EXPRESSION of the unique essence of Los Angeles did not end with the neo-Italian and Mission Revival developments. The former, as we have seen, was economically limiting in its considerations of scale and tainted by its amusement-park connotations. The Mission Revival style was briefly popular, then fell under accusations of artificiality. The next theme explored was the subtropical natural setting after which Lummis' publication, Land of Sunshine, had been named, and the social values he attributed to the days of a Spanish Arcadia: leisure, hospitality, sincerity, virility, dignity, anti-materialism, and simple living close to nature. The residential architecture which poetized the natural setting and enhanced those social values, the California bungalow, is grandly illustrated by the 1907 R. R. Blacker house, in South Pasadena, designed by architects Charles and Henry Greene (ILLUSTRATION 63). This mansion of elegant rusticity represents one of the finest examples of the new style. It enunciated the new values and the new aesthetic which swept the nation in the years between the turn of the century and the end of World War I. Both the style and the values found fertile expression in Southern California.

This new architecture, with its rusticity, simplicity, honest expression of both function and materials, unity of design, and invitation to a new living style also spread nationwide. For the first time, Angelenos chose houses that did not pretend to be stone castles or frosted wedding cakes, that did not disguise wood as marble quoins. The bungalow was a house built according to its function, a house designed to reveal the natural beauty of the materials of which it was formed. Instead of a gaudy Victorian imposition on the landscape, this house was designed to blend harmoniously with its setting. It did not represent an artificial history, as the Mission Revival did, rather it is rooted in the reality of its own time; it celebrated the beauty of the Southern California out-of-doors; and it echoed the leisurely pace of life sought by its inhabitants. What change in the people and their concept of the good life is responsible for this dramatic architectural shift?

In the closing quarter of the nineteenth century, the social fabric of America underwent a sudden, dramatic transformation. In terms of material progress, the national faith in rags-to-riches stories had been amply justified. More goods had been produced by more advanced machinery by companies which grew larger by the processes of cut-throat competition and takeover. These companies had hired increasing numbers of middle-level employees as supervisors, managers, accountants, attorneys, and efficiency experts. Educational requirements for such positions had driven an ever-larger group of

63. R.R. Blacker house, 1907

young people to pursue higher academic preparations. At first, the emergent middle-class had embraced the new opportunities with hopes of material success, whose requirements were ruthlessness, high-pressured competition, and a narrow self-service. Unrestricted by traditions of taste, the newly successful white-collar home-buyer had chosen a hard-sell display of his equally hard-won economic status in lathe-turned spindle work, excessive bric-a-brac, and eye-catching colors. (ILLUSTRATIONS 27 and 31). By the 1890s such catch-all decoration had given way to bombastic statements of self-promotion (ILLUSTRATIONS 40, 42, and 48).

Somewhere along the line, the diligent pursuit of things designed mostly to impress outsiders, began to lose its appeal. People of the growing middle-class could not escape the knowledge that real wealth was out of their reach, that Horatio Alger stories were only fantasies. They might have respectable row houses near Main Street in a middle-sized town, very similar to every other family's on the block. They might provide comfortably for their families, but they could not continue to hope for more. For people in this predicament, the dreams in which they had stood in a Vanderbilt's shoes, dreams they had expressed in castle turrets on their wooden houses, grew stale as the years passed. On the other hand, their security had reduced their fears of economic competition from the laboring class. The expanding middle-class, suspended between the ostentation of the rich and the subsistence anxieties of the poor, found itself in need of new measurements of self-worth and of goals more satisfying than the restricted possibilities for material acquisition. The Progressive Movement was the response.[2]

In the first two decades of the 1900s, spurred by an idealistic and optimistic belief in the possibility of progress toward perfection, reformers of all sorts attempted to correct a variety of perceived social and political ills. The elements of progressivism included women's suffrage (to purify politics), prohibition (to uplift morality), and U.S. participation in World War I (the war to end all wars, to make the world safe for democracy). Progressive reforms were, despite their name, conservative. Basic political and economic structures were not challenged. Most reforms were aimed at increasing the power and opportunities of the middle-class within existing structures. Although elements of a humanitarian concern for the less fortunate were voiced, the real emphases of reform actions were localized to the spheres directly affecting the lives of the activists. Underneath the righteous rhetoric, people were searching for a sense of moral superiority to justify attempts to better their own lives. The underlying spirit of progressivism was a "can-do" optimism; its primary ideological contribution was a shift from quantitative to qualitative values. Its base was a yearning for self-respect.

In Los Angeles, the housing style which came to embody progressive thinking was The Craftsman style, most specifically, the regional vernacular known as the California bungalow. One of its standard features was the masculinity of the living-room-dining-room-entry area. Paneled in low-gloss wood or half-timbering and burlap, furnished with rugged, simple Mission style or Stickley pieces, and decorated in warm earth tones, these rooms were as male-oriented as a hunting retreat or the smoking room of the Odd Fellows Lodge.[3]

The turn-of-the-century middle-class woman was better educated than her mother's generation. Much of the drudgery her mother had known was now eliminated by prosperity and the new labor-saving conveniences money could buy: hot and cold running water, electric or gas lighting, steam-radiator heating, an ice box refilled regularly by the ice man, home-delivered milk and groceries, and quick-to-fix breakfasts of oatmeal or farina. The up-to-the-minute modern family would have an efficient bathroom and kitchen with the latest plumbing gadgets, linoleum floors, Sanitas splashboards, and zinc-topped counters. The modern woman's husband was not home at midday expecting a huge meal. The children were away at school. The urban woman did not have chickens to feed or cows to milk. She was free to socialize with other women over a game of bridge, to go with a woman friend by trolley to the matinee or department store, or to attend a women's club meeting or suffrage rally. She was also free to spend considerable time reading, gardening, and at handicrafts, particularly if her husband or her budget limited her activities outside the confines of the home.

By the end of the 19th-century, technological advances in printing, wire services, an increasing revenue from advertising, and a growing middle-class readership, caused a proliferation of inexpensive periodicals and newspapers. In a fierce competition for readers, magazines and newspapers played upon the tastes, economic limitations, and socio-political concerns of the urban middle-class, purveying its tastes into demands, its limitations into chosen virtues, and its concerns into reform movements.[4]

The social scientists' newfound certainties that environment was a major determinant in human behavior and progress, and that environment, and its consequences, could be improved, were underlying themes in this literature. Women were persuaded by the periodicals that physical exercise and garments permitting freer movement would improve health, and styles changed. Women read that sanitary environments would improve their families' health. Housing responded with simplified modern interior arrangements featuring built-in cupboards and easy-to-clean surfaces, reducing dust and dirt, and housework as well. The new concern for providing a better environment for one's family emphasized the benefits of fresh air. It stood to reason that daytime sports activities were best complemented by nighttime access to fresh air. Houses featuring sleeping porches and window seats were called for by magazines and their readers. The woman reader was also convinced that she should accept the challenges of providing a more wholesome social environment, a homey refuge, for her urban family. The work-weary husband should have a comfortable chair, slippers and pipe ready, when he came from the office. The children should be warmly nurtured as blossoming people rather than relegated in Victorian fashion to isolated, occasionally displayed objects. A cozy family togetherness called for architectural features such as the open floor plan, an inglenook and the elimination of the formal parlor. These progressive ideals were realized in the California bungalow.

The progressive promotion of a better quality of life for individuals and their families went beyond an immediate sense of responsibility within the home to campaigns for improved external environments. The efficiency and cleanliness sought in the home was echoed in the community by campaigns for better streetcar systems, more street lights in residential neighborhoods, and improved sewer systems. Aroused citizens formed non-partisan political clubs to roust entrenched local politicians. Secure in its own prosperity, the middle-class turned its attention to the poor. It has been suggested that the depersonalization experienced by the newly-urbanized middle-class fed this hunger for the personal touch, and that a Protestant attachment of guilt to responsibility accompanied the new spirit. In any case, missionary societies, Christmas boxes for poor families, and crusades to improve safety conditions in factories, to eliminate prostitution, and to "Americanize" immigrants received journalistic encouragement and middle-class activism.

In this nationwide awakening, Los Angeles won attention as a progressive showplace. By the early 1900s the image of Los Angeles, to the reading public east of the Rockies, composed of advertising claims as well as descriptions of the built-up reality, coincided precisely with the progressives' spectrum of ideals.

Under muckrakers' exposures, civic leaders of the urban East had to face the downside of the Industrial Revolution: slums where immigrant unskilled laborers lived amid disease and vice; lagging public services; decaying and unsafe buildings, and political corruption. Los Angeles, however, was a new city. Most of the business buildings and residences had been constructed in the past two decades. In reality, as well as in the tourist literature, Los Angeles appeared the clean, modern model of what a city ought to be. It had few of the large factories found in the East; its labor market demanded more skilled than unskilled laborers;[5] and its agricultural workers lived dispersed in the surrounding countryside, not much in evidence. L.A.'s Chinese laborers did live in crowded and unhealthful conditions, but they were barred from voting and could be described as "picturesque." The only appreciably dilapidated sector was the outgrowth from the jumble of single-story shacks once known as Sonoratown, the polyglot district where transients and day laborers were concentrated. This one blighted area received the worried attention of muckrakers, visiting sociologists, and reform commissions, but its low profile and restricted confines made it easy for everyone else to overlook, especially after city charter reforms nullified its political clout. Its problems were largely invisible to the Eastern reader so it did not tarnish the image.[6]

Like other American cities, Los Angeles seemed to be controlled by a political machine, a machine identified by opponents as the Southern Pacific Railroad and allied interests. In 1897 the local business community triumphed over the railroad in a contest for federally funded harbor construction. Emboldened, non-partisan citizens' groups campaigned for structural changes in municipal government which they believed would prevent corruption by making government more directly accountable to the now politically-active middle-class. The new charter features, which went into effect in 1903, included the first provision for the initiative, referendum and recall in any American city government. The recall of a Los Angeles City Councilman in 1904 on charges of corruption was the first use of the recall anywhere. Armed with the new charter provision of recall, the backing of two newspapers, a secret fund, and a storm of accusations and innuendoes, the reform element succeeded in replacing the mayor and the majority of other municipal officers with their own candidates in 1909. They celebrated the triumph of "civic purity" at a mammoth banquet. In the first decade of the 1900s Los Angeles became the first city to put into practice a number of other progressive ideals. Its water system and public works were made municipal agencies. The first city agency for humane animal treatment, a nonpartisan civil service system, and municipal playgrounds brought Los Angeles fame as a model of civic progress.[7]

Los Angeles also proved a leader in the innovative and technical problem-solving characteristic of progressivism. Since the city's first decade as an American town, most voters and influential leaders in Los Angeles had become Angelenos by choice rather than by birth. Experimentalists in choice of living location, they had not been averse to experimentation in other ways. To keep up with the high rate of population influx, public services in Los Angeles were strained early and the challenges innovatively met. In water service, the most notable example, Los Angeles voters approved a bond issue in 1901 to establish a municipally-owned system. Charter safeguards protected the new Board of Water Commissioners from undue political pressures, ensuring efficiency and lower rates. A deeper problem was the inadequate supply of available water for future population growth. Again, Los Angeles showed ingenuity. First, the City sued for prior rights to all the surface and underground water in the L.A. basin, on the basis of the pueblo's original Spanish land grant and Spanish concepts of water rights, winning the case in 1895. Ranchers in the San Fernando Valley were thereafter legally forbidden to sink wells on their own property during drought periods. In 1904 a scheme was developed to obtain rights to the water of the Owens Valley, 234 miles away on the other side of the Sierra Nevadas. In 1905 and 1907 the voters of Los Angeles approved bond issues totaling a then-astronomical twenty-four-and-a-half million dollars to bring the water of the Owens River to the natural underground reservoir of the San Fernando Valley by 238 miles of aqueduct, through 142 tunnels, and over nine major canyons. Completed in 1913, the Los Angeles Owens River Aqueduct was regarded as an engineering marvel worldwide.[8]

To the new century's advocates of progress, Los Angeles appeared to be the City of Tomorrow. Here men of vision could meet and master any obstacles. By the end of 1913 Los Angeles had its new water system and the world's largest man-made harbor; it was producing one-third of the nation's oil; it was the heart of the new method of cooperative marketing (e.g., Sunkist) which pioneered the transformation of farming into agribusiness.

While he was thrilled by the pace of Progress, the modern man of the new century found it all a bit unsettling, the change a bit too rapid. Somewhat quixotically, he idealized the simple joys of rural life (though unwilling to give up urban money-making advantages), rosy-cheeked childhood innocence (while he reveled in cosmopolitan pleasures), individualism (long more ballyhoo than fact in America), and a leisurely lifestyle (which he passed by on his treadmill).

Virtue, an upright citizenry, and the American ideals of individualism and self-reliance had been identified with the rural life-style since the days of Thomas Jefferson. Only one or two generations removed from the farm or small town, the urban middle-class of 1900 had been taught to measure life against rural standards of morality. The depersonalization of urban living and corporate working, the intrusion of heterogeneous immigrants into an ethnically narrow

DEFINING AN IDENTITY

notion of Americanism, the stratified social structure, the brutality, filth and crime so prominent in a metropolis, all made cities abhorrent.

In his concern for an improved quality of life and as a positive influence on his children, the anti-urban progressive followed one or more of three paths. First, he could accept the advantages of city life while devoting himself to the reform of urban ills. Second, he could follow the Romanticist route of fantasizing about a by-gone rural or small-town life. A third option was to move to Los Angeles. Where but Los Angeles, demanded the booster brochures, could one find the energetic growth and future potentials of a city more modern than almost any other, and at the same time enjoy a home surrounded by flowers year-round? In Los Angeles one could expect to live the dream pictured by a progressive spokesman in 1909:

"We...firmly believe that the country is the only place to live in. The city is all very well for business, for amusement... But the home itself should be in some place where there is peace and quiet, plenty of room and the chance to establish a sense of intimate relationship with the hills and valleys, trees and brooks and all the things which tend to lessen the strain and worry of modern life by reminding us that after all we are one with Nature."[9]

Los Angeles was a ready-made paradise for the middle-class progressive. Here was the inviting out-of-doors in the best rural tradition, linked by streetcar line to the business opportunities of an expanding urban economy. The close association of streetcar interests with housing developers meant that new homes in delightfully situated neighborhoods were accessible to employment sites. Between 1900 and 1913, the population of the city trebled. In 1900, half the population of Los Angeles had arrived in the past decade. Most came from east of the Rockies intending to begin a new and different life in Southern California. In a nation starting to rethink its values, Angelenos were the vanguard, so committed to progressive ideals that they had been willing to physically uproot themselves to follow a quest for a better way of living.[10]

The visual record of these reordered priorities is the prevalence of the California bungalow, a style of housing advocated by The Craftsman magazine in the United States and drawn from earlier sources abroad, especially the English Arts and Crafts movement. It is not surprising that the new trend was identified with Los Angeles, a progressive city at the juncture of streetcar suburbanization, sunshine, and a swelling tide of middle-class settlers. A new aesthetic of simplicity arose in the new century to parallel the social, political, and technological reforms. One source was a middle-class moral turn away from material display.

In the 1870s and '80s, money newly gained from industrialization had sought expression in a multiplicity of patterns such as flowered wallpapers and boldly figured carpets and draperies. By 1900 there was a large, educated, reading public, neither rich nor poor, sufficiently cosmopolitan to appreciate the aesthetics of refined simplicity. In the 1870s and '80s, the social doings of the very rich had been topics of avid interest for the middle-class and the press. By the end of the century, muckrakers had so often linked tycoons with political corruption and unethical business practices that wealth itself fell into disrepute. Some segments of the middle-class were aggrieved by the journalistically-lampooned social airs put on by rich men, whom they were beginning to regard as no better than themselves. The middle-class asserted its own superiority in moral, not economic, terms. Condemning the vulgar display of wealth with which they could not compete, middle-class trend-setters took up righteous simplicity as the epitome of true good taste. The English paradigm, the Arts and Crafts movement, was at hand, accompanied by a rationale seemingly ready-made for American idealists looking for inspiration.

By the middle of the 19th-century, English thinkers, most prominently John Ruskin, were articulating concerns about the adverse effects of industrialization on both laborers and on Britain's national taste. The Industrial Revolution, they feared, was degrading workmen to a mere part of the machines they tended. These critics feared that the mass production of identical items isolated industrial workers from their fellows, robbed craftsmen of personal satisfaction, deprived society of beauty, and dehumanized mankind.[11] Writer-designer William Morris translated these humanistic and aesthetic concerns into action through a reform movement in building, furnishing, and decorating. Morris called for a unity of all the arts: for originality of expression rather than mere imitation of the past; for an art available to every level of society, which should bring joy and stimulate ideas; for an appreciation and retention of the natural beauty inherent in materials; for simplification and honesty in both art and living. He articulated his beliefs widely and effectively in lectures and publications: "Simplicity of life, begetting simplicity of taste, that is a love for sweet and lofty things, is of all matters most necessary for the birth of the new and better art we crave for; simplicity everywhere, in the palace as well as in the cottage."[12]

The movement was called the Arts and Crafts movement after the Arts and Crafts Exhibition Society, established in 1888 to exhibit the works of artists of the new outlook.

A magazine, <u>The Studio</u>, started in 1892 (later superseded by <u>The</u>

130

International Studio), and a growing enthusiasm for Arts and Crafts decorative concepts among wealthy British and Continental clients eventually brought Morris' ideas to American attention. An 1892 visit by Chicago soap magnate Elbert Hubbard to Morris' workshop inspired him to set up the Roycroft Institute in Aurora, New York. There, book printing, copper and leather work, and furniture were produced by a large community of craftsmen who shared an idealistic commitment to the simple life, listened to lectures, and worked as a guild with an apprentice system. Other guilds, working in various crafts, appeared. Artists, most notably Louis Comfort Tiffany, were influenced by the English trend and by the Art Nouveau style developing on the Continent. Their ateliers attracted like-minded craftsmen to produce pottery, stained glass, jewelry, tiles, fine books, and furniture. The output of these individuals was so limited in quantity and so elevated in price by the insistence on hand-crafting, that it might never have reached the attention of the general public if it had not been for general-circulation magazines.[13]

Gustav Stickley, a furniture manufacturer who visited leading Arts and Crafts practitioners in England in 1898, reorganized his furniture company near Syracuse, New York to carry out his own emerging version of the new craft concepts. In 1901 he started publishing The Craftsman, a magazine devoted to these ideals. The first two issues explained the ideas of Morris and Ruskin. Succeeding issues, until the journal's demise in 1916, traced Stickley's own philosophical development. They came to dwell primarily on architecture and interior design for middle-income homes, as well as to preach some of the progressives' ideas for political and education reform. Although the circulation of the magazine was never large,[14] it served as a forum of the architects who were to shape American styles on into the 1930s, among them Greene and Greene, Louis Sullivan, Frank Lloyd Wright, and Irving Gill. The Craftsman's commitment especially endeared it to the reform-minded sector of the reading public.

The Craftsman exhorted its readers to rededicate themselves to "right living" and "clear thinking." Stickley hoped to rekindle the self-reliance, initiative, individualism, and a pioneering "vigorous constructive spirit." The ultimate source of the good life would be the home environment:

"for it is only natural that the relief from friction which would follow the ordering of our lives along more simple and reasonable lines would not only assure greater comfort, and therefore greater efficiency, to the workers of the nation, but would give the children a chance to grow up under conditions which would be conducive to a higher degree of mental, moral and physical efficiency."[15]

While his contemporaries campaigned for new city charters and graft prosecutions, Stickley took up reform by way of domestic architecture. His vision of moral improvement through a simplified and humanized home environment was best suited for a rural or suburban context. Disparaging the decades-old drive for material luxuries, he claimed historical evidence that

"[the] people whose lives are lived simply and wholesomely, in the open, and who have in a high degree the sense of the sacredness of the home, are the people who have made the greatest strides in the development of the race. When luxury enters in and a thousand artificial requirements come to be regarded as real needs, the nation is on the brink of degeneration."[16]

In The Craftsman's view, creative self-expression, utility, and thrift established handicrafts as an important adjunct to the new lifestyle. Home craft projects would be fulfilling. And because creating beautiful and useful things with one's hands "is so important a factor in the growth of character that upon it depends nearly every quality of heart and brain that goes into what we may call the craftsmanship of life," The Craftsman became one of the leading proponents of manual arts courses in the schools.[17]

The principles so ardently propagated by Stickley's magazine were dispensed to the larger public by magazines with much greater circulation, such as The Ladies Home Journal, House Beautiful, and other home and women's magazines, which joined in after the movement proved popular. Family magazines such as The Chatauquan, Arena, and, in California, Lummis' Out West furthered the new taste and lifestyle, as well.

The homes these magazines recommended shared certain common features. They popularized practical aspects of the aesthetic: affordability, easy maintenance, efficient layouts and built-in storage, health consciousness, and harmony with nature. The new style also encouraged closer human interaction by insisting on open, flowing spatial arrangements and focal gathering spots such as the hearthside inglenook.[18]

The Arts and Crafts movement in America was termed the Craftsman style, after the periodical. It was so compatible with the feelings of the progressive middle-class that it transformed mainstream taste and style. But other contemporary and consciously interrelated currents also met in the style. One of these was the influence of Japanese art. The Western world's fascination with the recently discovered culture of Japan popularized books describing the features, functions, and artistry of its traditional homes. The use of a few muted colors carried throughout the interior decor, the spatial unity resulting from scaling all forms to multiples of the standard rectangular tatami mat, the coordination of an entire room to one focal object of beauty: these were exciting new concepts for jaded Victorian consumers.[19]

The Zen philosophy of beauty, too, appealed to those who would simplify life and its environment. As the 19th-century waned, the demand for lectures and publications on Eastern philosophies grew. If the tea ceremony served to illustrate Zen philosophy, its trappings illustrated Zen aesthetics. The hand-formed, rough-surfaced, tea bowl retained the beauty of its natural material and the individuality of itself and its creator's hand. Such thinking and the resulting art forms were compatible with western Arts and Crafts ideas, just as the Eastern path to serenity was appealing to America's pressure-ridden, machine-age middle-class.[20]

French Impressionist painting and sculpture also had an influence on The Craftsman style. The Impressionists' heightened awareness of the interplay of light, color, and texture were an influence seen in the finest examples of the bungalow. Shadows were part of the design, as were changing effects of morning to evening light on the surface colors and textures.

Another trend affecting the genesis of the bungalow was the Eastern Shingle Style of the Newport, Rhode Island, plutocracy associated with architects Henry Hobson Richardson and McKim, Mead and White. The simplicity and rusticity of houses sheathed in unpainted shingles were given high-style status by summering tycoons. In the East Coast luxury cottages of McKim, Mead and White in the 1880s, the public-access rooms opened off the entry hall as one vast flowing space through five to ten-foot wide doorways which could be closed off by recessed sliding doors. The casual lifestyle facilitated by this floor plan for vacationing millionaires appealed to the year-round middle-class as an enhancement of family unity.

The term "bungalow" was an English derivation of a Bengali term referring to the style of dwelling which housed the British Imperial presence in hot and humid portions of the Empire in the 18th and 19th-centuries. The pertinent characteristics were the central living room, the overhanging roof, and the verandas which brought the outdoors inside. The term was taken up and applied rather loosely to a variety of English and American cottages in the 1880s and 1890s.[21] Builder-advocate A. W. Smith described the type that had become known as the California Bungalow by 1906:

"The bungalow, as it flourishes in the balmy air of the Pacific Coast, is just now our especial pride. Its essential features are breadth, strength and simple beauty of plainness. It is mostly enclosed with shingles, shakes or rough sawn...clapboarding. There is a pleasing absence of 'mill work' and other fool ornamentation... It must have a wide projecting roof and always has a spacious porch."[22]

The California Bungalow was first embraced by self-styled artists and bohemians. By the 1890s, Los Angeles was just the sort of place to attract writers, poets, artists, intellectuals and non-conformists in general. It offered a life in closer communion with nature, in a new country where mores had not yet become confiningly rigid.

Charles Fletcher Lummis exemplified this element. He built his home on the Arroyo Seco (a Spanish term meaning dry riverbed or wash; the Arroyo passes through Pasadena and Highland Park). Stones brought up from the arroyo formed its walls and enabled the house to harmonize with its natural setting. The front door of rough-hewn wood, shown in ILLUSTRATION 56 contributed to the harmony. The calligraphic flourish of Lummis' initials, probably executed by his artist-friend Maynard Dixon, was as bold as the rustic wood on which it was mounted. Lummis extolled Native American cultures as closer to nature and more honest than his own. Their arts were adopted by The Craftsman aesthetic. Collectors sought Navajo rugs, pottery and baskets of all kinds. Designers and home decorators borrowed the designs and colors of traditional Indian craftsmen. Lummis' own foraging into Indian cultures was not limited to the American Southwest. In 1892 he accompanied the renowned anthropologist Adolph Bandelier on an archeological expedition to Peru. It was one of the highlights of his adventurous life. The hinges on Lummis' door are patterned on the sacred serpent motif found in the Incan ruins at Tiahuanaco. The bolt is reminiscent of early California or Mexico.[23]

The eccentric Lummis plotted a garden of native plants of the Southwest, ILLUSTRATION 57, and located his windows specifically for the enjoyment of favorite garden vistas. The idea of a garden approximating nature's wild beauty, concentrated by careful planning into the space of a suburban lot, was to become a symbol of good taste.

When bohemian intellectuals along Pasadena's rocky Arroyo chose to build out of river rocks, they did so because the material offered a cheaper house, and because the stones provided the cultivated rusticity illustrative of the values they advocated. The stonework, in addition to naturalizing the house, permitted an interplay of shadow and texture, the surface decoration of nature consciously invited by the designer. As the new architecture spread, the use of cobblestones, at least for the foundation and chimney, became a standard feature as "a device which is very effective in linking the house with its surroundings" — even when the surroundings were not rocky.[24]

DEFINING AN IDENTITY

Mass-circulation magazines called for homes designed for efficient upkeep. Lummis heeded the call in his own way. He created built-in cabinets and window-seats to reduce dust and cobwebs and to ease circulation. He also built niches into the walls for his art objects, and he cast a concrete floor so that, instead of sweeping, dusting, and floorpolishing, housework could be reduced to an infrequent hosing. The general public never went this far in its willingness to exchange amenities for simplicity.

The final step in architecturally linking the Arts and Crafts ideals, changing middle-class values, and the image of Southern California was taken by trained architects. It was they who devised an attractive blend of environmental considerations with the efficiency and aesthetic standards demanded by the Arts and Crafts philosophy. It was their work which was published, admired, and emulated on a smaller scale for the average homeowner. The architects and related artists most closely linked with the development of the California bungalow as high art had backgrounds in Arts and Crafts thinking.[25] But they were also able to understand and express their clients' special feelings for the distinctive Southern California context, and to explore beyond the popular styles of the times for an appropriate expression of those feelings for the place. In 1907 the California bungalow won national recognition as "the new American architecture,...as yet...hardly...a new style so much as a series of individual plans adapted to climatic conditions and to the needs of daily living, and in harmony with the natural environment and contour of the landscape.... [in a part of the country which] permits a life that is practically all out-of-doors, or, at all events, maintains such a friendly relation with out-of-doors that the house seems more in the nature of a temporary shelter and resting place than a building designed to be lived in..."[26]

The climate was finally realized as the primary inspirational source for an original expression of Los Angeles architecture. Architect Elmer Grey explained the new direction:

"Many eastern people seem to consider that we have a distinctive style out here... [It] is not because our architects have striven to be unique in their designing, but because they have tried to eliminate from it all features not properly belonging to their climate and to their local conditions, — because they have tried to be simply natural. The California architect is ... in a comparatively new country, the climate of which is radically different from other portions of the United States."[27]

Charles Lummis' house, (ILLUSTRATIONS 55, 56, and 57) and the architectural masterpieces of Charles and Henry Greene (ILLUSTRATIONS 63

through 68) tell the perceptive viewer a great deal about respect for the natural setting, an anticipation of a casual, indoor-outdoor lifestyle, and the embrace of new aesthetic standards and cultural values.

Greene and Greene built houses for wealthy clients who intended them as winter vacation or retirement homes. Simplicity and a certain rusticity were appropriate for these purposes, even for the rich. ILLUSTRATION 64 shows the back of the Gamble house, built in 1908 as a semi-retirement home for the Gamble soap heir, David B. Gamble. The leading considerations were climate and environment, by the architects' own statements. Low overhanging eaves to shade the exterior walls and terraces from the hot sun — an adaptation specifically inspired by the early California adobes — were supported by heavy beams. The new appreciation of simple beauty, influenced by Japanese aesthetics, led to the construction of the beams as design elements both on the interior, where they were exposed in a fine-finished state, and on the exterior. There, the joinery, though reminiscent of Japan, was an original treatment so elegant that no

64. Gamble house, 1908

65. Detail of Gamble house, 1908

further decoration was necessary. Posts built upon posts, as in Japanese tradition, were here held together with wrought iron straps and wedges.

A clear example of this method and its felicitous results can be seen in the Blacker House, ILLUSTRATION 67, over the second story window. The beam ends were rounded and shaped by hand, as were the supports and brackets of the Gamble house sleeping porch in ILLUSTRATION 65. Throughout the woodwork of the exterior, the interior, and the furniture, the screws that held together the component elements were transformed into decorative devices by sinking them and covering each with a rectangular peg in a contrasting wood (ILLUSTRATION 65).[28] In 1904, in answer to an earlier client's complaint about the projecting beam ends, Charles Greene had written, "The reason why the beams project from the gables is because they cast such beautiful shadows on the sides of the house in this bright atmosphere."[29]

These houses were hymns to that bright atmosphere. Shadows had become architectural elements of importance in a climate of perpetual sunshine. ILLUSTRATION 64 shows the diagonals thrown across the back of the Gamble

DEFINING AN IDENTITY

house. Light and shadow call attention to the rhythm of the descending beam ends in the Blacker house in ILLUSTRATION 67. Handsplit, 36-inch long shingles, exposing only 11 inches, provided both the exterior covering and the insulation. The rough-hewn shakes gave the hand-made quality preferred by John Ruskin over mechanical repetition. The use of clinker bricks (purposely overfired to produce the dark colors and uneven forms), sometimes mixed with the Arroyo's water-worn rocks, not only provided a natural bond between the foundations and the earth, but permitted a variety of tonal values. ILLUSTRATION 68 shows an exquisite modeling of light: channeled through the veranda, it glistens on the uneven surface of the brick terrace and outlines each beam and brace.

While the overhanging eaves provided cool shadiness to verandas and interior, inside layouts were planned around central hallways with screened openings front and rear (ILLUSTRATION 66) to encourage air circulation and a feeling of openness to the out-of-doors. The horizontal bands of windows (ILLUSTRATIONS 63 and 64) also contributed to air circulation. They were equally essential to the horizontality of the design concept, further extended by the cantilevered eaves, sleeping porches and the pergolas formed by extensions of the eaves (ILLUSTRATION 67).

66. Detail of Gamble house, 1908

The environmental setting was chosen for its natural beauties and then, as in Japan, tamed and enhanced. Two eucalyptus trees on the Gamble site were incorporated into the design, serving as the dual centerpiece of the rear terrace. A lily pool was nestled into the contour of the Blacker grounds, its colors and plant forms echoed in stained glass in the house, the clouds that it reflected repeated in cloud-motifs decorating the ends of the interior beams. The front door of the Gamble house depicts the gnarled oak trees dotting the surrounding vistas (ILLUSTRATION 66). The location and muted coloring of stained glass windows throughout the large Greene and Greene bungalows was purposely oriented to the sources of natural light. Stained glass turned the late afternoon sunlight into colors complementing interior decor. The cool shadowy interior, bathed in a glow of mellow tones, was a place of quiet beauty simply expressed in the medium of light.[30]

67. Detail of R. R. Blacker
house, 1907

68. Detail of R. R. Blacker
house, 1907

There was a sense of privacy and yet of a hospitable openness. There was also the realization of harmony with nature that was central to the quest which had brought Easterners here. The commodious, unpretentious chairs on the terrace in ILLUSTRATION 68 are indispensable to the lifestyle around which the house was built. The honest use of materials — so important to Morris — became the medium for art in praise of nature: rustic woods (stained to hues of aged wood), bronze patinaed as nature chose (not uncommonly hastened by etching), natural stone and chance-shaped brick (tended in the kiln to produce a natural look), vines planted and guided serving as nature's agents to reclaim the structure as their own.

A self-consciously Asian variant of The Craftsman style also appeared in Los Angeles but never rivaled the basic shingled rustic California bungalow in nationwide popularity. It was rarely built beyond California's urban fringes. Yet so many pagoda roof-lines, torii gates, stone lanterns, and other Asian design motifs remain since their conception in the early 1900s, that we must acknowledge their impression on visitors and prospective residents. Although

DEFINING AN IDENTITY

the Victorian desire for flamboyant ornament, inspiring the Newsoms' Chinese lions and moon gates, was discredited, the new appreciation for the simplicity of Japanese aesthetics lent legitimacy to Asian themes. Magazines extolled Asian traditions as compatible with the Arts and Crafts and Art Nouveau modes. A 1916 article in <u>The Craftsman</u> advised the reader to decorate her entire house around a single Japanese woodblock print. By reducing ornamentation to the spare simplicity of the print, and coordinating colors to the sensitive muted tones found in a good print — the "delicious 'twilight sky' blues, 'plum blossom' pinks,... 'wisteria' lavenders and purples, 'dried grass' browns...",[31] the average housewife could achieve the refined look of a professionally decorated home and accolades for good taste. Japanese aesthetics were fashionable among forward-looking individuals who refused to be shackled by old traditions, the very people who were flocking to Los Angeles in the progressive period.

Progressive Los Angeles had another interest in the Far East. Construction had begun in 1898 on the city's man-made harbor at San Pedro. It would be completed in 1913. The Panama Canal would be finished a year later, linking Pacific trade to the Atlantic. Between 1898 and 1914 the United States acquired important territorial possessions in the Pacific: Hawaii, Guam, Wake, the Philippines, and part of Samoa. Tremendous civic pride surrounded the city's growing importance in U.S.-Pacific relations and the city's own expected prosperity. The Chamber of Commerce was already anticipating this new future in 1900:

"When the harbor at San Pedro is completed, this city will share in the commerce between the Orient and the United Sates....[as] soon as [the harbor] is ready for business, ships from Japan, China, Australia, and the new island possessions of the United Sates will bring their cargoes of Oriental products thither..."[32]

Los Angeles' perspective on Asia had changed greatly since the 1880s. Then Asia seemed strange, exotic, mystifying; Chinese touches in architecture expressed a quaint outlandishness. In the new century, Los Angeles had become the portal of the nation. The new view was proprietary. Asia's new significance to Angelenos found expression in the work of leading local architects in the Craftsman mode.

Charles and Henry Greene deftly merged the new Asian imagery with Craftsman style traits and with older interpretations of Los Angeles as well. The Cordelia Culbertson house in ILLUSTRATION 69 was built by Greene and Greene in 1911, only three years after their Gamble house project and directly across the street from their R. R. Blacker house. At first glance, this seems a complete

69. Coldelia Culbertson
house, 1911

departure from the earlier grand bungalow style. The facade of this house is self-consciously Chinese. The entry lanterns (ILLUSTRATION 70) were directly modeled on Chinese antiques. Charles Greene employed rugs and fabrics of Chinese patterns throughout the interior to set off the Culbertson sisters' collection of Chinese artware. For wealthy clients with a unifying theme of their own, Greene and Greene proved readily adaptable.

For the roof, the architects used colored glazed tiles such as at the temples of both China and Japan, here in varied hues of green, blue-green and red. They crowned the gable ridges with a decorative tile coping, following East Asian tradition. Departing from the wooden surfaces which had won them fame, the architects chose a formed surface simulating historic Chinese temples and palaces. The walls were actually wood-frame covered in sprayed gunite left unfinished so that its texture should retain the natural look of its sand ingredient, and the contouring could exhibit the irregular flowing softness which would have been lost by trowelling. The original color was "a mellow rusty tan." The result was a harmony of house and earth, an artist's joy in the shifting sunlight and shadow across a grainy, irregular surface. The Arts and Crafts ideals had been preserved. The horizontality of the building mass was even more pronounced than in the architects' bungalow designs.[33]

Behind its Chinese mask, the Culbertson house expressed even more local ideals than had the earlier Greene and Greene houses. Built in a 'U'-shape around a courtyard, it harked back to the storied lifestyle of old California grandees such as Don Juan Templo. Like his adobe, this house of mixed heritage featured a formal Italian garden for the private pleasure of the inhabitants. Most of the Culbertsons' rooms opened directly onto the open corridor or veranda surrounding the courtyard, from which the gardens dropped away into successive terraces and manicured gardens. An extensive pergola partially closed off the open side of the 'U'. Life in the house was drawn out of doors not so much to the open-armed hospitality of the Hispanic adobe, perhaps, as to a sheltered refuge behind a wall of Chinese inscrutability. The house captured the cosmopolitan look appropriate to sophisticated clients in a city facing Asia. At the same time, it provided for the casual, outdoor lifestyle of Los Angeles. It was an eclectic, yet successful, union of diverse images.[34]

Whether developing the more popular shingled form of the California

DEFINING AN IDENTITY

bungalow or an Asian sub-style, the architect-pioneers of the new era were carrying out a set of principles which completely reversed those the Newsoms had followed in the 1880s. Art instructor and master tile-maker, Ernest Batchelder redefined the principles of good design for his students in 1904: "[In design,] success is quite dependent upon knowing what to leave out of a piece of work. We might almost define 'style' as direct, straightforward simplicity."[35]

A critic of the times, noting the "restraint and good taste" which characterized the bungalows of Greene and Greene and other architects who contributed to the elevation of the California bungalow to high-art status (such as Hunt and Grey, Heineman and Heineman, Walker and Vawter, and Louis Easton), concluded, "Taken all in all, the domestic architecture of the Pacific Coast...has grown close to the ideal, since it has succeeded in eliminating nearly all qualities that do not make for health, happiness and beauty, and in doing so has come to be a living art."[36]

70. Detail of Coldelia Culbertson house

The same principles characterized the vernacular bungalows. Since the mid-'90s, national magazines had been picturing houses that followed the Craftsman ideals. But they were dressed in a variety of borrowed styles — half-timbered Tudor, rustic cabin, Swiss chalet, and sometimes Mission Revival. The version known as the California Bungalow became widespread partly because, in the Southern California environment, it was inexpensive to build. It required no basement for furnace and fuel; foundations did not have to be sunk below a frost line; it required no other insulation than its shingle skin. Its low price, together with the modern ideas it represented and its attractive appearance, made it popular with the new Angeleno of the middle-class. It also became a popular style as far away as Vancouver, British Columbia, Helena, Montana and upper New York State, although it was not really suitable for climates other than California's. They must have caused successive owners many winter problems, with their thin outer walls and low-pitched roofs.

The restless, progressive perfection-seeker who left the East came to Los Angeles with a conscious image of a better quality of life. An important part of that image was a bungalow to call home. And it was a Pacific Electric streetcar that brought that dream within reach. Following the 1880s boom and bust, enterprising individuals had purchased the short streetcar and cable car lines built by boomtime developers to their real estate tracts. Available at desperation prices, these short lines were connected, consolidated and, in the mid-nineties, electrified by several competing companies. As part of the local campaign against the Southern Pacific Railroad's monopoly on transportation and politics, the citizens of Pasadena, Santa Monica, and Los Angeles favored the electric-car companies' successful bids to link the three towns in competition with the Southern Pacific's steam passenger lines. In 1900 the last of the Southern Pacific rail czars, Collis Huntington, died. His nephew, Henry E. Huntington, moved to Los Angeles, incorporated the Pacific Electric Railway Company as an interurban system, acquired control of the in-town Los Angeles Railway, and began to form a comprehensive electric rail system in 1901. Huntington's transportation network brought together communities as far inland as Redlands and San Bernardino, as far south as Huntington Beach (Orange County) and as far north as Owensmouth (now Canoga Park). Land served by commuter streetcars could be subdivided into 50 by 100 or 150 foot parcels and sold at many times its pre-streetcar price. Wherever the streetcar lines extended, especially after recovery from the national economic slump of 1907, communities of cheap versions of the California bungalow sprang up. The land companies often formed local utility services, banks, and even restaurants and other entertainments as they subdivided and sold the lots. Hamlets of a handful of houses left from the 1887 boom were transformed into fully-serviced suburbs. The telephone, gas and electric companies were immediately profitable, the banks and restaurants thriving — and the development companies soon sold them, as well, for high profits.[37]

Only a century before, Spanish officials and Franciscan padres had forged a fragile frontier on a remote wilderness coastline from a slender string of 21 missions, four presidios and three pueblos linked by a dirt track called El Camino Real. The complex knot of streetcar lines consolidated and constructed mostly between 1901 and 1911 under Henry Huntington's aegis transformed the turn-of-the-century town into a major metropolis of the modern age. The urban sprawl of which L.A. is now the infamous paradigm, can be blamed on the streetcars and on the streetcar riders' dreams. Wherever the tracks extended, so did settlement. The land developers associated with the streetcar systems sold small lots with room for a garden at prices designed to attract middle-class employees of downtown businesses. The streetcar marked out L.A. as a middle-

71. Bungalow tract, 1910s

class preserve. Thousands of families "of Very Moderate Means", as one advertisement went, were able to purchase lots and build houses miles away from places of employment. Eventually, as mass production brought the price of the Model T Ford down, garages became a standard feature on the back corner of every lot.

The unpretentious new Angeleno built an inexpensive California bungalow to house his vision of a new life complete with inglenook, paneled walls and zinc-topped kitchen counters. He had found his ideal home in the ideal setting. The California bungalow was cheap, yet artistically acceptable; it eschewed the vulgar ostentation he criticized; it embraced the family values he idealized. His bungalow, like each of his neighbors', was situated on a green lawn pierced with a palm tree and bordered with foundation plantings such as hydrangeas or geraniums (ILLUSTRATION 71). The single-family suburban dwelling with the cultural, social and employment advantages of the city as well as the country benefits of fresh air, open space, gardens, peace, and privacy — the 20th-century version of the American Dream — could become reality for the middle-class in Los Angeles.

Builders specializing in bungalows thrived for nearly two decades. Prospective homeowners often chose the plans from the flurry of popular bungalow books published in the 1900s and 1910s.

"Allen bungalows are built the world over. The THIRD EDITION of our bungalow book is without exception the most practical book on the market. Designs of homes costing from $800 to $2000 predominate in this edition. Send 50 cents today for a copy and be convinced.
W. E. ALLEN, Eleventh Floor, Story Bldg., Los Angeles, Cal."
— 1911 advertisement[38]

72. Bungalow vernacular,
1912

Do-it-yourselfers bought complete instructions and erected their own bungalows. The Sears, Roebuck catalog and a variety of smaller enterprises sold pre-fab kits.[39] In its nicest renderings, the small suburban bungalow retained the sense of individuality, the low profile, the harmony with nature the architect-designed houses had exhibited. The small bungalow in ILLUSTRATION 72 was completed in 1912. It has been kept in mint condition. The deep brown earth tone of the shingling, the clinker and cobblestone foundations and pillars, and the Japanese-influenced post and beam design are authentic touches. The horizontal feeling is there, even in so small a structure, due to the low sloping roof emphasized by the wide bargeboard, the horizontality of the gable beams, the windows and doors, and the rail line of the porch. At close hand, the gable beams reveal a roughhewn texture, and though the handkerchief patch of lawn may lack the pleasing slope of the Gamble house lawn, but for its time and for the budget and aspirations of newcomers from Eastern cities it represented a utopian life.

By the time the bungalow was institutionalized as tract housing (ILLUSTRATION 71), it had lost some of the charm of individuality and taken on a regimented look. Lawn after lawn sported a newly-planted palm in precisely the same spot. In this photograph, taken sometime around 1912, there appear to be three models. The first is a triangular-pedimented, one-and-a-half-story version, where attic-window corbels create a Swiss chalet look. A second model appears next door in a one-and-a-half-story house with a wide overhung dormer topped in Prussian points, sports pillars trimmed with a row of dentils. This model reappears five doors away. A two-storied model with daisies in the upstairs window box is the third style. It is repeated next door with a variation in pillar and eave treatments. Patterned similarity was compensated by affordability. Four hundred and more homes built as a tract from bulk-priced materials by workmen familiar with the construction specifications brought prices down. Very small bungalows could be purchased for less than one thousand dollars. Tract houses like these started at $2700, required a down payment of $200, and carried an interest rate of one per cent per month on ten-year financing. The typical lot was from 40 to 60 feet wide, 100 to 150 feet deep.[40]

"Southern California homes are cheap homes to build. A well built, five room bungalow with every modern improvement, on a good street, provided with water, gas, sewers, electricity, telephones, good car service, a twenty minute ride from the business district, can be purchased for $3,000. The result? A city of homes, the home idea being carried out for miles and miles along its streets, in its model communities, its subdivisions and its foothill valleys."

The final step in this process of bringing the bungalow within the means of almost everyone was the development of the bungalow court now attributed to architect Sylvanus Marston in 1909 Pasadena.[42] A grouping of identical units, often with a larger manager's or owner's apartment at the base of

73. Bungalow court, ca. 1913

74. Asian themed bungalow, 1914

the 'U' around a central court, each separated from the next by a landscaped walk or side yard (ILLUSTRATION 73), provided a small but present sense of privacy and the open green space often missing from urban working-class housing. The clustering of eight or twelve units on one piece of property brought the cost down to the laborer's rental level. Even on this scale, the values of the new era and their various sources could be acknowledged. The designer of the bungalow court in ILLUSTRATION 74 employed the consciously Asian touch, but only to accentuate the Japanese influence inherent in the California bungalow genre. The miniaturized post-and-beam porch supports and the exposed rafters were not directly Japanese, but they were compatible with Japanese tradition.

145

Facing West

The designer called attention to the Japanese styling of the buildings by adding a peak to each gable and by framing the property entrance in a torii gateway. These were additions tacked onto the basic bungalow style for the sake of commercial advantage. The owner of a rental court could appeal visually to the consumer's desire to reside in a stylish place depicting Los Angeles as wonderfully different from back home.

In ILLUSTRATION 73, a dilapidated Hollywood court pays cursory homage to the California bungalow's standard features in 24 by 24 foot units: triple windows forming a horizontal rectangle; walls shingled in natural tones; overhanging eaves supported by exposed beams; and a veranda shrunk to a stoop with one pillar. On either side, a poinsettia plant postures in flamboyant greeting. And a star pine, one of the foreign exotics introduced to gardeners new from the East, still draws the eye to the center of the court.

IN 1914 THE EUPHORIA which had accompanied progress in the Western world was shattered by the outbreak of a war more destructive and more widespread than any the world had ever witnessed. But in Southern California the war seemed very distant, the future bright. The business community's campaign to widen the economic base was poised on the threshold of success.

By 1914 the Chamber's drive for "Balanced Prosperity," a diversified industrial base, was off and running.[43] The Panama Canal had opened, stimulating shipping and trade. The federal harbor construction project at San Pedro had completed a two-mile breakwater and dredged inner and outer harbors for deep-draught ships. The City of Los Angeles had already built extensive wharf and warehouse facilities in both. The city's new aqueduct had been completed the previous year, bringing water for industrial growth along with cheap hydroelectric power. The same year, pipelines were constructed to bring natural gas from the oil fields of neighboring counties. Standard Oil Company had opened its refinery at El Segundo. Industrial fuel was thus both cheap and plentiful.[44] Three major rail lines gave local industries access to consumers west of the Rockies, making products cost-competitive with expensive-to-freight eastern goods. L.A. also offered industrialists relief from the pressures of organized labor. By 1911 the Times' publisher, trumpeting the advantages of his city, concluded:

"But among all her splendid material assets, none is so valuable, morally and materially, as her possession of that priceless boon, industrial freedom... [the term of the times for the open shop, i.e., no unions]."[45]

By 1916 the Chamber could report an estimated 2300 factories in Los

Angeles' city limits. While the Chamber's Committee on Manufactures importuned eastern factory owners with the city's merits and its Industrial Bureau labored to draw capital investment to this locality, fate intervened. Three newborn industries discovered Los Angeles on their own; oil, aircraft manufacturing, and motion pictures.[46] Their dynamic growth rates, all three spurred by the war, made possible the burst of expansion that quadrupled the city's population between 1910 and 1924.[47] Their characters, as the futuristic technologies of their day, and as risky opportunities for men and women of a gambling bent, played a major role in selecting the character of the immigrants who made up the expansion and who molded the city's new guise.

The oil industry was the first of the three to arrive. Settlers in the Hispanic period had roofed their adobe houses with tar, or brea, which they had found a mile away. By 1890 more uses had been found for this material. The high price of coal on the West coast had induced gas and light companies to switch to petroleum products; ferry steamers were burning oil instead of coal; and a number of San Francisco industries had converted to oil. The new market stimulated exploration and financing, resulting in spectacular new finds in both Ventura County and Los Angeles.

By 1895 the Los Angeles field was producing more oil than all the other oil fields in the state combined. A series of unprecedented oil discoveries in the area, beginning in Huntington Beach in 1919, and climaxing in the Santa Fe Springs and Signal Hill (Long Beach) discoveries in 1921, drew a throng of oil men and would-be oil men into Los Angeles. By 1922 Southern California produced one-fourth of the nation's oil.[48] To keep up with the furious pace of gasoline consumption, Southern California oil production leaped from 32,127,876 barrels in 1920 to 72,465,510 in 1922 to 208,325,121 in 1923. Of all the manufactured goods produced in the Los Angeles metropolitan area in 1923, oil ranked second in dollar value and third in weekly payroll.[49]

The second infant industry was aircraft manufacturing. It made its first appearance as a spectator amusement. The Wright Brothers' famous lift-off, man's first powered flight, had been staged in North Carolina in 1903. In 1909 a New York teenager named Donald Douglas traveled to Virginia to watch the Wrights demonstrate their latest flying machine. The youth was instantly "hooked" on airplanes. He was not alone. That same year the first international air meet was staged in Reims, France.

Appearing in Los Angeles that fall of 1909 was Roy Knabenshue, a dirigible exhibitioner who had been featured in the first moving picture footage shot in Los Angeles back in 1904. He convinced business leaders in the

Merchants and Manufactures Association (M & M) that another international air show, America's first, should be held in Los Angeles. They approved a site: an open expanse on the old Rancho San Pedro, Dominguez Field. It was strategically located near the Pacific Electric (P.E.) tracks, but it had a hill between the tracks and the field so train travelers were forced to purchase tickets in order to see the events. The passenger potential persuaded Henry Huntington, the P.E. magnate, to donate $50,000 toward the $80,000 prize money.

The Air Meet was held January 10-20, 1910. The crated airplanes had arrived by ship and train, the weather was clear, and some 20,000 spectators turned out for the opening day. Worldwide press attention was everything the M & M had hoped for. For eleven days the crowds were excited by balloon, dirigible, and glider performances and thrilled by the heavier-than-air flights of the international flying champions. New world records were set in distance, altitude, and speed.[30] Like Donald Douglas, there were many young men in those January crowds who caught the flying bug. The movie companies picked up on the flying craze and hired barnstormers to perform daring stunts in movie scenes. All the publicity about flying in Los Angeles persuaded a number of the early aviation developers to relocate to the region. L.A.'s weather offered the struggling inventor the temptation to build outside if necessary, and promised plenty of testing days throughout the year. This was a new field and no training or previous experience was available. Meager financing and trial and error methods doomed many of the would-be aircraft builders early but a few pioneers succeeded and formed companies that would become important foundations of the local and national economies a few years later.

Personal links between the individuals involved, such as Douglas, the Lougheed brothers (pronounced and later spelled 'Lockheed'), Glenn Martin and John K. Northrup, were another factor in the major aircraft companies' gravitation to Los Angeles. As a business, aviation lacked the get-rich-quick allure of oil and cinema, but it did have the rewards of inventive creativity and the new thrills experienced aloft. Rich and daring playboys, of which Los Angeles, with its traditions of flamboyant real estate promotion and flashy movie stars, had more than its share, bought flying machines and even built airfields of their own. L. C. Brand built one next to his mansion in Glendale. Charlie Chaplin's brother, Sydney, built one of the commercial fields convenient to Hollywood. By the mid-'20s the rise of commercial passenger airlines swelled manufacturers' orders. The aircraft industry and its related businesses were an important factor in the local economy. In August 1929 Los Angeles boasted

75. Japanese-Aeroplane
bungalow, 1913

fourteen aircraft factories and six airplane motor manufacturers. Southern
California as a whole had 53 airports and landing fields, and 26 aviation
schools.[51]

Long before the aircraft industry reached this level, the public
enthusiasm for flying was recorded in housing. ILLUSTRATION 75 shows one of the
many popularly called "Aeroplane bungalows" or "Japanese-Aeroplane
bungalows." True to its name, it served two current fads at once. Designed by a
prolific plan-service entrepreneur A.C. Smith, the eight-room Aeroplane
Bungalow in ILLUSTRATION 75 was built at a cost of $2,500. It is a shingled
bungalow, with all the features of the style. Its Asian look was achieved by
simplifying the post and beam gable support to a Shinto torii form and by
converting the chalet overhang into a pagoda roof line with the wide curving
bargeboard and the sloped lilt at gable and eave-corners. With or without its
wisteria screen it captured the popular theme.[52] At the same time, its nickname
reflected the current interest in flying machines.

Clay Lancaster traces the term "Aeroplane bungalow" to the T-shaped
floor plan employed by Frank Lloyd Wright and the Chicago School as early as
1901. He describes the contemporary interpretation, "It was a low, frame house
with cobblestone chimneys and porch piers, and exaggerated, reduplicated
fluttering eaves; the second story in the center of the pile contained 'flying'
bedrooms and sleeping porches."

The association of Japanese aesthetics, L.A.'s prospect as the gateway to
Asia-Pacific trade, and, the thrilling concept of man aloft: surely this was the
epitome of Modern and the progressive architectural design. Lancaster
concludes, "The Japanese-Aeroplane bungalow was a heterogeneous concoction
prompted by rank commercialism, seeking sales through appeal to two fads that
chanced to be raging at the same time."[53] It must have been a good seller, to
judge from the number that have survived to the present.

Of the three new industries, motion pictures played the biggest role in the imagination and economy of Los Angeles. In 1923 it surpassed the oil industry with an annual production value of $168 million, a weekly payroll of $1.3 million. It remained in first place for many years.[54] At first merely a penny-arcade novelty, moving pictures developed into an entertainment medium with story lines and dramatic action. The pantomime action won appreciative audiences among the working-class. Demand for the new entertainment led to five-cent movie theaters called Nickelodeons. By 1907 there were some 3,000 in the U.S.[55]

In the first decade of the century a film might cost only $150 to make, including actors' wages, film, and sets, but it could net $1,000 a week for exhibitors. High profits and the demands of theaters for a rapid-fire supply of new films stimulated film production. It was an easy business to get into. A camera, some film, a couple of actors and a cameraman was enough. Shot from a single angle with whatever story-line came to mind on the spur of the moment, very little reshooting or editing, and the adaptation into plot and picture of whatever local scenery presented itself for free (such as a passing parade or a building afire), it was not difficult to complete a film in a day or two. On a shoestring, ambitious young men left the garment trade, the bicycle business, or pool hall management or branched out from film exhibiting to go into film production. The competition was keen.

It was at this point that Los Angeles was "discovered". The primary attraction was the perennial sunshine. L.A.'s tourist literature claimed 350 sunny days a year, a most alluring prospect for filmmakers before the invention of mercury lights.[56] A second drawing feature was the varied scenery — the "difference." The search for new, unfamiliar, and more authentic looking scenery led movie-makers to the Real West of California. Los Angeles had nearly every kind of scenery imaginable — rugged mountains, chaparral-covered hills, valleys, plains, city, fishing villages, desert, and ocean, all in close proximity.[57]

The third factor in the westward migration of the fledgling industry was a result of competition. In 1908 eleven companies joined to form a trust, known as the Motion Picture Patents Company. Armed with patents on cameras and sprockets, and an agreement with Eastman Kodak to sell film only to its members, it attempted to control the film making, distributing, and exhibition phases of the industry, nationwide. California offered a haven from trust enforcement for independent film makers. At first, Los Angeles was only regarded as a temporary location for filming during the winter or for special scenery effects or pending a skirmish in business rivalry at a company's eastern headquarters.[58] By early 1909 the test period was over. Several companies constructed permanent studios — Selig Polyscope Company and the Bison Company located in Edendale (present-day Echo Park). In 1910 the Essanay and Kalem Film companies set up shop in nearby Glendale, and Vitagraph and Biograph moved into Santa Monica. Except for the western-making Bison Company, which arranged in 1911 to move to Santa Ynez Canyon (the edge of Pacific Palisades), vacating their Edendale facility to a sister company, Mack Sennett Comedies, all the early studios were to be found near streetcar lines — the same pattern of settlement followed by suburban housing developments. This cheap mode of access was one of the considerations that led the Horsely brothers to set up their studio in Hollywood in October 1911, the first studio there. Some of the other studios soon located nearby.[59] Geographically, Hollywood came to form the hub of the film-making circle, the center around which the famous settled and the tourists buzzed. The name Hollywood came to represent the film glamour aspect of Los Angeles. During the confident years of the early nineteen-teens, the new form of urban entertainment grew quickly in popularity. An industry spokesman claimed a weekly American attendance of 56 million in 1915. Historians estimate only 25 million a week, but with the national population at 100 million in 1915, even the lower figure indicates a sensational popularity for the new entertainment form.[60]

American drama critics refused to consider movies as worthy of attention before 1915, but the same was not true in Europe where film-makers were very conscious of the aesthetic possibilities and challenges of the new medium. The outbreak of World War I in Europe in the autumn of 1914 boosted the American movie industry just as it did the oil and aircraft businesses. The combination of economic drain, disruption and destruction, and the military draft temporarily halted European production. A number of leading directors and actors migrated to Hollywood. When peace returned, following the armistice of November 1918, the dominance of Hollywood in the international motion picture business was assured.[61]

In the '20s, these three industries, oil, aircraft, and motion pictures would be major elements in the dynamic economic and population expansions so long predicted by Chamber of Commerce boosters. They were also basic to the new aura of glamour imparted by the city. All three were futuristic; all three were risky, appealing to daring dreamers; and all three required innovation and adaptability. Each benefited materially from the First World War. Even before the war, though, each had contributed to the optimism with which Angelenos regarded their city's future. Those were the bungalow years, the progressive era.

PART FIVE

MOVIE STARS
AND
HARD TIMES

1920 · 1939

MOVIE STARS AND HARD TIMES

1920 - 1939

IX

REVIVALISM: INSECURITY AND PRETENSE

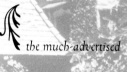

the much-advertised

City of Angels

was, after all,

a mere shadowgraph

of the place where the best

in current "Whoopee"

was invented and

the movies were made

IT WAS, QUIXOTICALLY, THE FINAL SURGE of Progressive idealism that carried America into the First World War in 1917. The premise of man's perfectibility through the improvement of his environment was extended to the world at large. The President asserted that the United States had no selfish war goals, no interest but to make the world a better place. For the sake of the nobler causes of freedom, democracy, and a just and permanent peace, Everyman turned from fading progressive causes of City charter reforms and street light campaigns to rolling bandages, buying Liberty Bonds, and observing "Wheatless Mondays" and "Meatless Tuesdays" to conserve food for "Our Boys" and the allies. The patriotic pride that had been such an important element of progressivism escalated to a militant nationalism. As the nation was swept into war, dissension was frequently stigmatized as "un-American." Worries about "hyphenated Americans," particularly German-Americans who might have divided loyalties, provoked near-fanatical protestations of loyalty by others. Out of the war came the slogan, "100% Americanism," which characterized the sum of ideals, pride, and traditions Americans (of whatever ancestry) believed in and felt worthy of fight and sacrifice.[1] Four million Americans joined the armed forces. The crusading spirit went so far as to achieve passage of the Eighteenth Amendment (Prohibition) while the old progressive zeal for reform was linked to wartime grain conservation. All the sacrificing, however, focused on the single goal of victory. When it came in November 1918, progressivism numbered among the war dead. The terms and after-effects of the peace treaty were disappointing. A sense of betrayal, of having fought for nothing, translated into cynicism and disillusionment. Americans were tired of unrequited sentimentalism, of self-sacrificing generosity.

The change in tone had sounded before the Armistice. Outrages against the idealist's sense of fair play had been committed by both sides in the war. The moral code of Horatio Alger and the McGuffey's Readers had been impugned. During the war, issues had been overstated in terms of clear-cut right and wrong, good and bad, leading to a postwar rejection of moralistic rhetoric.

The end of the war marked the end of individual life patterns, whether in small ways like doing without an extra pat of butter "for the war effort," or in major dislocations such as postwar unemployment and tension within newly re-united families. Thoughts of change now pointed to self-gratification rather than to society's betterment. For many, especially the young, there would be a con-scious revolt against the restraining values and principles of the pre-war period. Many Americans were ready to trade in their faith in progress and purity to settle for more tangible and immediate realities. The Roaring Twenties followed.

Revivalism: Insecurity and Pretense

Pre-war bungalow-dwellers had been righteous, self-appreciating optimists certain of a better tomorrow. The generation of the '20s saw those values as obsolete, along with the bungalow style housing that symbolized them. Over-popularized and over-produced, the bungalow had become a cliché. The workmanship standards of the Arts and Crafts movement had degenerated into hackneyed, commercialized, mass-produced wares sold in mail-order catalogs and magazine ads.[2] Tracts of monotonously similar California bungalows displayed hasty workmanship. Stickley's influential monthly, The Craftsman, went out of print in 1916. The term, "bungalow", itself became a slur synonymous with "mediocre" or even "plodding."[3]

Housing construction in Los Angeles, as in other cities, had fallen off during the war years to pick up again in 1919. A flurry of belated bungalows figured prominently among the new homes constructed. They represented a pent up market demand: pre-war dreams deferred in their realization. But after 1921 the cozy California bungalow was out of style and the word "bungalow," when it was used, usually referred to small houses in the Colonial Revival or Mediterranean styles.[4]

For Los Angeles, the Armistice of November 11, 1918 signaled not only the end of the bungalow era, but a turning-point in the formation of the city's image. The period that lasted from 1919 to 1939 was one of dynamic growth, of economic and social trauma. Major uncertainties of the era compelled a search for new answers and new images. During these two decades, a stock selection of historically-derivative architectural styles was adopted as a vernacular canon of styles. A ready reference library of approved characteristics of such styles was built along streets and avenues across Los Angeles. That set of references has served as the inspiration for home designs ever since. The period, not coincidentally, was also the Golden Age of the movies, which had a major effect on the style certification process. Paradoxically, the burst of energy which produced a fixed vocabulary of derivative styles also encouraged a burst of creative originality.

During the same period that silent movies poured out of Southern California studios raising a specter of low-cultural uniformity, a maturation of tastes, a sector of sophistication and cosmopolitanism flowered in Los Angeles, providing new patronage for design creativity. The decades between the wars are the watershed period which endowed Los Angeles with a rich spread of images. Broadly speaking, the buildings of the 1920s and 1930s, and the shadows they have cast on drawing boards, still outline the city's dreamscape today.

The transition from war to peace marked a threshold of change in

76. Colonial Revival
cottages, 1922

attitudes, values, and behavior. Flivvers and flappers, jazz and speakeasies marked new freedoms and defiant revolts of the Roaring Twenties. But another important ingredient of that decade was the desire to resuscitate the patriotism and reforming zeal, of moral certainty and suburban simplicity. Nationwide, as the building trades returned to a peacetime footing and home-building resumed, there was a demand by conservatives for a real American look: a flag-waving, motherhood and apple-pie nostalgia. The resulting Colonial Revival wave was a grab-bag of motifs from such early American styles as Greek Revival (or Plantation), Federal (or Adamsesque), Georgian (or Palladian), Dutch Colonial, and Cape Cod. In towns and cities across the country, including Los Angeles, Colonial Revival houses sprang up to give shelter to a disappearing sense of security. The row of small frame houses in ILLUSTRATION 76 was part of a development built in Santa Monica in 1922. All three have columns of the Tuscan order, each has the same small porch prefaced by the same flat rectangles of front lawn and foundation plantings. The designer did provide stylistic variations within the Colonial Revival medium. The house on the right has a gambrel roofline over the portal as a mark of the Dutch Colonial. Its neighbor to the left has a porticoed porch and a Palladian window gesture. The third house has been stuccoed over by some subsequent owner in an attempt to disguise its Colonial Revival intention.

The larger house in ILLUSTRATION 77, built in Glendale in 1926, with its Adamesque fanlight and its traditional dark green shutters, has been maintained and landscaped to perfection, declaring to passers-by a faith in an idealized national heritage unshaken for

77. American Federal Revival
house, 1926

over fifty years.[5] The architectural reaffirmation of patriotic pride and cultural conservatism found expression everywhere in America at this time. But Los Angeles never quite resembled "everywhere"; Colonial Revival architecture was soon overshadowed by more flamboyant styles.

Despite the conservative undertone, the dominant themes of the era of the '20s were fun and frolic, youthful flights of fancy, and escape from dull responsibility. Motion pictures, automobiles, and advertising provided the

Revivalism: Insecurity and Pretense

impetus for the changes in prevailing outlook that delineated the postwar from the prewar era and replaced regional provincialism with a nationwide culture. Each contributed to a new Los Angeles Boom. It was the motion picture industry, centered in Los Angeles, that contributed the most dramatically to the city's transformation.

Motion pictures offered one way of coping with the insecurity of a period of rapid and unsettling change: they invited escapism into a world of fantasies. After the Armistice no one wanted to watch movies on war themes. The film industry scrambled to identify and respond to new audience tastes. By the summer of 1919 they had discovered what the American audience wanted to watch: dashing adventures and comedies in which all problems were solved, all questions answered, all wishes granted; scenes of sex and decadence that surpassed the standards of the pre-war period; and wealthy sophistication or exotic historicism that offered vicarious dream worlds far from the mundane lives of average movie-goers.[6]

The public flocked to the movies. Entrepreneurs outdid each other converting neighborhood theaters into ornate temples to the imagination. A 1929 critic wrote, "The luxury of the contemporary moving picture theatre, the sense of richness in all the trappings of the show, the sanctuary the movie presents from all burdensome worries... it is the urban counterpart of the church sociable, the town...meeting, the county fair."[7] He might have added "the oracle of style and values." By 1930 there were 23,000 movie theaters in towns all over the United States. In 1922 the average weekly movie attendance was 40 million; by 1930 it was 100 million.[8] To many, the pretended gaiety so characteristic of the '20s, the preference for make-believe epitomized by the popularity of the movies, was synonymous with Hollywood. L.A. was the place, or so it seemed to the star-struck, where fairytale pretense was reality.

The rise of the motion picture industry and its concentration in L.A. by the 1920s had opened a new chapter in local promotionalism. The varied topography of hills, desert, orange groves, and beaches; the avenues of front-lawned houses among palm trees; the modern city center; and the clear, sunny skies became the setting for the moving fantasies of the screen. Their reality and perfection were impressed on every viewer. The movie messages of youth and beauty, of lively drama, of forbidden delights were added to the now familiar advertising themes, equating these new images with Los Angeles and adding more layers to its image. The new source of publicity was both free and effective. The build-up it gave Los Angeles, the attraction to the dream-prone, outweighed anything in American history, with the possible exception of the 1849 California

Gold Rush. The tourists who came in the '20s were sure they knew in advance what the place would be like: they had seen it in the movies.

By 1920 the star system was in full swing as well. The best-known and best-loved individuals in America became the men and women who starred in the films. Their love lives, parties, wearing apparel, perfumes, hair styles, automobiles, homes, health, pets, and peccadilloes were worldwide news items. At first, star-making publicity simply set up models for emulation. A publicity photo of actress Grace Cunard in a 1916 movie magazine was captioned:

"Grace Cunard Is a Beautiful Young Woman with Lovely Complexion, Big Expressive Blue Eyes, a Perfect Figure and Carriage and a Wonderful Head of Fair Hair, with a Tint of Gold in It. Grace Cunard Bids Fair to be a Wealthy Woman, for She is Accumulating Real Estate and Has Built a Beautiful Bungalow in the Hills of Hollywood. She is the Proud Possessor of a Big Automobile."[9]

By the late '20s, screen idols were adored by fanatical devotees, the "fans," who made pilgrimages past the homes of the stars in Los Angeles. In the nineteen-teens, an article by actress Virginia Pearson advised "Screen-Struck Girls" that their letters to producers arrived by the hundreds and were ineffective; that the way to "break into the movies" was to go to the nearest producer's studio in person and see the "engagement man" about a bit part as a means to "discovery." Hopefuls headed for Hollywood, with or without pushy mamas. By 1920 there were so many of them the studios had to set up offices to handle the crowds. By 1922 the Hollywood-bound migration of young and beautiful dreamers was such a universal phenomenon it could be lampooned indulgently in a hit Broadway play, Merton of the Movies.[10]

The new lights from the film industry joined the nouveaux-riches of the local oil industry in the city's night spots, and together they drew the onlookers like moths to an incandescent globe. A 1929 cynic noted the new focus of the L.A.-bound on the bright lights of Hollywood:

"...the much-advertised City of Angels was, after all, a mere shadowgraph of the place where the best in current "Whoopee" was invented and the movies were made. To bedazzled visions [L.A.] carried the promise of a richly victualed, plush-lined bandwagon on which there would be free and unrestricted seats... — a "Mediterranean" or a "Spanish" villa or a swell apartment on one of the fine boulevards — a front seat at the weekly cinema "premiers" in Hollywood... the joyous night-life, with leg-room among the other gay trippers on the crowded dance-floors...and the honor of calling the head-waiter by his first name."[11]

Revivalism: Insecurity and Pretense

Novels, non-fiction works, magazines, and newspaper columns added their prod to the cinema's pull. If rejection of pre-war idealism and traditions was the prime motivator of 1920s culture, it is not surprising that the leading cultural rebels, writers, screenwriters, critics, youth, and intellectuals, should concentrate their attacks on the strongest bastion of the old ways: the Protestant, rural, middle-aged, Midwestern ethos. One of the most recurrent themes of the 1920s iconoclasts was their contempt for the rural life and the Midwest heartland as dull, prudish, and ridiculous. The literature of the day, and the movies based on some of it, showed readers and viewers what they ought to jeer and wish to escape. To the 40 million Americans — heavily representative of the wage-earning class — who went to the movies each week and followed the news from Hollywood, Los Angeles seemed the most likely place to escape to. The critics who considered themselves among the intellectual elite described Los Angeles in scathing terms as a mindless tinsel-town filling up with rural, Protestant, aging Midwesterners. But to the ordinary person who had become restless and dissatisfied in Iowa, Los Angeles seemed a glamorous, fast-paced place of unfading youth and fantastic opportunities among ex-soda-jerk actors and exhandyman oil millionaires. Average movie-goers with above-average imaginations knew they would fit in and pulled up stakes for a new life of sun and fun, youth and romance, and perhaps fame and fortune as well.[12]

It was primarily by automobile that they came to Los Angeles, to see the sights and perhaps to stay. By the 1920s the horseless carriage, once the expensive toy of the rich, had been perfected to a more or less reliable necessity. By 1925 Ford's assembly line was turning out an automobile every ten seconds. The base price of a Model T dropped to $350. Credit buying put it within reach of nearly everyone, ending the isolation of farmers and widening Americans' experience through vacation travel. The automobile made it easier to pull up roots and make a new life somewhere else.[13]

The automobile and Los Angeles seemed made for each other. The number of sports-minded wealthy winterers here by the turn of the century, coupled with the possibilities of year-round motoring weather and scenic attractions radiating in all directions from the city center led to an early proliferation of the new toy and the formation in 1900 of the Automobile Club of Southern California. In its early intent to facilitate "automobiling" locally, the club sponsored tours and races for its members. As the machines became more reliable and membership grew, the club turned to lobbying for road construction and pavement, posting traffic signs, rating garages and hotels, printing maps and tour guides, and providing auto insurance. These activities stimulated public interest and led to extensive roadbuilding in California. As early as 1916, roads in the Los Angeles area were touted as the most advanced in the nation. They connected Los Angeles with other major tourist attractions in the state, such as Yosemite and San Francisco. By 1925 there were 465,950 autos registered in L.A. County, more than one car to every four people, the highest per capita ownership anywhere in the world.[14] In the post-war atmosphere of apparent prosperity and restless pleasure-seeking, Americans got in their cars and went places. They went to ballparks and movie theaters, for Sunday afternoon drives in the countryside, to other towns to visit relatives, and they went to California. A 1924 reporter described the scene:

"It is a common sight upon the highways leading into Southern California to see whole caravans of touring cars loaded with passengers and paraphernalia. At night these travelers are found in hundreds of municipal auto camps [camp grounds] conducted throughout the country by practically every city of any size. The auto camp has come to be a necessary institution..."[15]

Auto camps were not the only necessary institution. As travel became a way of life, gas stations, roadside eateries, billboards, and roadside hotels (or "motels") catering to passers-by (as contrasted to in-town hotels for those arriving by train) sprang up to meet the new demands.

By late 1922 it was estimated that tourists were arriving in Southern California at the rate of 420 private cars a day from out of state, three-fourths of them headed for Los Angeles. In the peak year of 1923, automobiles added 500 a day; the railroads delivered an additional 3,200 persons per day average, and steamships added another 200. A total of 1,350,000 tourists had arrived in L.A. by November. Based on past experience, Los Angeles officials could expect three out of ten arriving tourists to stay at least five months, and one out of ten to settle permanently.[16]

Between 1921 and 1924, peaking in 1923, the conditions in Los Angeles paralleled those at the onset of the 1886-87 boom: a flood of tourists with money in their pockets and a new mode of cheap transportation (a railroad price war in 1886, credit-purchased automobiles in the 1920s). Travel was opening to a naive element vulnerable to fast-talking sales pitches. This was a period of social change and prosperity with an ebullient confidence in upward mobility. Between the years 1920 and 1924 about 100,000 people per year took up permanent residence in Los Angeles City. The County, over the same period, increased its population by 712,215. Some of the most spectacular growth occurred in the smaller cities within the county, making Los Angeles automobile suburbs of former small towns. The rate of increase reached its zenith in 1923,

Revivalism: Insecurity and Pretense

but growth continued to the end of the decade.[17] A 1929 writer described the scene retrospectively:

"Nearly every newcomer was the seeker of a home. This resulted in a tremendous demand for, and a great speculation in, real estate. It has been estimated that during the fiscal years ending 1921, 1923, and 1924, the value of realty transfers in Los Angeles was $2,777,000,000... The real estate activity brought about the development of a great number of new subdivisions, many of them far removed from the center of the city. In 1922 and 1923 alone, within a ten-mile circle centered in the heart of Los Angeles, nearly 1400 new tracts were opened comprising 143,000 lots and covering nearly 29,000 acres. Prices of all kinds of property, both close-in and ultra-suburban, rose rapidly and large profits on quick turnovers were made. While no specific statement can be made about it, the opinion may be ventured that the ask-price for property doubled."[18]

The speculative frenzy was abetted by its coincidence with new discoveries of oil in 1919-1921. Excited fortune-seekers poured into L.A.. The 1923 peak in number and value of building permits and in population increase did not end in a sudden crash, but in a gradual tapering off of demand, another parallel with the 1880s boom. The initial momentum of the post-war mobility declined, building resolved the housing shortage, and those speculating in real estate for profits turned to the stock market where, by 1925, even higher returns could be realized.

One of our working proposals is that each era's building created the picture of Los Angeles that attracted and channeled the following wave of immigrants there. In the '20s, the city's image as perceived by outsiders was one of open space; single-family residences; newly-established industries; few apparent urban problems; and, best of all, the glamour, fun, and excitement associated with Hollywood, the film capital of the world, where actors and actresses "... are not infrequent sights upon the streets, and where castles, mountains, ships, and skyscrapers rise on the "lots"....This then, is California... a land that is different, a region where change of atmosphere, change of scene, complete change of environment assure that delightful difference of outlook which brings inestimable benefit to the traveler ....California with its stores of incalculable wealth in happy living, in storied wonder, in grandeur of nature — the call of California becomes, in effect, a delectable summons."[19]

The attracting image, with its close link to the tastes of movie-goers, would find expression in unrestrainedly imaginative housing styles. The image's reality as built into dwelling-places guided the selection of immigrants and housing development favorable to extended suburban living. The automobile brought such a dream within reach of salesmen, carpenters, retired farmers, auto mechanics, and factory workers.

In earlier real-estate flurries, suburb developers had invested heavy capital in street-car lines. Now suburbs could be planned beyond the streetcar lines, along roadways. The developers' costs were lower and the lots they sold were less expensive for the consumer with a car. Improved earth-moving equipment, trucks and steam-shovels could carve up the low ranges of hills that rimmed the basin and formed its interior valleys into terraced house-lots, impractical for low-fare streetcars or horse-straining buggies, but conquerable by Ford or Oldsmobile. The higher costs of leveling hillside lots made them more expensive, creating a paradox. In earlier years, the hills had been relegated to the shacks of chicken farmers; now they became prestigious homesites, advertised for their scenic views, montane exclusivity, and natural beauty. The new ability to penetrate the hills enhanced Los Angeles' appeal as a "City of Homes" — there were clusters of hillside houses for those who admired and could afford the view, tracts built in neat grid-patterned blocks in the path of urban expansion, subdivisions in gently rolling hills where the streets curved more graciously, semi-rural developments encouraging the keeping of goats and chickens, and communities planned for the moneyed elite. One could find a niche somewhere. Wherever it was, it should be a separate family dwelling. Of the 1923 residential building permits, 75.66% were for single dwellings, 5.15% apartments or flats, and 18.82% double dwellings, indicating the prevalence of the small-time speculator and of the lower income wage-earner now able to seek a new life in new surroundings.[20]

As the tide of arrivals swelled, shifting trends in tract development could be followed in newspaper advertisements. At first, close-in areas served by street car lines were laid out, streets paved, utilities brought in, and empty lots sold to buyers who would hire a builder to construct their houses. A February 1922 advertisement for Dahlia Heights, a new development in Eagle Rock, proclaimed:

> *"OUR SWITZERLAND" THEY CALL IT*
> *The Beauty and Exclusiveness of the Mountains — Conveniences*
> *of the City "Foothill Homesites," 75 by 1900 feet,*
> *less expensive "Mountain View Residence Lots," 50 by 150 feet,*
> *in the flatlands, and "Business Investment Lots" on Colorado Boulevard.*
> *Directions to the development: "Take the 'Eagle Rock City'*
> *Yellow Car to the end of the line."*[21]

Then more distant areas opened up, beyond the Pacific Electric tracks. If inaccessible by streetcar, distant developments drew tourists without their own transportation, or anyone else out for a weekend lark, could be drawn out to distant developments by the promise of free touring car rides and maybe even a free lunch. An August 1922 ad for Brentwood Country Club Estates, selling "large, picturesquely situated residence sites" for high prices, concluded with "How to Reach" in two columns, "By Trolley" and "By Auto." And in June 1923 the promoters of "The New Town of Girard" (located at the farthest end of the San Fernando Valley, at the junction of the Ventura State Highway and Topanga Canyon Drive) advertised a "Girard Free Educational Tour" with "free auto buses leaving Los Angeles daily at 9:30 a.m. and 10:45 a.m.," and a free lunch.[22] At first, advertising copy had been designed to appeal to the person who just wanted his own home, as in a 1920 ad for:

> *"40 Sand Lots in Venice*
> *$450 to $675*
> *10% down $10 monthly*
> *Some within 450 feet of surf, some on canals."*[23]

Prices went up as the number of interested newcomers grew. There was a surge of speculation in land parcels to be subdivided and in rental properties for those who could not afford the rising down payments or who were not ready to buy.[24] As real estate trade and profits rose, the competition mounted. Ads began to stress urgency, a pressure to "buy quick," in order to overcome the doubts and cautions of prospective customers. By 1922, speculative mania affected everyone. There was a temptation to buy two lots if one could afford to, build a house on one, wait until the rising houses in the neighborhood had driven up the price on the second lot, and then sell it for a profit or build a rental house on it. The promoters of Torrance attracted the small-time buyer by coupling the expectation of rising property values with the possibility of wealth in oil royalties:

> *"TORRANCE — THE MODERN INDUSTRIAL CITY OIL*
> *LANDS & HOMESITES*
> *Big Money is being made in land deals every day. Here is your*
> *opportunity to participate in this wonderful era of prosperity.*
> *Full Size Residence Lots*
> *on 60-Foot Streets With All Oil Rights*
> *$395"*[25]

Increasing property value was a major goal of both the buyer-resident and the buyer-speculator: it was the premise of the investment. Unsightly buildings, "undesirable" neighbors, or too many vacant lots in a development would retard the expected rate of value escalation. To prevent such blights, a growing number of tract promoters by 1923 were restricting architectural styles, following the examples set by the exclusive Palos Verdes Estates; others were erecting "spec" houses (built on speculation, a buyer to be found after completion) scattered throughout the tract to set the tone of the neighborhood; some limited sales on the bases of race and ethnicity — a practice covered by the polite phrase, "restricted residential property." The house pictured in ILLUSTRATION 78 was located in such a development. The tract's 1922 advertisements were also indicative of the high pressure technique:

> "WILSHIRE HIGHLAND SQUARE
> —Dont [sic] lose the best opportunity you will ever have to buy improved, restricted residence property in the Wilshire District at prices far below the present market.
> —You must hurry if you intend to buy in Wilshire Highland Square. Large lots $2100 to $2700.
> Small Deposit, —
> Easy Terms
>
> INSPECT THIS TRACT TODAY
> —There are only a few lots left and each one is a profit maker for you. We expect to be sold out shortly.
> You must act quickly.
> THOS. C. BUNDY & CO.
> 236 Merchants Natl. Bank Bldg. Phone Bdwy. 8388
> Salesmen at Every Corner of the Tract
> —For Sale—
> Two beautiful stucco bungalows in Wilshire Highland Square. Both nearly ready to move into. These bungalows are charming in design and location and are models of convenience. Unusual bargains at the low prices and terms we are asking. Inquire of our salesmen on the tract."[26]

78. Detail, Spanish Colonial tract house, 1929

Revivalism: Insecurity and Pretense

By mid-1923 land developers teamed with construction companies, built large numbers of homes in a limited choice of floor-plans, and sold finished houses, realizing profits in volume production and simultaneously avoiding the threats to property values posed by empty lots. Ads for the Baldwin Hills development of Angeles Vista Heights showed a drawing of a small Hansel and Gretel style house and announced:

"A HIGH CLASS HOME AT A LOW PRICE
...artistic new home...high sightly location...
overlooking the city and mountains...
Prices $6000 to $7950
Terms as Low as $900 cash and only $60 a month"[27]

With so many competitive developments, so many attention-seeking ads, tract salesmen turned to entertainment and give-aways to draw the crowds, quite often for the grand openings and sometimes on a periodic basis. Palos Verdes Estates featured stunt flying exhibitions. The opening festivities for Whitley (in present Sherman Oaks) had everything:

"TODAY'S PROGRAM AT WHITLEY
Free Lot Given Away Today
Register before 4 p.m. Winner announced at 5 p.m.
Free Entertainment
Grauman's "Covered Wagon" in Realistic Action
Indian Chiefs (in Person) —
Jack Hoxie
and Cowboys (Universal) Races and Contests
Free Spanish Dinner —
Band Concert
Free Bus from 6034 Hollywood Blvd Every Hour."[28]

Those who responded to these sales pitches, competing offers, pressures to buy quick, entertainments, easy credit, and clap-on-the-back assurances that "you can't go wrong with this deal" did not tend to be worldly-wise or experience-hardened skeptics. They had come to a place unlike their former homes. As the decade passed, more and more of them came from the Midwest. A disproportionate share of the newcomers were retired people.

Among the newcomers were large numbers of real estate men, high-pressure salesmen, and their less reputable counterparts, who expected to flourish.

The single largest classified heading in the 1925 membership roster of the Los Angeles Chamber of Commerce was "Real Estate", with 1187 listings not including related but separate headings such as "Real Estate-Income Property," "Real Estate Exchanges," and related occupations. By 1930 only a quarter of the city's population had been born in California, 37 percent were transplanted Midwesterners.[29]

Wherever they came from and whatever their original intentions of settling, vacationing, or making a quick gain, their cultural tastes lay exposed in the successful style of advertisers' appeals. The Whitley tract promoters could count on an enthusiastic response to movie cowboys, races and contests, and Indian Chiefs (In Person!). They understood the tastes of the average Angeleno. So did the merchants who enlivened the cityscape with "programmatic" commercial architecture: eateries in the shape of a hot dog in a bun, a coffee pot, a giant doughnut, and other enterprises more or less appropriately built to resemble a giant dog, a Brown Derby hat, or a Big Red Piano.

Even preachers and a cemetery in Los Angeles resorted to stage sets and cinematic techniques. At Forest Lawn Memorial Park the infant section, Lullabyland, features a sculpted fairytale castle and heart-shaped flowerbed; the mortuary is in the 16th-century Tudor style; and the chapels are movie-set doubles of Annie Laurie's church at Glencairn, Scotland ("The Wee Kirk o' the Heather") and the English church that inspired Gray's Elegy ("Little Church of the Flowers").[30] Evangelist Aimee Semple McPherson dramatized her sermons with fully staged tableaux, backed by painted backdrops, elaborate props, a costume department, a band and pipe organ, a huge choir, wire-suspended angels, and professional stage lighting — all worthy of the town where the world's movies were made.[31] These novelties caught attention, patronage, and delight. The slice of humanity that was moving to Los Angeles loved them and exclaimed, "Ain't that cunnin'!"

In retrospect, we suspect that the loneliness and insecurities the "100 Percenters" voiced in their Colonial Revival houses were an ever-present ingredient in the vivacious hedonism we more often equate with the Jazz Age. The fun-seeking carried a hint of desperation, the jollity a sense of pretense, perhaps to convince oneself as well as the rest of the world that one wasn't afraid and insecure in a rapidly-changing, confusing world. On the surface, the lively and entertaining worlds of films, fans, preachers and Forest Lawn, flivvers and the forbidden seemed to come together in the City of Angels. There, fantasy and

Revivalism: Insecurity and Pretense

79. Castle, 1925

80. Apartment house, 1936

real life were one. Dream-drenched escapees from sobriety and responsibility looked to Los Angeles for their own happily-ever-after denouements. They would come here and build storybook houses that expressed their childlike credulity, lively imaginations, and irrepressible gaiety.

The result was the transformation of Los Angeles into Wonderland in one decade. The city took on the appearance of a huge movie lot, its avenues crowded with stage-set houses where dreamers could play out their pretenses. Little stucco castles sprang up right and left. ILLUSTRATION 79 captures an owner-designed-and-built castle of 1925 in the Hancock Park neighborhood. Though limited in size (seven rooms and a two-car garage), it has turrets, a formidable front door, and a family of gargoyles serving as spotlight holders.[32] A less striking but more inviting use of the tower entry occurs on a small, developer-built Santa Monica house (ILLUSTRATION 81), in a style labeled the "French Normandy Look" in 1923. By the mid-'30s, when building single-family homes was rare, investors turned their empty lots and extra cash into apartment houses. The proven popularity of the castle theme helped Depression-era investors in the competition for paying renters. The turreted apartment house in ILLUSTRATION 80 was constructed in Hollywood in 1936.

Castles were only one of the styles enlivening L.A. in the '20s and '30s. There were Middle Eastern harems, Egyptian temples, Tudor manors, and Hopi pueblos. Most of all there were Spanish haciendas. All were stage sets for dream lives set in distant times or places that seemed more imaginative, adventurous, romantic, or exotic than the present reality. They were the products of wonderfully wild and wistful imaginations.

We said at the outset that recycled styles permit us to gauge the changing tenor of different eras. The wide range of outrageous styles had all figured into the L.A. scene around the turn of the century. The chart on page 169 allows a comparison of the earlier renderings of each style with their 1920s counterparts and major differences are apparent at once.

At the beginning of the century, fantasy revivals had been expressions of well-heeled imaginations. In the 1920s, each of these style selections framed average-income imaginations. Instead of a few enclaves of expensive homes in

STYLE RECYCLING

Style	1890s-1900s	1920s-1930s
Castle	Illus. 42, 43	Illus. 79, 80, 81
Tudor	Illus. 45	Illus. 82, 83, 84
Beaux Arts Italianate	Illus. 53, 54	Illus. 85
Colonial Revival	Illus. 47	Illus. 76, 77, 86, 87, 88, 89
Middle Eastern	Illus. 48, 49	Illus. 90, 91
Mission/Mediterranean	Illus. 55, 58, 59, 60, 61	Illus. 78, 97, 98, 99, 100, 101, 102, 104, 105, 106, 107, 108, 109, 110, 111

81. French Normandy tract house, 1923

exotic styles, set back on extensive lawns, neighborhoods to which tourists were taken as impressive L.A. monuments, 1920s Los Angeles spawned hundreds of suburban avenues lined with miniature versions of French provincial towers, half-timbered Elizabethans, American Colonial time pieces, Scheherazade sets, and Mediterranean memories. These styles were not limited to their most numerous middle-class renditions, but extended upward to the high-priced developments of Windsor Square and Beverly Hills and downward to apartment houses and tiny workers' row cottages. The acceptance of the same styles by all classes reflected a homogeneous taste, a consensus of exciting fictions in which all wished to participate.

If we compare 1900s Tudors to 1920s Tudors, 1900s Middle Eastern to 1920s Middle Eastern, and so forth, we can detect a difference in intent across the span of time. The earlier projections attempted to impress the external viewer, to express authority, grandeur, and a certain air of class superiority. The lines are heavy and sure-handed, the surface areas large in proportion to the total house. Style sources were often incongruously mixed. It was the effect of magnificence rather than historical authenticity that was sought. In the 1920s the same styles, even when executed in large and expensive homes, give off a movie-set look of "cuteness." They demonstrate the fantasies of the internal occupants; they create a fiction about those occupants for the external viewer. The style-determining decorative details are as historically consistent and mood-evoking as stage sets should be. The details are crowded more closely together, and greater attention is paid to immediate comprehension. The diversity of interpretations possible in the 1894 Mooers House (ILLUSTRATIONS 39-41) is replaced by style congruity. While the facades of the turn-of-the-century Barmore and Brand residences (ILLUSTRATIONS 45-46, 48-49) are imposing, those of their 1920s counterparts are fragmented into a

Revivalism: Insecurity and Pretense

complex of mini-stages for dramatic action: balconies, towers, walled patios, a number of gables, and so on. More eye movement is required to take in all these surfaces, making the later houses seem more exciting and active, less staid and monumental in overall flavor. Rather than intimidating the passerby as the earlier houses had, the revival houses of the 1920s and '30s work magic on the passing audience; like any successful stage-play or film, they suspend disbelief and bring the viewer into the mood of the production. They give him a vicarious role in a delightful, exciting entertainment. They are contagiously happy homes.

Motion pictures were a major and direct inspiration for the revival styles. They were, to the public, the primary authority on how a "French Norman" country house or a sheik's palace, or a Southern plantation ought to look, and they popularized a given look by associating it with favorite film stories.[33] In the days of silent movies characterized by a fast-moving plot, a director needed to communicate the nature of the scene of action, and the relative status of his characters, immediately, so that no confusion or waning of audience interest could set in. A princess wore a coronet so her position could be immediately grasped; a castle looked undeniably, flamboyantly, like a castle. The set would be reduced in scale so it could be effectively framed behind the action and would not dwarf the actors. A concentration of identifying details such as turrets, crenelated battlements, moat, and so on, identified a castle. Other period revivals were similarly defined by cinematic style references and set construction constraints. By the end of the '20s, certain hallmarks of style had become standardized. A glimpse of a round tower with conical roof was a sufficient trigger to transport an audience of experienced moviegoers to the setting and mood of a fairytale castle.

In Los Angeles, the physical presence of movie sets provided constant additional style references. The Babylonian set of Intolerance (1916) stood for years near the intersection of Sunset and Hollywood Boulevards, with its rows of elephants atop bulging pillars shaping Angeleno aesthetic standards. Ben Hur's (1923) coliseum loomed at La Cienega and Venice Boulevards. The Norman castle sets for Fairbanks' Robin Hood (1922) dominated his lot on Melrose Avenue. For Angelenos, sets such as these were not fantasies, but part of their visible surroundings. The studios themselves were built to period references to convey certain tones and to double as sets. The Ince studios were inspired by Mount Vernon; the Goldwyn studio was modeled on a pillared Roman temple; Chaplin's looked like an Old English village street.

The houses of the leading actors and actresses further reinforced the taste for particular styles. In the nineteen-teens, few film people built mansions, partly because their source of wealth was so new there was no assurance it would last. By the close of World War I, though, some of the screen stars and studio moguls were renting or purchasing older houses in expensive Los Angeles neighborhoods. The available stock of local mansions, dating from the 1900-1915 period, were often in the Tudor or Beaux Arts Italianate style. By the 1920s, fans across America avidly followed the stars' personal lives, one reason, perhaps, for the nationwide popularity of Tudor and small-scale Beaux Arts Italianate styles in the 1920s.[34]

Film stars' rental patterns cannot be given all the credit, however. The public had been exposed to twenty years of illustrated newspaper coverage of high society and had learned to associate these styles with affluence. When movie makers wanted to portray rich living, they were obliged to use Old English or Beaux Arts backdrops for comprehension and legitimacy. A home buyer whose imagination ran to scenes of elegance and pretensions of class and stability would build in one of these styles.

By the time the star system had reached major proportions in the '20s and movie stars were constructing the houses the tourists came to see, their studios and agents were fully cognizant of the importance of their houses to stars' created images. Great attention was given to creating houses that would showcase their occupants to best advantage. Few screen stars came from privileged backgrounds. Their only acquaintance with opulence had been formed by movie props, their wealth had come too suddenly to permit a gradual acceptance into a high society of old wealth. In fact, despite their wealth, movie actors and producers were largely shunned by the local upper crust in the early days. By the '20s the wealthy element in Los Angeles was suddenly and preponderantly composed of nouveaux riches like themselves — movie, oil, and real estate people. Many of the newly successful turned for guidance to the examples already made acceptable by earlier association with wealth. They merely revived their revival styles, and were, in turn, emulated in reduced scale at the vernacular level.

Its convenient proximity to the Hollywood core of the movie industry, the availability of spacious lots, and its pre-planned air of exclusivity made the community of Beverly Hills an attractive location for new wealth in the '20s. Three superstars were among the first movie people to settle there: Gloria Swanson in a quasi-Italian neo-Renaissance mansion and newlyweds Douglas Fairbanks and Mary Pickford in "Pickfair." Pickfair was a Tudor design credited to a Hollywood art director, one of the first of many overlaps of film industry and the architectural profession in Southern California. In 1926-34, Pickfair was

Revivalism: Insecurity and Pretense

modernized to the Regency style by architect Wallace Neff.[35]

Aristocratically pretentious styles popped up all over Los Angeles, their size and amount of decorative detail revealing their true place on the economic ladder. The small version of the Old English house in ILLUSTRATION 82 was built in Beverly Hills in 1926 by architectural designer John Byers. Clearly, neither owner nor designer felt obligated to bombard the passer-by with period details.

82. Old English style house, 1926

With self-assured restraint, the house states its claim to a Merry Old English heritage with a slight overhang of the upper story, one half-timbered gable, a planked look to the door, and a steeply pitched roof. These hallmarks were enough to assure style recognition; there was no need to decorate the other gable, shutter or lead-pane the windows, or insist on an English garden.

Other builders went to more trouble to assure a quaint look. The 1926 Old English house in ILLUSTRATION 83 was built by contractor H. Denman Schmitt, on speculation. Spec houses became an important feature in the investment scramble of the 1920s. They fared best in the real estate market if they had instant eye appeal, if they were "cute" or quaint or different from others in the area. Here, brick facing, a bay window, an exaggerated roof slope, and the artistic chimneys call attention to the structure.[36]

Such Hollywood-set touches were found at every level. From tracts of small houses in which Tudor was one of the ready-made images set before the prospective home-buyer, to multiple-family courts of small detached units. The look was certified by half-timbering, rustic doors with strap hinges, diamond-paned vertical windows, tall chimneys, and steeply-pitched or even inwardly curved roofs.

When the high-spending '20s were replaced by the economic depression of the '30s, period revival styles like the Tudor underwent a transformation. The sculptured surfaces of '20s' houses were dissolved to minimal or basic planes. The viewer's eye was no longer required to flit between a dozen decorative details. Architects selected only a few style ornaments and applied them sparingly to what were actually functional modern buildings. The erasure of decoration and the reduction of the labyrinth of small rooms to an efficiency-engineered interior took away some of the "cuteness" built into the

83. Old English style house, 1926

earlier period houses. But the new look met two requirements of the '30s: it cut building and maintenance costs, and it exuded the fashionable look the decade labeled "modernistic." This was the era's over-worked term for anything that was new, efficient, scientific, and streamlined in both appearance and utility.

ILLUSTRATION 84 shows a 1937 "Tudor" model in a large tract development in Santa Monica. In keeping with depression economics, the historic look was expressed with greater austerity than during the preceding decade. The developer here appealed to the cost-conscious buyer who still liked the Tudor look, but was willing to accept fewer decorative touches for the sake of a lower purchase price. The half-timbering is minimized. The casement windows merely hint at an if-not-quite-Tudor-at-least-Jacobean flavor. The eaves have been sheared back to the walls to reduce material cost and smooth the visual lines of the building. The chimney and the slope of the roof are barely reminiscent of the previous decade's flair. But the illusion of Old

84. Tudor style tract house, 1937

England is still present. The sales agent might have played on the buyer's vanity by emphasizing the stylishly modern look of the plainer surface, rather than its lower price. Architectural historian David Gebhard termed the 1930s' versions of period styling "bland."

The other style of high-class pretension, the tile-roofed Beaux Arts Italianate, is frequently indistinguishable from the Spanish Colonial style. But "Villa de Leon," the graceful mansion in ILLUSTRATION 85, could never be confused with styles indigenous to primitive colonial frontiers. From its site on the edge of the palisades overlooking the Santa Monica Bay, its buff-colored walls

Revivalism: Insecurity and Pretense

85. Villa de Leon, 1927

and red tiled roof strike a harmonious balance against the dark greens of the hillside vegetation and the blue of the ocean below, bringing it to the notice of the public passing beneath on the Pacific Coast Highway (then known as the Roosevelt Highway). As a familiar landmark to travelers since 1927, it has established its own legitimacy as a standard of refined taste.[37]

The American Colonial style might be viewed as a statement of storybook pretense as well as one of patriotic conservatism. A recent analyst of nationwide housing trends, noting the general preference for the Old English and the American Colonial styles in the interwar years, credited it to "racial and ethnic sentiments" and a perceived need for families "to establish their heritage and their place in the world."[38] Pedigree claims to English gentility and colonial patriots were socially enhancing in a time of social flux. An American Colonial house might be a true statement of one's ancestry; it might imply an ideological position; or it might be pure illusion, an attempt to build into reality an assumed identity of Anglo-Saxon or Founding Father roots.

The stately mansion of ILLUSTRATION 86 was built in Glendale in 1922 by a socially prominent attorney from Kentucky, Mattison Boyd Jones. "Belaire"

86. Belaire, 1922

87. Merrie Land, 1924

was a public announcement of plantation heritage, although with California concessions, especially in the tree-lined approach, where eucalyptus substituted for magnolia or live-oak trees.[39] "Merrie Land," the estate with the Federal Revival portico in ILLUSTRATION 87, was absentee-owned for years by a prominent Glendale auto dealer. Perhaps its ready-made image was designed to attract a politically and/or socially desirable stratum of tenants.[40] The sedate 1921 brick house in ILLUSTRATION 88, by architect J. A. Melton is an antiquarian collector's piece, which could pass as an authentic 1715-1740 Georgian if it were located on the Atlantic Seaboard instead of in Beverly Hills.[41] The Colonial Revival house in ILLUSTRATION 89, was built in 1922 for Armenay Kurkjian, apparently as an income property at first, later as his own family residence. The exterior of the house revealed no clue of Armenian heritage, referring only to American Colonial history.

How can an outside observer today gauge the motives uppermost in the minds of builders or buyers of the past? Did one mean to wave the flag, another to honor his ancestry? Did some consciously pose to win social acceptance; were others hoping to escape to a romantic dream of an earlier America as a finer time than the present? We can only guess. But some borrowed styles were clearly intended as magic carpets for the imagination. Islamic architectural traditions have been put to use as a Hollywood apartment house (ILLUSTRATION 90). "Miradero," the 1902 home of L. C. Brand which we looked at earlier (ILLUSTRATIONS 48-50), borrowed its inspiration from similarly exotic

88. Georgian brick house, 1921

89. American Colonial house, 1922

traditions, but with different results.[42] There the scalloped arches and pointed domes seemed to flaunt their owner's power and wealth. Here, the unfamiliar window shapes and repeated minarets hint of interior mysteries and cubbyhole retreats.

The dramatic discovery in 1922 of Tutankhamun's Tomb and its treasures sparked American imaginations — especially those of Angelenos easily

90. Middle Eastern style apartment house, ca. 1925

91. Detail from Doheny Mansion

92. Pueblo style house, 1939

inflamed by film fantasies and hopes of oil fortunes under tract lots. Decorative arts, women's fashions, and architecture picked up ancient Egyptian design elements shortly after the tomb's discovery. Los Angeles contributed its monuments to this fad, most notably in its Central Library (1922-25, Bertram Goodhue, architect) and the crowning pyramid of its City Hall (1927-28, John Parkinson and Albert C. Martin, architects), but also in scattered examples of domestic architecture (ILLUSTRATION 91). Too few of its residential landmarks remain in unaltered condition today to more than record a passing fancy and to add another image layer to the increasingly bizarre cityscape of the 1920s.

Another choice of style came from the native cultures of the American Southwest. The house in ILLUSTRATION 92 is patterned after the Pueblo Indian dwellings of the New Mexico-Arizona mesas and canyons. Completed in 1939, it conveys a convincing sense of great antiquity. The stucco walls are molded to resemble eroded mud construction, the beam ends (vigas) seem to have weathered in place for 500 years. Interestingly, the form native to the desert mesa is sited in a woodsy Calabasas dell. The depression-era owner-builder may have sought the soothing sense of continuity expressed by structures of great lasting power. He may also have ascribed to an isolationist current favoring architecture of native American inspiration, an All-American Architecture.[43]

Finally, under the category of "Fairytale Dream" houses, we must include the cloying cottage look which architectural historians Gebhard and Winter so aptly term the "Hansel and Gretel" style. A more sweetly romantic hideaway can scarcely be imagined than the 1923 duplex in ILLUSTRATION 93, designed by architect Einar Petersen in 1923, with its undulating roof, stenciled flowers over the windows, and a barnyard gate to disguise the driveway. The house in ILLUSTRATION 94, while related in flavor, could alternatively be described as a large Anne Hathaway Cottage. It was built in 1926 in Pasadena by H. Denman Schmitt.

Overall, the 1920s and '30s offered a wide range of houses in which

MOVIE STARS AND HARD TIMES

93. Duplex, 1923

94. Hansel and Gretel style house, 1926

dreams were literally constructed as domiciliary stage sets for the acting-out of colorful, light-hearted, escapist fantasies. Some were distinctive expressions of individual dreams. The gateposts of the elegant villa we looked at from the Pacific Coast Highway in ILLUSTRATION 85 are highly personal. Local lore says the four draped statues, four views of the same woman in four contrasting theatrical poses, represent the original home-owner's movie-actress aspirations, the gateposts serving as a stand-up portfolio (ILLUSTRATION 95).[44]

Other houses in make-believe styles were built by developers and building-plan service contractors in alluring styles to catch the attention of people eager to move into ready-made dream-sets. ILLUSTRATION 2 shows a 1925 development where a Tudor, an American Colonial, and a Spanish Colonial are offered smorgasbord-style. The result of this kind of streetscape was a newly enlivened Los Angeles inspiring the sneers of iconoclastic eastern critics:

"The residential people of Los Angeles are cultivated enervated people, lovers of mixturesque beauty — and they like to express their emotivation in homes that symphonize their favorite historical films, their best-beloved movie actresses, their luckiest numerological combinations...Here you will see a Pekinese pagoda made of fresh and crackly peanut brittle — there a snow-white marshmallow igloo — there a toothsome pink nougat in the Florentine manner, rich and delicious with embedded nuts. Yonder rears a clean pocket-size replica of heraldic Warwick Castle — yonder drowses a nausey old nance. A wee wonderful Swiss shilly-shally snuggles up beneath a bountiful bougainvillea... And there a hot little hacienda, a regular enchilada con queso with a roof made of rich red tomato sauce, barely lifts her long-lashed lavender shades on the soul of old Spanish days....And the Be-Happy-with-a-Home Realty Company is just a brokenne-downe olde picturesque cobwebby comfy shacke recalling the cute olde clockmakers of Nuremberg who would plan you a little gingerbread cottage...for about $9,000..."

—Edmund Wilson, 1932[45]

95. Detail of Villa de Leon

Revivalism: Insecurity and Pretense

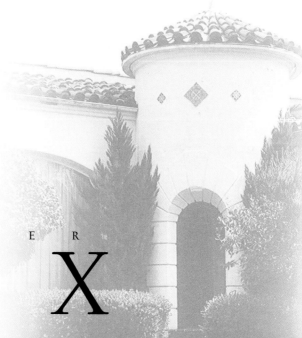

X

LOS ANGELES FINDS ITS OWN STYLE

I feel we should retain

as much as possible

the Spanish,

or I should say Mexican

or early Californian feeling.

Failing this,

Italian is the

next best thing.

— MARY PICKFORD

THE LOS ANGELES BASIN OPENS onto a seventy-mile stretch of beaches, bracketed by the picturesque developments of Castellamare in Pacific Palisades, near one end, and Palos Verdes, near the other. Each presents a scene of rolling hills descending to the seashore, hills decorated with cascades of cream colored stucco houses with clay tile roofs, graceful arches and serenade balconies, liberally embellished with polychrome tilework, wrought iron and bougainvillea. The scenic charm of Palos Verdes and Castellamare is due to the stylistic preferences of the developers. Of all the fanciful imagery given architectural form in the '20s and '30s, the one that came to dominate the spectrum was the Mediterranean Colonial, to use today's polyglot term for the style then variously referred to as "Spanish," "Californian," "Italian Villa," "Mediterranean," or, most often, "Spanish Colonial." The Palos Verdes Homes Association and its Arts Jury specified the Mediterranean Colonial Revival style, reviewed plans, and enforced adherence through deed restrictions.[1] The style it mandated was, in any case, the leading choice of home-buyers throughout Southern California in the 1920s.

After the major population influx of the 1880s, Angeleno dreamers had settled down to their own search for identity. They had sought a housing style that would express the full spectrum of images they identified with L.A. while accommodating their own pre-existing tastes and their new patterns of life. This had demanded a certain eclecticism, to say the least. After some flamboyant trials and some landmark errors, they had discovered the California Bungalow. While well suited to certain themes of the Los Angeles good life such as leisure, nature and simplicity, the California Bungalow revealed some confusion about its mixed inspirational sources: the Swiss chalet, the British-Indian bungalow, Japanese joinery and progressive morality. Mass production fatally challenged its claim to individualistic craftsmanship, and the Jazz Age rejected the Progressive Era values it represented.

The 1920s swept another major population tide into the L.A. basin. Its imagination was more fantastic than that of the Victorian era. The houses built in the 1920s and 1930s explored a wider range of more distinct architectural statements. Among these mixed statements was an architectural acknowledgment of the Spanish past. The Spanish statements were stronger because they had roots in the Southern California soil. By the mid-'20s, it was clear that the tile-roofed casita of Spanish inspiration was the favorite of all classes. Over the next decade or so, civic buildings, commercial buildings, churches, hospitals, and especially houses built in the Spanish or Mediterranean Colonial style blanketed Los Angeles. A common architectural expression of the

Los Angeles Finds Its Own Style

peculiar diversity of dreams that had brought so many to Los Angeles had been established.

Why did this one style come to be favored over the others? First, it capitalized on the indigenous historic myth, unlike any of the other borrowed or created styles; second, prominent patronage and the selection of this style for civic monuments gave it a seal of approval; and, third, it dovetailed with the decade's youth-mindedness, health-faddism, and enthusiasm for the active outdoors life.

The Spanish Colonial houses of the '20s did not really represent an unbroken lineage from a Spanish past. The historic truth of the matter was that houses in the Spanish pueblo of Los Angeles had been small and squalid affairs by American standards of the '20s. The small, rural pueblo of the Mexican period boasted a few commodious adobe ranchos and smaller townhouses with some amenities. This was the Los Angeles a handful of American traders and seamen had chosen to settle in the 1820s and 1830s. Accepting the local way of life, they modeled their own dwellings after those around them, though adding some New England cultural notions of what a home ought to include, such as wooden floors, formal parlors, and indoor kitchens. The architectural fusion of the accepted images of the new culture with the values brought from home became the new visible image for the next wave of immigrants. We have called this layering.

In the case of Hispanic architectural traditions, however, there was a break in the layering process from about 1850 to about 1890. This break we attribute to the hostilities of the Mexican-American War and a rising American nationalism, the selective nature of settlers in the early American period, and a late 19th-century Victorian emphasis on material display. It was nearly the turn of the century before Angelenos again expressed an affinity with the Hispanic history of Southern California. By that time, the adobes of the Spanish and Mexican periods had largely disintegrated, or had been demolished or disguised beyond recognition. Drawing upon the ruins for inspiration, popular writers in the 1880s and 1890s had discovered, or actually invented, a romantic Spanish past which became a central theme in the Los Angeles essence. At the turn of the century, the search for a more genuine, simple, and honest life led to the Mission Revival Style. Its popularity was brief. Attempts to adapt significant mission motifs, the tile roof, for example, to more current styles such as the bungalow, were not very successful. An example of an Asian-themed bungalow with mission overtones, built by architect Robert A. Farquhar in 1910, is seen in ILLUSTRATION 96. [2]

96. Gorham house, 1910

Even if there had been many well-preserved and authentic examples of the adobe and wood housing from Spanish and Mexican times, Angelenos from the 1890s through the 1920s would find few of them worthy of emulation. What they really admired was not the factual Los Angeles past, but a fictional past largely created by professional advertisers to increase tourism, business patronage, real estate sales, and motion-picture ticket sales. A romanticized account of the Spanish past so perfectly merged with the emotional needs of Angelenos that we have, over the generations, shaped the city's substance to reflect that fiction.

Early in the '20s a new generation of Angelenos, many of them only recently arrived, became interested in the Spanish heritage. Angelenos knew what they wanted to believe of that Spanish Arcadia: a Ramona-like myth of a languorous life in perfumed Mediterranean air, the romance of the Spanish señorita, the masculine bravado of the adventurer on horseback. The houses in the myth were grand haciendas with walled patios, splashing fountains, and grilled balconies. Spanish Los Angeles, in the myth, was a time of plenty and graciousness, in which no one seemed to work and everyone was happy. The image was given substance by novels and anecdotal accounts from Helen Hunt Jackson's Ramona through the writings of Lummis and his circle to regional magazines like Sunset and Touring Topics. Throughout the '20s there was a thriving market for fancifully-embroidered "histories" of the missions.[3] The popular version of Old California was illustrated in bank ads and library-wall murals.[4] It was acted out by horsemen and mantilla-bedecked beauties in parades from the early La Fiesta festivities through Pasadena's Rose Parades and in theatricals like the perennial Mission Play in San Gabriel and Ramona in Hemet. It was picked up by the motion picture industry in films such as The Mark of Zorro (with Douglas Fairbanks, 1920), movie versions of Ramona (a Cluné version in 1916, an Inspiration Production starring Dolores Del Rio in 1927), and over a dozen movies depicting Cisco the Kid (1914-1947). Southern Californians were steeped in this myth of a romantic Spanish past, and they loved it. It was very close to the dreams that had brought them to Los Angeles:

Los Angeles Finds Its Own Style

beautiful people in a warm, beautiful environment, freedom from Puritan conventions, semi-rural open space, leisure, and romance.

The renewed enthusiasm for the romantic past as an escapist fantasy was popular but it rarely admitted the historical link between L.A., Mexico, and Mexicans. One of the new Angelenos in the 1920s boom, Mrs. Christine Sterling, having found the tourist literature "appealing with its old Missions, palm trees, sunshine, and the 'click of the castanets'", was particularly distressed to find that the heart of the original pueblo, the old Plaza, was run-down, filthy, and forgotten. "Life in Los Angeles before the Americans came was an almost ideal existence," she nostalgized. "People lived to love, to be kind, tolerant, and contented. Money of which there was plenty was just for necessities. The men owned and rode magnificent horses. The women were flowers...in silk and laces. There were picnics into the hills, dancing at night, moonlight serenades, romance and real happiness."

Mrs. Sterling launched a one-woman campaign to preserve the two historic buildings which remained on Olvera Street, a one-block lane opening off the Plaza, and to convert the street into a Mexican market place as a "gesture of appreciation to Mexico and Spain for our historical past."[5] Her efforts succeeded. The historic buildings were restored; the facades of other buildings were altered to harmonize with the Mexican village theme; *puestas* (small stalls with awnings) offered ethnic food, and Latin American wares were sold by Mexican Angelenos wearing traditional Mexican costumes. The business community applauded the introduction of a downtown tourist attraction offering non-competing consumer wares and admitted a new appreciation of Mexicans, especially those with a "facility in our language and thought".[6]

With the rare exception of the patronizing attitude toward Mexicans at Olvera Street, however, the popular dichotomy between "Spanish" and "Mexican" remained in force, the latter a pejorative term describing an underclass, the former referring to an unreal, idealized past and a (presumed-complimentary) reference to any Hispanic. In a history of the city commissioned in the 1950s by a major banking firm, the entire historic period up to 1848 was described as Spanish. In fact, Mexican had rule replaced Spanish rule after 1821. The book concluded with a description of the bank's new branch then under construction at Olvera Street, its carved doors, wrought-iron and tile trim, and antique weapons display representing a return to "the kind of atmosphere which only gracious Spanish culture can bequeath."[7]

It was to memorialize this idealized "Spanish" graciousness that restoration of several old adobes took place. In some cases the myth was memorialized at the expense of historic accuracy. Oil and sports tycoon Earl Gilmore hired John Byers, an architectural designer specializing in the new Spanish Colonial style, to renovate the 1828 Rocha adobe. The result was charming, but the original structure was hardly evident among the major structural changes.

Other restoration efforts were aimed at recapturing the past as it was. In 1930 a group of volunteers rescued the disintegrating Sanchez Adobe in Glendale (ILLUSTRATION 9). The same year, Dr. M. R. Harrington of the Southwest Museum was at work restoring the Andres Pico house. In both cases, educated guesses had to fill the gaps left by incomplete records, the ravages of time and changes by later owners. In order to appear old and hand-made, replacement hinges had to be beaten, the plaster had to be uneven, the underlying adobe bricks exposed in places. No one, in the movie era, could have imagined a statement of antiquity without clear, if affected, evidences of aging.[8]

The family that owned Jonathan Temple's Rancho Los Cerritos (ILLUSTRATIONS 11 and 12) took pride in the accuracy of their 1929-1931 restoration, but chose to replace the shingle roof with clay tile. Either they wished to improve on the original, or they, with the majority of the public, had learned to think of the clay tile roof as the authenticating stamp of a Spanish heritage. It was ironic that the private houses in the Spanish period had not really been roofed with tiles, but with homelier tar and cane.

In 1925 an organization called the Hispanic Society of California completed a representative replica of an early 1800s hacienda, which they called the Casa de Adobe, and presented it to the Southwest Museum so that every Angeleno could know what life was like in the days of the great ranchos. The Society could find no existing model that pleased its members, so they ended up patterning the patio after an adobe in San Diego county, the floor tiles after the San Juan Capistrano Mission, doors after other sites, the washroom and polychrome tiles from a hacienda in Mexico, the kitchen layout after a composite drawn from various California missions, and so on. No reality was ever as elaborate as such an ideal. Housed in a museum, the Casa de Adobe purported to portray historical accuracy. The many visitors to private restorations, and particularly to the Casa de Adobe, saw the idealized life as fine and desirable. They wanted for themselves the architecture that enshrined such a life. The administrators of the Casa de Adobe expressed pride in the model's acceptance:

"We are happy to know that the Casa has apparently filled a real need, architecturally speaking, as it has been copied in full or in part in many portions of the country, both for homes and for 'movie' sets. Very many architects visit

Los Angeles Finds Its Own Style

the Casa. Since it is not a copy of any one California home, but rather a composite of various homes of our earliest residents, this interest is very gratifying."[9]

In 1909, the Mission Revival style of architecture, which had first appeared in the 1890s, was still flourishing as a commercial style throughout Southern California. The Santa Fe and the Southern Pacific railroads built depots in the style from 1910 to 1915. The Herald Examiner's Mission style headquarters opened in 1912, and through 1915 many public schools, libraries, factories, and hotels were designed to resemble those church-state outposts of the Spanish frontier.[10] It was in 1909 that the small city of San Diego, a hundred miles or so south of Los Angeles, started planning a major exposition to celebrate the opening of the Panama Canal, scheduled for 1915. Considering the link with Latin America represented by the canal, they naturally considered Mission Revival buildings. But forms that might function well as 18th-century frontier posts or 20th-century train depots, were not flamboyant enough for a fair which is intended to entertain and to attract attention. Thus, San Diegans were open to new ideas.

The architect selected for San Diego's Panama-California Exposition, Bertram Grosvenor Goodhue, consciously sought to embroider romantic dreams into the fair's buildings:

"everything that met the eye and ear of the visitor [was] meant to recall to mind the glamour and mystery and poetry of the old Spanish Days....for it must be remembered that Exposition Architecture differs from that of our everyday world in being essentially of the fabric of a dream — not to endure but to produce a merely temporary effect. It should provide, after the fashion that stage scenery provides — illusion rather than reality."[11]

Scorning the simplicity of Spanish frontier architecture which could claim historical relevance to California, Goodhue turned to the Churrigueresque or late Baroque style of Spain that had been favored for church and palace construction in Spanish Colonial Mexico. Named for Spanish architect José de Churriguera (1665-1725) and his sons, the style contrasts plain expanses of wall with concentrated masses of florid sculptural ornament. The vitality of the focal ornamenture takes command of the viewer's eye and energy. Carleton M. Winslow, who designed most of the temporary buildings of the exposition under Goodhue's guidance, consciously borrowed architectural elements from selected Spanish Colonial churches and palaces in Latin America.[12]

The Panama-California Exposition was a memorable success. It drew attention to San Diego and promoted the region's economic and population

97. Casa Madre, 1923

growth. It also left a lasting visual impression — a vision drenched in Spanish romance and particularly cherished by Southern Californians searching for new roots. Since the Churrigueresque version of Spanish Colonial architecture had drawn such favorable and profitable business in San Diego, it was naturally soon put to use attracting attention and profits for Los Angeles businessmen who constructed a number of grocery stores and a motion picture theater in this mode.[13] While this ornate and elegant style was well-suited to the palaces of commerce and to cathedrals, it was less adaptable to domestic structures. Such heavy decoration was difficult to employ on the smaller scale of a house without overwhelming it. Only a few houses in the Churrigueresque style appeared in Los Angeles, and these had the elegant scale and Baroque grandeur befitting the owners' social status. The house seen in ILLUSTRATION 97 was built in 1919-23 as a winter residence for an Eastern socialite, Mrs. E. N. Halliday.[14] It was illustrated in Rexford Newcomb's authoritative book, The Spanish House for America... (1927), where it was credited to architects Pierpont and Walter S. Davis.[15]

A Spartan alternative to the formality and ornamentation of both the Churrigueresque and the Mission Revival styles was introduced by architect Irving Gill. He sought a means of retaining the usable tradition of the patios, the color and texture of adobe, and the graceful form of the arch without compromising modern efficiency and his own creative integrity. By 1910, he had developed a minimalist paraphrase of the Spanish mission, an ascetic modernism (ILLUSTRATIONS 98 and 113). The purity of Gill's version of Hispanic historicism was a timely antidote to the Churrigueresque trend. But its simplicity was too stern for most Angelenos.[16] Simpler houses with open floor plans characteristic of old houses in Southern Spain and in Colonial Mexico were closer to the romantic image envisioned by Angelenos. A number of books published between 1915 and the mid-'20s convinced the prospective home builders that these were appropriate models for Los Angeles house designs. One of these, dated 1915, was written by Walter S. Davis, who had traveled to Europe expressly in search of a compatible source model for small-scale building. He studied the old homes

98. Detail of Horatio West apartments

99. Tinglof residence, 1925

in the Andalusian towns of Algeciras, Ronda, Seville, Granada, and Cordoba. Since Andalusia was remarkably similar to Los Angeles in climate, and because the Spanish conquistadores and padres had embarked for the New World from Andalusian ports, he concluded that no more appropriate housing model could be found. Besides, Davis found in Spain all the romance Southern Californians hankered for:

"With memories of the Alhambra and of their own homes fresh in their minds, the Spanish Dons who settled California built their new houses around cool, beflowered patios. Today several examples still remain... Who has not, charmed with the beauty of these patios, thought to himself, 'I, too, will have a home like this!'[17]

The eleven householders who had settled Los Angeles in 1781 would hardly have recognized themselves in this description. The clients of Davis and his brother, A. Pierpont Davis, however, wanted homes like those he described.

By the time the construction industry was recovering from its World War I slump in 1919, the shelves of local building contractors and architects carried a number of reference books on authentic building types persuasively linked to the Spanish Past of Los Angeles. Well-informed individuals considering building their own homes might well have read this literature. Architects and contractors pleased clients with patios, fountains, window grilles, balconies, fireplaces, a wrought-iron candelabra drawn directly from sketches, a photo, or memory of historical models. Some designs copied entire facades and even floor plans, with modifications for modern living.

Los Angeles architectural firms began to win commissions in this genre on the basis of their published expertise on the domestic architecture of Spain, Italy, and Mexico. The firms of Marston & Van Pelt along with Johnson, Kaufmann & Coate, solidified their reputations with books and articles on the historic architecture of these countries. Johnson called for an eclectic blend of originality and various Mediterranean historic source models to meet the particular requirements of site and climate. The argument permitted him to call into play his own direct knowledge of Italian architecture drawn from five years' residence in Europe.[18]

John Byers' reputation did not rest on architectural training, but on his extensive knowledge of Spanish culture as a professor of Romance languages. His designs were veritable textbooks in authentic architectural folk-culture. ILLUSTRATION 99 represents one of John Byers' Santa Monica projects, a house built in 1925. Byers' early Spanish Colonial houses were constructed of adobe, showing his insistence on authenticity. A patio and balcony detail of the adobe house he built for himself in 1922 may be seen in ILLUSTRATION 100. The design's inspirational source was the 16th-century Toledo residence of the painter El Greco.[19] Other designers looked closer to home for their inspiration. They rejected European sources and championed a Monterey Revival style. Named after its introduction in Northern California by Thomas O. Larkin in 1835 and carried out in Southern California by Jonathan Temple, it combined the Hispanic frontier adobe's simplicity and outdoor orientation with the two-story symmetry, pillars and covered shutters of the American Greek Revival. Although Monterey style had a stronger claim to historical authenticity in California than Andalusian, Mexican, or Italian derivations, as a revival style it was less popular in the '20s than the more imaginative Spanish or Mediterranean Colonial style. But in the Depression '30s stucco and wood-frame Monterey Revivals appeared, not only on the basis of historical accuracy, but because their simpler box-like form, shingled roofs and restricted ornamentation made them cheaper to build than the multiple forms, fragmented surfaces, ornament and tile roofs of the Mediterranean Colonial style.

100. Byers house, 1922

101. Monterey style house,
1923/29

The Monterey Revival house in ILLUS-
TRATION 101 has more than a token historicism about
it. The property was originally part of the Verdugo
land grant and later continued in the Verdugo family.
In 1867-70, a Verdugo descendant and her husband,
Tomás Sanchez, had built an adobe house in the
nostalgic style of her ancestors, with an outbuilding
in back. After further subdivision of the property, new
owners built this wood-frame house in Early
California mode on the foundation of the old
outbuilding.[20] The Monterey Colonial style, with its
links to the past, was ideal for expressing continuity
of this historic site.

The more popular Mediterranean Colonial
style was also appealing on the bases of un-
pretentiousness and simplicity of form. Successful
architects brought out the sensory pleasures of
contrasts in color and surface texture; modeled white
or off-white plaster; fired clay roof and patio tiles with
their dull red luster; and polychrome tiles of energetic
pattern, used sparingly and set off by dark,
unvarnished wooden doors and beams. Foliage,
flowers and bubbling fountains served as integral
features of the house in patios and terraces onto
which various rooms opened and balconies
overlooked. When clients demanded greater
formality, the leading practitioners incorporated
elements of Italian villa architecture, compatible in
terms of arches, tile roofs, and environmental
symbiosis, but rigidly symmetrical, employing the
formal orders of columns and carved corbels,
patterned marble floors, and coffered rather than
rough-beamed ceilings.

Wallace Neff, a native of Southern
California, and a scion of the McNally publishing
family, was a particularly successful practitioner. He
had been educated and widely traveled in Europe. He
studied under Ralph Adams Cram at M.I.T. and

102. Berg residence, 1926-27

apprenticed with George Washington Smith in Santa Barbara. His first solo project was a Spanish Colonial house there for his mother. This project, combined with family social ties among affluent Pasadenans, eventually brought his Pasadena office so much business that he could afford to turn down any project valued at less than $50,000. Neff was commissioned by Augustus Busch to build a house, ILLUSTRATION 102, as a 1927 wedding gift to the brewer's granddaughter. Neff consciously designed the house after a Tuscan villa he had seen and sketched.[21] An Italian Renaissance formality is apparent in the formal pillars, the doorway framing, and the structural symmetry. Illustration 1 shows the arch of a garden gateway at this same residence, embellished with a formal cartouche. Although it was inspired by the country estate of an Italian Renaissance courtier, the 1927 Pasadena mansion is usually referred to as "Spanish Colonial." It is easy to see why Southern Californians in the 1920s were so expansive with that label. A house with arches, an exterior surface of uneven plaster, a clay tile roof, balconies, fountains, patios, wrought-iron grilles and light-fixtures, a house which is, furthermore, located in a city with a Spanish name, founded, as everyone knew for fact, by Spanish dons on silver saddles — it had to be a "Spanish" house. Only a rare informed client, a few perceptive passersby, and the architect himself would have any thought at all of Italy or the Renaissance. Perhaps the most appealing element of the Spanish Colonial style was its patio, accommodating the 1920s enthusiasm for outdoor activity and echoing on the domestic level, the city's new booster themes.

In 1921, seeking to spur summer tourism to catch up with the long-established winter seasonal influx, the business community launched an "All-Year Club" with a million-dollar budget for a three-year program to advertise the continued attraction of Los Angeles. Still active in 1928, funded by business contributions and county tax revenues, it turned tourist-luring into a science of statistics, graphs, and charts on demography and spending.[22] The All-Year Club and the Chamber of Commerce shifted their advertising themes to outdoor activities and sports. They highlighted many outdoor amphitheaters that took advantage of the region's balmy evening skies. Dramatic and musical productions stages outdoors, if not too slow-moving or cerebral, attracted throngs of tourists. The Pilgrimage Play, featuring "noted artists from the speaking stage and silver screen" proved a huge success.[23] A nearby canyon was developed by Hollywood business leaders into an amphitheater for musical galas and Easter Sunrise Services. This was the Hollywood Bowl, completed in time for Easter, 1922, and the setting for the local orchestra's Symphonies under the Stars. It was taken over by the County of Los Angeles in 1924. The Greek Theater opened the same year in nearby Griffith Park.[24]

The All-Year Club played on the Jazz Age fetishes of perpetual youth and fast-paced activity, and made new promises to lure tourists to L.A.. The new emphasis on outdoor activities represented an updated version of a half-century-old health claim.

"Notwithstanding the even quality of the climate, it is invigorating, strengthening and tonic. The climate of Southern California produces many of the world's athletic champions....Women respond quickly to the vitalizing combination of sunshine and breeze here and display unusual vim in golf, swimming, tennis and other sports. Many noted men and women come every year...to rejuvenate themselves...."[25] They publicized sports events: golf tennis and polo tournaments; college football matches and local baseball tams; yacht races and lawn bowling.[26]

The proven drawing power of sports events and the complementary nature of the new sports theme with the traditional L.A. sunshine theme persuaded civic leaders to propose hosting the ultimate sports event, the Olympic Games. In 1923 the burgeoning city was designated as the site for the 1932 Games. With tourist potential in mind, a Coliseum was built, then expanded, partly paid for by a 1928 statewide bond issue for one million dollars. After the stock market crashed in October, 1929, Los Angeles business leaders looked forward to the money to be made during the approaching Olympics. They estimated that during 1929 Southern California had entertained 1,066,722 tourists, who had spent $418,526,392 while they were here; surely the Olympic games would bring visitors and dollars in far greater numbers. L.A.'s climate, attractiveness, and sports activities were expected to win worldwide attention as magazines and newspapers reported on the Olympics. Along with this free publicity, the Olympics would bring profits to businesses and jobs to the unemployed.

However, by 1932 the Depression had worsened, and the world economic picture was bleak. There was even talk of canceling the games. A number of nations indicated an economic inability to participate. The Olympic Committee quickly devised the concept of an Olympic Village which would provide housing, food, and local transportation for all the athletes and their trainers for only two dollars a day. Two thousand athletes from 39 nations participated, and up to 110,410 spectators per day watched the contests. In the end, the 1932 Olympics Committee had over $200,000 in profits to give to City and County governments. Better yet, it was estimated that some $60 million had been pumped into the local economy by the visitors and subsequent publicity. Thousands of visitors, liked what they saw and went home to say so. More than 700 news correspondents converged on Los Angeles to cover the events, and, in addition to their accounts of the triumphs and defeats of the athletes, they filed colorful accounts of the local scene that were read worldwide.[27]

Advertisements in the pre-war progressive period had frequently appealed to the moralist: one ought to visit Los Angeles for one's health, for a cultural exposure to "Our Italy", and for a purifying immersion in old missions and fields of wild flowers. By contrast, ads of the '20s and '30s focused unabashed attention on personal pleasure, without moral justification. The photographs of Los Angeles in the 1920s booster literature and newspaper coverage of stars, sports, and the Olympics pictured people at play: happy crowds at spectator events, rows of bathing beauties performing calisthenics at the beach, a smiling starlet sampling a fresh-picked orange, a dance marathon, an actor with a bevy of admiring fans.[28] The purely hedonistic resort appeal was visually verified by its appearance. The city was dominated by palm trees and the various forms of Mediterranean architecture, two elements foreign to the vacationer's roots.

From across the nation, a generation hungry for change and excitement headed for Los Angeles. The movies depicted life more dynamically and dramatically than it really was and 1920s newcomers expected to find a sensory feast waiting for them in the city where films were made. The visitors, chugging along L.A.'s streets, were bombarded on every side by exotic images in disparate housing styles, stores built as giant ice-cream cones and hot dogs, cemeteries alive with movie-set imagery, sunlit colors of tinted stucco houses amid year-round lawns and flowers, movie palaces with their roving Kleig lights, and automobile traffic unlike anywhere else in the world. In order to be noticed, hard-sell advertising had to escalate the visual assault on already overwrought senses. To appeal to the competitive and materialistic values of the era, real estate developers, architects, builders of spec-housing and apartment-house investors stretched to more and more novel imagery. They also discovered the patio.

103. Detail of Krotona Court apartments, 1914

The patio provided a private respite from the buzz of modern life. The still water in a patio's fish pond offered tranquillity (ILLUSTRATION 103). The mellow, time-worn and naive appearance of well-designed Spanish Colonial patios counterbalanced materialism that dominated the '20s (ILLUSTRATION 100). Life at home could be simple, casual, comfortable and relaxed. In the midst of urban density, the sense of openness to the heralded sunshine and its contrast with the cool interiors that communicated with it were a source of enjoyment for Angelenos. Surrounded by tropical palms, banana plants, geraniums and bougainvillea, one could truly believe in a New World Garden of Eden.[29]

The attitude toward leisure, closely linked in the vision of Los Angeles with its outdoor living, had also undergone changes. Early American observers had noted the fact that the Californios did much of their living, cooking, eating,

104. Detail of Byers house, 1922

entertaining outside the four walls of their homes, and that their houses were consequently small and simple. Early ranch houses (ILLUSTRATION 6), town houses, and even the houses of social leaders (ILLUSTRATION 13) were little more than crude shelters. The gente de razon of Los Angeles in the Mexican period spent most of their time in leisure activities such as picnics, visiting, gambling, resting, and horse-riding, all of which was criticized by Yankees, hard-bitten by the Puritan work ethic, as innate laziness. Simple houses and outdoor living were ascribed to lack of initiative and an inferior culture. Only a few Yankee visitors admired the simplicity as refreshing and the leisure as the mark of the grandee.

By the 1920s, average Angelenos led a busy life. They worked at a demanding pace in a mechanized world hustling in their automobiles at the pace of the traffic. They viewed their leisure as deserved self-pampering. They would have a house where they could give themselves the freedom to loaf on a balcony outside the bedroom, lounge on a patio with a fountain, and smell the flowers grown in walled gardens (ILLUSTRATION 105 and 111).

The patio emerged as a major selling point for '20s and '30s real estate.

192

105. Griffith house, 1924

Builders added patios to Tudors, American Colonials and fairytale castles. But the patio truly belonged to the Mediterranean Colonial style. It was a hallmark of the Spanish look and myth.

The authors who were defining and illustrating the "correct" historical elements of the style made a distinction between patio and garden. The patio was an outdoor living room, enclosed within the structure of the house and its extended walls. It was paved, contained outdoor furniture, and was planted to small palms, patio-scale potted trees and shrubs and everywhere a blaze of brightly colored flowers. A fountain was often the centerpiece. ILLUSTRATION 105 allows us a peek at the patio of a 1924 house designed by Johnson, Kaufmann and Coate. The turned wooden grille or *reja* we are looking through was, according to the literature, an Aragon departure from the wrought iron rejas found in Catalonia and Andalusia.

Scholars traced the origin of the patio to two sources in Spanish culture: the self-sufficient farm compound and the seclusion of women. The farm compound, known in Spain as a *cortijo* (or, in the case of olive-growers' compounds, a *hacienda*), dates back as far as the Roman colonia. Like other Roman-influenced building forms characterized by a closed compound around an open center space, it served both convenience as well as defense.

More specifically Spanish were townhouses built to meet the Islamic religious stricture on the seclusion of women with its origins in the Moorish conquest of Spain in the 8th-century. Muslim wives and concubines could not go out in public unveiled, nor be seen by outsiders, a custom that spread beyond the Islamic community to Spain at large. The stifling confinement women surely experienced could be relieved in a house with secluded gardens, splashing fountains and flowers, all the pleasures of the outdoors — except freedom — brought within the harem walls. Grilled *balconets* and *galerias*, which typically fronted the street, permitted observation of the outer world without violating the seclusion. Open balconies facing the patio or the walled garden extended a feeling of freedom to the occupants of upstairs rooms. Usually, in back of the house surrounded by high walls, was a real garden where fruits and herbs could

Los Angeles Finds Its Own Style

be cultivated by the women of the house for pleasure or kitchen needs, again without violating taboos.[30]

Houses with such features, beautifully designed by gifted architects and carrying out the principles of the books on Mediterranean and Spanish Colonial design, appeared along the avenues of Pasadena, Santa Monica and Beverly Hills. Photographs of tile-roofed mansions of prominent social leaders, hidden in the depths of large estates, appeared in local newspapers. Tour guides reeled off big names in the motion-picture business as busloads of tourists were driven by the Spanish style Homes of the Stars. Clearly, persons of refined tastes, with wealth and power, who were role models — preferred the Mediterranean Colonial style.

Director Thomas Ince built Dias Dorados, his 25-room Spanish style mansion in 1923-24. Rudolph Valentino's Falcon Lair, above Benedict Canyon, was a tile-roofed extravagance with Italian gardens. Razor magnate King C. Gillette built his 22-room Italian Renaissance mansion in 1916, but by the time Gloria Swanson bought it in 1919, its cream-colored stucco walls and clay tile roof qualified it as "Spanish style." Director Ernst Lubitsch brought a crew of Mexican masons back with him from a shooting location to build a Mexican hacienda for himself in Los Angeles. John Barrymore bought a Spanish style house with a Moorish balcony which had been designed by set designer Cedric Gibbons. A list of other high-profile occupants of Spanish Colonial houses in the '20s would include Cecil B. DeMille, Harold Lloyd, Charlie Chaplin, Deanna Durbin, W.C. Fields, Bette Davis, Francis X. Bushman, Roland van West, Buster Keaton, director Fred Niblo, and Jesse Lasky.[31]

In an era when, it seemed, everyone was star-struck, the Southern California Chapter of the American Institute of Architects invited Mary Pickford to address them in November 1926 on the topic, "Spanish Architecture, Ideal for the California Home." It was her opinion that "English and early Colonial, with red bricks and heavy pillars, have no place in Southern California....I feel we should retain as much as possible the Spanish, or I should say Mexican or early Californian feeling. Failing this, Italian is the next best thing. I have long felt that the Spanish influence in California is one of the greatest charms our state possesses, a precious heritage second only to our climate, and that it should be preserved in every way possible."[32]

She went on to decry the kind of stylistic contradictions captured in ILLUSTRATION 2 where the "effect" of one's house and its choice of style could be spoiled if a neighbor erected a house in a style of "bold and glaring contrast." The actress called for urban planning to include style consistency, for land developments with deed-restrictions on style as in Palos Verdes, and for

194

developments in which the developer filled all the lots with harmoniously designed structures, leaving no empty lots for owners' whims. She applauded the City of Santa Barbara, which had set up strict guidelines for rebuilding in the Spanish mode following a disastrous earthquake in 1925. Santa Barbara's style controls successfully captured the air of Old Spanish romance she admired.

Two of the tract developers in the Los Angeles area who adhered to Miss Pickford's vision were H.J. Whitley and Alphonso Bell, Sr. The former developed Whitley Heights, a hillside tract of Mediterranean villas near the Hollywood Bowl, which still provides a pleasant vista to freeway drivers, and a less expensive tract, Whitley Park, across the ridge on the San Fernando Valley side. The 1923 advertisement announced:

> "RESTRICTIONS on TYPE of architecture only — not on cost.
> ...the architectural restrictions permit only Spanish or
> Italian homes, primarily artistic."[33]

Bell's Castellamare and Miramare developments in Pacific Palisades, platted in 1925 and 1927, offered more or less precarious hillside sites on winding streets for tile-roofed Spanish villas with ocean views. One of the most formal houses built in the Castellamare section was Villa de Leon, pictured in Illustration 85. Most, however, expressed the relaxed, rambling ideals drawn from Southern Spain and Mexico, with polychrome tiles, thick walls, uneven plaster, balconies, patios, and beamed ceilings.

In 1927 the Los Angeles Times sponsored a Demonstration Home in the Miramar unit. Architect Mark Daniels was lauded in the Times as an artist, musician, and poet as well as a successful architect and landscaper, with a background including extensive studies in situ of the architecture and gardens of Spain, Italy, southern France and North Africa. Thus accredited, Daniels built a two-story, tile-roofed house with a view of the ocean and the foothills, incorporating decorative wrought iron and colorful tile, Moorish grilles and a flagstone patio. He also added innovations to thrill modernists and the gadget-minded, such as automatic garage doors and built-in roller window screens. The Demonstration Home, or Villa Aurora, as it was christened, was opened for public tours in April 1928. As many as 20,000 visitors saw it in a day. Clearly, there was a lot of public interest in Mediterranean Colonial housing.[34]

The '20s witnessed the construction of city halls in Beverly Hills and Pasadena, the interior of Los Angeles' city hall, schools, post offices, shops, gas stations, grocery stores, banks, and churches of various denominations in

106. Detail, Spanish
Colonial tract house, 1931

107. Detail, Spanish
Colonial tract house, 1924

Mediterranean-inspired architecture. As congregations discussed church plans, professors and provosts pondered college layouts, and elected officials argued civic center designs. Arguments in favor of the romanticized Spanish heritage were drummed into the public consciousness. The Mediterranean Colonial style, endorsed and re-endorsed by leaders of taste, had become not only stylish but the average homebuyer's automatic first choice. Newcomers seeking temporary apartments, retirees looking for a small cottages, factory workers looking for his own affordable home, the white-collar middle-class, intellectual purists, and the wealthy chose Mediterranean Colonial as the ideal expression of Los Angeles.

The building industry responded to this new market. Contractors employed skilled artisans to add fine details such as reflecting pools and the thick window wells, corner buttressing, and uneven plaster simulating adobe walls (ILLUSTRATION 78).[35] Tract houses with a mixture of classic quoins and keystones, polychrome tile trim, arches, and tile roofs (ILLUSTRATION 106), or arcaded entry patios, square mission columns, projecting vigas, and casement windows (ILLUSTRATION 107), met the voracious public demand.[36] The popularity of Spanish Colonial extended even to rows of working-class cottages, where a single row of tile coping might stand in for a tile roof, and troweled patterns had to satisfy the desire for the adobe look (ILLUSTRATION 108).[37] The Spanish Colonial style was also extended to the bungalow court (ILLUSTRATION 109).[38] Although the Spanish past might have been a gimmick that was over used in the '20s in hard-sell images battering already overwrought imaginations, it remained commercially attractive for investors in Depression-era ventures (ILLUSTRATION 110).[39] The Spanish Colonial replication of a fictionalized past also served occupants as a restorative antidote to the pressures of the present. Renters and buyers preferred models in this style and in so doing, expressed themselves and contributed to reshaping Los Angeles in terms of a romantic historical myth. ❧

108. Spanish Colonial row
houses, 1920s

110. Detail, Spanish Colonial
apartments, 1935

109. Spanish Colonial
courtyard housing, 1927

111. Detail, Spanish Colonial
house, 1928-30

Los Angeles Finds Its Own Style

XI

DARING ORIGINALS

California has an astounding

sum of significant creative work; ...

... Among the reasons for this

is certainly the freshness, the newness,

of this coastal civilization,

its freedom from

inhibiting tradition,

its readiness to experiment.

—PAULINE SCHINDLER

THE TWO INTER-WAR DECADES saw the creation of a stylistic canon that would guide housing forms to the end of the century. The fairytale gamut including Tudor and castle, Middle Eastern and Hansel and Gretel styles climaxed in the Spanish or Mediterranean Colonial style. There was another significant style: Modernism. Like the others, it eventually spread to a broad price range. It started with high-art monuments and gave rise to small, inexpensive versions of the popular Streamline Moderne style shortly before the outbreak of the Second World War. In the case of Modernism, however, the high-art examples remained in the majority and they and their architects drew acclaim worldwide.

At the close of the First World War, Los Angeles had found itself the gathering ground of a significant element of creative artists, power figures in the pioneer film industry, and innovative architects. This was one of those rare moments in the history of the arts when technological advance, political and economic climates, and a spring of new ideals combine to produce a fertile flood of artistic expression bringing about the rise of Modern architecture is such a rare moment. It is difficult to arrive at a precise definition of the international term, "Modern Architecture," when such a term must be broad enough to encompass both ILLUSTRATION 112 and ILLUSTRATION 113. However, there are a number of traits common to the works of architects who have considered themselves moderns: anti-historicism, minimalism, functionality, originality, reform idealism and an industrial design orientation.[1] These features appealed to the new patronage establishing itself in Los Angeles in the interwar period.

In Europe, the First World War nearly halted artistic endeavors. Ballet and symphony concert schedules, salon exhibits and theatrical performances were disrupted or canceled, and the work of artists of all types was next-to-impossible, given the military draft and wartime priorities. Creative artists in many media, and, eventually, those who hovered about them as critics, admirers, and patrons, were drawn to Los Angeles for one reason: this was the heart of the world's film industry. That industry was the principal, monied patron of the arts in the 20th-century, as Florentine bankers and textile guilds had been in the 15th-century.

As we have seen, movie sets and the well-publicized houses of the film stars in 1910s and '20s favored fanciful renditions of historical styles. But actors and actresses were the contract-bound pawns in the motion picture business. The real power brokers were the producers, corporate moguls and financial backers. The key creative artists in the film industry were behind the scenes as directors, composers, and screenwriters. When inspired monuments of modern

112. Hollyhock House, 1919-1920

Daring Originals

architecture first appeared in Los Angeles, it is worth noting how many of them were commissioned by these powerful and creative figures. This influential element of newcomers apparently agreed with the writers who lampooned fairytale houses. They employed daring, original architects to design their houses which tested, stretched, and sometimes shocked or offended the passerby's sense of what was attractive or even acceptable domestic architecture.

By 1929 Los Angeles was acclaimed as one of the few U.S. showplaces of modern domestic architecture. This had come about because personal links between architectural colleagues drew a number of early modernists here from other places and because of the tendency for an architect's initial work to lead to a string of commissions among the client's associates.

On a hill in Hollywood in 1919 a mansion designed by a famous architect to resemble a Mayan mausoleum was under construction. (ILLUSTRATION 112) A few miles away in Santa Monica another architect was overseeing completion of an airy apartment house of clean, uncluttered forms. (ILLUSTRATION 113) The two architects had apprenticed together in Chicago. The apartment house is still admired as a model of modernist tenets. The mansion largely violated those tenets, catering instead to theatrical escapism. The diverse trends signaled by these two projects heralded L.A.'s receptivity to modernism and led to a series of modern masterworks by a generation of younger architects and their successors.

It was Frank Lloyd Wright who designed the moated Barnsdall house. Irving Gill built the Horatio West apartments. Wright drew fame, critical interest, and three important disciples to Los Angeles. Gill demonstrated the functional and aesthetic advantages of real modernism in the local environment. However, Wright's project acknowledged more of the new ideals than appear at first glance, and Gill's gave a nod to historicism. These two projects represent a range of creativity that attracted a clientele for innovative house forms which, in turn, reshaped the Los Angeles image.

Frank Lloyd Wright had met Aline Barnsdall, a 32-year-old oil heiress, in Chicago in 1914. He already had a body of local work to his credit and a reputation there. He had won international acclaim from the 1910-11 European publication of his Portfolio. Miss Barnsdall was active in local theater and she discussed her ideas for a new building for the Chicago Little Theatre with Wright. After a trip to California that year, she changed her mind about her offer: she would uplift the cultural level of the new movie capital of the world by establishing her Little Theater in Los Angeles instead. By 1916 she had moved to L.A. and was producing stage plays there with her own company (each of

113. Horatio West apartments, 1919

114. Detail of
Hollyhock House

whose members later went into movies). The Hollywood atmosphere had a stimulating effect on the plans she continued to discuss with the architect by long-distance correspondence. Her vision expanded to encompass an entire artistic complex, including her own dwelling; housing for resident artists, staff and an artistic director; a 1250-seat live theater; a motion picture theater; a row of commercial shops, a terrace restaurant; and extensive gardens.

In 1919 Ms. Barnsdall purchased a site for the complex, a 36-acre undeveloped rise in Hollywood. Her own residence, Hollyhock House, would be built first (ILLUSTRATIONS 112 and 114). Thus it was that an internationally famous architect first made his mark on Los Angeles. In more than one sense, Ms. Barnsdall's choice of Wright as her architect was an historic mistake. Although her plans for the complex had been developed in close give-and-take between them over several years' time, dissension marked the construction period. Her unhappy experiences with her architect and the home he built for her led her to change architects midway through completion. She lived only briefly in the house Wright designed, then moved to a more comfortable home. She offered Hollyhock House to the City as a park two years after its completion. Nevertheless, it remains one of the landmarks of American architectural history.[2]

When Ms. Barnsdall selected Wright for her project she had probably never heard of Irving Gill, a former colleague of Wright's, who had moved to California some years earlier. While Ms. Barnsdall's hilltop mansion was taking shape, Gill was at work on a small apartment complex near the beach. (ILLUSTRATION 113) Each of Gill's apartments offers light, efficient, comfortable living space. The clean, simple lines of the exterior form a unified design, yet each living unit is individualized. The starkly simple arch (ILLUSTRATION 98) is a barely perceptible nod toward historicism. It is a fine and confident example of modern design for 1919, belying the iconoclasts' depiction of Los Angeles as a cultural wasteland.

Only three years apart in age, both Gill and Wright had trained in the Chicago office of Louis Sullivan (1856-1924). Concerned about the quality of American architecture, Sullivan had advocated steps for its improvement. First, "It would be greatly for our aesthetic good, if we should refrain entirely from the use of ornament for a period of years, in order that our thought might concentrate...upon the production of buildings...comely in the nude." Second, he yearned to create a truly American architecture, freed from style-dependence on European historicism.[3] Irving Gill, achieved the first goal; both Gill and Wright strove to meet the second. Each looked to native American architectural traditions and then beyond, to an individuality freed of derivative sources.

At the age of 23, Irving Gill heeded the hard-sell health claims of Southern California's boosters, left Chicago, and moved to San Diego. For the first few years he designed homes, churches, and commercial buildings in various derivative styles, ending up in The Craftsman camp after the turn of the century. His debt to Sullivan was expressed in his restriction of ornament. As he matured, and as he fell under the spell of Southern California, he began to evolve a personal, experimental style that predated the avant-garde modernism of his better-known counterparts in Vienna, Germany and Holland. After 1906, Gill produced a series of buildings guided by what he called "the luminous idea of simplicity." They were made of concrete and stucco and reduced in form to simple, interrelated cubes, relieved by openings which were merely pierced rectangles or arches.[4]

Writing in The Craftsman in 1916, Gill summarized his crusade for simplicity:

"If we, the architects of the West, wish to do great and lasting work we must dare to be simple, must have the courage to fling aside every device that distracts the eye from structural beauty, must break through convention and get down to fundamental truths."

He defined these truths as "the straight line, the arch, the cube and the circle." And he called for an architecture of pure, unadorned form:

"Any deviation from simplicity results in a loss of dignity....If we omit everything useless from the structural point of view we will come to see the great beauty of straight lines, to see the charm that lies in perspective, the force in light and shade, the power in balanced masses, the fascination of color that plays upon a smooth wall left free to report the passing of a cloud or nearness of a flower..."[5]

Gill's aesthetic philosophy was persuasively demonstrated in a number of buildings in the San Diego area. In 1911 developers called him to the Los Angeles area to do much of the planning for the community of Torrance. Partly due to his eclipse in San Diego by the highly ornamented version of Spanish Colonial architecture popularized there by the Panama California Exposition of 1915, he confined his major works to the Los Angeles area in civic buildings, houses, housing courts, and apartments, until his return to obscurity in San Diego in the late 1920's.

The Horatio West Apartments, completed in 1919 in Santa Monica, illustrate his principles in the use of balanced cubic volumes, their relationships accentuated by depth and shadow, and the simple horizontal band of windows. His own words capture the emotional content communicated by the habitational sculpture he had created:

"There is something very restful and satisfying to my mind in the simple cube house with creamy walls, sheer and plain, rising boldly into the sky, unrelieved by cornices or overhang of roof, unornamented save for the vines that soften a line...[in this case, well-placed podacarpus and other foundation plantings instead] I like the bare honesty of these houses, the childlike frankness and chaste simplicity of them."[6]

Gill took special pride in designing his houses for efficiency and easy care. He eliminated projections that would catch dust, fitting door moldings flush with the walls, eliminating baseboards, picture moldings, and paneling. The floors were treated concrete slabs, rounded up at the walls to prevent cracks where dust or vermin might lodge. The sinks and bathtubs were sunk into molded magnesite to prevent the accumulation of dirt or dampness. He invented built-in vacuum sweeper systems, garbage disposals, ice-boxes and mail-boxes with access from outside, even a car-wash system for the garages, in the interest in the occupants' quality of life.

Daring Originals

The use of new materials and building techniques likewise confirms Gill as a pioneer modern. He often used thin, fireproof walls of hollow tiles, filled with concrete, covered with stucco or a thin layer of concrete. He was an innovator of the tilt-slab method in which reinforced concrete walls are poured in place and tilted into position. He must be credited with pioneering designs for steel door and window casings. Even in his larger commissions, economy was a prime consideration. Even a multi-unit apartment house where cost effectiveness is critical, could, in Gill's hands, achieve a sense of quiet beauty. Small apartment units, where utilitarian principles were applied to the conservation of space, seemed large.

Irving Gill won local approbation in Southern California for the modest structures he designed for moderate prices. Only recently, decades after his death, have architectural historians accorded him recognition and brought him world attention. Frank Lloyd Wright, on the contrary, was already apotheosized before he arrived in Los Angeles in 1919 to commence work on Miss Barnsdall's artists' colony. In part, this was the result of proven performance in the Chicago area, where his work, ranging from "interesting" to "breath-taking" spanned the transition from the Arts and Crafts movement to the Modern movement. In part, Wright's fame was the result of his own knack for publicity. After 1910, when his works were published in Europe, he became a major international architectural figure. The Barnsdall project in Southern California came at a time of crisis in the architect's personal life, offering him a welcome change of scene.[7]

His client had her own reasons for seeking a refuge in California. She was chronically restless, "possessed by incorrigible wander lust" as Wright put it, never pursuing any one interest for long. She frequently exhibited the eccentricities of an independent heiress with liberated notions, a few years too soon for the flapper era. But at the time Hollyhock House was on Wright's drawing board, Ms. Barnsdall was under particular stress. Her father had died in 1917 and the settlement of the estate was a long and trying ordeal. She was still unmarried at 35, a socially awkward matter in those times. Then, in 1917 she gave birth to a daughter of unclear paternity. The air of scandal in her personal life was further fueled by her association with Movie People, still viewed suspiciously as bohemian, arty, and outrageous. The oil heiress was rumored to be a Bolshevik sympathizer. She was besieged by reporters, gossip columnists, and fortune-seeking flatterers. Wright sensed a close parallel between his client's interests and needs and his own in this period. Instead of following his earlier style of the "broad shelter in the open", he designed a cave-like hiding place for her withdrawal. In his autobiography he described Aline Barnsdall in her new setting as "a princess in aristocratic seclusion." He built for her a royal headquarters from which she could orchestrate a renaissance of theater arts, but one which could also serve as a formidable fortress where she could take refuge.[8]

The location, which Ms. Barnsdall had herself selected, was a steep hill rising alone from the flatlands of Hollywood. The house was set on the crown of the hill and the approaches on both sides were guarded by Residences A and B, built in 1920-21. If a would-be invader succeeded in getting past these outposts, he found a real moat protecting the west end of Miss Barnsdall's citadel. Thwarted there by the architect's cunning, he would have to reconnoiter past suspended balconies, walled courtyards and terraces screened by impassive walls before he noticed a low and dark tunnel-like opening that led to the main entrance. The door itself, in the depths of this tunnel, was massive and forbidding. Inside, the main entertainment rooms — dining room, music room, living room and foyers — are airy, open, and tranquil. But beyond them, the rest of the commodious house for one woman and a child — 17 living and sleeping rooms plus 7 bathrooms — entraps the visitor in a tangled maze of trapezoidal hallways and small rooms at various levels.

If architect and client had chosen the form of a Medieval European castle for this impenetrable retreat, it would, perhaps, have drawn less attention. There were, after all, quite a number of fairytale castles of varying sizes under construction in Los Angeles by the mid-'20s. But Hollyhock House was a remote and mysterious Mayan ceremonial center of eighth and ninth-century Mezo-America. It is curious that the architect who prided himself on his originality should have chosen the Mayan world as a source of inspiration. It was not his client's doing: she had left the style up to him. He may have been a searching for an indigenous American style.

Since 1841, books, newspapers and National Geographic had been entertaining the American reading public with accounts of intrepid jungle explorers uncovering ancient Mayan ruins. Other architects, working in Los Angeles in the mid-'20s, enthusiastically embraced pre-Columbian architectural models as appropriately American architecture.[9] Wright himself never acknowledged a Mayan compromise to his creativity. His son, Lloyd Wright, denied the Mayan inspiration, claiming the Native American Southwest as the source instead. Regardless of his reticence, Frank Lloyd Wright was clearly indebted to classic Mayan forms.[10] Hollyhock House was a composite of Mayan styles familiar to this public.[11] In some ways the Mayan theme was appropriate. From the sumptuous palaces of the privileged Mayan elite sprang the arts, including the dramatic rituals which embroidered Mayan culture. These centers isolated the aristocratic class from the masses; they were defensively secure; their monumentality was symbolically and psychologically imposing and authoritative; and their decorations were so highly stylized that they were awesome to the excluded classes. Ms. Barnsdall, the patroness of a theater renaissance, in need of a refuge and a shielding mystique, was well served by Mayan forms.[12]

Were it not for the architect's reputation, Hollyhock House would qualify as another example of fairytale architecture. The Mayan temple-palace which looks so massive and permanent was actually built of wood frame, hollow tile, and stucco. It was a flimsy movie set for the staged illusion of Mayan grandeur, authority, and permanence. In fact, it actually was a stage. The two main wings of the house enclose an open-air theater (ILLUSTRATION 114). The courtyard-facing sundecks of the upstairs rooms provided loggia seating; orchestra seats were placed where we now see windows. The grass in the foreground is the stage, elevated three steps above the level of the house floor. In this house the line separating the staged drama from real life had ceased to exist.

Because Frank Lloyd Wright's name was synonymous with modern architecture, viewers have examined Hollyhock House for evidence of the modernist tenets its Mayanism denied. As the ornamental motif inside and out, Wright did incorporate cubist abstractions of Ms. Barnsdall's favorite flower, the hollyhock. The furnishings, which he also designed, carry out the same theme. The bold frieze and accentuating finials which both ornamented and unified all elements of the structure were repetitions of the flower's stylized stalk. In the Los Angeles of 1920, this may have been the man-in-the-street's first encounter with abstract art.

The Barnsdall house also demonstrated new materials and design concepts such as indirect lighting, split-level interiors, and a cast concrete front door. The frieze was made of pre-formed units of cast stone. It was the intermediary step in Wright's development of textile-block construction, employed on the four residential commissions in Los Angeles which followed the Barnsdall project. There, pre-cast concrete blocks, some smooth, others with cast-in patterns, were woven together on vertical and horizontal reinforcing rods, then filled with mortar. This development was Wright's response to the region's frequent earthquakes. The surrounding moat, ingeniously channeled to reappear indoors as a miniature, spark-arresting moat surrounding the living room fireplace, was one of several fireproofing innovations.

Despite its Mayan reference, Wright's Hollyhock House has been heralded as the genesis of modern architecture in L.A.. It brought an acclaimed modern architect to the local scene and it was directly responsible for bringing to

Los Angeles three other outstanding architects of the Modern school: Lloyd Wright, R. M. Schindler, and Richard Neutra, and, after them, full acceptance of Los Angeles as a mecca of Modern architecture, to which many other important Modern architects came to work.

The Los Angeles commissions of Frank Lloyd Wright and his three immediate successors gave coherent form to three apparently conflicting desires emerging from the depths of the nascent Los Angeles psyche: the desire to be admired as fashionable and sophisticated; the need of the lonely newcomer for a cathartic expression of his anxiety; and the wish for the kind of self-confidence that permits true freedom of individual expression.

In 1925 an important exhibit was staged in Paris, the *Exposition Internationale des Arts Decoratifs et Industriels Modernes*. The furniture, machinery, jewelry, textile patterns, glassware, metalwork, book bindings, and illustrations brought to world attention in this mark of Europe's rebirth after World War I popularized a new aesthetic style which came to be referred to as "Art Deco", after the name of the exhibition. The most prominent characteristics of the new look were the thin, crisp line; the highly stylized cubist design elements in which a nervous angularity largely replaced the relaxed and sensual curves of Art Nouveau; the flat-relief which took the place of realistic depth; and a hedonistic focus on luxurious materials. Architectural historians sometimes descriptively label the Moderne of the '20s "Zig-Zag Moderne" to distinguish it from the Streamline Moderne of the '30s. When films in the '20s wished to portray high sophistication, Art Deco sets were used. Surprisingly, few houses were built anywhere in this short-lived style. Los Angeles, however, favored Art Deco commercial buildings, and still exhibits many noteworthy examples of the style.[13]

115. Sowden hose, 1926

Art Deco's flourish of popularity in the mid-'20s illustrates a case of belated public acceptance of what had been fresh and original. Lloyd Wright, the eldest son of the famous architect, was working in his father's artistic footsteps just as Art Deco became popular. The frieze of stylized hollyhocks on the Barnsdall house (ILLUSTRATIONS 112 and 114), the crisp, linear patterns in the concrete blocks of the son's Sowden house (ILLUSTRATION 115), and the stepped angularity of its central opening are part of the Art Deco vocabulary. High fashion had caught up with Lloyd Wright and he gained a series of commissions for the

Daring Originals

fashion-minded in the film-capital of the world.

To Frank Lloyd Wright may also be due the rather dubious credit for introducing intense emotional expression to L.A. architecture, both directly and through his impact on his son. Lloyd Wright, the firstborn in the family Frank Lloyd Wright had abandoned, trained briefly in Irving Gill's office and served as the original construction supervisor for the Hollyhock House. He opened his own architectural practice in Los Angeles in 1921. Defending his father's art and revealing his filial dependence, he modeled his work on his father's ideas of space, beauty, and material, making those ideas his own by exaggerating their elements and heightening their emotional content.[14]

The emotional intensity of the Sowden residence, designed by Lloyd Wright in 1926, not only exceeds that of Frank Lloyd Wright's works, but identifies Lloyd Wright with the Expressionist movement. Painters and writers we call Expressionists, such as with Van Gogh, Münch, and Nietzche, devoted their art to the expression of their own deep and powerful personal emotions. In the case of the Sowden residence, the house presents its own jagged mouth, open in the terror and relief of the primal scream.[15] Penetrating the cave-like entrance to Frank Lloyd Wright's Barnsdall house is a child's game compared to the Sowden entrance engineered by Lloyd Wright. Once inside this cavity one groped one's way up a spiral stairway in underlit and musty confinement. The disorienting, deep cave entrance, often obscuring a stairway, was found in several of Lloyd Wright's works of the 1920s. For the curious, however, these houses reveal not only the emotional states of the owner and his architect, but something else as well: the histrionic affectation of Hollywood. In silent film, as in Greek drama, actors were obliged to exaggerate their facial expressions and body movements in order to communicate emotional content. The drama schools which sprang up all over L.A. during the early days of the motion picture industry trained movie hopefuls in the art of exaggerated emotional display. Lloyd Wright was a film-industry insider. He understood and built in its language.

In 1916, Lloyd Wright had moved from San Diego to Hollywood to become head of the Design and Drafting Department at Paramount Studios. In that capacity, he was directly responsible for the concentrated images of medieval castles, sultans' palaces, and those larger-than-life versions of far-away and long-ago places which filled the imaginations of movie-goers. He also became part of the social life of Hollywood. He met Aline Barnsdall and became part of her theatrical circle. He married Kira Markham, one of the actresses in her stage company. The people with whom he was acquainted were making movies. When he opened his own architectural practice in 1921 they were his clients. He built houses for Ramon Novarro, John Derby, Martha Taggert (whose daughter became his second wife) and a number of others. John Sowden was an actor, film director, and proprietor of a drama school. His house was intended to project a dramatic posture for fan publicity. It served as the location of his acting school, and his private entertainment complex, with a screening room and stage theater for his guests.

Lloyd Wright employed the Mayan look and the patterned concrete blocks his father had made famous. Visitors experience the same kind of thrills in this house that they would under the spell of a movie. After they survive the ordeal of the entry passage, they find themselves in a huge room, with a pitched ceiling originally painted in copper. Along with all the other rooms of the house, it opens through a pillared portico onto a central courtyard which served as an outdoor movie theater with a retractable screen for movie-viewing. The Sowden House stood outside the conventions of Art Deco in the intense emotional involvement it required of both occupants and onlookers. Its histrionic statement was comprehensible to a small new segment of the population which was versed in European Expressionism. Few people other than thespians and drama coaches, would want to make such a personal psychological statement, in the form of their residence.

The equally daring, but emotionally cool creations of Rudolph Schindler and Richard Neutra were admired by L.A.'s growing enclave of artists, musicians and writers as inspired works of art, original and modern. The work of Schindler and Neutra could also be accepted by sophisticated and fashionable Angelenos who were not necessarily acquainted with avant-garde arts because they found it compatible with the crisp lines, the cubist design elements, and the detached coolness they had come to regard as good taste. The high-fashion of Art Deco had educated Angelenos so that high-culture could be admired, if not fully understood.

In some of his other projects, Lloyd Wright eschewed psychological extremism and Hollywood exhibitionism to join Schindler and Neutra in winning the patronage of a narrow stratum of confident, cultured literati who settled in Los Angeles in the '20s and '30s. It was in this period, at last, that high fashion and high culture found themselves at home in a town so long castigated as low brow.

In the decades when Hollywood's versions of life and opportunities were beckoning the typical movie-goer, and in doing so, selecting for Los Angeles a population specifically by mediocrity of taste, the movie industry was also drawing the cream of the cultural world to Los Angeles. In the 1920s the film industry began to hire acclaimed American authors and Broadway directors. It absorbed the European film producers, directors, technicians, actors, musicians and composers who fled the First World War, post-war economic crises, then Nazism. Many of the era's best-known writers such as Hemingway, Steinbeck, O'Hara, Saroyan and Faulkner, came to Los Angeles, some for a few months at a time, others making it their long-term home. The Garden of Allah was one of their Hollywood watering spots and author-humorist Robert Benchley, who arrived in 1926 to make his first film and stayed to make over 40 others, served as its resident bon vivant. Budd Schulberg was writing here, along with Nathaniel West, James M. Cain, and Raymond Chandler. Director George Cukor came to Hollywood from Broadway in 1929 under contract to Paramount Studios to engineer its transition from silent movies to talkies. He stayed until his death in 1983.

The list of European émigrés included filmmakers Fritz Lang, Erich von Stroheim, Maurice Tourneur, and Ernst Lubitsch, writers Kurt Weill and Lion Feuchtwanger. The advent of sound in motion pictures created an unprecedented job market for musicians, conductors, and composers. Arnold Schoenberg came to stay in 1934 and his contemporary, Igor Stravinsky, stayed in Los Angeles until 1969.[16] Within this urbane, highly cultured community,

116. Studio Residence A, 1920

MOVIE STARS AND HARD TIMES

experiments in abstraction, expressionism, primitivism and futurism were discussed and appreciated. When Lloyd Wright, and occasionally Schindler, created works in the Expressionist mode, they could count on a positive response by an articulate and knowing minority. The succession of commissions among this cosmopolitan element which Lloyd Wright, Schindler and Neutra enjoyed served to familiarize average Angelenos with the avant-garde.[17]

Rudolph Schindler trained under two of the most important early modernists in Vienna, Otto Wagner and Adolph Loos. Near the end of his training he discovered Frank Lloyd Wright's published Portfolio. Wright's emphasis on free-flowing space, the extension of living space to the outdoors, the horizontality of the Prairie House, and his persuasive writing on the role of house design in the expansion of human potential had a dramatic effect on the young Viennese and he yearned to work with Wright.

In 1914 he won a trip to Chicago as a contest prize. After four years' effort, Schindler was accepted as a draftsman in Wright's Chicago office. Wright delegated the on-site supervision of the Barnsdall complex first to his son Lloyd and then, in 1920, to Schindler, who was obliged to move from Chicago to Hollywood to complete the job. In the meantime, construction began on the next two buildings in the complex. The plans for Studio Residence A, The Director's House (ILLUSTRATION 116), were drawn by Schindler and submitted to Wright, who approved them unchanged.[18]

The Studio Residence was designed to be compatible with the Hollyhock House. Schindler employed the unifying frieze and a clear reference to the Wrightian idiom in his design. In both houses the frieze ties together the constituent modular units, but in this case it does so without dominating. Here the frieze is reduced to a continuous containing band. Mayan references are eliminated in favor of Wright's earlier style marks — the cantilevered roofs, the horizontal window bands. The Studio echoed the daring clarity and simplicity of the less-noticed Gill project. Schindler went further: he simplified the roof and lightened it to a thin cantilevered slab. With that step, all forms other than the rectangle are eliminated, and the house is unified by the repetition and variation of that one geometric form.

The house is restricted to a set of simple cubes, the bordered windows reduced to rectangular surface patterns. The rhythm created by the relationships of a series of rectangular shapes is controlled by the horizontal bands of the eaves and the frieze. The feeling that Studio Residence A imparts is more intellectual, dispassionate, and self-possessed than L.A. was accustomed to. The best of Irving Gill and Frank Lloyd Wright had joined in a worthy successor.[19]

Daring Originals

Rejecting the massive and enclosing cave feeling of the Hollyhock House, Schindler employed his own concept of expanding space for human activities. Individuality, privacy, light, and extension of living space to the out-of-doors were accomplished by surrounding the entire sleeping end of the house with a strip of clerestory windows set high enough to ensure privacy but low enough to see trees and sky. Such windows needed no curtains. They admitted light and fresh air. The living room, at the other end of the house, is two stories high with a wall of windows overlooking the view of the nearby mountains while maintaining privacy. Although Studio Residence A and the Hollyhock House still keep harmonious company with each other, their effect on the viewer is a study in contrasts. The Hollyhock House forms a solid bulwark reinforced by its reference to antiquity; the Studio, with its thin edges and its attention to surface skin appears almost fragile.

117. Schindler-Chase house, 1921-22

By 1921 Schindler was easing out of Wright's employ and building up an independent practice. Once on his own, he proved to be a truly daring original. ILLUSTRATION 117 shows one wing of his own office-home combination, the Schindler-Chase residence. Schindler built the complex in 1921-22 and occupied it until his death in 1953. In it we can see that this new Angeleno had perceptively recognized the major aspects of the Los Angeles essence. His contribution to the layered image was to repackage that essence with an originality consonant with the international movement of modernism: ahistorical, without ornament, functionally beautiful. It was an experiment in efficient industrial design and the use of new materials and techniques, and a very earnest exploration of social ideals.

The Schindler-Chase Residence represented an experiment in engineering a new lifestyle which would suit the individuals involved — an unconventional lifestyle permissible in such a forward-looking, fast-growing place. The house reflected the L.A. theme of the healthful climate. It was this generation's reinterpretation in Modernist terms of the regional enthusiasm for indoor-outdoor living. The tourist brochures' assurances of sunny weather as a dependable norm made shelter seem of little consequence. Schindler absorbed this propaganda and built for it.

He and his wife had visited Yosemite as one of the regional high points on tourist agendas. The Curry Company, which had developed the visitor facilities in Yosemite Valley, built inexpensive housekeeping units of concrete on concrete pads, with canvas roofs. Each structure, similar in floorplan to an 'H', accommodated two families. The open ends of the 'H' were screened by canvas curtains which could be drawn for privacy. Around each open end a fence was built to enclose the extended cement pad as a patio, on which were located a wood-burning stove, some shelving, and a table and chairs. An awning of canvas roofed the whole complex. The double unit permitted each family an acceptable level of privacy, while giving each access to the open air, the starry sky, and the surrounding trees. There were no doors or gates, thus encouraging a flow of activities to the spectacular natural features of Yosemite National Park. This lifestyle seemed ideal to Schindler and he was inspired to create a vacation environment for year-round occupancy.

Two couples, the Schindlers and Mr. and Mrs. Clyde Chase, were to co-habit the residence. Each of the four was an artist and each was regarded as an individual of worth. So, there would be five major rooms in the house: a studio for each of the four occupants and a guest room. A common kitchen was to be cooperatively used by the two couples. Instead of parlors for social effect and kitchens for onerous duties related to maternal martyrdom, Schindler's ideal was a private room for each occupant where he or she could "gain a background for his life."[20]

There were no bedrooms. Over each couple's end of the house was an elevated porch for sleeping — what Schindler referred to as "sleeping baskets". The sleeping basket for the Schindler's wing is seen in the photograph. The floorplan of the house forms an angled, three-armed spiral. Three "garden living-rooms" open from the three wings. On the front of the property, the Chase wing, extended by a planted hedge, wraps around a patio with outdoor fireplace. On the back, another patio with outdoor fireplace forms an outdoor living room between the open walls of the Schindler wing and the back of the guest wing. All of the glass-paneled walls were originally fitted with sliding panels of canvas, which were removed seasonally, creating three-walled patios instead of conventional rooms. The Schindlers' patio pictured in ILLUSTRATION 117 has Rudolph Schindler's studio on the right, and Pauline Schindler's adjoining it on the left.[21]

The already-established regional favor for indoor-outdoor living was prominent in L.A. housing when Schindler arrived. Schindler carried that tendency to an extreme. His house has been described as nothing more than "a

Daring Originals

118. Detail of Schindler-Chase house

series of loosely grouped pavilions."²² This does not follow <u>The Craftsman</u> concept of the house nestling into its natural site, rather, the Japanese idea of creating a miniature, tranquil version of nature in which man could seclude himself (ILLUSTRATION 118).

Schindler's interest in expanding living space beyond walls was more than aesthetic and psychological, however. In the course of his work on the Barnsdall project, he had become acquainted with what we might call a "health nut". Dr. Phillip Lovell wrote a popular syndicated column, "Care of the Body", which advocated exercise, natural foods, holistic medicine, and fresh air. Schindler became an avid proselyte of his views. And, in turn, Lovell lionized Schindler for his ideas on domestic architecture:

"When we consider that we spend at least half of each day hours in the home, the importance of building a structure for health purposes is evident. In the past, such elements as beauty, convenience, and comfort have played the dominant parts. Houses for health are even yet relatively unknown. Mr. Schindler's views on house construction are of a daringly liberal kind. Our entire architecture would be changed to conform to a greater utility and to a larger purpose were we but to follow his teachings."[23]

In a series of six articles he wrote for Lovell's column, Schindler described some of the features a "house for health" should have. He was convinced that breathing air exhaled by others was chemically and bacteriologically unsound. In Southern California's benign climate houses needed only be an "open shelter against the rain." They could be built with thin walls, no attic, no furnace, and a maximum of fresh air circulation. To avoid the drafts from small window openings, the entire wall could be of sliding or casement glass windows.[24]

The sleeping basket, the canvas walls, and the lack of artificial heat called for a more rigorous devotion to natural living than most Southern Californians have been willing to endure, as was his insistence on natural materials — the gray concrete revealing impressions from the formwork, unfinished redwood wire-brushed to accentuate the grain, composition board, and glass. However, the introduction of this environmentally oriented architecture was an important contribution adopted in less dogmatic form by later architects.[25]

Even though their most noted commissions were from the financially well off, the architects of the '20s Modern movement shared a concern for the masses. They perceived that society's responsibility to provide adequate shelter also carried the larger challenge of satisfying the psychological needs of modern man in congested urban centers. Providing for privacy and individualism in housing that could be inexpensively mass-produced posed a problem that required innovative solutions.

Schindler's own small house, built on a very limited budget, was a laboratory experiment in solving this problem. His basic material was low-grade reinforced concrete, poured on the site in four-foot-wide slabs and raised into position. Irving Gill had used this tilt-slab method earlier in the Dodge house, which stood across the street from the Schindler-Chase residence. Some of the vertical three-inch spaces between panels were filled with masonry, others with opaque glass. The clerestory windows between the top of the concrete panels and the eaves permitted light and ventilation and a view of the treetops while excluding a view of traffic. The fact that they were formed of intervening space rather than by carving them from the structure, as windows have traditionally been created, reduced construction cost and created a spontaneous sense of continuous space. The interior walls were non-load-bearing movable partitions which permitted flexibility. The cantilevered beams which supported the roof and the eaveline of each of the three-walled rooms doubled as the track for sliding light fixtures and movable partitions. Economical in material and construction, efficient in function, and unified by the repetition of one simple form, the Schindler-Chase House pointed to the future. Schindler commented on its significance:

"The house is a simple weave of a few materials which retain their natural color and texture throughout. Each room in the house represents a variation on one structural and architectural theme. It is the beginning of a building system which a highly developed technical science will permit in the future."[26]

Schindler's later houses refined and brought to public attention the most successful elements of the Schindler-Chase experiment. Most of his commissions in the '20s and '30s were for small houses, usually of stucco, on hilly urban lots around Los Angeles. They helped popularize a number of new features for eventual acceptance at the vernacular level: the clerestory and casement windows, the glass curtain wall, the concrete surfaces, the thin cantilevered slab roof, the concrete floor extending out of doors. All of these were inexpensive, readily available, and aesthetically integrating features.

Restricting himself almost entirely to rectangular forms, with only the rare appearance of a curve or diagonal, Schindler's works of these two decades look like statues in motion. They are sculptural arrangements of volumes, advancing and receding in an asymmetrical but harmoniously balanced pattern. The relationship of volumes has a rhythm of its own, sometimes forming a flow of interlocked cubes poised in orderly descent down a steep hillside, sometimes in a surprising set of contrasting surface planes and recessed volumes. Often, interpenetrating planes form the horizontals of slab rooflines, parapets, a stylized lath patio roof, or strip windows. Occasionally a Schindler house is instead unified by a series of narrow vertical rectangles. The interlocking of the volumes, the eventual acknowledgment of balance and harmony of forms are knowing and confident.

Of all his completed projects, none receives more attention from today's architectural students and historians than the house he built for Dr. Phillip Lovell in Newport Beach south of Los Angeles in 1925-26 (ILLUSTRATION 119). Elevated above the beach on five pilotis, which are themselves pierced cubist planes, the Lovell Beach House is a cantilevered cube of glass and concrete slid apart to reveal constituent dark and light planes of glass and concrete. There is a clear relationship to the contemporary paintings of Mondrian and the De Stijl school — the asymmetrical placement of rectangular planes of unequal sizes,

119. Lovell Beach house,
1926

highlighted in contrasting values, to create a dynamic but harmonious balance between opposing parts. While the Lovell Beach House is ranked today beside the greatest works of Gropius, Le Corbusier, and Mies van der Rohe, it was not so influential in its own time as another house for the same client by architect Richard Neutra, completed in 1929.

How fitting it is that this house which drew Los Angeles into the spotlight on the international architectural stage, the Lovell Health House, should have been built for a health faddist and that it should have been designed by a recent arrival from Austria. In 1919, in Zurich, Richard Neutra had seen a travel poster with the slogan "California Calls You". The words reinforced a dream, conceived in his Vienna youth during his association with Adolf Loos (1912-1914), heightened by his exposure in 1914 to Frank Lloyd Wright's Portfolio, and hardened into an obsession that same year when his friend Rudolph Schindler left for America. Neutra wanted to make such a trip himself, to see first-hand the skyscrapers of New York City, the architectural monuments of Chicago, and the wonders of industrial society. Like his friend Schindler, he dreamed of apprenticing with Frank Lloyd Wright.

His plan, which might have been carried out after his graduation from the Vienna Technische Hochschule in 1915 under ordinary circumstances, had to be postponed because of the war. Correspondence with Schindler kept the dream alive. In 1919, the year Neutra saw the California poster, Schindler relocated to Hollywood to work on the Barnsdall commission. His letters described the climate, the lifestyle, and the opportunities for a young architect there. The visual picture of Los Angeles that Neutra formed from Schindler's descriptions contrasted vividly with his own surroundings in war-damaged Europe. California called.[27]

Finally, in 1923, his long efforts to obtain a visa were rewarded and at the age of 31 Neutra left his pregnant wife in Europe and sailed for New York. Once in Chicago he landed a position as draftsman with the pioneer skyscraper

Daring Originals

designers, Holabird and Roche, visited the architectural monuments of Wright's earlier Prairie period, and met the declining Louis Sullivan. In 1924 Neutra had a brief reunion with Schindler on the occasion of Mrs. Neutra's arrival from Europe. With Schindler's advice and encouragement, Neutra finally made contact with the peripatetic Frank Lloyd Wright. Wright invited the Neutras to settle at Taliesin, the workshop of the Master. They spent two pleasant and stimulating months there. The Neutras arrived in L.A. in February 1925.

120. Lovell Health house, 1929

Schindler met them at the railroad depot and took them to his house on Kings Road. They moved into the vacant Chase wing, and Richard Neutra joined Schindler's practice. His ten-year quest had been rewarded.

In 1928 Dr. Lovell was ready to build his primary dwelling in Los Angeles. As with his earlier Beach House, it was to be an experimental house where his theories about the relationship between environment and health could be demonstrated. Although he had been very pleased with the beach house Schindler had designed, he chose Neutra instead for the Los Angeles commission. The controversy over how and why this happened is less important than the fact that two houses for the same client, one by Schindler in Orange County, the other by Neutra in Los Angeles, are two of the most significant landmarks of Modern Architecture.[28]

The property Lovell had selected was a steep canyonside covered with natural vegetation. It commanded a spectacular view from Griffith Park to the Pacific Ocean. Neutra met the challenge of the site with steel frame technology — the first steel-frame house in America. A cage of steel, prefabricated off-site, was lowered section by section onto the site from the street above and bolted together in less than 40 hours. The two-and-a-half-story structure extended horizontally from the lip of the hill, its weight partially borne by ferro-concrete foundation and pilings. The form of the house was the undisguised steel structure itself, scantily wrapped in a thin skin of glass and shot-concrete to afford the basic amenities of privacy and shelter. The balconies extending beyond the steel frame were supported by wire cables from the roof structure above. The

218

asymmetrical surface pattern of concrete, glass, and void which reflected the functional arrangement of interior space, provided the aesthetic dynamics of a masterpiece (ILLUSTRATIONS 120 and 121).

The house joined the European theories of replicable, inexpensive, and efficient housing with the American realities of mass-produced, off-the-shelf building parts. The cool efficiency of a design based on industrially-fabricated, standardized parts is exemplified by the windows. Ordered from Sweet's building supply catalog, they were merely slipped into place in a steel-frame made to measure. Industrial technology and art had met and merged.

Neutra developed a theory of the interrelationship of architectural environment with physiological and psychological health which he termed "Biological Realism" or "Biorealism." The goal of domestic architecture, he felt, was to bring modern man back into a symbiotic harmony with nature. In later projects the transparent walls — wrapping around corners, incorporating waterways — eliminated the distinction between indoors and out. He came to use walls, moats and terraces as "tentacles of structure to catch or hook some surrounding feature of the land."[29]

He called for simplicity: minimization of shapes and materials, elimination of extraneous detail, a maximally functional layout. The unifying repetition of a few, crisp, geometric shapes was effected with economy and clarity by employing only three materials — concrete, steel, and glass. Interiors as well as exteriors were simplified to the point that they contained nothing unnecessary for comfort of the occupants, performance of human activities, and harmony with the site. With each client, Neutra developed a detailed study of personal habits, lifestyle, and goals. Every possession was accorded a place; every habit was accommodated; every housekeeping peccadillo was minimized.

121. Detail of Lovell Health house

Neutra's creative vision could not have been carried out so effectively in any other part of the United States but urban Southern California. The thin walls and extensive use of glass were meant for life in this temperate climate. The flat roofs, so essential to the architect's aesthetic expression, were possible in an area of little rain and no snow. The balcony and garden extensions of living space and the use of landscaping to tie together the structural elements on the site were local architectural traditions. It was more than climate, however, that inspired Neutra. There were the Angelenos.

Neutra's biographer, Thomas Hines, quotes Neutra's appreciation of the selective settlement of Southern California as a source of clientele:

"[in] Southern California, I found what I had hoped for, a people who were more 'mentally footloose' than those elsewhere, who did not mind deviating opinions...where one can do most anything that comes to mind and is good fun. All this seemed to me a good climate for trying something independent of hidebound habituation..."[30]

The characteristics of Neutra's work quickly associated him with "the International school" architects Walter Gropius, Ludwig Mies van der Rohe, and Le Corbusier. The Lovell Health House radiates the same cool, crisp logic, the same dedication to rational order, the same quiet confidence as the best of their work. Like theirs, it gave no voice to emotional expression or stagy illusions — it was a pure articulation of technological functionalism. Gropius summed up the new ideals so well exemplified by the Lovell Health House:

"Spatial harmony, repose, proportion are the conditions which animate and humanize a building. They must be ideals of architecture. In the progress of our advance [toward] the dictates of structural logic, we have learned to seek concrete expression of the life of our epoch in clear and crisply simplified forms. The New Architecture throws open its walls like curtains to admit a plenitude of fresh air, daylight and sunshine....not in stylistic imitation or ornamental frippery, but in those simple and sharply modeled designs in which every part merges naturally into the comprehensive volume of the whole. Thus its aesthetic meets our material and psychological requirements alike."[31]

Dr. Lovell loved the house. He devoted his newspaper column to describing it and its accommodation to the lifestyle he advocated. As a demonstration of his environmental theories, he invited the public to guided tours of the house upon its completion. Fifteen thousand Angelenos accepted Lovell's invitation, proof of local receptivity to avant-garde designs for living.[32]

The consequent newsworthiness of the house and its architect soon reached international proportions. Richard Neutra, in contrast to the modest Gill and the individualistic Schindler, was a diligent and successful self-promoter. In 1930 Neutra completed a book proclaiming his architectural ideals, largely illustrated by the Lovell Health House, and then set off on a world tour. En route to Brussels to attend the meeting of CIAM (The International Congress of Modern Architecture), he visited first Japan and then each of the European cities where Modern architecture had already been successfully recognized.

Everywhere, his books, acclaim in professional journals, and his own lectures won him fame and further invitations. He served as guest lecturer at the

Bauhaus. He met the industrialist and patron of Modernism, C.H. Van der Leeuw, who would later commission Neutra to build an experimental house in L.A., and he developed personal ties with other leaders of Modern architecture.[33]

Shortly after he returned to Los Angeles, New York's Museum of Modern Art opened its epochal exhibit, "Modern Architecture". Neutra was one of the five American architects featured in the exhibit. Schindler was not.[34] By this time, Richard Neutra was a celebrity, and particularly cherished in Los Angeles. By the mid-1930s, Neutra enjoyed the busy design practice that fame had brought him. Neutra's 1930s residential clients included several film industry insiders: director Josef von Sternberg (a 1935 house later acquired by writer Ayn Rand), director Eugene Frenke, film editor Leon Barsha, screenwriter Anita Loos, film score composer Edward Kaufman, and writer-director Albert Lewin. Another in this elite was Galka Scheyer, psychologist and art collector.

It is also noteworthy how many of his commissions were for scientists and teachers: Charles Richter (the Cal Tech professor who "fathered" the earthquake measurement scale) was one. Others taught economics, science, physical education, and art at Cal Tech, Occidental College, and other local institutions. The technical precision, the emphasis on functionalism and the status of high art appealed to a select clientele. The crisp, clean look and the operational efficiency of Neutra's buildings won him many commissions for commercial, educational, and civic buildings to the point that their appearance was accepted as the ubiquitous norm.

Fame and commissions also brought followers. Among those architects who studied under Neutra and went on to become leaders in their own right were Gregory Ain, Harwell Harris, Raphael Soriano and (indirectly) Craig Ellwood. Gregory Ain designed the Edwards House seen in ILLUSTRATIONS 122, 123 and 124. Ain had studied under both Schindler and Neutra, and this early

122. Detail of Edwards house, 1935-36

123. Detail of Edwards house

124. Detail of Edwards house

work reflects both masters, as well as Ain's own creative originality.

In 1935, Pauline Schindler, in the role of guest editor of a special edition of California Arts and Architecture devoted to modern architecture, had recognized the special affinity of the Los Angeles cultural scene and architecture's daring originals:

"California has an astounding sum of significant creative work; no region of the United States has a greater number of outstanding and internationally known architects building modern houses. Among the reasons for this is certainly the freshness, the newness, of this coastal civilization, its freedom from inhibiting tradition, its readiness to experiment. This perhaps is why so large a proportion of modern work is to be found in the southern part of California.... Gradually, however, the spirit of the new architecture, with its simplification of forms to their essentials, its freedom from irrelevant ornament, its functional candor of line and mass, pervades new regions."[35]

Simplification and elimination of ornament also reduced cost, and Depression era economics encouraged further experiments in Modernism, including a vernacular form referred to as Streamline Moderne. The great Depression began in 1929 and reached its nadir in 1932. The personal values so prominent in the '20s, having a good time, acquiring material things, living for the moment, and the attendant wish to believe that a day of reckoning would never come were useless in the face of unemployment, lost investments, and foreclosures. A great many who had pursued success with every expectation of betterment found themselves suddenly destitute. Those who lost jobs and savings suffered from feelings of helplessness and insecurity, embarrassment, anger, despair or bewilderment. All worried. Some sought panaceas, other scapegoats. Some withdrew from reality into a fantasy world; and some stoically refused to get ruffled, resolving to make it through somehow.

Houses and housing patterns in Los Angeles during the Depression reveal several forms of withdrawal syndrome. The Edwards house (ILLUSTRATION 122) illustrates one of those forms. C. H. Edwards was in the hardware business. In 1936 he hired a young architect just establishing his practice, Gregory Ain, to build a two-bedroom house on a small hillside lot on a narrow, winding street above Hollywood. The total cost is said to have been $7,000, of which $700 was the architect's fee. The side view of the house reveals a set of pleasant patios, one for each bedroom, which extended room space beyond confining walls. ILLUSTRATION 123 shows the front of the same house. Other than the frosted glass shoji panel in the entry, the only window on the public side of the house is a round porthole on the blank wall hedge-hidden from our view. The house allowed its owners to shut out the threatening times and withdraw behind a terse mask that divulged nothing about its occupants' dreams, emotions, or identity.[36]

Here, a middle class merchant chose an architecture which met all his own needs, yet acknowledged no obligation to conform to social expectations such as an unused front yard, windows that breached privacy, or historical staginess in styling. Presenting a stoic minimalism on the exterior, the house had an interior which permitted an open and pleasant life for its hidden occupants. ILLUSTRATION 124 shows the back of the house: a wall of glass. Ain had worked for both Schindler and Neutra. That he learned from each, and went beyond their ideas, is evident in this first, completed project. The living room and dining room compose a three-walled pavilion curtained with panels of glass which can be opened if desired. The playroom, on the left, extends the transparent walls beyond the building, forming a box of glass, ceiling and all. Beyond a small swimming pool and lily pond, the backyard drops off to a steep canyon, leaving an unobstructed view of the Los Angeles Basin by day and a sea of city lights by night. Ain wrapped three sides of the house in a subtropical environment with plantings of avocado, orange, palm, and jacaranda trees. By contrast, the street facade's landscaping was restricted to unadorned rectangles of lawn, bracketed by cedar hedges which extended down the side boundaries. The patio gardens on the bedroom side, their privacy assured by the hedges, became Schindlerian outdoor living rooms. The interior rooms radiate from the entryway with wide openings to facilitate human interaction.

In the 1910s, the California Bungalow had opened up the house form, facilitating an easy flow from the inside to the outside. In the 1920s, popular historical fantasy houses had postured to attract outsiders' attention into the supposed doings of occupants inside. The Edwards house, as did many others in the 1930s, turned an inhospitable back to the passerby and opened up the real use of the house only in the interior and the rear-facing elements for its residents to enjoy in private, privileged seclusion. Nevertheless, this particular idea exhibits several clues of a not unhealthy form of withdrawal from society: the stark simplicity and avant-garde modernity attest to a sense of confidence; the openness of rooms and ease of flow inside, the glass wall extension of the living environment to a panoramic view, testify to individuals who are at ease with themselves and within the family group. The occupant re-entering the uncertain mainstream each morning from this tranquil retreat came renewed for coping with the day's troubles. The closed forms created a few years before by Frank Lloyd Wright and his son had expressed insecurity and escapism in

Daring Originals

claustrophobic entries, a maze of hallways, and busy surface patterns. The impassive austerity of the Edwards facade gives way to entirely open forms, expressing a confident wait-out, an avoidance of senseless confrontation, a rational serenity.

By the late '30s, the economy had severely restricted building activity locally as well as nationwide. Even in those cities like Los Angeles where some individuals could still contemplate new houses, thrift was a leading consideration; it had become an important social value once again. As we have seen, a thrifty reductionism was applied even to the favored fantasy styles like mock Tudor. Of the houses that were added to the Los Angeles scene during the lean decade, a remarkable number were Streamline Moderne. It was economical, it was modern-looking (the popular word was "modernistic"), and it emanated much the same message as the Edwards house. ILLUSTRATIONS 125 and 126 give us two vernacular versions of this 1930s style.

Since the late 19th-century, naval architects and physicists had investigated the principles of airflow, fluids in motion, and wind resistance. The wind tunnel was invented as an instrument for studying these phenomena. The new sciences of hydrodynamics and aerodynamics had appeared in the curricula of advanced institutions such as M.I.T.. These sciences led to the cigar-like shape of the Zeppelin airships, oceanliners, German U-boats, and wind-tunnel tested automobile prototypes. The new forms were described by the term "streamlined", meaning those shapes discovered to offer the least resistance while in motion; the word came from the "stream lines" that formed around an object in a wind tunnel. In the public mind, streamlining indicated man's technological thrust into the future.[37]

Between 1927 and 1934, American industries, in an attempt to boost sales in a flagging economy, employed former theatrical set designers, advertising illustrators and others who began terming themselves "industrial designers." They were hired to update the external appearance of consumer products such as camera bodies, radio sets, and toasters. Although refrigerators and pencil sharpeners are not normally mobile objects, the new aerodynamic principles, as well as the term "streamlined", was applied to their housings: all extraneous details were eliminated; curves were employed to merge one element into the next to prevent wind-resistant sharp angles. One of the early industrial designers preferred the term "cleanlining" for this kind of design. Often without change to the inside works of a product, the new external look caused sales to shoot up by factors of four, five, even seven. Why? Advertisers throughout the '20s had programmed the American public to appreciate newness, fast pace, and certainty

125. Ulm house, 1939

as appropriate factors in selective purchasing. The Depression was teaching two additional shopping criteria: efficiency and economy. The streamlined image appealed to all these consumer values. A kitchen toaster that looked really new, unlike any previous toaster; that had rounded edges and flush-mounted controls suitable to high-speed projectiles; and which made a statement of bold, unified coherence — looked better to the customer, even if it toasted bread no better than the older model.[38]

By the mid-'30s, the streamlined look was regularly appearing in Los Angeles architecture. Not only did it emerge as the most popular style for local commercial buildings from the mid-'30s to the mid-'40s, but it was a major choice of house and apartment builders.[39] To this day, Los Angeles retains an unusually large stock of Streamline Moderne architecture. Moderne houses are invariably simple stucco boxes, originally colored white or near-white as if to emphasize their message of antiseptic cleanliness. Their severely plain exterior wall surfaces were controlled and unified by narrow banding at the top. Their rounded corners and curved walls were an architectural obeisance to the principles of aerodynamic engineering. Their transportation motifs, especially the metal ship railing and portholes, were carried inside with nautical bathroom decor and compact built-in furniture reminiscent of ocean-liner cabins. They utilized the newest industrial products: glass block, linoleum, plywood, chromium plated steel, vitrolite, bakelite, magnesite, and Monel (an alloy of primarily nickel and copper). Steel casement windows were standard to the style, and thin horizontal slab canopies often projected over focal windows and doors. Private decks and balconies were tucked here and there in asymmetrical overall schemes.

The two examples we selected illustrate these features well. The Ulm

126. Hamilton house, 1941

house, ILLUSTRATION 125, was built in 1937 on a steep hillside lot near Griffith Park. The glass blocks of the foreground tower pour light into the curving magnesite stairwell inside, yet shielding the occupants from the clamorous world. Pipe railings surround private patio decks. Steel frame windows, thin canopy projections, and a banded parapet roofline are common to both the Ulm house and the smaller Hamilton house seen in ILLUSTRATION 126. This house, built near Douglas Aircraft in 1941 after the local recovery from the Depression was well under way, is still a pristine example of the Streamline Moderne years after its original palm trees had grown out of sight.[40]

While one factor in the style's popularity was its close relationship to the well-known architects of the International School and their acclaimed masterpieces — made comprehensible, even whimsical, to the public by recognizable similarities to modern modes of transportation, the new style also related to a popular form of fantasy literature.[41] Science fiction was popular in the '30s because it provided an escape from present realities to another time frame, just as romanticized historical fiction did. Escape from reality to a make-believe world is a passive form of withdrawal, as well as a source of delight and entertainment. Science fiction had appeared in comic strips such as "Buck Rogers", not coincidentally, in the first year of the Depression.[42] Like comic characters' space ships, Streamline houses had appeared on the scene. Houses are stationary objects. Is there any valid point in reshaping a house corner to the curve we see in the Hamilton house? In a moving object, such a design reduces friction and permits higher speed with less energy expenditure. In a house it becomes an artificial, purely aesthetic touch. Is it possible that some Angelenos who selected this style for their residences wished to imagine themselves on a world cruise, or were they thinking of farther flights of fancy in their aerodynamically advanced machines?

Streamline Moderne, and its more sophisticated relative, the high-art monuments of Modernism, convey contradictory messages of escapist fantasies and of confidence. But at all levels, the modern houses of the '30s expressed confidence in technological solutions to the human problems of their times. Streamlining permitted trains, ships, cars and planes to travel more rapidly, to operate more economically, to provide smoother, quieter rides. The streamlined house reflected these themes. It appeared to be a machine in motion, a well-tuned transportation machine headed purposefully into the future. The simplicity, the well-planned economy of function, space and material that characterized the Moderne house reassured a generation awakened to the values of thrift, utility, and efficiency. The house imparted a sense of smoothness, of cool unflappability, that was desirable in times of crisis. Complexities were erased, angular movement in conflicting directions reshaped to a smooth, guided flow. Undercurrents of emotional significance to colors were replaced with a clean, laboratory white. The streamlined house imparted a renewed confidence that man, utilizing technology, was in control of his emotions, his environment, and his destiny. Modernism looked to the future rather than dwelling in a nostalgic past.

At the end of the decade, the Eastern architecture critic, Henry-Russell Hitchcock, summed up West Coast modernism: "...what appears most promising is the general consistency of aims combined with a wide variety of means and the extent to which the essentials of plan and structure and expression are already established and even to a certain degree accepted by the public."[43]

CHAPTER

XII

ORDINARY DREAMS

. . . I like to think how nice

it's gonna be, maybe, in California.

Never cold. An' fruit ever' place,

an' people just bein' in

the nicest places, little white houses

in among the orange trees.

I wonder — that is, if we all get jobs

an' all work — maybe we can

get one of them little white houses."[25]

HENRY-RUSSELL HITCHCOCK HAD GOOD REASON for his optimistic assessment of Los Angeles in 1940.[1] L.A.'s low-rise profile, low-density, pattern of single-family houses, and its extended suburbs accommodating all social levels had resulted from careful planning. Los Angeles' suburban lifestyle stood as the model for students of city planning elsewhere. L.A. had by far the highest percentage of single-family detached houses of any industrial city in the nation, at comparable cost to less desirable living quarters elsewhere.[2] To guarantee the permanence of this ideal lifestyle, planning pioneers had very early on imposed zoning and height restrictions on the city representing a conscious commitment to horizontal growth, open space, and the suburban way of life. As early as 1904, after an exhaustive study by a special committee, the Los Angeles City Council legislated a building height limit, varying from 55 feet to 150 feet, depending on the class of construction and intended function of the building. Later locked into the City Charter to prevent variances, it remained in effect until 1957, dictating the future look of Los Angeles. The only exceptions were City Hall, completed in 1928, and a 1925 amendment permitting height variances in industrial zones outside the central district.[3]

In 1909, Progressive activism had led Los Angeles to set up zoning restrictions (distinct from nuisance-abatement acts such as ordinances against saloons or pool halls); it was the first City in the nation to do so. Between 1909 and 1915 successive legislative acts had divided the City into three zoning categories: one open to any kind of industry, one restricted to residences, and one which permitted both residences and certain kinds of light industry. The effect was the creation of islands of industrial activity, with the bulk of the city dedicated to purely residential use. By 1922 the City had developed comprehensive zoning ordinances that spelled out building construction codes, proportion of open space to building footage, height, specific minimal sanitary facilities, and setbacks of buildings from property lines.[4] These dictated the way the 1923 industrial and population boom would affect the city.

Until the 1920s, Los Angeles had not been known as a factory town. But behind the scenes of the movie-set town, Los Angeles was becoming an industrial center. Each of L.A.'s three novel industries — oil, aircraft, and motion pictures — had spawned subsidiaries, such as pipeline and drilling equipment; aircraft engines, gaskets, and sheet metal; cosmetics, fashion garments, and photographic equipment, respectively. Other industries and an expanding service trade followed. Between 1920 and 1939, Los Angeles experienced more rapid manufacturing development than any other region in the nation. The manufactured product value for the City of Los Angeles, which had been $103,457,993 in 1914, was $610,166,093 by 1927, an increase of 490 per cent. By the mid '20s, balanced prosperity, the goal of the business community's crusade to attract new industries, had been achieved. Employment opportunities expanded rapidly at every level.[5]

Newcomers poured in, filling industry's expanding employment opportunities and increasing the local market for goods and services even further. The exuberant expansion of the 1920s saw the population of the City of Los Angeles leap from 576,673 to 1,238,048 in one decade. The spread of suburban development meant an even higher growth rate for the County as a whole: in 1920 it had a population of 936,455; by 1930, 2,208,492.[6]

By 1923 the region was drawing not only prospective investors and factory owners, but a crowd of blue-collar job-seekers as well. Work in foundries and assembly plants might not seem glamorous to everyone, but the security of plentiful job opportunities, coupled with prospects of home ownership, seemed ideal to many. Such hopes differed from the rebellious dreams which had formed the major building blocks of the City of Angels for so long. Generations of newcomers had been pulled to Los Angeles by the strength of restless imaginations. The new group was as much pushed as they were pulled. Disadvantages at home, paired with new economic opportunities in Los Angeles formed a classic demographic catalyst. The housing that sprang up around the new industrial centers in Southern California was not only tailored to the workingman's wallet, it was stylistically reflective of a new set of prosaic hopes for adequacy, security, and domestic contentment. These newcomers were perhaps not expecting a new life in a turreted castle or a Spanish hacienda. Minimal marks of style, such as the slightest hint of Colonial or Tudor or Mediterranean influence in the trim of a porch or the treatment of a window, were enough. Small houses, so scant on imagination they could have blended into much less exciting towns than Los Angeles nevertheless, represented dreams as brilliant as those of any castle-builder. A safe harbor, freedom from need and the most basic of living conditions could be glorious ends in themselves.

One might think that new, laboring-class arrivals to Los Angeles would search out inexpensive down-at-the-heels lodgings, even slums, to serve as home until savings could be built up. However, Los Angeles did not have the backlog of dilapidated housing of older industrial cities, partly because many of the immigrants prior to 1925 had been retirees, white-collar workers, glamour-seekers, and highly-paid, skilled construction workers. Office workers lodged modestly in the numerous apartments and boarding houses profitably constructed in the first two decades of the century near downtown and still in good condition in the 1920s. (ILLUSTRATION 47). There had been little demand for sub-minimal housing or shacks. Furthermore, the newness of the city found few old and shabby neighborhoods ripe for conversion to slums by the '20s or '30s.⁷ The pattern of city building, with available open land surrounding the

127. SouthCentral L.A. Bungalow tract, 1923

city's core that could be subdivided into new tracts priced at rates accommodating low incomes, also worked against the formulation of slums.

Developers' decisions about curved or gridded street layout, sewer line diameter, and the size of lots and garages predetermined occupancy, as did decisions about construction quality, house size, and degree of ornamentation. In areas zoned for combination residence and light industry entire tracts of gridded streets were laid out where cheaply constructed houses with few trimmings, each with its single-car garage, were built. Such housing was within reach of a factory worker's budget (ILLUSTRATIONS 76, 108, and 127).⁸

The constraint of distance from work places was overcome in time for the 1920s boom by the extension of streetcar lines and of paved streets for now

Ordinary Dreams

mass-produced automobiles. Books about Los Angeles rarely failed to mention the omnipresent garage, even in the most modest tract developments: "...seemingly endless sections of unpretentious but attractive small houses, each with its own pocket handkerchief of lawn and flower-bed, and, incidentally, its garage."[9]

The building boom and competition among tract developers reduced prices to the point where most wage earners could afford to buy, or at least rent, their own single-family residences. There was a brisk resale and rental market for the previous decade's bungalows, as their original occupants "traded up" for new houses in more distant suburbs.[10] This transfer made available good home buys for factory workers and minorities who could never have hoped to own houses in Eastern mill towns and Southern rural communities. Although the prevailing anti-union stand of L.A. merchants and manufacturers kept wages lower than they were in many other cities, the lower costs of heating and building made tight budgets manageable. Even the lowest wage earner could expect to find: "living expenses considerably less...if he joined the ranks of the great majority of his fellows, bought a bungalow on easy terms and became a home owner. He became...a capitalist. He expected to sell his home at a profit, so it seemed. That produced an interesting psychological effect in the city; even the workers were boomers and boosters."[11]

A wave of new Angelenos began to buy up the bungalow tracts in the 1920s (ILLUSTRATION 127). A 1923 advertisement for a nearby tract of new houses appealed to workers: compact conveniences, a garage, and capitalist prospects. The tract of four- and five-room houses was named "Goodyear Park" because it was next to the Goodyear Tire factory at Florence and Central.

> "PERFECT HOMES $600 DOWN,
> $40 PER MONTH, 5c CAR FARE
> ...modern in every particular and built either of stucco or wood. Each
> has garage, cement drive and walks, gas, electricity and water.
> Hardwood floors throughout. Pullman breakfast nook and all proven
> built-in conveniences.
> Profits as high as 400% on resales are being taken in this wonderful
> subdivision. Here you can save rent and make money on increasing land
> values."[12]

A tiny palm tree was planted in front of each house. Today, the palms rise tall above the houses: they are L.A.'s trademark vista from freeways and

MOVIE STARS AND HARD TIMES

inbound airplanes. A contemporary writer sketched the dream life that drew buyers to houses like these:

"On his lot, the wage earner could have a garden or keep some chickens....He could have a lawn, some trees. The family maintained a flower garden. He bought a small automobile, and the family used it daily on the good roads, in all seasons, because of the good weather. The family lived an out-of-door life, was healthy and happy. There were the beaches that they could reach one week end, the mountains they could visit the next.... Out here everybody made a new start. For the time being, at least, everybody was equal. The spirit of the place was contagious. In less time that it took to realize it, the newcomer had become a Southern Californian and was beckoning to others to come and join in the fun of life in the sunshine."[13]

The dynamic metamorphosis of Los Angeles into a thriving industrial center, while providing job openings in factories for mainstream workmen and farmers' sons, also opened opportunities in transportation and service work for other newcomers in the 1920s, including Blacks. L.A. had had a Black minority for over two centuries: four of the eleven family heads who had founded the settlement in 1781 had been *negro* or *mulato*. In line with L.A.'s Spanish Myth their descendants and city publicists preferred to downplay that fact, so we have wrongly come to think of all Black Angelenos as later migrants from the American South. The 1910 census reported 2.4% of the Los Angeles City population as Black.

Few Blacks moved from the Southern states (where 90% of Black Americans lived until 1910) to the far West before the First World War.[14] The cost of transportation was high and the poverty of Southern Blacks was severe. None of the tourist literature was aimed at them, nor was it easily accessible to rural Black Southerners. Chinese, Japanese, Mexicans, and, later, Filipinos already filled the lowest-paying jobs in California. Most Southern Blacks who fled the economically troubled South prior to the Depression headed for the band of Northern industrial cities east of the Mississippi. Especially after the onset of the European war in 1914, which curtailed the supply of cheap immigrant labor, industrial recruiters actively promoted what has been called the "Great Migration" of Blacks from the South to the cities of the North.[15]

Between 1915 and 1918, a series of economic disasters hit the Deep South. The tide of displaced Black Southerners who had responded to job opportunities in Northeastern and North-Central industrial centers found themselves compressed into ghettos and increasingly subjected to antagonism over strike-breaking controversies and neighborhood segregation. Race riots in

Illinois and New York in 1917 preceded 39 riots in other urban centers in the next two years. It was then that Black attention was drawn to what Los Angeles offered.[16]

Before World War I, Blacks in Los Angeles were dispersed throughout the city, living in dwellings ranging from racially-mixed, working-class rooming houses, to small cottages, aging Victorians, and on up to the imposing houses of Black physicians, lawyers, and real estate entrepreneurs. However, inexpensive land toward the southwestern edge of town had brought enough settlers of color by the turn of the century to make the Ninth Ward a center of Black Republican political strength. By 1920, the growing number of Black-owned businesses along Central Avenue made it the 30-block spine of a significant Black community. Central Avenue connected Los Angeles proper with the independent community of Watts, where many new arrivals settled in the 1920s.[17] A 1913 reporter declared:

"[The Blacks of Los Angeles are] without doubt the most beautifully housed group of colored people in the United States. They are full of push and energy and are used to working together....I saw the business establishments of the colored people. There was a splendid merchant tailor shop with a large stock of goods...a contractor who was putting up some of the best buildings in the city with colored workmen; physicians, lawyers and dentists with offices in first-class buildings and, above all, homes — beautiful homes."[18]

The Los Angeles Black press and a number of Black realtors and preachers began to spread the word: Los Angeles was a new Promised Land. Although Black employment opportunities in skilled factory, sales, and professional positions were, in fact, meager in Los Angeles in the 1920s, rumors and beliefs to the contrary stimulated a dramatic influx of Blacks during the '30s. Among the basis for this powerful set of beliefs were the positive reports from acquaintances and relatives and an initially higher employment rate. Blacks here earned three to four times what rural Southern Blacks could make, a wage comparable to the highest wages available in Northern urban centers. Then too, the State of California, and the County of Los Angeles in particular, paid higher unemployment relief than most states of immigrant origin. Although by mid-decade residency qualifications barred many newcomers, earlier reports lingered in the belief structures of the California-bound. The persistence of these rumors was facilitated by the lack of racial friction of headline proportions. The Black population of Los Angeles more than doubled from 1910 to 1920, continuing with a higher rate of Black immigration than White during the Depression. Of the total City population of 1,238,048 in 1930, Blacks accounted for 3.1%, or

38,894. In 1940 the total City figure was 1,504,277, of which 4.2%, or 63,774 were Black.[19]

Housing was the single most attractive aspect of the vision guiding Blacks to Los Angeles during the hard times of the '30s. The widely reported ability of Black Angelenos to purchase a house, either for their own residence, or for investment as a rental property or profitable resale, was unparalleled: historian Lawrence De Graaf found that in 1930 over one-third of L.A.'s Black families owned their own houses, whereas only 10.5 percent in Chicago, 15 percent in Detroit, and 5.6% in New York did so. The possession of a neat bungalow, on a pleasant avenue, similar to those in ILLUSTRATION 127, represented a rare opportunity for Black advancement, pride, and dignity. Upper middle-class Blacks formed model neighborhoods. True urban slums did not develop, even where barriers of prejudice, restrictive covenants, and discriminatory laws confined Blacks to crowded sections. Single-family, low-density land-use patterns prevailed.[20] Most were neatly kept, the streets were clean and wide, lawns were green, and a sense of community prevailed — and does to this day, albeit with bars on the windows.

Mexican immigrants and their families formed another distinct element of the Los Angeles populace, some 30,000 strong in 1920. Some were recruited laborers, others came as refugees from the Mexican revolution of 1910-1917. Their dwelling places signified the temporary quality of their residence or the haste of their relocation to Los Angeles.

Beginning about 1900 and peaking in 1912, the Southern Pacific and Santa Fe Railroads had sent recruiting agents into Mexico, at times providing special-rate boxcar transportation to El Paso on its Mexican subsidiary lines, to entice laborers to cross the international border, where they could sign 6-month work contracts without violating federal contract labor laws. From Texas, Mexican workers were brought by rail to whatever line needed cheap laborers. They worked for wages lower than the going rate, and they worked hard. By 1906 two and three boxcar loads of laborers (*cholos*) were being brought into Southern California per week. The Pacific Electric streetcar system was largely built by their labor.

As late as 1930, 70% of the section crews and 90% of the extra gangs on the western railroad systems were Mexicans. Such workers lived in railroad work camps at the construction sites. These usually consisted of temporary clusters of tents and boxcars at first. In some locations the rail companies later built more permanent row-houses. Since much railroad work is seasonal, and — in those days of new construction — temporary, the Mexican rail worker would

Ordinary Dreams

find himself looking for other work, often in agriculture, where he became the preferred, underpaid, seasonal employee of agribusiness. The rail camps gave rise to the formation of many *colonias* (colonies) and *barrios* (neighborhoods) in the Los Angeles area. Around the initial camp site, Mexican rail workers, ex-employees, acquaintances, and relatives would buy or squat on small lots and build their own shacks. For example, the town of Watts had a sizable Hispanic population at one time, traceable to a 1906 rail camp for the construction of the Pacific Electric line.[21]

By the end of the First World War, the systematic importation of Mexican laborers was superseded by waves of dispossessed refugees from the violent revolution which raged in Mexico from 1910 to 1917. Some were disappointed that the dreams and visions for which they had fought proved slow to materialize and nearly all were desperate victims of an agrarian economy in such a state of disarray that survival itself was in question for those who stayed. The appearance of thousands, eventually tens of thousands, of field workers willing to work hard for little pay was a blessing for California's major growers.

The timing was perfect, coinciding with the decline in the number of Chinese due to immigration restrictions and the trend toward self-employment by the Japanese, both of whom had served as the main sources of agricultural employees before 1917. By 1919, nearly a third of the workers in the citrus industry was Mexican. By the mid-'20s, an average of 58,000 Mexican field workers poured into California's Central Valley each year for temporary employment. Between crops, especially in the winter months, the seasonally unemployed field workers found their way to California towns where there were existing pockets of Mexican residents, where Spanish was spoken, where relatives and acquaintances might make room for more, where markets and churches and cultural patterns were comfortably familiar. Los Angeles was the primary destination of this seasonal influx.[22]

For many of them, home here would consist of two tiny, overcrowded rooms (1.73 to 2.22 average persons per room) in a house court. A typical house court was described in a 1920 study: 26 two-room habitations were located in three rows (10 units in one row, 4 units and the two restroom structures in a center row, and 12 units in the third) on a grassless lot 80 by 145 feet. These house courts were popularly called "cholo courts." A 1913 study found that one of the worst and dirtiest of these was a Southern Pacific Railroad court on New High Street.

"The [units] are constructed of rough 1x12 pine boards with battened cracks. Thin board partitions... separate one habitation from the other.

MOVIE STARS AND HARD TIMES

The plumbing ...consists of 6 hydrants with hoppers connected with the sewer, 1 hydrant without hopper and 4 double flush toilets [in the two structures located in the center of the court]. There is one window in each room of each habitation. One room is used for a kitchen and the other for living and sleeping."

Other newcomers from Mexico set up housekeeping in shacks built from crates and scrap lumber or in the deteriorating remains of work camps left behind from railroad construction days. A 1920 study of Mexican residences of the city found that 28% had no sinks, 32% did not have indoor toilets, and 79% did not have a bath tub.[23] The shacks and small communities (*barrios*) were physically isolated by river, railroad tracks, or walls from the majority community. Relegated to out-of-the-way locations not often passed by Anglo Angelenos, few recognized that Los Angeles between the wars was once again becoming an important Mexican town. Their dwellings were later razed to make way for low-cost public housing projects, erased from the cityscape. To us, today, looking for architectural clues to the waves of incoming people who have contributed to Los Angeles, their disappearance is misleading. But the people were here and they did come with dreams.

In the years surrounding World War I, another group of minorities, this time from Europe, arrived: Russian, Armenian, Jewish and other victims of war, economic distress, and persecution emigrated to Los Angeles, many of them skilled craftsmen, artists, or professionals. Some had life savings with them, while others, particularly the Jewish immigrants from Eastern Europe and New York, were assisted by local resettlement organizations. Many moved into the small, older houses and a group of new rooming houses in the harbor area, Crown Heights, Beaudry Hill as well as Boyle Heights — a once sophisticated 1870s suburb just across the river from the Civic Center. The older neighborhoods, where few ethnic barriers existed, changed not in looks, but in culture, with the new inhabitants. The small but charming 1880s cottage in ILLUSTRATION 37 might have enshrined the new generation of immigrant hopes in multi-ethnic Los Angeles.

As their Americanized offspring and their own economic security matured, these ethnic minorities dispersed geographically. By the 1930 census, the foreign-born owned more houses per capita than any other segment of the Los Angeles population. Whether because their cultural memories were too bitter to build replicas of home, or because, in the case of Jewish history, of centuries of experience at adapting to majority dictates in urban housing styles, the houses they built were indistinguishable from those of their American-born neighbors. Census records were the only way to discern ethnicity: Russians,

European Jews, Armenians and other minorities were invisible to one searching for social clues in residential forms. At least in terms of dwelling places, our targets for learning of the dreams of new groups, they had assimilated completely.[24]

A group very different from the educated Europeans in culture and social status, but also fleeing to Los Angeles as a safe haven, was the "Okies," farmers from the Southern Great plains states dispossessed by the Dust Bowl conditions of the '30s. They chose California because they wanted farm work. Since California was the most prosperous agricultural state in the Union, all believed they could find jobs there, or at least a warm place to sleep outdoors. Just as important, they chose California because they believed in a picture of paradise created by years of publicity, and motion picture rumors. Ma Joad, the matriarch in Steinbeck's The Grapes of Wrath gave voice to the dream:

"...I like to think how nice it's gonna be, maybe, in California. Never cold. An' fruit ever'place, an' people just bein' in the nicest places, little white houses in among the orange trees. I wonder — that is, if we all get jobs an' all work — maybe we can get one of them little white houses."[25]

Dust Bowl conditions brought an estimated 375,000 homeless to California during the '30s. They made up a third of the state's population increase, with most arriving more or less as a group from 1935 to 1938. That fact, along with their poverty, their regional speech patterns and their social customs, set them apart and made them seem more numerous than they actually were. They headed for the major growing regions, especially the San Joaquin Valley, but also Los Angeles County, which at that time was important in citrus, grape, dairy, and vegetable production. Unlike the Mexican field hands, whom they largely replaced, they had brought their families with them. In spite of preferential hiring, there were too many for the number of field jobs. Clusters of near-destitute families camped alongside rural ditch banks, sleeping on the ground, sometimes in tents, sometimes with blankets strung between trees for privacy; cooking over open fires or oil-drum stoves; and drinking polluted water, thus subject to disease. They were cold, muddy and miserable in rainy weather, dirty and despairing the rest of the time. Local officials tried to destroy the dirt bank settlements and routed their inhabitants, but they relocated. As it became apparent to the newcomers that their poverty and migrant status would not be as temporary as they had hoped, "Little Oklahomas," as migrant camps were sometimes called, more frequently located around the edges of towns, where the migrants hoped their children could at least attend school.

In the Los Angeles area, there was no distinction between the "Little

Oklahomas" (such as those in Sawtelle and in Bell Gardens) and the "Hoovervilles," the popular term for the huddled makeshift shelters at the edges of towns and cities where the urban homeless took refuge. Long-time County Supervisor John Anson Ford recalled the daily arrival of bands of underfed boys who rode the rails or hitchhiked into L.A., and the innumerable unemployed men of all ages who drifted in singly. For each of them, removal from home had left one less mouth to feed. They were lured by the rumors of jobs and, failing jobs, at least the certainty of warmer weather in which to sleep in doorways or under cardboard shelters. Besides, they had been exposed to three decades of "Ramona"-style, romantic orange-crate pictures certifying plentiful fruit throughout Southern California, implying that surely one could neither freeze nor starve in the City of Angels. Overnight, communities of packing crates and cardboard sprang up in empty lots and along railroad tracks.[26] Homelessness confirmed the bitter reality: the Great Depression had taken the place of the Roaring Twenties.

The kind of people who had for years been coming to Los Angeles were exactly those worst equipped to cope with the unexpected disaster of the Depression. The Los Angeles population was made up of the kind of people who had always refused to face unpleasant (or even merely dull) realities. These were the people who, instead of facing their problems at home, had fled in search of better prospects in the glittering West. They had chosen to trade in their certainties for high expectations, now destroyed by the Depression. Each had to work out alone the disparity between brilliant dreams and dull realities.

The Los Angeles Chamber of Commerce insisted that things were going to get better in no time and, anyway, even "in the blackest times, there is business to be had by hustling." A local banking leader advised businessmen to build new commercial buildings while they could take advantage of the fact that unemployment had forced labor costs to an all-time low. The owner of the Los Angeles Times insisted that the best way to stimulate the economy was for employers to cut wages and hours, presumably forcing employees to spend a larger percentage of their pay at local businesses.[27] By the beginning of 1933, one-fourth of the nation's work force was unemployed. By March 1933, four-fifths of the nation's banks were closed. The jobless, the homeless, and the investors and depositors who had lost everything wandered the streets and sat in parks, ashamed and embarrassed to ask for charity, but desperate for help. Public charity was nearly non-existent. The mayor of Los Angeles, noting that San Francisco had set up free soup kitchens, bragged that there were none in Los Angeles: "We do not find it necessary to feed our unemployed men here."[28]

Ordinary Dreams

California's governor met the challenge of the economic crisis by calling for a regressive state sales tax, which squeezed the unemployed and the poor, vetoing an income tax which would have shifted the burden to those most able to pay.[29]

Health officials and humanitarians expressed concerns about the homeless clustered in shantytowns of packing crates at the southern edge of L.A.. Taxpayers feared they would have to foot the bill for their less fortunate brethren. The police dispersed the "Little Oklahomas" and "Hoovervilles." The merchants who made up the Hollywood Boulevard Association petitioned the City Council to keep their district free of beggars; their presence was bad for business. Los Angeles' City fathers tried to discourage down-and-outers by ordering them arrested for vagrancy, as many as 15,000 in a year.

The number of suicides off Pasadena's Colorado Street bridge prompted the posting of guards and erecting of fences.

The hard times of the '30s intensified the need for group security and for the reassurance charismatic leaders could offer. Many Angelenos turned to demagogues and charismatic religious figures who offered often simplistic answers to their problems.

Californians rallied to unusual political alternatives. Upton Sinclair, long-time muckraker and inveterate socialist turned Democrat, ran for governor in 1934 on the slogan "End Poverty in California" (E.P.I.C., for short). His advocacy of state-operated farms and factories and the redistribution of property, among other things, branded him a radical and catalyzed an imposing opposition. Even so, his opponent's margin of victory was not wide.[30]

The Townsend Movement was a simplistic program proposed by an elderly Long Beach physician that appealed to many older people who had retired to sunny Southern California, then lost their savings in the stock market crash and subsequent bank failures. His plan promised to restore prosperity and, at the same time, guarantee a pension of $200 a month to every unemployed citizen over sixty. Older people nationwide subscribed to the Townsend publications and placed their hopes in the Plan. The movement's greatest strength was in the Los Angeles area.[31]

In the spring of 1932, the hunger of homeless men coincided with troubled orchardists who could not afford the cost of labor to pick their fruit, but who worried about theft and tree damage from overladen branches. At first informally, growers around Los Angeles agreed to give up to half of the fruit to anyone who would pick it. Within a few weeks a self-help association had been formed to regularize this innovative movement. It soon extended to providing labor for businessmen in exchange for surplus goods, and then to cooperatives

128. Krotona Court, 1914

where surplus fruit, milk, old clothing, household goods, gasoline, and services could be exchanged. The cooperative movement was largely abandoned as federal work relief projects began generating regular employment projects. But at its peak the grass roots return to a barter economy had sustained some 200,000 people.[32]

Los Angeles, so long populated by recently uprooted newcomers had developed unique institutions for the homesick, from the annual Iowa picnic, which drew as many as 150,000, to a variety of cults and communes.[33] Some of them left long-lasting marks on the city. An apartment house in Hollywood

129. Gates to Malibu Colony

sporting cusped arches and small cupolas once housed the Theosophists' retreat, Krotona. Its dome and prayer balcony can be glimpsed in ILLUSTRATION 128.[34] Columnists and calumniators have long delighted in colorful descriptions of such sects. One of these, Duncan Aikman, described L.A.'s population in 1925 as: "A rare mixture — of evangelical mountebanks, new thoughters, swamis, popular novelists, movie persons, solemn pamphleteers, realtors, ku kluxers, joiners of the thousand-and-one fraternal orders of good will and everlasting sunshine, artists, consumptives, music lovers, cripples, retired farmers, [and] ex-beer magnates...Also there are the cults. It is beyond question that there are more nonsense cults in the environs of this city than anywhere else on earth."[35]

Cults flourished in the Depression. They offered a form of group retreat from harsh realities. Others, who could afford it, retreated physically, building their homes behind walls that shut out the homeless and those the residents regarded as socially undesirable. At Malibu Colony, the residents, many of them film stars, fortified themselves behind a wall and guarded gate (ILLUSTRATION 129).[36]

Masonry walls were not the only defensive deployments of the interwar decades. The period saw a rising pattern of rejection and exclusionism clearly evident in the 1920s and increasing in the Depression decade. In these years Angelenos, by neighborhood and by silent general agreement, erected paper walls to keep out people different from themselves. The Ku Klux Klan was very active in Southern California during the '20s and '30s. Black residents met acts of violence from neighbors who objected to their "intrusion." Major civic and social bodies such as the Chamber of Commerce, businessmen's clubs, country clubs, and fraternal lodges — many of whom had numbered Jewish leaders among their founders — began to exclude Jews.[37]

True to form, Angelenos' houses were powerful vehicles of expression of these hostile social attitudes of racism, rejection, and exclusion. Restrictive clauses on residential property deeds appeared in the 1920s. By the mid-'20s, Black residents were moving into newer suburbs as far as Slauson.

MOVIE STARS AND HARD TIMES

Neighborhood resistance confined it there until World War II. In the same decade, a growing Black middle-class expanded its residential concentration from West Jefferson to West Adams. Meanwhile, the original Central Avenue district was down grading into deteriorating rentals and conversions of older houses into multiple-family dwellings. The dynamics of Black expansion aroused alarm about declining property values among older homeowners. In response to these perceived threats, residents so effectively barricaded their blocks against minority intrusion through restrictive covenants that by the end of the decade 70% of the Black minority found itself confined to an increasingly congested area north of Slauson in a long strip centered on Central Avenue.

A sociological study undertaken in 1927-1928 of a neighborhood near the University of Southern California provides invaluable insights on how and why restrictive covenants were employed. Eighty-four per cent of the residents of the area bounded by Normandie Avenue, Jefferson, Vermont, and Exposition Boulevards were interviewed. Some of the houses of this middle-class section dated back to the 1887 Boom, but most were of the single-family bungalow type. They were set back on quiet, respectable lawns on tree-lined avenues. Streetcars put the area within twenty minutes of the civic center. The neighborhood had undergone some changes since 1914. Construction of a number of bungalow courts, an apartment house, division of houses into flats and addition of rear houses had altered its character. The high demand for housing at the onset of the 1920s had made such conversions an attractive investment for property owners. In January 1928, 364 lots had single dwellings, while 105 had more than one building. By 1927-28, Blacks were moving into the northwest corner of the study area.

The researcher recorded the pride and self-identity the established residents felt for their homes and neighborhood. Yet a number of homeowners were seriously contemplating leaving. They confessed that a leading consideration was the approach of Blacks and Japanese who they feared would lower their property values, as well as lower their social standing. Those interviewed frequently expressed the opinion that the minorities ought to be "kept in their place." A number objected to their children attending integrated schools. They revealed a tension among neighbors over suspicions of intent to sell to minorities.[38]

Concerned discussions led to petition circulation, meetings, and a formal organization known as the University District Property Owners' Association, which drew up a legal document restricting the sale, rental, or occupancy of property to any "non-Caucasian." Pressure was applied to property

Ordinary Dreams

owners to sign the agreement and file it as a legal amendment to their property deeds, to be permanently binding on current owners, heirs, as well as future purchasers. The significant clauses of the "Agreement and Declaration of Restriction" were as follows:

"That no part of any of said lots or parcels or land shall ever at any time be sold or rented to any person other than of the white or Caucasian race. That no part of any of said lots or parcels of land shall ever at any time be used or occupied or be permitted to be used or occupied by any person other than of the white or Caucasian race. Provided, that said restrictions shall be perpetual and binding forever upon all of the said lots or parcels of land and upon the parties hereto, their heirs, devisees, executors, administrators, and assigns." Such restrictive covenants were widely instituted in neighborhoods across the Los Angeles Basin in the '20s and '30s. They were not outlawed until 1948, when the U.S. Supreme Court declared them unenforceable.[39]

The widespread deployment of paper bulwarks against minority occupancy effectively bottled up Black, Asian, and, in some cases, Jewish communities into declining neighborhoods. In the exclusionary spirit of the inter-war decades, local governments enacted laws to erect further barriers against certain minorities. In 1922, the City of Los Angeles rezoned the Central Avenue area to permit factories, thus relegating the two elements unwelcome in the majority of neighborhoods, Blacks and factories, to each other's uneasy company. The City of Glendale legislated that Blacks employed within its limits could only work between dawn and dusk, housemaids had to be day-workers rather than live-ins. Glendale residents boasted, "No Negro sleeps overnight in our city." Even City boundaries were redrawn to reflect racial exclusionism. By the mid-'20s, so many Black voters were moving into the predominantly Caucasian city of Watts that inhabitants feared they would soon find themselves a voting minority under a Black city government. Thoroughly aroused by an emotional election campaign, they voted in 1926 to merge by annexation into the City of Los Angeles. Other discriminatory acts in the '20s and '30s, such as segregated firehouses, the closure of public beaches to "persons of color," and a ban against use of public swimming pools except on the day before the water was to be changed, laid a base for a festering sense of majority hostility which would eventually break out in the Watts Riots in 1965.[40]

The Depression decade witnessed official actions designed not merely to confine or restrict, but to send away those "undesirables" already settled here. In February 1936 the City's Chief of Police, responding to taxpayer concerns about the mounting costs of public relief, set up a departmental task force to prevent the indigent from entering California with police officers posted at state border crossings from Oregon to Arizona. They detained needy-looking California-bound travelers and subjected them to questions about financial resources and employment prospects, rejecting those whose economic status seemed unsatisfactory. Most of them were migrants from the South-Central United States displaced by severe drought. The local press applauded.[41]

The "bum blockade", as it was called, was dismantled after two months and ruled unconstitutional when the case finally reached the Supreme Court in 1941. While it lasted, though, it received media attention nationwide. A new aspect of the L.A. image was emerging: the warning of rejection in place of the tradition of open-handed hospitality which had been an important part of L.A.'s culture since its beginning.

Public officials, as well as the citizenry they represented, anxiously searched for ways to reduce unemployment and to stem mounting state and county relief expenses. In the fall of 1930 President Hoover called for the formation of local citizens' relief committees to coordinate charities and find ways to reduce unemployment. One of the first actions of the Los Angeles relief committee was a proposal to rid the region of Mexican aliens in order to free up jobs for needy citizens. The availability of cheap Mexican labor had been a key factor in the success of Southern California's agribusiness. But in the depths of the Depression, growers could not pay even their low wages, in some cases. The seasonal ebb and flow of field workers between crops periodically gave them a high visibility in the L.A. barrios that made them vulnerable in hard times when their employment might be resented by the unemployed. Few Mexicans had applied for visas or U.S. citizenship, nor had there been particular incentive for doing so. Politicians, knowing they had no vote, focused on Mexicans to solve economic problems.

L.A.'s relief committee obtained the cooperation of federal immigration officials in a highly publicized series of raids early in 1931 on the Mexican barrios of Los Angeles. Those without papers were deported to Mexico. Although only 230 aliens were actually deported out of the three to four thousand people detained, the exaggerated rumors in the press, the awakened hostility of the host population, and the air of imminent danger led others to flee. Those who did included many who had lived here a number of years but who had no papers, as well as children born here who were thereby U.S. citizens. After the federal task force departed in March 1931, the Los Angeles County Bureau of Welfare substituted its own program for expelling Mexican residents. It made railroad arrangements to transport trainloads of Mexican Angelenos deep

Ordinary Dreams

into Mexico. Some went voluntarily and others were rounded up by law officers, often without legal subtleties. At a one-way price per head of $14.70 from the County treasury, it was generally considered a bargain.[42]

Local government welfare resources were exhausted soon after the onset of the Depression, private charities strained.

The history of Los Angeles business and government was marked by a booster outlook. Even admitting problems by addressing them openly could tarnish the polished luster of the Los Angeles image. Thus, the public-sector response was very small, over-reliant on the efforts of private charity organizations, and quick to grasp at innovative self-help measures such as the cooperative movement. Local government spent little on direct relief compared with many other U.S. cities. The largest sum, a county bond issue of $5 million for emergency relief measures, was exhausted by 1934. Federal government programs established after 1933 such as the Public Works Administration (PWA), the Federal Emergency Relief Administration (FERA), and the Works Progress Administration (WPA) promised to eventually relieve the hardships of the unemployed, possibly as much as 20% of the local workforce.[43]

Local governmental reluctance to face the problem of housing the homeless was also eventually resolved by federal intervention. Local officials, citing health reasons, evicted the squatters and destroyed the Hoovervilles. The county set up an emergency shelter in a warehouse, altruistically dubbed "American House." Cots, pine tables and benches constituted the amenities of this temporary shelter and soup kitchen.[44] A federal agency, the PWA, was responsible for razing slums and erecting multi-family housing projects between 1934 and 1937. PWA projects eventually housed thousands of families in urban centers around the nation, but not one of them was built in the Los Angeles area. A major factor in this omission was that PWA programs required local administration and the cooperation of local government. Local government refused to cooperate. The opposition of the real estate trade was a key factor. Facing the highest vacancy rate in thirty years, they feared government housing would add to the surplus.[45] The primary purpose of

MOVIE STARS AND HARD TIMES

130. Harbor Hills housing
project, 1941

the PWA's public housing program was to create jobs; housing was a by-product. The federal government's interest in housing as a primary cause was sparked by the wide attention given to a passionately delivered sentence in President Roosevelt's Second Inaugural Address in the spring of 1937, "I see one third of the nation ill-housed, ill-clad, ill-nourished."[46]

In August of 1937, after two years of wrangling, Congress passed the Wagner-Steagall Housing Act creating the United States Housing Authority (U.S.H.A.) and authorizing long-term loans for low-cost housing. Its provisions overcame the resistance of real estate and banking interests. First, it required the razing of one unit of existing sub-standard housing for each new unit constructed (results: no change in vacancy rate; reduced pressure on slumlords to upgrade deteriorating rentals; and an upgraded cityscape). Second, it required public housing tenants to have an income level at least 20% less than was

Ordinary Dreams

required for the least expensive private housing in the community. This was a gap so large that the private rental market could not be impacted by public housing; a provision that would leave an unfortunate element of the population betwixt and between, whose incomes fell just short of the one provision, just over the other, with no place to go.[47]

Under these mollifying conditions, ground was broken late in 1937 for Ramona Gardens, the first public housing project in Los Angeles. As it neared completion late in 1940, the Housing Authority of the City of Los Angeles reported that the average income for the 610 families qualified for occupancy would be around $700.00 per year. Rent would run $11 per month for one bedroom units, up to $18 for three bedrooms, including utilities, a stove, and a refrigerator.[48] By the end of 1941 there were twelve such projects completed or under construction in Los Angeles. ILLUSTRATION 130 gives us a view of the Harbor Hills project, completed in 1941 near San Pedro. Although a striking austerity marked the architectural design, the site planning provided the same sense of pleasant outdoor orientation that private home-dwellers prized in Los Angeles. The three hundred original dwelling units were not arranged in tightly-regimented rows, nor were they stacked into the vertical boxes their Eastern counterparts so often were. The federal government, which was putting up 90% of the financing of projects such as this one, had four key considerations in evaluating project plans: functionality, longevity, minimal site and building cost, and low cost of maintenance and operation. The least expensive arrangement of buildings on a site, was straight rows of buildings, parallel to the streets. Operational policies were designed to foster traditional family lifestyles in apartment layout and tenant-selection standards; racial segregation (de jure stipulations were rigidly followed until 1949; general de facto policy lines not curbed until 1962); and, some would say, social stigma. By clustering housing units stylistically drab and distinct from that of the surrounding neighborhood, tenants were made to feel marked as government dependents, a self-assessment reinforced by rigid rules of conduct and housekeeping. One writer assigned this architectural message to the typical U.S. housing project:

"Public housing, as architecture, was visibly permanent — a solid investment of the taxpayers' money — while the individual units were usually small and Spartan, since they were not supposed to encourage the idea that this was a place to settle into for long."[49]

What factors allowed the distinguishing humanization remarked of government housing design in Los Angeles? First of all, federal standards did permit site planning to be shaped by climate, local social institutions and housing customs, with lower density where land costs were lower. Thus, in Los Angeles, available open land; local low-density traditions; and *de rigeur* grass lawns, the ingrained local custom at every social stratum, affected project design and layout.[50] Then, too, the late start of government housing construction in the Los Angeles area meant that before much design could be done in an attitude of condescending charity, the objective had changed.

The Depression was replaced locally with a build-up of military industries, creating a sharp housing shortage for defense workers by 1939, swelled by housing needs of military dependents by 1941. So, as early as 1939, government housing here was being designed largely for defense workers, with an attitude reflecting patriotism and a desire to provide pleasant living conditions for "those who are doing their share in the Arsenal of Democracy." Finally, there were a number of planners and architects who saw housing projects as a challenge to creative innovation in design and/or an opportunity to blend their own social ideals with their professional expertise. Noted architects devoted themselves to projects with idealistic social purposes, such as Gregory Ain's 1935 design for prefabricated shelters for farm workers, and the creative designs of Lloyd Wright and Richard Neutra for public housing projects.[51]

The Harbor Hills project was designed by a team of architects working under Reginald Johnson, renowned for his work in traditional styles during the '20s and in modified traditionalism in the '30s. Cost standards and preference turned the architectural team to the International or Modern style. Local weather, which did not require storm windows, persuaded federal administrators to relax their ban on steel casement windows, so that their sleek modern look could be incorporated. The use of concrete block for the lower fifth of the building, along with cantilevered roof lines and canopies accentuated horizontality and contributed functionally. The renowned New York designer, Clarence Stein, whose training was based on the Ecole des Beaux Arts and the English Garden City traditions, assumed responsibility for site planning. To the despair of many other Eastern project planners, he insisted on low-density suburban layouts instead of the uniformity and efficiency which they felt was more enlightened. In L.A. he retained the natural contours of the site and called for large open areas between buildings, some of which are arranged diagonally rather than at right angles to each other to reduce the sense of regimentation.[52] Although they incorporated positive physical features, these public housing projects did not fulfill idealists' goals of social betterment for the poor. As soon as they could be completed they were filled with newcomers, this time recruited for the nation's war efforts. ❧

PART SIX

DREAMING ON

DREAMING ON

XIII

ROSIE AND JOE AND A HOUSE IN L.A.

Oh, Boy, when I get out

of this jungle,

I'm going to build me a sweet

little cottage in California

and stay there the rest

of my natural life.

It won't be big but it'll have

every convenience

I can cram into it

ON SEPTEMBER 1, 1939, Hitler's forces invaded Poland; on September 3 Britain and France declared war. A second World War had begun in Europe. In the Far East, Japan moved to create its New Order in East Asia. While the Nazis headed for Warsaw, Japanese troops engaged two Soviet divisions in combat far away on the border between Outer Mongolia and Manchukuo. World War II would be a global struggle.

In sunny Los Angeles, attention was elsewhere. MGM was rushing the finishing touches on Gone With the Wind for its premiere showing. The Wizard of Oz was screening at the Carthay Circle Theater. The local economy seemed to be recovering from the Depression with almost 20% more employed than in 1938, 50% more than the 1930 figure. On the day Europe went to war, the Nippon Maru and three other Japanese tankers were in Los Angeles Harbor loading 302,000 barrels of locally produced oil for the Japanese military build-up.[1]

The city was on the verge of a metamorphosis. The war would soon bring hundreds of thousands of servicemen, G.I.s named Joe or Jack or Bill or something else, through Los Angeles en route to battle posts in the Pacific. Employment opportunities in defense plants and shipyards would draw thousands of men and women as war-workers — Rosie the Riveter and Wanda the Welder and Tom, Dick and Harry. Los Angeles, as formed by the imaginative builders of the 1920s and '30s, would make a vivid impression on these newcomers, enhanced by the wartime circumstances under which they were introduced to the city. Their perceptions and interpretations of the essence of the city proved sufficiently attractive to persuade many of them to settle permanently in the post-war period. Their numbers, their concept of the city and their relationship to it, and the houses they built there changed the L.A. they had first met into something quite different. The vernacular housing of the 1940s was less fanciful, less sculptural, and less interesting to look at than that of the preceding decades. Historical references were restricted to a vaguely "traditional" look not identifiable with any particular historical setting, unless they were safely "American" — no French chateaux, Old English houses, or Spanish haciendas. Even the return of imaginative styling in the 1950s was restricted by an unprecedented uniformity of vision.

The clear contrast between pre- and post-war vernacular housing points to the 1939 to 1950s period as a major evolutionary stage for Los Angeles. The volume of new housing built to accommodate the war and post-war immigrants was far greater than any previous accretion to the built environment. Between 1940 and 1950 the population of Los Angeles County increased by 49%;

between 1950 and 1960 by another 45%.[2] The physical magnitude of this wave of newcomers had a more dynamic impact on Los Angeles than that of any previous era. The architectural contrast reflected three factors: how G.I. Joe and Rosie the Riveter saw and experienced the good life in Los Angeles; how they expressed that image in architectural terms; and how their post-war housing irrevocably altered the nature of Los Angeles.

The initial effect of the war on Los Angeles was a positive one. War production cured the remnants of the Depression. The city, like the rest of America, had suffered through the lean '30s. At the 1932 nadir there had been 344,000 unemployed in Los Angeles County. But by 1938 and '39, as other nations prepared for war by purchasing such local products as airplanes and oil, the local economy began to improve. Airplane manufacturers, concentrated in the Los Angeles area since 1910, were clearly beneficiaries of distant wars. But theirs was a gambler's business, dependent on trial-and-error technology, uncertain investment sources, and luck. When World War I and its military orders ended, the aircraft companies had found themselves dependent on slim air-mail contracts, chancy passenger airline endeavors, and sporadic military contracts for experimental aircraft. Then in the late '30s, as international tensions mounted in Europe and Asia, their prospects brightened once again. The possibility of war anywhere on the globe considerably increased the likelihood of lucrative warplane orders.[3]

Foreign demand for planes and, later, orders from the U.S. Government, replaced the Depression, locally, with a war industry boom. Prosperity returned first to those suburbs clustered around the airframe factories and the shipyards: towns such as Burbank and Santa Monica, San Pedro and Wilmington. In January 1932 Burbank's Employment Relief Department had 3,500 homeless and hungry people registered, and could only manage to solicit $2,200 in contributions to feed them for a month. By 1936, the WPA (Works Progress Administration) was employing one-third of Burbank's work force. Lockheed Aircraft, located in Burbank since the First World War, employed only 64 people in 1932. Beginning in 1936 the company was awarded a succession of federal contracts for experimental military aircraft. It started hiring new employees. Then, in 1938, the British government ordered 200 of Lockheed's Hudson bombers in anticipation of war. Lockheed's work force swelled to 2,300. To increase efficiency and output, the U.S. Army Air Corps put together intercorporate pools, such as the 1939 pool of Boeing Aircraft in Seattle, Douglas Aircraft in Santa Monica, and Lockheed, which together built B-17 bombers for a French and British contract. Between 1939 and 1940

Lockheed's labor force was expanded to 7,500; Douglas grew 140% to a work force of 15,000; North American Aircraft doubled to 5,000. In May, 1940, President Roosevelt went before a joint session of Congress and asked for $1,182,000,000, calling for an incredible output of 50,000 war planes per year. Aircraft plants added second and third shifts. They built new facilities and expanded across former beanfields and dairy pastures. By the beginning of 1941, the Los Angeles area aircraft builders together had a $1 billion backlog of business, an annual payroll of $100 million, and 57,000 workers.[4]

The shipbuilding industry also flourished as the war approached. Los Angeles Harbor was a man-made port completed only at the outset of World War I. No large ship had been constructed there since 1920. In 1940 contracts were awarded to three local shipyards, and by the end of 1941 shipbuilding was L.A.'s second largest manufacturing industry. Oil, aircraft, shipbuilding and related industries nearly tripled L.A.'s industrial work force between September 1, 1939 and December 7, 1941.[5]

One local industry initially appeared threatened by the effects of war. The motion picture business had weathered the Depression in good health. In 1939, 85 to 96 per cent of the world's movies were made locally and 31,000 people depended on the film industry for their pay checks. The economic health of the city itself depended in large measure on the continued prosperity of the motion picture business. Movie stars and producers had a particular solicitude for the outlook of the industry. Admittedly, Hollywood had benefited by the influx of European cinematic talent in flight from Nazi persecutions and cultural restrictions since 1933. But the outbreak of war portended the loss of Hollywood's foreign markets, which accounted for approximately 35 per cent of its film rentals. Furthermore, the withdrawal of foreign investments in the film industry necessitated a financial readjustment. And, finally, foreign governments were expected to place restrictive wartime controls on film content, exhibition, and importation.[6]

But production for Europe's war revitalized Hollywood's glamour industry along with the other elements of the local economy. The war-industry boom caused a critical labor shortage, wages rose to attract workers. Average weekly wages in L.A.'s manufacturing industries increased from $28 at the beginning of 1939 to almost $40 in December 1941. With much of the nation still living in Depression conditions, Southern California's expanding job market and rising wages were powerful inducements to relocation. The combination of well-paying jobs and the well-advertised climate and charm of Los Angeles was irresistible. Los Angeles County swelled by 150,000 new residents from other states in 1941 alone. Between April 1940 and April 1944, 780,000 arrived. There was an in-state migration, too. Many of the refugees from the agricultural Depression in Oklahoma, Texas, and southern Kansas who had come to California in the late '30s in search of farm labor work relocated from the fields of Central California to the growing industrial suburbs of Los Angeles between 1938 and 1941.[7]

The expansion of industry and the influx of job-seekers was good for business. Workers spent their paychecks in local stores and movie theaters. Movie attendance picked up. With the best wages in years, few minded the fact that ticket prices were higher than ever. Domestic movie profits more than compensated for the wartime dislocation of the foreign film market.[8]

Building trades were also stimulated. A surge of building activity, the largest in seventeen years, took place between 1937 and 1941. A locally-financed school construction program, initiated in 1936, had started the construction industry on the road to recovery. With the approach of war in Europe, the federal government began granting contracts for the construction of aircraft plants and shipyards. Together with industrial expansion of aluminum plants, steel mills, oil refineries and other operations related to war preparation, these yielded over 100 million construction dollars by September 1942. Between 1940 and 1942 building contracts for military bases, training camps, and coastal defense facilities brought another 50 million dollars into the local economy. 1943 and 1944 saw these figures multiplied several times over, as direct American involvement in the war called for a dramatic military and industrial build-up.

The flood of newcomers created a considerable market for new homes, especially for single-family residences the industrial worker could afford. The Los Angeles life, as every newcomer knew from its portrayal in movies and his own immediate visual impression, was inseparable from the single-family residence, set apart from its neighbors by perpetually green lawns and an obligatory driveway. The question was, how to obtain one on a factory-worker's salary and without a large down-payment? Two New Deal measures made it possible. Congress had passed the National Housing Act in 1934, creating the Federal Housing Authority (FHA). Although slow to be implemented, it was providing guaranties for home mortgages up to 80% of the valuation (later changed to 95%), at 5 or 6% interest, for terms up to 20 years by the time it was in full operation in 1937. Since commercial loans rarely extended to over 50% of valuation, and were usually repayable in five years at higher rates of interest, the FHA program gave a tremendous boost to the housing industry as did the 1939 amendment to the income-tax laws which permitted a tax deduction for mortgage interest.

The FHA loan ceiling was $20,000, but in practice in the late '30s and early '40s, the agency rarely guaranteed loans over $8,000.[9] The result was that numerous buyers, anxious to take advantage of the new mortgage terms, would not look at houses much over $8,000. Builders scrambled for ways to build more house for less money. Enterprising contractors experimented with new construction methods in order to reduce the time and cost of home construction. They tried new materials, such as plywood for interior paneling and cupboards; they turned increasingly to fabricated parts; and they adapted the assembly-line method to producing large numbers of almost identical houses, either pre-fabricating units off-site, or utilizing a division of labor on-site so that each worker would perform the same limited task on each house in a row. The lumber industry, plumbing firms, the building trades and architects' organizations, Better Homes in America (BHA), and civic bodies researched new techniques and materials to increase quality and decrease costs.[10]

In Los Angeles, the market for low-cost houses was very good. The most marketable were those under $8,000 including the lot, with innovative solutions to storage space, indirect lighting, or other amenities. The most

131. Regency Revival stucco box, 1939

profitable builders were the largest-scale contractors who could take advantage of economies of scale. They built houses like the one pictured in ILLUSTRATION 131. The typical practice was for the developer to build a model and prepare the sites for a large number of houses. Visitors to the model would financially commit themselves to a selected lot, choosing one of the variants of the floor plan and exterior trim packages from a set of illustrations. The house pictured (ILLUSTRATION 131) was constructed in West Los Angeles in 1939 by such a developer-contractor. The five-room house on a 50 by 150 foot lot, measured 39 by 38 feet, with a detached, two-car garage. The cost of the structures alone was $3,700. Typical of these small houses, the styling details were quite conservative. FHA loan considerations included resale value, and houses that appeared unusually modern to the appraiser were often rejected as a passing fad, whereas houses of Colonial or other traditional styling were considered to have lasting appeal. One writer has termed the resulting hodgepodge of colonial images

Rosie and Joe and a House in L.A.

132. Mar Vista tract
house, 1940

"California Monterey", and streamlined reductionism, "Hollywood Regency." In this model, the green shutters and the pre-formed porch canopy provide safely traditional touches to a house with factory window sashes, modern horizontality and asymmetrical balance.[11]

As the need for defense worker housing became more urgent, huge housing tracts were planned. The houses in ILLUSTRATION 132 were part of a tract built in 1940 in the Mar Vista area — centrally located between Douglas Aircraft, Hughes Aircraft, and the movie studios in Culver City. The land had formerly produced potatoes, celery, beans, and onions. The tract was composed of fifteen square blocks of houses built on four floorplans and mirror-images of these: eight plans in all. The houses were further differentiated by color, several choices of pastel stucco with contrasting wood trim. These structures were simple stucco boxes with minimal references to Anglo-American traditions: the house on the left has a paneled door and louvered shutters, the porch of the house on the right makes a nod to the Monterey style.[12] An even bigger development, under Fritz B. Burns, located on former bean fields and chaparral-covered bluffs between the El Segundo aircraft plants, Mines Field, and Hughes Aircraft, numbered 5,000 houses. It was started in 1942 and christened Westchester. The scale of repetitive developments such as that in ILLUSTRATION 133 contrasted with the smaller, lively and irregular pocket developments of the 1920s.

The tracts of look-alike stucco boxes could not be built fast enough to accommodate the demand. At the end of 1942 the shortfall between available housing units and newly arrived workers was forcing some 65,000 families to "double-up", that is, take in lodgers or move in with relatives. Many families occupied substandard housing units. Rents on older structures skyrocketed. A lucky Lockheed employee might pay $25 a month for a thirty-year-old bungalow in Glendale, eight miles away. A Douglas Aircraft worker in Santa Monica might buy a trailer in a nearby trailer court on monthly payments.[13]

After ten years of Depression, few private investors had sufficient resources to capitalize on this critical market situation. Insurance companies were an exception. Three of them, Aetna, Prudential, and Metropolitan Life, financed private, multi-family housing projects. The latter's 10 1/2 acre development near Wilshire and Fairfax, Park La Brea (ILLUSTRATION 134), built in 1941-42, was more or less compatible with the low density land-use patterns

characteristic of Los Angeles at that time. The two-story height and the dispersal of the rest of the units in a park-like setting was sympathetic to locally favored housing patterns. Like the contemporary builders' tracts of stucco boxes, these were differentiated by pastel colors. To provide interest, diagonal streets were introduced, along with staggered offsets of the wall planes. However, the New York architect placed the units which faced on Sixth Street and Fairfax Avenues directly on the sidewalks, an Eastern tradition which had been shunned in lawn-loving Los Angeles. The units were so efficiently minimalist that they appeared stark and institutional by contrast to the existing houses nearby. Reference to traditional styling was reduced beyond the accepted norm: only a flat entry canopy on thin posts provided a hint of what the architects claimed was the Southern Colonial tradition. Under the stress of the housing shortage, bland and uniform dwelling units, whether in tracts of stucco boxes or in institutional apartment complexes, were changing the face of Los Angeles in the early war years.[14]

After Pearl Harbor, the housing shortage grew more critical as military priorities created a shortage of materials and government regulation restricted private housing developments and projects. The War Production Board (WPB) set regulations on lumber, cement, and metal goods. A few examples indicate the

134. Park La Brea, 1941-42

severity of the impact these were to have on homebuilders: bathtub manufacturers were forbidden to use metal; residential structures were limited to 30 pounds of copper wire each; household appliance manufacturing was curtailed; the extension of water, gas, and electricity lines to new structures was restricted. More directly, the WPB asserted control over construction permits, rejecting any housing project not located close to expanding war plants and public transportation, or exceeding new wartime construction standards limiting use of critical materials. Finally, in November 1942, the entire construction industry was brought under price control. Building activity in Los Angeles County immediately plummeted. By May 1943 the number of dwelling-unit permits was down to 220 for the month, as compared to an average of 4,550 units per month during the peak of spring and summer, 1941.[15]

If the pressing problem of a housing shortage for war-workers was to be resolved, it was clear by 1942 that the government would have to do it. The federal government's Depression-era housing projects had provided thousands of dwelling units, but, as we have seen, none in Los Angeles, due to the resistance of local business interests. That resistance had been overcome by the provisions of the Wagner-Steagall Housing Act of 1937, permitting the construction of the first public housing project in Los Angeles, Ramona Gardens, completed in 1940. By that time, the return of prosperity and the influx of war-workers had altered the objectives of government housing programs. Harbor Hills, completed in 1941, (ILLUSTRATION 130) was conveniently located near the shipyards, rather than in a blighted area. Reflecting the new economic conditions, rent was tied to net family income. By the end of 1941 twelve projects were completed or under construction in the city. After Pearl Harbor, all but one of them were converted strictly to war-worker housing. To be eligible, applicants were required to be American citizens, employed in a certified war industry, and earning less than one dollar per hour. Signs outside rental offices read, "Now Open, Low Rent Homes for American War-workers."[16]

While Harbor Hills was typical of these projects, the pressing need for war-worker housing also led to the construction of lower-standard government housing. These were the "duration city" and dormitory projects of Banning Homes and Wilmington Hall, both in the harbor area. Banning was a 2,000-unit domicile for childless couples. Wilmington Hall was a dormitory for 3,000 single men. Both were frame and plywood structures slated for demolition at the end of the war. In spite of their homely appearance, there were waiting lists for these apartments.[17] By the end of 1942, the system of priority permits and the restrictions on building materials had slowed down building activity associated with the influx of war-workers and the build-up of war industries. But by that time the face of Los Angeles had changed. The huge number of new residential structures had added large swatches of new material to the L.A. fabric: tracts of low-cost single-family houses, private multi-family dwellings, and large-scale public housing projects. These were all typified by low-profile, pastel-colored, simple box-like forms set in a uniformly proportioned expanse of open space minimally landscaped with grass and a few young shrubs and seedlings. The preference for single-family dwellings, the low profiles and low density were expressive of a continuity with past eras of Los Angeles development but, the repetition and uniformity of these structures contributed a new ambiance to Los Angeles. The proliferating war plants were likewise low and boring.[18]

Although building programs ceased in 1943, life in Los Angeles had not stabilized. The 1942 rush program that had produced Banning Homes and Wilmington Hall had overlooked a significant element of the civilian workforce: single women. By the end of 1942, 15 million women were part of the American labor force, 3 million of them having joined in the previous 18 months. The combined Allied demand for military equipment required an enormous advance in productivity at the very time when American men were being drafted away from industry into the armed services. Women would have to fill the vacancies and expanding openings in the factories. The War Manpower Commission and the Office of War Information (OWI) launched a campaign to sell women on the idea of taking jobs such as riveting aircraft parts, operating heavy machinery, and repairing trains. In the process, the image of womanhood changed. The OWI distributed pamphlets, magazines published articles and recruitment pitches, and radio stations broadcast advertisements. A typical radio ad went:

"This is (name) speaking...to the housewives of (city). I'm a housewife, too... never worked outside my home until this year. Feeding my family and buying war bonds just didn't seem enough. So I got an 8-hour-a-day job, and managed to run my home besides. My husband's proud of me...and I've never been happier. I feel I'm really helping to make the war end sooner... and maybe saving the life of just one boy from home."[19]

Recruiting women for war industry was particularly vital in Los Angeles. During the war, the work force in the local aircraft plants increased thirteenfold. As the industry sought more workers, it lost 100,000 male workers to the draft. By May 1943, after eleven months of recruitment, more than 30 per cent of the industrial wage earners in Los Angeles County were female. Before the year was out, 60 per cent of the Douglas Aircraft work force and 35,000 of Lockheed's 94,000 workers were women.[20] Women in slacks, women with their

Rosie and Joe and a House in L.A.

hair wrapped in bandannas, women with lunch pails, and women operating machinery appeared everywhere. They could be seen on every passing streetcar. They wore their overalls and carried their lunch boxes as badges of their contribution to the war effort. They had pay checks of their own and they felt a spirit of camaraderie the stay-at-home war wife lacked. Magazine and newspaper illustrations focused attention on the new industrial woman out of all proportion to her actual numbers. Female office workers were ignored. It was the new industrial worker, the woman performing a man's job, who was interesting and written about. Hollywood movies such as "Swing Shift Maisie" glamorized Rosie the Riveter. She was described as able, independent, and contributing nobly to the war effort. Articles, ads, and films portrayed her as glamorous in a new way, no longer the fluttering, fragile woman or the femme fatale, but self-confident, energetic, and down-to-earth. Women's magazines and advertisements for cosmetics and clothing persuaded readers that it was possible to build airplanes and be beautiful too.[21]

Women who served in the armed forces were also a new phenomenon, and, like their male counterparts, numerically concentrated in this strategically located city. WAACs, WAVEs, and WAFs, like G.I.s, were treated as guests of honor in Los Angeles. They were portrayed in movies and periodicals and recruitment posters as patriotic and daringly adventurous, as well as capable and confident.[22] The barrage of publicity, and the creation of such positive images, gave Rosie the Riveter and the servicewomen a sense of self-respect and independence which would affect their post-war lives. The primary message was that Rosie's working outside the home would end the war sooner, enabling the fighting men to come home and bring life back to normal. Her job was to be temporary, a brief aberration to normal life patterns. The public housing projects erected for war workers provided no space for single women workers. Planners saw no need for permanent structures for women, since they were only temporarily working in industry. After the war it would be their patriotic duty to "make way" for returning veterans. Many women apparently agreed. A Los Angeles Times survey of the area's aircraft plants in 1945 found that between V-E Day in May and V-J Day in August, 1945 the number of women workers had dropped from 51,000 to 34,000 as women returned to homemaking.[23]

ON SUNDAY MORNING, December 7, 1941, the Japanese bombed Pearl Harbor and America found itself in the war. The City of Angels, the city of sunshine and good health, vacation frolics and film fantasies, darkened with fear and hatred that belied its name. Angelenos of Japanese ancestry were the first to feel the chill. By 1940 there were 36,866 Issei (first-generation immigrants) and Nisei (second-generation Japanese-Americans) residents in Los Angeles County.[24] Japanese immigrants to Los Angeles, beginning in the 1880s, had experienced legal and social discrimination, but they had worked hard to Americanize and to get ahead. Many owned their homes as well as small businesses or agricultural lands (registered in the names of minor children, to circumvent a 1913 state law prohibiting "aliens ineligible for citizenship" from owning land). Their children took piano lessons, played baseball, and earned UCLA degrees.

The morning after Pearl Harbor, FBI agents and military police showed up in twos and fours at Issei doors. Sometimes they only asked questions and made notes. Sometimes they went through all the cupboards and drawers and confiscated cameras, radios and ancestral samurai swords. Sometimes they took away the man of the house or a Kibei (educated in Japan) son. Japanese employees of the movie studios were sent home and told not to return. Soldiers were posted on 24-hour guard outside Japanese businesses. Local newspapers fanned rumors and fears of a "Jap" fifth-column. The Monday morning Times editorialized on the danger of "spies, saboteurs and fifth columnists." Pointing to the large numbers of Japanese in Los Angeles, it concluded that "Some, perhaps many, are...good Americans. What the rest may be we do not know, nor can we take a chance in the light of yesterday's demonstration that treachery and double-dealing are major Japanese weapons." In the days that followed, other newspapers and radio commentators sensationalized rumors of Japanese espionage, signals to offshore submarines, and plots to poison the populace. On January 29, 1942, restricted zones were delineated from which enemy aliens were barred. On February 19, President Roosevelt signed Executive Order 9066 authorizing the forced removal of all West Coast residents of Japanese ancestry, including the 77,000 who were natural-born American citizens, to internment camps for the duration of the war. Beginning March 2 some 110,000 of these American victims of wartime hysteria were relocated. They were allowed to bring with them only what they could carry. In Little Tokyo, San Pedro, Gardena, and the Westside, and in isolated farmhouses throughout the county, davenports, washing machines, pianos, clothes, cribs, and sewing machines were sold at desperation prices, given away, or left behind in vacated houses. Children with identifying tags pinned to their clothing lined up with their families to be bussed to temporary Assembly Centers, where they would remain under Army guard until permanent inland camps could be constructed. Santa Anita Race Track served as an Assembly Center, each horse stall, altered hastily by the Army

Corps of Engineers to plans by architect Stiles O. Clement, serving as a one-room apartment. By August, 1942, all West Coast Japanese had been removed from their homes; by November they were all in camps such as Manzanar in the Mojave Desert, Topaz on the stark plateau of Utah, or Heart Mountain in Wyoming.[25]

War had changed Los Angeles. The empty apartments over boarded-up sushi restaurants and Japanese grocery stores in Little Tokyo were occupied by Black families spilling over from the overcrowded Black ghetto along Central Avenue. The new residents were poor and underemployed. The war industries' spectacular rate of growth between 1939 and 1941 had stimulated an unprecedented migration of Black job-seekers to Southern California. Between 1940 and 1945, while the Caucasian population of Los Angeles rose by 17.7 per cent, the number of Blacks in L.A. increased by 109 per cent. Racially restrictive covenants on property deeds, not outlawed until 1948, prevented a natural expansion of Black neighborhoods. The opening of Little Tokyo by the exodus of the Japanese was a rare case of open housing. Job opportunities were more restricted. The aircraft industry was typical. As an experimental and close-knit economic sphere before the war build-up, it had employed few Blacks except in janitorial capacities. Employers openly told them that only Caucasians were being hired. Significant minority hiring and training programs did not occur until 1943, after a summer of activism by Blacks themselves and the pressure of a critical labor shortage.[26]

When the Japanese, who had specialized in labor-intensive crops like celery and strawberries, were gone, Mexicans moved into their empty farmhouses in Culver City, Arleta, Whittier and Palos Verdes. Los Angeles County held the record as the most productive agricultural county in the nation, partly due to such small-scale truck-farming, but even more to large-scale commercial growers. Mexicans had served as the major source of farm labor for these growers throughout the '20s and '30s, despite the influx from the Midwest Dustbowl, and despite the 1931 Mexican repatriation drive. The war placed new demands on agriculture and tripled the value of California's crops. The major growers and canners of California pressured the federal government into a program which imported farm workers, *braceros*, from Mexico to work at subminimal wages. The initial program lasted from 1942 to 1947. Over 100,000 Mexican nationals were transported across the border by the U.S. Government and turned over to growers and to railroad companies throughout the Western United States. They lived in house-cars in railroad camps, in the few remaining housing courts in town, or in farm-labor camps near the fields they tended, and thus formed part of the changing face of Los Angeles during the war years. Long-resident Angelenos of Mexican descent found themselves competing with these federally-subsidized braceros. Making up about ten per cent of L.A.'s population at the time, Mexican-Americans did not find compensatory openings in industry for their losses in farm work during the war. The intensive hiring programs of the aircraft, shipbuilding, and secondary war material plants practiced hiring policies that were preferential to Anglos.[27]

The Second World War fundamentally altered the lifestyle of a population grown dependent on the automobile. Since the 1920s, Los Angeles tracts, factories and stores had been laid out for a population of automobile owners. By 1939, 80 per cent of the passenger miles traveled in Los Angeles County was by automobile, and in many outlying sections there were no alternative means of transportation. The war disrupted this pattern. A few days after Pearl Harbor a freeze on the sale of tires and inner tubes was ordered, followed later by a strict rationing program. In February 1942 all new auto production for civilian use was halted. In July 1942 gasoline rationing began. It turned more stringent in November. Three gallons per week was the limit for an average car owner with an "A" ration card. Driving was sharply curtailed, and the busy traffic downtown and along major thoroughfares was a thing of the past. Ridership on the Pacific Electric's Red Cars and on motor coaches reflected the changing nature of Angeleno mobility.[28]

War spread an atmosphere of fear over Los Angeles. The day after Pearl Harbor, blackout and dim-out regulations were issued. That very night Los Angeles experienced its first blackout drill. Air-raid sirens wailed and mass confusion resulted. Afterwards, officials assured the public that there would be no further blackouts unless there were reports of approaching unidentified aircraft, which only intensified fear in subsequent blackouts.

Blackout orders converted busy streets into eerie haunts, only emergency vehicles with masked lights moved through the darkness. The electric utilities issued blackout rules for homes and businesses. Their tone was alarming: "Don't light cigarettes outdoors during a blackout." "Most blackout drapes ...are not a protection against flying glass, so if explosive bombs start falling proceed to the safest room in your house away from window areas." The imminent danger of enemy attack was confirmed almost immediately. On December 21, 1941 a Union Oil tanker was attacked and sunk by a Japanese submarine off the coast near San Luis Obispo.

Public fear turned to hysteria in February. On February 12th Walter Lippmann editorialized in favor of incarcerating Japanese residents: "It is the fact

Rosie and Joe and a House in L.A.

that the Japanese navy has been reconnoitering the Pacific Coast... It is the fact that communication takes place between the enemy at sea and enemy agents on land. These are facts which we shall ignore or minimize at our peril...The Pacific Coast is officially a combat zone: some part of it may at any moment be a battlefield." His "facts" were wrong, but he spoke authoritatively. Later the same day, a Japanese I-17 submarine surfaced off Elwood, an oil facility near Santa Barbara, and fired 15 rounds, though without major damage. On February 25 at 2:23 a.m. the air raid sirens sounded in Los Angeles. 10,000 neighborhood air raid wardens and auxiliary police officers turned out to handle the emergency. Anti-aircraft guns fired over 1,400 rounds. Five people died of heart attacks or falls. Shrapnel fell in several backyards. An unresolved dispute among officials the next day as to whether there really had been anything to shoot at, did little to dispel a bad case of what was termed "war jitters." It was more than jitters, it was a case of war paranoia, and it was contagious. Police departments were sandbagged. Skylights were painted black. Malibu beach was placed off-limits to allow military maneuvers. Set technicians from the studios were put to work camouflaging the sprawling aircraft plants to protect them from Japanese bombs. Concrete bomb shelters lined the median strip of Santa Monica's Ocean Park Boulevard in front of the Douglas plant. Concrete bunkers dotted the coastal bluffs. Signs went up everywhere: "Warning! Zip Your Lip on Military Information."[29]

Into this city, already transformed by post-Depression prosperity, by the construction of war plants, shipyards, refineries, and tracts of look-alike houses for war-workers, by the exacerbated issues of racial hatreds and disappointments, by war-bred fears and suspicions, came the General Issue Soldier, the average Joe, now committed to arms in the service of his country. He came, for the most part, by train, and he arrived at Union Station. Just opened in May 1939, its lofty beamed ceilings and mission tile floors, its courtyards planted to poinsettia and pepper trees, its red tile roofs and palm-tree-flanked arches confirmed the reputation of Los Angeles as a Mediterranean paradise.

He and every other soldier and sailor arriving from induction centers and training bases in other states were put aboard Pacific Electric troop trains and taken to their assigned bases in San Pedro, Long Beach, Santa Ana or elsewhere for training or for processing out to the battle line in the South Pacific. From the streetcar windows he could see the actual city he had known only as movie backdrops. The 1940s reality formed a dazzling contrast to the 1930s movie view. It was not at all like his home town, wherever that might have been. While the effects of the Depression might still be lingering back home, here, thanks to the war industries boom, the stores bustled with business, the downtown sidewalks were crowded in mid-day with shoppers and businessmen and bareheaded girls in the new knee-length cotton dresses instead of the muffled and coated look of colder climates. He saw a thriving urban center, but one with open space and touched with the magic of association with the movies he had watched. Except for City Hall, the buildings were limited to a height of 150 feet and separated by wide streets, permitting the California sunlight to set off bright facades with strong shadows. He could link the business buildings he passed with the one from which he had seen Harold Lloyd dangle or those in which movie detectives had their offices. Depending on his destination, he might pass a gargantuan ice cream cone or a bug-eyed stucco dog serving as eateries. As the streetcars passed from downtown through the suburbs, they offered views of the palm-lined streets. There were the Tudor and Spanish and Colonial and Moorish, the Hansel and Gretel and fairytale castle houses, big and small, that spoke of unrestrained fancies and exhibitionism of a sort he had believed, all along, he would see in Los Angeles. He knew he was about to have a holiday, maybe his last holiday, in a place built on dreams.[30]

As many as seven million servicemen passed through California on their way to war. They spent a few days or weeks in Los Angeles, San Diego or the San Francisco Bay area before they went to face the traumatic test of their lives. There were several major military bases within weekend pass range of Los Angeles. They processed vast numbers of young men. The intensity of the seven or eight-week military training period and the emotional apprehension about the war duty ahead charged furloughs with an urgent hedonism. Passes, usually for a weekend or for one day, were issued to 25 to 50 per cent of the men on a base. Such a leave, or "liberty" was too important to waste in camp, especially for a G.I. lucky enough to be stationed near the most glamorous and publicized place in the world: Hollywood.[31]

Hollywood films and star imagery during the war enhanced the serviceman's image of himself. This was a universal phenomenon among American military men, but the G.I. who saw duty, even briefly, in the heartland of the motion picture industry identified most directly with the heroic model projected by the films of the forties, because he himself had felt welcomed into a special and personal relationship with the people and places of movie fame. Motion pictures, as a communications form of unprecedented mass impact, presented the war and the G.I. in a glowing light. Immediately after Pearl Harbor, the studios moved to capitalize on war themes with films like "V for Victory" and "Remember Pearl Harbor." President Roosevelt, while insisting that "the motion picture must remain free in so far as national security will permit," set up a Bureau of Motion Pictures under the OWI in December 1941. It subjected every prospective motion picture to the basic question, "Will this picture help win the war?" By May 1942 the Bureau had decided that Hitler and Hirohito should not be portrayed as personal villains, but that movies should teach the American public to blame the German and Japanese people. The OWI established six categories of films and decreed that every movie should relate to at least one of them in order to inform and unite the public behind the war effort. OWI guidelines called for American men in uniform to be portrayed as handsome, heroic, tough, good-humored, and winning the war. They required that allied peoples be depicted as likable and worthy comrades. And they obliged film-makers to treat the enemy so negatively that the viewer could condone hating and killing him.

Although movie-makers expressed some fear that overregulation would ruin them, this was not the case. Movie-goers enjoyed the vicarious identification with heroic, handsome winners. It was comforting to believe that all French and English people were trustworthy. Troubled consciences were relieved by the persuasion that every Japanese and German was a dastardly villain. The public favored films featuring patriotism and personality to those depicting realistic terror. Box office receipts soared.[32]

The military services, with 11 million men and women under their command, sought to mold a single-minded fighting force. Orientation officers were provided with weekly indoctrination material. The officers preface to a 1944 Army orientation bulletin whose objective was to build "confidence in the home-front and a feeling of unity with the civilian production worker" as "essential to the morale of the soldier" went on to direct officers to "clear up any misconceptions [their] men have on this matter and direct their hatred against the enemy instead of the home-front." The average serviceman accepted the simplified and clear-cut images presented by motion pictures and military indoctrination and believed in himself and the cause he fought for.[33]

"Clark Gable Now Abroad", read a first page headline in 1943. The article updated the public on the doings of "Captain Clark Gable, former screen actor...[now] attached to the gunnery group of a bombardment squadron" and portrayed him as just "one of the guys" looking forward to brave action over Germany. Gable was only one of many male role models from the film and sports world who saw military action — action well-publicized by agents and newspaper reporters. If young men before the war had modeled themselves on movie actors, now their models were, like themselves, sailors or soldiers: they wore the same uniforms, they served the same cause, they were, in a sense, members of the same club. The identification of self-image with heroic and virile movie characters was confirmed by this common ground of military service.[34]

The G.I. who passed through the city where the movies were made found this self-image directly reinforced by his first-hand introduction to Hollywood. The number-one destination for any G.I. on leave was the Hollywood Canteen, a ramshackle building on Cahuenga Boulevard near Sunset which had been converted into a social club for servicemen. It was decorated like a Western film set, with rough wood paneling and wagon wheel light fixtures. It had a small stage, a dance floor, and a snack bar, and it offered live entertainment every evening. 6,000 actors, actresses, musicians, writers, directors and studio secretaries signed up to operate the Canteen. They performed on stage; they danced with the G.I.s; they served potato salad; they cooked and washed dishes; they signed autographs; they sat and listened to homesick soldiers; and they were even known to sew on buttons. The movie people were supplemented by some 3,500 young women volunteers — all of them carefully screened and chaperoned. Between them all, they treated the ordinary Joe like a Somebody.[35]

War films such as "Winged Victory" and "Guadalcanal Diary", were filmed on location at local military bases. This direct interaction with the movie-making process blurred the line between fantasy and reality for the soldier, the line between the scared, lonesome kid facing war, and the hero-winner he identified with in the movies. His interaction with the movie world in Los Angeles cast him in a role larger than himself, and one that won the adulation of the American public, just as if he were himself a movie star.[36]

G.I. weekend leaves in L.A. formed lifetime memories for a generation of young men. One of the renowned features of L.A. was evangelist Aimee Semple McPherson's dramatized sermons. She played to the new audience: "...Sister will preach an illustrated sermon using as her theme the song, 'Coming In On a Wing and a Prayer.' Parents of Servicemen and their loved ones will especially appreciate it." The Hollywood Bowl's Easter services, usually featuring performers of screen fame, were well attended by military personnel. The summer concert seasons were one of the popular tourist attractions provided free to uniformed servicemen.[37]

Los Angeles gave some servicemen their first taste of sin, too. A tawdry collection of bars, burlesque houses, dance halls and movie theaters hummed into the late hours at the intersection of Spring, Main and Ninth Streets. Across town on the Sunset Strip high-priced nightclubs hosted name bands and entertainers. Areas like these were considered "sore spots" by military police because of drinking problems. By late 1942, with arrests for drunkenness in L.A. 27 per cent higher than at the time of Pearl Harbor, Army, Marine, and Navy commands for the West Coast set up joint regulations limiting the hours for the sale of liquor to servicemen.[38]

The contradictions of L.A. added a certain tense energy to the atmosphere: a long-established tourist mecca for leisure, hedonism, and nonconformism in which the G.I. was bound by rigid military orders except for the brief respites afforded by weekend or 24-hour passes. It was a city of neon nights and sunshine, but with blackouts; more cars per capita than anywhere else in the world but with gasoline rationing. It was a center of Japanese settlement without Japanese — only the Kanji characters on shop signs and grave markers testifying to their recent presence. It was a city with a Spanish name and a history as a provincial Mexican settlement with a romanticized Spanish past. The quaint Olvera Street tourist attraction was frequented by G.I.s. Dancers with castanets and lace mantillas performed there on weekends, yet most citizens of Mexican descent were relegated to menial labor. Some Mexican youths expressed adolescent rebelliousness combined with a revolt against the depersonalization of underemployment and discrimination by affecting an exaggerated clothing fad, the zoot suit. In June 1943 fights between sailors and zoot-suiters escalated into five nights of military mayhem and several days of racist headlines in local newspapers. Police failed to protect the targeted victims. The conflict ended only when the Shore Patrol and Military Police declared the downtown area off-limits to servicemen. The press quickly downplayed the "Zoot-Suit Riots" as a case of "boys will be boys" and the servicemen returned to the bars and movie houses.[39]

Los Angeles was the place where G.I. Joe first met Rosie the Riveter. Few cities in the United States had such a high proportion of women in the industrial workplace as this center of war production. As one of the major transit and training centers for the military services, the G.I. on his weekend pass could not miss the 'California girl'. The war brought women into public places at a new rate. The favorable image of the serviceman as a suitable partner was enhanced by his centrality to the patriotic efforts of every war-worker, volunteer, and war-bond purchaser and by motion picture idealization. There were quick shore-leave romances and a high marriage rate. Wartime in Los Angeles was both romantic and liberating.[40]

While servicemen's image of Los Angeles centered on glamour and good times, accommodating the contradictions and tensions as well, it also included the warmth of personal kindness extended by average Angelenos.

DREAMING ON

Women's clubs brought books and checker games to military posts. Individuals knitted helmet liners and darned socks. U.S.O. volunteers played the piano, poured coffee and made servicemen feel at home in centers all over the county. The Grey Ladies wrote letters and read aloud for hospitalized veterans. The Red Cross served coffee and doughnuts to nearly 500,000 military arrivals and departures in Los Angeles in the course of the war. Military regulations forbade servicemen thumbing rides, so civic organizations and the Automobile Club urged local drivers to stop and invite G.I.s to ride. At Thanksgiving and Christmas, L.A. wore its heart on its sleeve: the newspapers coordinated a program of inviting servicemen to be guests in Los Angeles homes. Hundreds of homes adopted G.I.s for holiday dinners. 15,000 "sunshine baskets" were taken to men in military hospitals. The 34 U.S.O. posts in Los Angeles hosted home-cooked holiday dinners. And L.A.'s Santa Clauses handed out thousands of Christmas gifts to boys in uniform.[41]

The young American who came through Los Angeles during World War II had an experience here that changed his life and outlook. He had never been so honored, indulged, petted, pampered, or free as he was on his brief shore leaves in the City of the Angels. It was a short nirvana juxtaposed with the hell of war, the contrast only magnifying his rosy nostalgia.

ON AUGUST 14, 1945 Japan surrendered. In Los Angeles, people danced and hugged each other in the streets, tooted horns, rang church bells, showered papers from the windows, and rejoiced. Life in Los Angeles never returned to what it had been before the war. Rosie's home-front efforts and Joe's military presence had transformed the city visually and economically. The war had changed Joe and Rosie and their feelings about themselves, too. These changes would be reflected in the post-war cultural tone of Los Angeles.

The soldiers, sailors, and marines who had fought the war came home, many of them through Los Angeles. The wave crested in December, 1945. On December 17 there were 17,000 servicemen in Los Angeles waiting for paperwork and transportation. Twenty more ships with an additional 14,000 servicemen arrived the next day, and 90,000 more were expected by Christmas. It was not possible to handle discharge papers fast enough, and thousands were forced to stay aboard their ships in the harbor. USO entertainers performed for the shipbound G.I.s from a harbor patrol boat.[42]

The war had had a vital impact on the Los Angeles economy. War industries had lifted Los Angeles out of the Depression early and had gone on to bestow a spectacular prosperity on the city. Employment and productivity had soared but with the victories in Europe and Asia, military contracts were canceled. Between V-E Day in May 1945 and the end of that year almost 200,000 Angelenos lost their industrial jobs. At first, many of them were women and older people who quit willingly in order to rejoin returning servicemen or to return to retirement after "doing their part." Then massive layoffs followed, hitting the remaining women production workers hardest. Douglas Aircraft laid off 90,000 workers in one week, most of them women, only a fraction of them housewives happy to return to what columnist Hedda Hopper had called their "real job" of homemaking.[43] Return to peace disrupted the home-front worker's routine patterns and stability as well as the G.I.'s military regimen and role-certainty.

Peace did not catch Los Angeles unprepared. Planning for the potential impact of peace had occupied civic leaders, industrialists, builders and architects, and federal officials throughout the war years; dreaming of peacetime had occupied everyone. Since the beginning of the war, business and civic leaders in Los Angeles had worried about the rapid build-up and the urban problems that might ensue. They had expressed fears that an economy over-reliant on military contracts might suffer a severe local recession when peace returned. As early as 1940, the Mayor and members of the Planning Commission had begun calling for the development of large-scale post-war public works programs such as freeway construction, housing projects, school construction, urban redevelopment, flood control projects, and park creation. Their dual intent was to rationalize and shape the runaway growth of the city, and at the same time provide replacement jobs for the sudden and massive layoffs expected from military cut-backs. Boards, commissions, and City government departments worked on proposals for post-war funding and implementation. They were plagued by gadflies and politicians who labeled coordinated planning "utopian," "bolshevist," and "totalitarian." The political process itself tended to fragment future planning as special interests applied pressure for pet projects. Finally, jurisdictional division impeded effective long-range planning. The Los Angeles basin contained 46 political divisions with separate jurisdictions and, in some cases, overlapping constituencies; it was not easy for them to coordinate area-wide plans for transportation, water works or land-use. In spite of these obstacles, advance planning by state and local government made possible a freeway network and a waste-treatment system paced to post-war population growth, and it provided for the construction of elementary schools and playground facilities to accommodate the post-war baby boom.[44]

The effects of these peacetime conversion policies on the physical and visual identity of the city were perhaps most apparent in transportation. The war had severely reduced driving in an auto-dependent city, but that proved to be temporary. The first freeway had opened in 1940 and as tires, gasoline, and car parts became available again at war's end, it proved popular, leading to the post-war construction of an entire network of freeways. In 1947 automobile ownership reached a new high, with the equivalent of one car for every three residents in the county. The private automobile dramatically affected the image of Los Angeles in the 1940s and '50s. It contributed the sense of random and rapid movement that marked the cityscape at all hours. It added something unpleasant to the air quality, first identified in 1940 and designated "smog" in 1943.[45] The communal ridership of public transportation was replaced by the isolated compartments of private automobiles, thus adding to the depersonalization some observed. The Pacific Electric system, which had enjoyed peak profits in 1943, showed deficits for 1946 and 1947 and eventually terminated its streetcar system. Union Station, which had served 100 trains a day during the war, dropped to 66 at the end of the decade as commercial air travel became popular. Wartime Mines Field was converted into a major commercial facility, Los Angeles International Airport.

War industries themselves had also planned for peacetime. Months before hostilities ceased, war-plant management had tackled the problem of conversion. Aircraft leaders had started engineering work on commercial aircraft designs and some had taken contracts for motor casings for refrigerators or tooling contracts for other consumer goods manufacturers. The automobile plants in Los Angeles, which had been constructing army jeeps and parts for other military equipment, began retooling for a return to automobiles. The metal industries began developing new products for the post-war market, such as steel beams, pre-cast bathroom units, and aluminum window-frames. Research and development for such transitions was financed by V-Loans authorized by the Federal Reserve Board for companies holding military contracts. Because 1945 saw a wind-down to the war effort, rather than a sudden global victory, contracts were canceled over several months rather than all at once. The trained workers who were laid off at an aircraft company were often recruited by companies staffing up for consumer products.

The war build-up had produced permanent facilities which would serve as a core for new development. Henry J. Kaiser had constructed a major steel plant in Fontana. Tire companies had developed new synthetics for the military from which they had gained new equipment and market lines for post-war production. The military had extended the harbor facilities and breakwaters of the Los Angeles and Long Beach Harbors, ushering in the post-war expansion of commercial shipping. The large stretches of undeveloped land available for building large factories and the wartime formation of a large pool of skilled labor in experimental and advanced technology fields had been brought to the attention of industrialists nationwide. The physical facilities for a major expansion of the local economy were in place, thanks to the war.

In spite of layoffs at aircraft plants and shipyards, leaders of the Los Angeles business community greeted 1946 with confident optimism. They predicted a huge demand for consumer goods after four years of wartime shortages coupled with increased wages and unspent wartime savings. They noted an expansion of almost 30 per cent in the local population since 1940, and translated that into prospective consumer sales figures. They were right. Los Angeles became a regional hub, manufacturing consumer goods for a market extending to the entire West, whereas before the war the market had been local. Between 1945 and 1948, 1,300 plants expanded and 850 new plants were constructed. By January 1948 factory employment in the Los Angeles area was on the rise again. In September 1948, employment in all manufacturing industries combined, excluding aircraft and ship-building, broke new records, surpassing the war-time peak. By that time, the Cold War arms build-up and then the conflict in Korea breathed new life into the airplane industry. By 1950, that industry's concentration of engineers and scientists and its extensive plant facilities drew government contracts for missiles and other military hardware and California emerged the aerospace and electronics leader of the nation. Already, by late 1948, Los Angeles enjoyed full employment, high incomes, and record business activity.[46]

The war-workers and soldiers who had experienced Los Angeles during the war years also had plans for peacetime. They dreamed of family life in small houses in Los Angeles suburbs. The brief period that G.I. Joe had spent in Los Angeles en route to the war zone had been a high point in his life. It was the place where a recent adolescent, a general-issue soldier, had been important, free, and certain. He had basked in the attention given to him by America's reigning screen idols, by volunteers and local drivers, and by young women like Rosie.

Many G.I.s who had passed through Los Angeles had dreamed of returning after the war. That dream may have reflected a subconscious desire to regain the euphoria associated with wartime memories and make it a way of life. For war-workers who had come to Los Angeles for defense-industry jobs, life in Los Angeles with overtime pay had contrasted with the dreary depressed conditions they had come from; the climate was usually a favorable contrast, too;

and they had been singled out by the press, by military indoctrination, and by war bond publicity as homefront heroes, vital to victory. To the women in their ranks, the war years in Los Angeles had represented even more: the peak of personal independence, sense of self-worth, and romantic experiences. They, too, had won attention and admiration then, as they might not anywhere or anytime else.

The Los Angeles of their wartime memories was a city of neat pastel houses set back on green lawns among palm trees and other exotic plants. During his stint in the South Pacific, the G.I. fixed his gaze on a vision of peacetime life, a vision shaped by what he had seen. A 1943 ad (ILLUSTRATION 135) spoke to that dream: "From a Foxhole in New Guinea Pvt. Houston Dreams of Home," the copy began, "Oh, Boy, when I get out of this jungle, I'm going to build me a sweet little cottage in California and stay there the rest of my natural life. It won't be big but it'll have every convenience I can cram into it...a handy little kitchen — and a certain girl named Sally who knows how to make a juicy steak sit up and say papa."[47]

Rosie the Riveter also had dreams. In the midst of her war work years, a local newspaper poll determined that two-thirds of the women then working in Los Angeles hoped to continue doing so after the war was over. But the same poll showed that 80 per cent of them also believed that marriage was necessary for happiness, and that if they had to choose between marriage and career, the former would win. When interviewed in 1944 in a women's magazine, the nation's women war-workers agreed that "If the American woman can find a man she wants to marry, who can support her, a job fades into insignificance beside the vital business of staying at home and raising a family — three children is the ideal number...." As a woman who had

135. Advertisement, US Steel, 1943

FROM A FOXHOLE IN NEW GUINEA
PVT. HOUSTON DREAMS OF *Home*

"OH, BOY, when I get out of this jungle, I'm going to build me a sweet little cottage in California and stay there the rest of my natural life. It won't be big but it'll have every convenience I can cram into it . . . a shower with *hot and cold* running water for each bedroom . . . a handy little kitchen . . . and a certain girl named Sally who knows how to make a juicy steak sit up and say papa."

What kind of homes will the boys want when they get back from the wars in 194X? They've been fighting for a memory of home—a home better than anything else they've found in foreign countries. They'll be tired of strange places—and they'll want something not *too different* from the home they left behind.

One thing you can be sure of, this mechanized war has given our fighters a healthy respect for the value and versatility of steel.

For post-war houses, steel will be increasingly important. Because it lends itself to mass production methods, steel windows, steel kitchen cabinets, pressed steel bathtubs, sinks and lavatories can be made cheaper and will cost less to install.

Prefabricated steel stairs, clothes closets, shower cabinets will reduce costs. Steel roofing, gutters, and down-spouts will give the most economical service obtainable over a period of years.

Porcelain enamel, in a variety of colors, will give the architect something new to work with. It can be made into attractive paneling for bathrooms and into colorful wainscoting, tile, shingle for roofing and a host of other product. The war has speeded development of new steels, many of which will be available when the fighting is over. Our booklet, "US Ways to Make a Better Home" will show you what's new in steel products. Write for a copy.

U·S·S
BUILDING STEELS

COLUMBIA STEEL COMPANY, *San Francisco*
CARNEGIE-ILLINOIS STEEL CORPORATION, *Pittsburgh and Chicago*
TENNESSEE COAL, IRON & RAILROAD COMPANY, *Birmingham*
United States Steel Supply Company, *Chicago, Warehouse Distributors* · United States Steel Export Company, *New York*

already had the experience of working in a man's world, she could view her new uniform, the ruffled apron, as the conscious choice of the independent woman. She could be content with a vocation of serving her husband's starring role because she believed it was by her own choice.[48]

The generation which had come of age in time to fight the Second World War had grown up with motion pictures. Hollywood's films had been the national cultural arbiter across all regional boundaries. In the late 1940s the movies reinforced dreams of marriage, home and family. Under the influence of the war, the number one cultural institution of Los Angeles, the movies, had also changed. Pre-war movie stars were generally portrayed as remote idols, unapproachable dream objects, particularly for fans far from Hollywood. At the Canteen, and in shows brought to bases, the men and women in the armed services discovered a new image for the stars. Actors who had gone to war, just as they had, were buddies. The movie industry understood the new level of fondness and played on it. Stars were portrayed as freckle-faced and clean-cut kids; movies focused on middle-class family life. The top Oscar winner for 1947 was a movie about G.I.s returning to middle-class family life, "The Best Years of Our Lives."

As soon as the war was over thousands of individuals began to act on these personal plans for family, home, and a movie-perfect life in Los Angeles. Twenty-five to thirty percent of the servicemen from other states who were being processed through military separation centers in the Los Angeles area indicated plans to settle there. The newspapers interviewed families crossing the state line at the Needles and Blyth checkpoints and found that many of those intending to settle in Los Angeles were headed by out-of-state veterans who had seen the place during their military service. In December 1945 local headlines announced: "New Residents and Sun Seekers Pour into California by Thousands," "Swelling Migrant Tide Poses Perplexing Issues." The United States Employment Service issued a warning bulletin: "There is no acute labor shortage in Southern California, there is an extremely critical housing shortage in this area...[Unless you have a job prospect] and can make arrangements for living quarters in advance, temporarily postpone your trip to California." The advice fell on deaf ears. Between 1941 and 1949, 949,585 new residents settled in Los Angeles County. They faced a severe housing shortage.[49]

To meet that shortage, another element had been engaged in planning since the early war years. Architects, builders, and producers of building supplies had suffered during the lean years of the Depression. Although the war brought a renewed demand for housing, they had found themselves restrained by FHA

276

DREAMING ON

loan policies, government restrictions on building permits and critical materials, and finally a 1944 ban on private residence permits. Recognizing the escalating demand and its portent for the building trades as soon as controls were lifted, they considered future strategies.

In January 1944 Architect and Engineer carried an editorial by architect Michael Goodman addressing the prospects for his profession in the post-war period. Admitting that a large amount of home-building was a certainty, he took issue with the ebullient prognostications of most of the professional journals. He predicted three possible futures for the architectural profession. Architects might use the new housing demand as an opportunity to express artistic visions of avant-garde aesthetics and social reform ideals. He argued against this tendency, rejecting extremist designs as intentionally shocking and unlikely to be livable, buildable, or acceptable to the general public. He castigated the modernists as artistic dictators imposing their own aesthetic principles on the public rather than building for occupants' needs and preferences. A second possibility, to which he also objected, was that the need for large quantities of housing under conditions of material shortages would turn over the design process to building-material corporations. Pre-fabricated units would be factory-built, and design decisions would be governed solely by cost and machine-production factors. The architect would be reduced to "rendering clerical services to the Industry." The third possibility, to which he clearly ascribed, was that this war, like the previous one, would be followed by public conservatism: a demand for the revival of "the sentimental house...French, English, Spanish, not to mention our own Cape Cod strain of cottages," and only those technical improvements already confirmed by usage would be accepted. Goodman wrote the editorial as a plea for architects to join together in forming a joint position that would popularize the architectural profession, resist surrendering creative independence to industry, and prepare to capitalize on the realities of popular taste.[50] Goodman's plea failed to produce a united front. Los Angeles architects divided along the three paths he had predicted: their experimental projects and preparation for peacetime contributed significantly to shaping the housing forms that would sweep a new look over Los Angeles in the post-war years.

Goodman's article had specifically attacked the Case Study program. Under the editorial direction of John Entenza, California Arts and Architecture, a magazine devoted to modern architecture, had won international admiration for Southern California's coterie of modern architects by showcasing their works of the 1920s and '30s. In 1943, the magazine announced a competition, "Designs for Post-war Living." The intent was to elicit good designs for the typical post-war American worker/veteran. Contestants were reminded that the typical American would have been conditioned by the war experience: "He will be better trained, more technically aware, and more conscious of himself in terms of the economy under which he lives than any worker in history." As a result, he could be expected to demand "simple, direct, and honest efficiency" in his material environment. Encouraged to experiment with new materials and innovative construction methods, contestants were cautioned that they were to submit designs for houses that could actually be built at war's end, taking into account the regulations and shortages and the average wage-earner's budget.

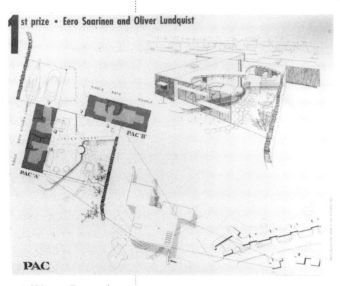

st prize • Eero Saarinen and Oliver Lundquist

PAC

136. Winner, Designs for Postwar Living, 1943

Contest entries were submitted by architects who had accepted the modernist credo: they viewed the social, economic, and technical problems as a challenge calling for original architectural solutions. Winners were announced in the August, 1943 issue. The jury had rejected entries it considered "architectural clichés," that is, entries with references to work of the past. It showed a preference for designs that incorporated pre-assembled components (PACs). The first prize winner, unanimously selected, was a design composed of two PACs with connecting curtain walls enclosing patio space as extensions of the interior (ILLUSTRATION 136). The plan drawing called readers' attention to the austere simplicity of line and form, the inclusion of two baths, sparse furnishing, and the presence of a helicopter in the garage.

In January 1945, the same magazine, now re-named Arts and Architecture, followed with a study in which architects were commissioned to "get down to cases" and actually build models. Thirteen "Case Study Houses" were to be chronicled from the design stage through the construction process in the next several issues. The featured architects were to create replicable, budget-restricted houses within the current material and building code limitations. Each house was to be financed by an actual prospective occupant willing to open his house to the public for inspection for several weeks after completion. The Case Study program was one that could have taken place only in Los Angeles. First, Los Angeles, had attracted a number of outstanding modern architects including

Richard Neutra, Rudolph Schindler, J.R. Davidson, Gregory Ain, Raphael Soriano, and Harwell Hamilton Harris. Second, the film industry, educational institutions, and pioneer technology had brought together an element of innovative individuals who formed a client base. Since the 1920s, the built-environment in Los Angeles contained a number of avant-garde architectural masterpieces, legitimizing the form. Only under circumstances such as these could an editor like John Entenza have found enough interest in modern architecture to sustain his magazine.

Government regulation, price controls, and material priority classifications dogged the Case Study Houses from the beginning. The first house was not unveiled until July 1946, almost one-and-a-half years past the projected completion date. One intention of the Case Study project was to demonstrate the preferable livability, economy and aesthetics of the modern house over the historically derivative styles that had previously marked vernacular housing. Although 360,000 people toured the first six Case Study Houses, none of the designs led to tracts of replicated versions to house returning G.I.s. The Los Angeles Times Home Magazine featured the first three Case Study Houses prior to the public tours. The Times felt obliged to explain "even what constitutes the fundamentals of this strange new futuristic type of building."[51]

While the Case Study Houses did not produce an immediate rash of vernacular versions at the tract level, the program's publicity and tours helped convince the public of the desirability of a number of features, some of which the Times writer summarized: "its maximum use of glass, its arrangement of courts, patios, terraces, sun decks and rambling wings...allowing large areas of the house, which otherwise might be corridors and dark hallways, to be exposed to sunlight and fresh air." Entire walls of glass, overhanging roof extensions calculated to maximize sun on the walls in winter and shade in the summer, extremely simple interior spatial design and furnishing to reduce drudgery, house plans in which the social areas were open to outdoor spaces and removed from street noise, and a second bathroom were all features implanted in the popular mind by the Case Study Houses and other modernist works publicized in the architectural magazines. The high-art connotations of these avant-garde models served to legitimize the minimalist lines and lack of ornament of the stucco box, vernacular tract house built strictly to budget. Their publicity exposed a wider public to a new aesthetic standard: all of the Case Study houses were crisp, rectilinear forms stripped of fussy ornament and historical reference, made beautiful by means of geometric form and textural contrast.

137. Mar Vista tract
house, 1948

Although post-war prosperity and eventual relaxation of controls resulted in thriving practices for the modernist architects in Los Angeles, their residential work was mainly limited to private commissions for one-of-a-kind houses, rather than to replicable, inexpensive houses in large numbers. One exception was a 1948 tract by the office of Ain, Johnson and Day for the Advance Development Company (ILLUSTRATION 137). Fifty-two houses were built in Mar Vista. The area of each was 1,050 square feet. The same basic floor plan, varied by turning it on its site to present different sides toward the street, and multiplied by offering mirror images, resulted in eight different appearances while preserving the cost-efficiency of identical construction steps on all 52 houses. Clerestory windows on the street side provided light without sacrificing privacy, sliding glass walls opened the houses to back terraces. Sliding interior walls permitted flexible spaces. Asymmetrical forms employed occasional diagonals for dynamic interest. But neighbors complained that the houses "stuck out like sore thumbs," and banks were reluctant to extend loans. Eventually, the developer suffered a severe financial loss. Understandably, few other tract developers were willing to invest in such "strange new futuristic type[s] of building."[52]

Goodman's second prediction, that architects might be subsumed by industry, did not seem implausible in the 1940s. Plywood and plastics manufacturers, lumber companies, and public housing agencies looking forward to the post-war market, employed designers to improve on the pre-fab concept. Renowned architects experimented in designs for housing modules which could be factory-produced. Houses incorporating pre-assembled components won prestigious architectural competitions. In 1943 and 1944 pre-fabs looked like the course future housing would take (ILLUSTRATION 138).

In Los Angeles the housing shortage reached critical dimensions by the spring of 1946. Building material shortages were curtailing the construction of new houses, reflected by the fact that the Los Angeles Times could garner no more than one page of display advertisements for new houses. Among them were several for pre-fabs aimed at the first-time home-buyer: "Veterans! You Can Find a Place to Live! ... Hamill and Jones Production Homes, pre-assembled material for quick erection. $1994..." Another company offered pre-cut, ready-to-assemble houses from $225 to $1750. Some listed a dozen or more dealers.

Pre-fabs claimed a number of positives: a construction time of six hours per unit, cost equal to an automobile, the possibility of combining modules to permit expanded and individualized dwellings. But they were stigmatized by their association with the factory-made trailers and housing modules developed too quickly during the war for military families and war-workers. The haste and cost-guidelines under which those pre-fabricated structures were developed had resulted in a poor-quality product. The popular perception of pre-fabs was the regimented sameness and shoddiness characteristic of emergency military housing. Advertisements which confirmed this negative perception pictorially outweighed the positive aspects. Building trade magazines warned that the quality, resale value, and financing of pre-fabs were unpredictable. Government controls on materials and financing made it impossible for many of the pre-fab manufacturers to deliver to prospective customers. By 1947, articles, references and advertisements for pre-fabs were rare.[53]

138. Plywood Ad

A number of Los Angeles architects followed Goodman's third course and prepared designs in readiness for the post-war market, designs with sentimental references to historical traditions, and with only those gadgets and design features already market-tested in the earlier war boom. Illustrated plan books, presenting prospective home buyers with a variety of small-house ideas, poured off the press between 1945 and 1950. Some of these were basically promotional portfolios for particular architects. Some were really catalogs: for $40.00 the reader could send for "a complete set of specifications, [and] working drawings...complete and ready for any builder to work from." Others presented collections of editorially-selected sample houses from the files of architectural or family magazines. Most of the small "Dream Houses" illustrated in such books reflected conservative tastes.

Los Angeles architect Paul R. Williams published one of these in 1945, "The Small Home of Tomorrow." Among the 40 houses illustrated with floorplans and elevations were a "Cape Cod," a "New Englander," a Monterey Revival, a Spanish Colonial, a French Provincial mysteriously labeled "The Regency," and a small house with shuttered windows, a paneled Dutch door, and stone trim meant to capture "a subtle domestic character" and "the charm of the old" which was even more mysteriously labeled "Contemporary." Williams profited from this advance preparation: when the housing shortage was at its peak in April 1946 he advertised his already-available plans for sale for the do-it-yourself builder. A reviewer's summary of one of these small house books could apply to most of them: "the ultra-modernist and the seeker for radical, unorthodox or socialized departures...will not find them here." "There is not very much [in this book] that is experimental, untried, novel or tending toward practices to which the general public has not at least given the nod." These safely middle-of-the-road house designs were ready and waiting when the post-war housing shortage hit Los Angeles.[54]

THE NATION THANKED its war veterans by giving them the opportunity to buy a home. In 1944 Congress authorized the Veterans Administration to set up a mortgage guarantee program. The program, which was administered by the FHA, enabled veterans to borrow the entire appraised value of a house with no down payment. The returning soldier or sailor, who was thus encouraged to dream of a house in Los Angeles as the reward for war service, received a rude awakening. There was a severe housing shortage and he was going to have to wait until houses were built before he could buy one. In the meantime, he had to find a place for himself and his family to live. The influx of newcomers which the Los Angeles Times had counted and interviewed at the state border in December 1945 arrived to find hotel and apartment rates in Los Angeles skyrocketing. The Office of Price Administration (OPA) extended rent control regulations to war-surplus pre-fabs, remodeled chicken coops and railroad cars. Would-be homeowners were reported sleeping in automobiles and city parks. Los Angeles estimated an immediate shortage of at least 90,000 housing units. The State Reconstruction and Reemployment Commission determined that a minimum of 280,000 new houses would be needed in Los Angeles County between 1945 and 1949. The colleges were besieged by veterans returning to school who could find nowhere to stay. UCLA contracted for seven disassembled apartment buildings that had been built for shipyard workers in Vanport, Oregon and had them set them up on Gayley Avenue. The City of Burbank spent $40,000 to house 100 veterans' families in trailers. In April 1946 the Los Angeles City Housing Authority started selecting 1500 veterans on a hardship basis to move into Rodger Young Village, a veterans' emergency housing project of war surplus Quonset huts erected in Griffith Park. There were 13,000 applicants. In July the Census Bureau estimated there were still 50,000 married veterans doubling up or living in makeshift quarters.

139. Brentwood apartment house, 1952

New construction, however, was hampered by war-time price controls and shortages in construction materials. In January 1946, the Federal Government issued new regulations designed to stimulate the building of moderate-cost housing for veterans. A selling price ceiling of $10,000 or rent of no more than $80.00 per month would qualify a builder for priority release of regulated materials such as lumber, pipes gypsum board, and bathtubs, if he offered the finished house exclusively to veterans for the first 30 days. In April 1946, new federal regulations mandated that one-fourth of all new residential permits go to rental units; new rent controls were instituted; and the price ceiling for a single-family residence was reduced to $7,000 for the Los Angeles area. But materials remained scarce, even for priority projects. Few contractors could afford to build and sell under this ceiling.

In the 1946 election, affordable veteran housing emerged as a volatile political issue. Early in 1947, the new Congress removed controls on certain materials for houses under 1500 square feet, and permitted a 15% rent increase. There was an immediate surge of activity on the local construction scene, with 32,000 dwelling units completed in the first five months, compared with 35,000 for the entire year of 1946. Rent decontrol and the one-fourth-permit rule favored apartment house construction. Between April and October, 1947 the number of monthly permits for multi-family dwellings rose from 674 to 2,256.[55] Block after block of look-alike apartment houses sprang up along thoroughfares in Culver City, Santa Monica, West Los Angeles and other communities. Repetition and similarity made them seem even less interesting than they were. (ILLUSTRATION 139).[56]

Vast tracts of small single-family dwellings replaced fields and orchards in Westchester and Panorama City, Covina and Azusa, and other outlying areas. They shared that tone of look-alike, mass-produced, machine-age products. They were studies in cost-cutting efficiency and built quickly of light, cheap material: wood frame, tar paper, chicken wire, and stucco. Fritz Burns, the builder of war-worker houses in Westchester, teamed with Henry J. Kaiser, the metals and ship-building magnate who had constructed worker housing in the Northwest, to form Kaiser Community Homes. The company bought 500 acres in the San

140. Ponty Homes under construction, 1947

141. View of San Fernando Valley

Fernando Valley and built 2,000 small homes. Company literature boasted that they had devised 700 variations on one floorplan. Developers Louis Boyar, Ben Weingart and Mark Taper built 17,000 homes in Lakewood. Large tracts of small, look-alike houses, altered slightly by applied trim and a rearrangement of modular units were built by similar development firms throughout the county. On this scale, builders could operate like a huge assembly line: lumber arrived pre-cut, conveyor belts carried shingles to the roofs, and carpenters put together the frame units with automatic nailing machines. At Lakewood, as many as 100 new houses were started per day.[57] With the houses and housing projects built in the 1939-1943 period (ILLUSTRATIONS 131, 132 and 134) and those built on this gargantuan scale in the post-war years (ILLUSTRATIONS 133, 139-140) the magic once attached to Los Angeles by movie-set houses went flat, the valleys filled in with smog and suburbia (ILLUSTRATIONS 141).

If vernacular housing expresses the dreams of a generation, then what was so different about the 1940s? First, if one were viewing Los Angeles in 1948, one would have to consider the role of government regulation. Regulations on price, size, financing, permits, and materials curbed expression. They channeled building toward small houses and apartment houses. They limited price and size, favoring huge developments of monotonous efficiency. They favored stylistic references to historic traditions.

Second, the unusual circumstances of war-time population boom and prosperity coupled with restricted home-building and veteran home-buying benefits stimulated such a high demand for new affordable houses that developers could hardly build fast enough. It was not necessary to engage in costly advertisement or promotional campaigns. It did not matter what a competitor developer offered. Whatever was built would sell. All the developer had to do was make houses which satisfied institutional standards, and qualified for G.I. or FHA loans. Those standards were conservative, based on tastes generalized to the nation as a whole.

Third, the homogeneity of Los Angeles housing of the 1940s, relates to the new population wave of the 1939-1950s period. Every previous wave of settlement had involved a stage in which the prospective settlers were convinced — before they ever left home — that Los Angeles offered something better and different than life back home. They had been convinced by rumors of agricultural wonders or miraculous cures in the 1870s, for example, or movie glamour and frolics in the 1920s. The Second World War brought job-seekers fleeing desperate Depression unemployment back home, a push of necessity as much as a pull of promise. The war also brought involuntary visitors in military uniforms. Instead of a selective slice of the dreamers, the misfits, and the overly imaginative, the 1940s wave involved a median sample of the healthy young men of America. The 1940s exposure to Los Angeles was much less selective, much more a representative sample of the general American population, than any previous period of city growth. Of course, not every worker or soldier forcibly exposed to Los Angeles chose to settle there in the post-war period. That stage of the selection process remained voluntary. But since the exposure sample was broader, it is reasonable to assume that the respondents represented a broader sample, too. Also, the generation of war-workers and G.I.s had been subjected simultaneously to the same war-time fears, indoctrination, government-standardized movie images, and G.I. loan-based and advertisement-stimulated dreams of a post-war house in the California suburbs where an adoring wife was happy to fix her hero-husband a juicy steak. There was a sameness about this generation that had gone through so much together that even their ideals of where to live were identical — for many it would be that place of the last furlough before heading out, Los Angeles. These were people that conformed to institutional regulations . They bought assembly-line look-alike houses without demurring.

BY THE END OF THE 1940s, Angelenos proved ready for a more expressive form of housing: the Ranch style. In 1949, Congress declared that "A Good Home" was not just a dream for the average American family, but "a Democratic Right." The Housing Act of 1949 was designed to ensure "the realization as soon as feasible of the goal of a decent home and a suitable living environment for every American family." It launched a new federal loan program under the Federal National Mortgage Association (Fannie Mae), offering loan guarantees for larger and more expensive houses than ever before.[58] In Los Angeles, the new financing and the removal of the last federal material restrictions in 1948 coincided with soaring industrial wages. The boom in cracker-box tracts and apartments had eased the worst of the housing shortage. Los Angeles builders geared for a more demanding clientele, and one willing to pay more for its dream houses.

The Ranch style or Western Ranch style had been identified during the 1930s. It had appeared in plan books and magazines as early as 1936. It was offered as one possibility in Paul R. Williams' 1945 book. The style as it came to be applied in the 1950s was marked by rustic surface materials such as

142. Extended Ranch style house, 1960s

fieldstone, used brick, or board-and-batten siding. The Ranch style house was, at first, a single-story building forming an 'L' or a splayed 'U' around a backyard patio. Sliding glass walls opened the rooms onto these out-of-door living spaces. Even in the later and more elaborate developments of the style featuring split-level floor plans (especially on hillside sites) or one-and-a-half story living rooms, the Ranch style usually fit the term, "rambling," in reference to its informal grouping of volumes as opposed to a tight mass. A long, low-pitched roof, extending to overhanging eaves, unified the house horizontally, creating an illusion of extended size. The interior was open without internal corridors or formal walls separating the social rooms. The ruggedness of the exterior was often echoed inside with flagstone entries, stone or used-brick hearths, exposed beam ceilings, and knotty pine paneling. The total effect was one of informality and outdoor living (ILLUSTRATION 142).[59]

The origins of the Ranch style are the subject of some debate. To the passerby studying these houses for clues to the Los Angeles past there is no debating their significance as expressions of cultural synthesis. The immediate inspiration for the California Ranch Style was Western Americana, both the

DREAMING ON

historical reality and as romanticized in motion pictures, the fiction of authors such as Zane Grey, and, later, television series. One of the earliest examples of the style (sometimes credited as the progenitor), was the 1927 Gregory house, a rural retreat built near the northern California community of Santa Cruz by architect William Wurster. The Gregory house was intentionally patterned after the agricultural buildings of the American Western frontier. The vernacular Ranch houses which proliferated in the Los Angeles area from 1948 into the 1960s drew upon the same rural traditions. Even the simplest models featured wood siding. In the more elaborate examples, board-and-batten is used, at least on the street front. Dove cotes, split-rail or board fences, barbecues, and barrel planters were favored touches of ranch-life rusticity.[60]

Every American G.I. who had come through California on the way to war between 1942 and 1945 had grown up on the legends of the Wild West and the Cowboy Hero. He had identified with the Cowboy Hero in Tom Mix or William S. Hart movies in the '20s and '30s and he had learned to measure himself in relation to the values represented by the fictional cowboy. The relationship was symbolically acknowledged by the wagon-wheel light fixtures in the Hollywood Canteen. Westerns had been one of the most successful motion picture genres from the start. They matured with the generation that settled in Los Angeles in the '40s and '50s. In the 1940s, producers explored new varieties: Westerns that portrayed the rebel or outlaw sympathetically; Westerns with heavy sexual overtones; humorous Westerns; and Westerns with a social-conscience message. The typical cowboy hero was laconic, unquestionably masculine, and heroic. He lived in an informal environment and his social relationships were direct and uncomplicated. For a generation dosed on nationalistic fervor and xenophobic suspicions, the cowboy, as a singularly American creation, provided a safely uncomplicated folk hero. The G.I.'s wartime self-image, confirmed by the admiration and attention showered upon him by civilian society, was very similar to the cowboy image as portrayed in motion pictures. The female roles in Westerns admitted a wider range: from Dale Evans, who, in 1946, had not yet been kissed on screen after 17 Westerns, to Jane Russell, who played a spicy siren in "The Outlaw" the same year. At both extremes, however, and characteristic of '40s Westerns in general, filmmakers had abandoned the "shrinking violet" type in favor of independent and outspoken female roles more acceptable to post-war viewers and closer to the self-image of Rosie the Riveter.[61]

The boom in Ranch style tract housing that began in 1948 and extended through the 1950s was naturally concentrated in the largest remaining open spaces in the L.A. basin, areas such as West Covina, Torrance, and especially the San Fernando Valley. In the case of the Valley, the historic and motion picture associations of the area dovetailed with the make-believe imagery sought by middle-class home buyers as well as tract-home builders. In the 1850s and '60s ranchers such as Vicente de la Osa, Miguel Leonis, and the Van Nuys-Lankershim interests had raised livestock and dry-farmed grain in the Valley. Butterfield stagecoaches had stopped at the Encino Tavern. Bandit Tiburcio Vasquez had haunted its borders. The San Fernando was the real Old West. Ranching had declined by the end of the century for want of water. But when, in a burst of progressive era optimism, the voters of Los Angeles had authorized the construction of a 238-mile aqueduct to bring water from the Owens Valley to Los Angeles, they had also unwittingly voted the transformation of the dry San Fernando Valley into a lush orchard paradise, to the benefit of the business and civic leaders who had bought up the acreage for just this eventuality. The water arrived in 1913. Speculative land-owners began to sell small irrigated farm plots for good prices so that the Valley was soon covered with a patchwork of walnut groves, poultry farms, and citrus orchards. Barns, sheds and little farmhouses of board-and-batten construction typified Valley life in the 1920s and '30s. The Valley truly represented the simple, rural life.

The availability of rural scenery, and, even more importantly, the large land expanses at low rural prices yet close to the Los Angeles urban center, drew several of the motion picture studios to locate in the Valley in the 1910s and 1920s. Warner Brothers, R.K.O., and Twentieth Century Fox each set up ranch lots where their Western films and other rural scenes were shot. R.K.O made a number of films at the old de la Osa ranch house in Encino. Elaborate Western sets were erected at Corriganville, in a northwest corner of the Valley. The backdrop for Wild West adventures in the films was the San Fernando Valley.

In the 1920s and '30s, motion picture stars and famous directors began buying and building rustic ranches in the San Fernando Valley. These retreats were usually not working cattle-ranches or citrus farms, but weekend retreats with white rail fences and simple wood-sided houses in which actors could relax, away from the pressures of autograph seekers. Some actors and actresses lived out their movie fantasies on these ranches, riding horses for fan-magazine photographs. A few developed ranches for breeding horses. Stars such as Ernest Borgnine, Monty Montana, Barbara Stanwyck, and Betty Grable were among them. During the '40s era of tract development in the valley and other outlying areas in the Los Angeles basin, the proximity to these "ranchettes" of the stars stimulated real estate sales. The predominance of the Ranch style in the tracts built in the San Fernando Valley during the 1948-1950s building boom was, in the style's reference to the historic land use and movie mythicization of the area, quite appropriate. Ranch style houses rooted the fantasies of the '40s generation to the realities of site.[62] The population of the San Fernando Valley increased nearly six-fold between 1940 and 1960. The citrus and walnut orchards, horse ranches and open spaces of the Valley were plowed under and planted with rows of make-believe ranch houses. Few commented on the irony.[63]

143. Ranchified stucco box, 1952

By 1948, the reduction of the housing shortage forced developers to seek gimmicks to win buyers in a newly competitive market. The answer proved to be the Ranch style house, produced in the same industrially-rationalized methods that had produced the stucco boxes, but laid out and ornamented as a stage set for resident dreamers of Western dramas. The star attraction of the Los Angeles Home Show of 1947 was a board-and-batten Ranch style house, with knotty pine paneling inside. Builders of extensive tracts of small low-cost houses began facing their stucco boxes with rough wood siding and forming their floorplans around backyard patios in order to claim the luster of the Ranch style label (ILLUSTRATION 143).

The popular imagery of Western Americana and the psychological needs of the G.I. generation for the simple solutions associated with it by films and fiction were not the only sources of the Western Ranch style. The Ranch style served as this era's way of acknowledging the Spanish Heritage of Los Angeles as well. Builder Cliff May, one claimant to founder of the style, insisted that it was directly inspired by the adobe houses of the early California rancheros. He was himself the descendant of the Estudillo family, and he enjoyed childhood memories of an aunt's historic adobe. The first house he designed in 1931 while the Spanish Colonial style was still in full swing, had won attention for its authentic historicity. May's use of clay tile roofs and stucco walls to simulate adobe, the pillar-supported extension of the roof beyond the house wall to form the traditional corridor, and the arrangement of rooms in a single-depth string around a patio as a loose 'L' or 'U'-shapes were direct echoes of early California forms. Years later, summing up his building career, he reminisced,

"To me, when we lived on the [Las Flores] ranch, with cross-

Rosie and Joe and a House in L.A.

ventilation and rooms spread out and around courtyards, [in the] basic old California plan, it seemed to be a much better way to build and live.... [T]hat, of course, is the ...whole California way of living [—] protection [from and/or] trapping the sun and for having privacy... [It is] what the early Californians did and what I...did and still do."

In the mid-'30s he built several such houses in the Los Angeles area, some of them with shingled instead of tiled roofs and with board-and-batten sheathing similar to the American era "improvements" to the Mexican era adobes. These were brought to national attention in House Beautiful, House & Home and Sunset magazines in the early '40s. Although their illustrations showed some Spanish Colonial features, the national-circulation magazines usually ignored reference to these regional historical traditions, instead publicizing May's houses as the ideal homes for "Western living," a term they regularly used to indicate a casual, leisure-oriented, outdoor lifestyle. Thus recognized as authoritative, the designs of May and a partner, Chris Choate, became the most widely built versions of the Ranch style. Beginning in 1953, their designs were purchased on a royalty commission basis by large-scale developers for reproduction by the thousands.[64]

In the use of the concrete slab floor to bring the interior level close to the patio level, and in the layout of a string of rooms opening to the outdoors, as well as the concept of cross-ventilation which this permitted, the ideal versions of the Ranch style represented, consciously or unconsciously, a direct relationship with the adobe ranchos of Mexican California. The life for which these houses were designed echoed the spirit of Old California. Again, there is an irony. Nineteenth-century American observers had disparaged the laziness of the leisure-enjoying Californios and of the crudity of cooking, eating, and washing out-of-doors. Angelenos of the '20s had acted out the ease of fictionalized Spanish grandees of old California in private patios. Angelenos of the '50s brought leisure and its architectural setting around full circle with barbecues and ramadas. Similar to the simpler houses of the adobe period, the '50s Ranch style houses were only loosely wrapped around or backed by patios or terraces which were rarely more than paved portions of their back yards. Families spread their daily activities out to this arena — they cooked on brick barbecues, ate on patio furniture, and refreshed themselves in backyard pools. Utilization of outdoor space by Angelenos in the period from 1781 to 1848 was from practical necessity: interior heat, smoke, and lack of plumbing. For Angelenos in the post-war period outdoor pursuits were considered pleasurable privileges.

While the Ranch style house incorporated the spirit and some of the

144. Historic Los Encinos
Adobe in 1948

forms and functions of the historic Spanish past, they distinctly shunned the copying of historic models which had been so popular in the '20s. While they accommodated the romanticization of the Western frontier America with barrel chairs, ruffled lamp shades, and braided rag rugs, they refused to continue the romantic myths of the Spanish past so popular in the '20s and '30s. Clay tile roofs became the mark of houses no longer new. Arches were incompatible with the vernacular form of the Ranch style house. Symbolic of the postwar generation's attitude toward the early California legends, Rancho Los Encinos (ILLUSTRATION 144) was subdivided in 1948. The developer set up field headquarters in the shabby remains of the de la Osa adobe. No mention was made of lace mantillas or silver-studded saddles.[65]

The 1950s ranch house also represents, in some ways, the vernacular modification and acceptance of modernism. Features of High Art Modernism adjusted for mass-production, had produced the Case Study experiments. There, art and new living arrangements were tamed by practical considerations of volume building, limited materials, and salability. The connecting themes are especially clear if we recall R.M. Schindler's 1920 house on Kings Road, a

Rosie and Joe and a House in L.A.

rambling arrangement of three-sided pavilions extended on the fourth into outdoor living areas (ILLUSTRATION 117). It was built on a concrete slab, at ground level for direct transition between interior and exterior. The floorplan was made open and flexible by means of movable partitions. Clerestory windows on the street facades permitted light and cross-ventilation without sacrificing privacy. The Schindler design accommodated a casual life-style and the California sunshine in a way quite similar to the 1950s vernacular ranch houses. The two booms in stucco box houses — the war-worker tracts and the immediate post-war tracts such as Kaiser Community Homes — had been aesthetically legitimized by their association with the stark lines and efficient use of space

145. Moore house, 1965

drawn from the High Art Moderns and Case Study publicity. They had been popularized by the application of shutters, paneled doors and other minimal references to historic traditions.

The Ranch style house was the final compromise between the modern canon and vernacular tastes. The modernist features of horizontality, floorplan and siting considerations, construction efficiency, and minimal details on the interior, were popularized by the easy process of tacking to the facade a number of popular decorative motifs that played upon the sentimental attachments of the general home-buyer for the All-American Cowboy mystique. In this way, the simple stucco box, so long as it opened onto a small back patio, could be called Western Ranch style by applying a bit of wood siding on the front surface, an artificial dove cote on the gable, or an eave extended to cover a front porch. The interior of the typical ranch house and the experimental moderns shared such features as slab floors, layouts drawn from efficiency studies, lack of unnecessary moldings, a use of machine-made components and new materials. Ads for Ranch style houses, even those with the most quaintly decorated street elevations, often used the words, "modern" and "new."

Even the least modern feature of the Ranch style, its decorative rusticity, was redeemed by its association with the work of modernist leaders such as Neutra and Schindler. Schindler began experimenting with wood exteriors in the 1930s; Neutra and others turned to wood as the war curtailed the use of other materials. Lloyd Wright's adoption of his father's Usonian forms resulted in an extreme expression of the ranch idiom (ILLUSTRATION 145). Their explorations of wood as a medium for avant-garde design condoned rusticity as high fashion. A taste for rustic wood, open floorplan informality, the functional benefits of built-ins, horizontality, and the extension of living space to the out-of-doors were expressed in the first two decades of the century by The Craftsman Movement and its housing form, the California bungalow. The California bungalow, which had so deftly accommodated the values and dreams of the middle-class homeseekers to the climate and culture of Los Angeles in the 1900s and 1910s, had favored these features as means to realizing the movement's values. It had encouraged the health-seeking settler to enjoy fresh air activities as did the Ranch style. The best bungalow architects had manipulated light and shadow to create textural works of art. The best examples of the Ranch style houses, with their brick and rough-textured boards, their light-filtering patio roofs and overhanging eaves, and their multiplicity of volumes did likewise (ILLUSTRATION 142). Finally, the California bungalow had enfolded its occupants in a cozy affirmation of the family unit, of the father's dominant role, and of folksy security in a rapidly changing world. The Ranch style, reinforcing the roles of G.I. Joe, Rosie the former Riveter, and the family as idealized in post-war motion pictures and television series, met the same kinds of needs for the post-war generation.[66]

Like the bungalow of the earlier period, the Ranch style house proliferated. In every suburban open space, tracts of houses were built bearing the marks of Western imagery and incorporating layers of previous architectural

responses to a unique city. As with the bungalow, builders and homeowners interpreted the Ranch style for a range of income levels with variations all loosely related to the rural ranch house of the fictionalized American West. They might incor-porate American Colonial references such as diamond panes or overhanging jetties. They might add touches of whimsy: an exaggerated dove-cote or rippled bargeboard (ILLUSTRATION 146). A tract located, appropriately, between Warner Brothers and RKO studio lots combined fancies in miniature Hansel-and-Gretel in-the-Wild-West settings (ILLUSTRATION 147). Others referenced the Ranch style to the vacationer's A-frame (Illustration 148) or celebrated rusticity in the ultimate degree: the house as barn (ILLUSTRATION 149). Like the bungalow before it, the Ranch style tract house spread to the rest of the nation, appearing even in regions where its frontier and sunshine references were inappropriate. It became, by the 1960s, the archetype of the American middle-class dream.[67] Between 1939 and the 1950s Los Angeles had experienced its third major population boom, far exceeding those of the 1880s and the 1920s.

146. American Colonial ranch house

147. Hansel and Gretel ranch houses

The stucco boxes of 1939-1943 and 1946-1948, and the Ranch style houses from 1949 through the 1950s reveal several things about Joe and Rosie and their generation. The look-alike character of the 1940s stucco box was a response to the controlling influence of governmental regulations, reflected the regimentation of a generation. Even when controls were relaxed, and the 1950s generation of home-buyers could express themselves more freely, they continued to express a war-formed homogeneity by choosing one ubiquitous form, the Ranch style. The Ranch style house revealed an understanding of L.A.'s meaning as it had been built up layer by layer in the past, accommodating style features and layouts developed by previous waves of settlers.

148. Vacation style ranch house

149. Barn style ranch house, 1952

150. Front yard wishing well, 1950s

Finally, the Ranch style houses that dominated suburban Los Angeles by 1960 reveal beliefs and dreams unique to the generation for which they were built. The Ranch style exuded an aura of permanence because it appeared old, or at least old-fashioned. There was a gingham sentimentality to it that spoke of security and of "coming home". Its open, relaxed interior and patio extension made a person feel bigger than they were. Its Western flavor seemed to confirm sex roles that labeled the male as a Marlboro Man and denied the threatening ambivalence of changing women's roles. Feminists have pointed out that a den, with masculine decor, was a frequent feature of the Ranch style house, while women's personal room was the kitchen. However, women also enjoyed a new independence in the Ranch style house, because of technological advances and modernist simplification of detailing which reduced housework. In the insecurity and fear common to a polarized world in the nuclear age, the generation that had been indoctrinated to simplistic views of American goodness and international villainy found refuge in a house that was All-American, a house without Japanese motifs or Spanish tile roofs, but instead echoed the American cowboy myths of machismo and moral certainty . The Ranch style house and its sunny, Southern California setting became the paradigm of the American dream. ❦

C H A P T E R

XIV

IS THIS THE END OF THE RAINBOW?

. . . an endless plain

endlessly gridded with

endless streets,

peppered endlessly

with ticky-tacky houses

clustered in

indistinguishable neighborhoods.

"AS L.A. GOES, SO GOES THE NATION." By the 1960s, news commentators, popular magazines and students of urban development frequently cited Los Angeles as both the trend-setter of national culture and the initial test tube of national urban problems. Two decades later a British observer remarked that Los Angeles is the "most American of American cities." Comparisons are made to Los Angeles wherever arterial boulevards are bordered in low-profile commercial buildings, car sales lots, shopping strips, signs and logos connect urban centers to extensive tracts of look-alike houses, each with its patch of lawn, its garage, and its strip of driveway. The American dream and the Los Angeles image sometimes seem synonymous. But their merger was neither sudden nor is it complete.[1]

In the 1920s, radio, motion pictures, and automobiles served as vehicles of a nationalizing culture. Film publicity and advertising projected to the rest of the nation an image of the Los Angeles lifestyle as a lively alternative to tradition-bound regional cultures.

The Ranch style house that flourished in Southern California in the 1950s symbolized the diffusion of the Los Angeles allure to accommodate the American dream in general. Ironically, while a trend toward uniformity was being imposed on Los Angeles, the style that had drawn together so many earlier expressions of L.A.'s unique identity was being exported for adoption by the nation at large. Wartime fears, demands, and unity; post-war regulation; Cold War nationalism; and television hastened the trend toward a uniform national culture and its local expression in tracts of ubiquitous stucco boxes and Ranch style houses. The latter, which so aptly synthesized the various strands of earlier L.A. imagery, but in a nationalistically pure and safely traditional rubric, was adopted and promoted as the ideal home in national-circulation women's magazines in the '50s and '60s. The layered themes that had drawn generations of dreamers to California, and which were so well expressed by the Ranch style house could be appropriated to a national culture because of the all-American style references to cowboys and patriots. New Englanders, Southerners, Middle Westerners could (at least, in season) wear the clothing, tend the barbecues, cultivate the suntans, and build houses expressing the L.A. dream, all without leaving home. As tracts of Ranch style houses appeared in new suburbs across the nation in the '50s and '60s, the rest of the nation became more like L.A.. What is the meaning of Los Angeles, under these circumstances of regimented sameness and nationwide appropriation of L.A.'s imagery?[2]

That question took on a new urgency in the '60s and '70s as it became clear that Los Angeles was filling up to overflowing. By the 1960s, the basin and

Is This the End of the Rainbow?

interior valleys had filled in. The coastal palisades were crowded to the edges. Hillsides had been carved into terraced building sites. Marshes had been drained and filled and built upon. Houses had been constructed even where there was no ground to build them on. And still the metropolis continued to grow, spreading beyond political boundaries and pouring over into neighboring Orange, San Bernardino, and Ventura counties.[3] In 1984, architectural historian Esther McCoy summed up five decades' observation of the perennially transitory imagery of Los Angeles. Through the 1950s, she observed, Los Angeles had remained "a huge and loose experiment being built," rather than a place with a fixed referential meaning. Only in the '60s did a significant number of Angelenos begin to notice that the process of city-creation was drawing to a close. Long-resident and newly-committed Angelenos began studying their urban environment in a critical, proprietary way, taking stock of what kind of place it had become, and calculating what its future prospects might be.[4] They found Los Angeles to be a city of unassimilated and sometimes alienated minorities, a city where anomie and mediocrity were countered by defiant outbursts of flamboyant individualism, cooperative efforts at social and aesthetic reforms, and newly-appreciated traditions.

Civic and business promoters and national circulation magazines had long described Los Angeles as the City of Tomorrow, indicating the Southern California lifestyle as the harbinger of future national cultural patterns. Planners had used the same label in predicting that problems experienced by Los Angeles in transportation, air quality, water supply, and other areas portended problems soon to be faced by other cities. Realistic natives concurred with the basic premise of these professional prognosticators, for Los Angeles really was the city of the future. After the Second World War it had emerged as an acknowledged hub of advanced technology. In a city where truth and fiction had often been difficult to distinguish, the Buck Rogers fiction of rockets and spaceships which had informed the design of 1930s Streamline Moderne buildings, became an industrial fact of the 1960s.

At the close of World War II, local defense industries had set their engineers and scientists to develop new products. Thriving research, aerospace and electronics industries date back to 1947 in Southern California. It was in that year that the American public was apprised of a new, polarized balance of power in international relations, a situation termed the "Cold War." The Cold War and the ensuing Korean Conflict, the space race initiated by the 1957 Sputnik launch, and then the war in Vietnam produced a flood of government contracts for missiles, electronics, data processing systems, and aircraft which brought a new surge of prosperity to the area. Los Angeles firms took the load in these fields.

Such a concentration would make the regional economy vulnerable in times of military cut-backs, but through the 1980s commercial diversification enabled these "high-tech" industries to adapt and thrive. An aerospace slump from 1967 through the early 1970s forced a redirection from military systems into computer technology, advanced communications systems, and precision instruments which were intended to inure the local economy to future defense budget cuts. Southern California companies continued to receive a high proportion of the military and space contracts awarded each year by the federal government.[5]

L.A.'s acknowledged leadership as a center of advanced technology has drawn a narrowly specialized group of settlers. Beginning in the 1940s, high-tech industries offered academic environments and high salaries, in order to stimulate creative thinking and to entice leading physicists, chemists, engineers, and mathematicians from across the country to join their staffs. In the first three decades following World War II, California's professional and technical workers more than doubled. By the 1980s America's highest concentration of Nobel Prize winners, scientists, engineers, mathematicians and skilled technicians resided in the Los Angeles area. The newcomers' educational specialties and their professions were predicated on a faith in high technology.[6] That faith quickly became visible in architectural form.

A respectable stock of buildings in various modernist forms already marked Los Angeles. The general public had become familiar with architectural statements of avant-garde ideas dating from the 1920s and associated with the international colony of intellectuals, artists, and film people. The 1950s and '60s witnessed new experiments in futuristic structures by a new generation of architects. The same period also saw a popular acceptance of vernacular forms of modernism far exceeding the Depression era's brief interest in Streamline Moderne. Minimalist single-story structures with walkway canopies supported by steel pipe-columns, serving as small office buildings, schools, and public service facilities were so commonplace by the 1960s that they drew little notice.

To match the luster of scientific intellectuality conferred by L.A.'s state-of-the-art technology, a more visionary architecture was called for. John Lautner and others rose to this challenge. 'Chemosphere,' a 1960 residence (ILLUSTRATION 151), expresses a truly "out-of-this-world" excitement about the technocratic era. The very functional "flying saucer" hovers at the rim of a steep hill, supported by a slender steel and concrete stem. It commands a breath-taking

151. Chemosphere, 1960

view of the San Fernando Valley and is, in turn, a highly visible icon to high-tech futurism.[7]

Lautner's 'Chemosphere' was a symbolically extreme statement of the new era's faith in technology, human engineering, and the machine aesthetic. In Los Angeles that faith was so widely shared and so little challenged that it could be effectively stated without such flamboyance. Modernism, once practiced only by Daring Originals, was taken up by teams of technicians employing the scientific design approach.

The house in ILLUSTRATION 152 is a product of that scientific design approach. The owner, Anne Strick, a transplanted Philadelphian, liked Los Angeles for its mountains and untamed vistas. She chose a canyonside lot with a mountain view, but one which posed engineering challenges to builders. With a previous experience of living in a "beautiful piece of architectural sculpture" and with a higher priority this time of providing livability, she rejected the single artist approach for the cooperative laboratory process. She created her own floorplan, as she herself knew best the functions the house was to serve. Oscar Neimeyer served as the original architectural specialist, setting up sketches, plans and models, none of which was totally satisfactory to the owner. Some of his ideas for the exterior were incorporated, so it is not incorrect to say that the house is "after the design of" Neimeyer. Ulrich Plaut, a designer of industrial buildings, was brought in to revise and carry out the construction. Others were consulted for ideas and solutions to particular problems. David Travers recommended designer Amir Farr, who resolved a number of inconsistencies in the interior. Ms. Strick and Farr designed the landscaping with the advice of a professional gardener. Inside, bright colors, a high living room ceiling, and an entire wall of glass and vista free the spirit without sacrificing a warm nesting feeling. The house communicates the best aspects of the technological faith. Its design process illustrates the rational approach to solving unique problems and planning for particular applications. It brings together functional integrity, harmonious proportions and textures, an aesthetic unity of house, site, and landscaping.[8]

Technological innovation found new means of naturalizing housing to the unique local climatic conditions. In the 1900s, Greene and Greene had incorporated shadows as architectural forms in their shingled Craftsman masterpieces. In the house in ILLUSTRATION 153, a new material, textured concrete in pre-formed sections, is contrasted with tropical foliage to accentuate shifting patterns of light and shadow in the Southern California sunshine.[9]

The geological jumble of mountains, canyons and alluvial valleys that compose the Los Angeles landscape are signs that Nature has not yet finished shaping the place. Significant earthquake damage in 1933, 1971, 1987, and 1994 are proof of that.[10] Periodically, temblors, brushfires, floods, and ocean storms have destroyed large numbers of houses. Phoenix-like, the demolished structures are soon replaced by new ones, the replacements representing dreams refined by time and experience. In 1961 a disastrous brushfire destroyed dozens of houses in the Bel Air hills. After the fire, the hills were gradually transformed by a blanket of new houses. The house in ILLUSTRATION 154 is one of them. Constructed between 1966 and 1969, it typifies the 'ideal house' of Los Angeles in that period and "L.A. Living" as described by home and architecture magazines through the following decade. It is a spatially isolated single-family house situated on a hillside with an ocean view, but within a five-minute drive to a high-density center of business and commerce. While its facade is solid and closed at the street level, to provide privacy for the occupants, the view sides are open. Its Schindlerian legacy of the deconstructed geometric unit permits an open interior plan, inviting at once to informality, light, and the outdoors.[11]

152. Strick house, 1964-65

153. Babcock house, 1956

Somewhere between the immediate post-war visions of replicable, functional, reasonably-priced (but sometimes institutionally bland) modern housing which had motivated Gregory Ain and the Case Study program, and such individualized ideals as the Chemosphere, the Strick residence, and the Bel Air phoenix, there was room in Los Angeles for a

Is This the End of the Rainbow?

154. Wood and glass
modern, 1966-69

155. Balboa Highlands, 1963

vernacular adaptation of high-tech modernism.

Balboa Highlands, a tract of about one hundred houses that opened in 1963 in Granada Hills, was one such adaptation. Tract developer Joseph Eichler had already successfully marketed tracts with avant-garde styling in Marin County and the San Francisco peninsula area now referred to as Silicon Valley. For his first venture in Southern California, Eichler's firm employed architects A. Quincy Jones and Frederick Emmons. They designed post-and-beam pavilions with exposed beams and plank ceilings, flying A-frame entries, and interior atria. They buried the heating and air-conditioning ducts in the concrete slabs. The interiors formed bold sculptures of natural light and plastic forms marked by vertical slit windows, clerestories in long horizontal or dynamic triangular shapes, and the long thin lines of the exposed beams. Posts, beams, indirect lighting, and glass walls brought modernist minimalism to the middle-class, mass-produced level, without sacrificing a certain sophistication.

A tract of houses such as the Balboa Highlands model in ILLUSTRATION 155 is testimony to a common meeting ground between the competitive concerns of the building industry and the futuristic concepts of a unique home-buying element. Between the late '50s and the early '70s, large-scale tract developers struggled competitively for survival. Tighter credit and expensive-to-implement building codes put new houses out of reach of many of the wartime baby-boomers just reaching the family-formation stage in the early 1960s. The war generation was beginning to retire and sell its empty nests. Real estate activity focused on resales and apartments. Investors turned to apartment-house construction, which was enhanced by tax shelter possibilities. The large-scale builder who wished to remain in single-family tract housing needed to create a unique commodity that would attract the population element most likely to seek a new single-family residence: young professionals in high-tech industries or related services. Marketing-minded developers, "merchant builders," as Eichler's son called them, succeeded commercially with dramatically modern tracts such as Balboa Highlands because they had discovered a new "community of taste," a well-

156. Marina City
apartments, 1972

educated buyer element that appreciated futuristic styling and technical solutions to functional specifications, an element that knew what it liked and was able to pay higher than median prices to get it. Fifteen years earlier, tract versions of modernism had failed for lack of consumer appreciation. But by 1963, they were well received.[12]

The apartment building boom from the late '50s into the '70s was slower to adopt sophisticated elements of modernism, but significant landmarks emerged in the '70s and '80s. One of these assumed symbolic significance, as it marked both a departure from L.A.'s characteristic low-spread look and a change in land-use patterns.

Marina City's three towers form the distantly visible masthead of Marina del Rey, a recreational harbor facility developed between 1957 and 1966 under the direction of the County of Los Angeles. The marshy 800-acre site where the harbor was excavated was once a county dump. In the early '50s, Hoppyland, an amusement park on the theme of TV's serial cowboy, Hopalong Cassidy, occupied the site. Marina del Rey was designed for more sophisticated and higher-priced outdoors leisure activities. A complex plan for coordinating land and water traffic patterns permits 6,000 boats, 5,800 apartments, numerous restaurants, hotels, and other businesses, and thousands of visitors to come and go efficiently by land or water. Marina del Rey operates like a clean, functional machine. The site's references to a discarded or a fictionalized past have been obliterated.

Paralleling the imagery of the marina, the three towers of Marina City are modern solutions to the desire for sun, fresh air, and leisure living (ILLUSTRATION 156). The apartment complex was developed by Summa Corporation, a corporate offspring of Hughes Aircraft. The architect, Anthony J. Lumsden, for Daniel, Mann, Johnson & Mendenhall (DMJM), created forms resembling split stacks of rings. Each apartment has balcony access to the sun two times a day. Each has a view of the marina channel, even if only through the split in the ring. Each faces inward to the city-within-the-city community. And each faces the outer world alone. Since the '20s, organized outdoor leisure activities have been an important feature of Los Angeles. In the '70s L.A.'s most extensive playground was marked by a secular axis mundi — modern housing

Is This the End of the Rainbow?

157. Pacific Townhomes,
1982

for the good life, a trinity of symbolic markers visible from long distances like the cathedrals that had marked medieval market towns.[13]

Outstanding examples of high-modernism added new dimensions at the more intimate neighborhood level as well. The stark industrial lines and colors of a set of four townhouses by Stafford and Binder (ILLUSTRATION 157) contrast sharply with the folksiness and fictional historicism of the older bungalows and apartments around them, riveting the attention of viewers. The contrast dramatically underscores the rationality of the machine aesthetic. The colors are those of a new age: red stacks and rails against factory gray walls. They accentuate the repetition of shapes which attest to the unwavering modernist credo of replicability, use of industrial stock parts, ahistoricism, experimentation, and concern for health, hygiene, natural light, and functional organization of space. It is appropriate that the cool logic and steady rhythms of the machine are reflected in housing in L.A., the seat of advanced technology.[14]

There are other connotations of technology and the machine as well. Dehumanization. A struggle for identity. Topics whose associative context shifts, while the potential anguish of their interaction remains constant. The advanced technology sector offered little to L.A.'s Black and Hispanic minorities in 1960. Public schools in minority neighborhoods displayed a dismal record of high drop-out and delinquency rates, a low ratio of academic classes to technical courses, the least experienced teachers, low student and staff morale — all exacerbated by cultural and economic counterforces to the educational system. As a result, inner city minorities were often underqualified for jobs in technology. Racial stereotypes extended the perception to other applicants of the same ethnic origin. By the mid-1960s the expansion of electronics and related industries led to new industrial parks on the outer edges of the metropolis. Residents of the economically depressed inner city were left behind, without reliable transportation, too distant from the limited assembly line jobs these industries might offer them. Caught in a spiral of unemployment, poverty, welfare, discrimination, and hopelessness, racial minorities in Los Angeles, as in many other American urban centers, exploded.

In August 1965, fiery riots broke out in Watts and nearby areas. Thousands participated, 34 died, over a thousand were injured, nearly four thousand were arrested, and $40 million in property damage was recorded. Afterwards, a blue-ribbon commission was appointed to study the causes of the Watts Riots. It found serious inadequacies in police-community relations, social services, employment, education, transportation, health care, and in housing. The underlying problems were poverty among the Black minority, and the alienation from the Anglo majority which perpetuated and worsened that poverty. Houses record social history. After the riots, Watts was marked by empty lots among the small tract houses off Central Avenue where houses had burned while angry mobs, letting out the frustrations of years as an underclass, confronted all-white fire department crews.

In 1985 the County and the City of Los Angeles set up another blue-ribbon panel to conduct a follow-up study. It found continuing problems of a serious nature in police-community relations, only a short-lived improvement in social services, significant but insufficient improvement in health and transportation, and an educational system perhaps worse than it had been twenty years before. Housing that had been aging and in short supply in 1965 was even older and scarcer in 1985. One-third of the study area's residents lived in public housing projects. Only 300 new housing units had been built in the area in twenty years, none of it single-family dwellings. The one positive note

Is This the End of the Rainbow?

was a job-training program which had resulted in the rehabilitation of 600 existing residences. The 1985 commission concluded that, again, the basic problem was poverty; that critical problems remained unresolved because the Black community in South Central Los Angeles was a low-priority concern by government bodies dominated by Anglo interests.[15] At the same time, it was noted, record numbers of Black families were moving out of the inner city into suburbs such as Inglewood and Pomona.

In the decade following the Watts Riot, a larger proportion of L.A.'s Black population moved from city to suburb than in any other metropolitan area in the nation. Those who have remained by the necessities of economics and inertia, internal despair, and external disinterest, experience new forms of alienation.[16] Houses in South Central Los Angeles are defensive redoubts under siege. Windows are barred, doors reinforced, walls covered with graffiti. On some blocks, every house has bars on the windows, testimony to the fear of the police, the gangs, the drug-dealers, and the desperate who practice violence as a way of life. The bars outline disintegrating dreams.

In another aging neighborhood not far away, the dreams of a second alienated minority were affirmed and reinforced in a burst of color on housing project walls. The loose term "East Los Angeles" is widely applied to the area extending east from Civic Center, an area which includes Lincoln Heights, City Terrace, Boyle Heights, Brooklyn Heights, Whittier, and Belvedere, as well as East L.A. proper. It is the largest Spanish-speaking barrio in the United States. The area is poor, politically underrepresented, cut into sections by five freeways, and socially fragmented by differences in language, national origin, immigration status, and by economic competition.

Until 1972 Estrada Courts looked like any other thirty-year-old wartime housing project.[17] Then a blaze of brilliant pictorial expressions of rage, revolution, sacrifice, and the stylized patterns of pre-Columbian art burst out on its walls. Houses talk. Estrada Court's eighty murals shout. They shout across language barriers. They shout with the voices of barrio youths as they styled themselves in rebellion against their parents' passivism.[18]

During the era of ethnic activism, the '60s and '70s, Mexican American youth suffered from an identity problem deeper than that common to adolescence in general and more acute than that of many other ethnic minorities. Unlike the turn-of-the-century Old World ghettos of New York or Chicago, the barrios of cities in the Southwest retain connections to immigration sources. Neighborhoods remain culturally and linguistically Mexican because there has been a continual influx of newcomers from the homeland, an obstacle to

158. Murals, Estrada Courts,
1972-82

acculturation. The Anglo Angeleno majority, perceiving common cultural patterns, language and appearance, fails to notice the individuality of the Hispanic and sees only a stereotype. Immigration policy and regulations regarding the employment of aliens turn the stereotype into economic oppression. The brand, or the suspicion, of the undocumented alien is extended to all Hispanics. An employer may prefer to hire someone who does not look or sound Hispanic, rather than risk penalties for employing illegals. Or he will take the risk of hiring illegals knowing he can pay them less than minimum wage for long hours in substandard working conditions because economic desperation and vulnerability to deportation will keep them cheap, hard-working and docile. A young person of Hispanic ancestry entering the job market for the first time must compete for employment at the level of the exploitable undocumented alien.

Education is not a clear-cut solution. Restricted opportunities, linguistic limitations, and a community not fully able to supplement or support academic study, coupled with economic necessity, result in a higher high school drop-out rate among Hispanics than for any other group.

In the late '60s Chicanos began painting murals on barrio walls. An unemployed art teacher painted her grandmother, "Mi Abuelita," on a park bandshell. Two brothers painted a mural, "The Birth of Our Art," on the front of a small storefront to debut their art gallery business. In 1971 Willie Herron expiated his grief at his brother's stabbing in a gang action by painting a giant rip on the alley wall where his brother had fallen, a rip bursting with blood, Chicanos killing each other, an anguished grandmother, pre-Columbian symbols, and gang *placas* (insignias marking territory). Such murals touched a deep responsive chord within the Hispanic community. Young people began participating in mural projects all over East Los Angeles, on the walls of housing projects, parking lots, stores, vacant buildings, and retaining walls, creating some 350 murals by 1976.[19]

For these Angelenos, murals were more than decoration. They were more than a means of communicating messages about loved ones or art or commerce. They went beyond the individual or group need to make a mark.

159. "Innocence",
mural, 1973

They were a statement of cultural heritage, and pride with a linear descent from pre-Columbian Mezo-American fresco forms and the revolutionary *muralistas* of Mexico.[20] It was in this tradition that the mural painters at Estrada Courts intended their murals to arouse minority consciousness and activism among residents and speak to passersby about injustices, pride and hopes (ILLUSTRATION 158). Murals designed by trained or self-taught artists, approved by wall owners or housing-project directors as a deterrent to graffiti, as beautification, or as alternatives to gang violence painted by neighborhood youngsters under artists' guidance, provided a rallying point.[21]

Many of the murals developed youthful themes of fantasy paradise, bright futures, and high hopes, always with dark shadows or dangers lurking in the corners. Norma Montoya's mural, "Innocence," (ILLUSTRATION 159) is one of these. In a style as simple as a children's book illustration, the artist portrayed the innocence universally idealized to childhood, sunny and untroubled. But there are clouds ahead, the responsibilities and concerns inevitable to adulthood. It is a mural that faces a major thoroughfare, Olympic Boulevard, and it speaks across ethnic stereotypes, creating a bridge between minority and majority, a bridge of understanding of shared human experience. Other murals are more militant in content. While they may appear antagonistic and threatening to outsiders, they molded support within the barrio for "La Causa", the cause of revolutionary opposition to oppression.[22]

Even the simplest arrangements of stylized ancestral designs, as in ILLUSTRATION 158, opened a dialogue within the barrio. The youngsters who worked on the sidewalk walls questioned, researched, learned, and celebrated their shared roots. The residents of the project and the larger community responded warmly to the murals. They gathered to watch, criticize, ask questions, and admire the murals as they were painted. The murals provided a new community bonding. In turn, the public responsiveness and the act of creating as a group of peers encouraged the painters. The murals transformed drab, standardized housing units into colorful and lively landmarks, each structure unique.

The Chicano murals of the 1970s contributed a special meaning to the theme of houses as a means of expressing occupants' dreams. The murals converted residential clusters into galleries of intense pictorial messages. Some of the artists first acclaimed for their murals have found success in mainstream art circles. Advertisers, the entertainment industry, and politicians are adjusting to the upward mobility and numerical strength of Hispanics in Los Angeles. However, the murals at Estrada Courts are beginning to fade and peel. No new murals have been executed there since 1983. The Housing Project Manager attributes this to upward mobility. Instead of painting angry messages on housing project walls, "the kids here are more interested in getting degrees in business management." "Cultural heritage is on a back burner." Statistics on education, under-employment, birthrate and immigration contradict him.[23]

Los Angeles is the second largest Mexican city in the world, after Mexico City and ahead of Guadalajara.[24] It has been populated by Mexicans since 1781, a hard-working people with genuine human concerns. While American prejudice substituted a myth of Spanish grandees, Anglo Angelenos had ignored the real Hispanic residents. The 1970s murals confronted the local majority with the real people, their problems, and their power. The murals' bold colors and intense messages attracted international attention. Outdoor art and bright colors served as free publicity for L.A.'s number one feature, its climate.

The gratifying attention to Los Angeles did not go unnoticed by civic leaders. They paraded dignitaries past the East L.A. murals. As the 1984 Olympics approached, they observed that murals were a cheap means of beautifying the urban landscape. Moreover, colorful pictures discouraged graffiti and encouraged pride. For all these reasons, public and private funds were poured into mural art. Concrete freeway canyons bloomed in colorful murals — not paintings of defiant pride or anger or pain, but bland and sunny murals from which all reference to dark clouds, powerful emotions, and conflict was excised. Still, the adoption of the mural form for Olympics beautification and its widespread identification as an essential ingredient of the visual experience of L.A. represents a fusion of cultures.

While the Black and Hispanic populations formed compacted growths in the center of the metropolitan mass until they erupted in fire, riots, and painted walls, a very different demographic movement was taking place on the urban peripheries. There, the rest of Los Angeles, not defined by minority label or common cultural identity, was diffusing outward to lower-density housing tracts and low-rise apartments. There they engaged in lawn-mowing, television-watching, and the compulsion to fashion themselves and their houses after their neighbors. Conformity marked their utopia.

Ownership of a single-family, suburban house surrounded by landscaping, had been identified as the American dream at least since the post-war G.I. Bill brought it within reach of middle Americans. It had been The Los Angeles ideal from the beginning.

In the 50s' and 60s' a growing economy and materialistic values, a suburban tract house in Torrance or Northridge or West Covina offered dream-fulfillment of several kinds at once. Houses were a sound investment, where a sure-fire increase in equity brought phenomenal returns. "Moving up" to a larger and more expensive house was widely recognized as the way to leverage an owner-investor's nest-egg ahead of the rate of inflation. Upward social mobility assumed a sacrificially righteous tone when it was rephrased as "providing our children with advantages we didn't have."

Traditional gender-roles, challenged by the actual experience of the war years, were reinforced in the post-war period by the demands of suburban home maintenance, as well as in the visual symbology of the Ranch style. The Veblenesque value of conspicuous consumption as one consideration of homeownership, fueled an urge to buy ever bigger and more luxurious houses, to devote primary attentions and energies to home decor and front-yard landscaping, or to engage in home-improvement projects which would enhance appearance and resale value. The demands of home care and the exercise of consumer skills related to home decoration presupposed the traditional one-breadwinner-one-housewife family. Social homogeneity marked the post-war suburbs, until economic downturn, the spiraling demands of upward mobility, and the burdens of single-parenthood caused growing numbers of women to enter the workforce, and curtailed new building and upward speculation. In the '50s and early '60s, the houses in a given tract were the same age; similar in size, price and style. They attracted families of approximately the same size, income level, and tastes. Three and four-bedroom houses with generous backyards appealed to families with two or three school-age children.

Government contributed to this homogeneity. Freeways were routed to connect suburban pockets of settlement with centers of urban concentration. They channeled movement to the same shopping, working, and entertainment areas. Zoning regulations, conservatively designed to protect property values and the single-family lifestyle, isolated housing tracts from multi-unit residences and commercial development, locking in bedroom-community uniformity. Local building codes, attentive to union and building material lobbyists, affected price and limited variety. Aerospace contracts to Los Angeles firms swelled employment of engineers and technicians at the same times in the same suburban areas where the recipient plants were located, diminishing human variety within neighborhoods. Federal and state financing regulations for veterans and small homes, bankruptcy protection for homeownership, and income tax deductions for home loan interest all conspired to spur single-family housing within a middle-range economic level.[25]

On the valley floors and flat coastal mesas of the Los Angeles outlands, the orange orchards and the eucalyptus wind-breaks were plowed under, the bean, celery and strawberry fields graded for house sites. Landmarks and color were replaced by undulating drab seas. From the air, coming into Burbank Airport over Sepulveda and Van Nuys or into L.A. International Airport over Torrance and Hawthorne, there is a boring sameness about the roofs and their attendant rectangles of front and back yards. On smoggy days, the colors flatten, the lines of houses and shadows blur into a nondescript uniformity. Lewis Mumford decried it: "Los Angeles has ... become an undifferentiated mass of houses, walled off into sectors by many-laned expressways..." Reyner Banham noted the worldwide image of Los Angeles as "an endless plain endlessly gridded with endless streets, peppered endlessly with ticky-tacky houses clustered in indistinguishable neighborhoods..." And, although these descriptions are at odds with L.A. as a whole or in many of its parts, and although clearly an over-generalization, the spread of war and post-war tracts lent the image of monotonous uniformity a certain credibility.[26]

Color concentrated instead on the boulevard commercial strips. Potential customers were not pedestrians, but the drivers and passengers of automobiles passing by at 35 miles per hour, intent on destination rather than on intermediate vistas. To call attention to their product or service, strip businesses resorted to aggressive signs and logos, or to flamboyant architecture. As the strips filled in, they became a forest of flashy signs, each designed to outbid the next in the competition for the motorist's eye. The use of symbols, pictures, bold colors, gigantic scale, neon, and movable elements created a visual assault productive of emotional upset, if not physical fender benders. They are central to the charge that Los Angeles is the capital of "kitsch" (meaning everything someone else castigates as cheap and tasteless). Building shapes joined the compensation for motorists' attentions, their roofs tilted at rakish angles or pitched in steep A-frames, their logo themes demanding to be noticed. The flamboyant new forms marked coffee-shops, bowling alleys, and even apartment houses.[27]

The 1960s saw a new boom in apartment construction. For many young people born in the post-war baby boom and ready to form families, single-family dwellings were out of reach. They set up housekeeping in new apartments. So did newcomers to L.A., attracted by the growth industries. Southern California housing costs were escalating more rapidly than the national cost of living. Even professionals who relocated to Los Angeles found that the equity brought from the sale of a home elsewhere would not purchase a comparable home here. They might rent an apartment until they could adjust to the disparity. The rise of suburban industrial parks also brought lower-wage earners to the suburbs in search of housing near their jobs. Their salaries mandated apartments. State regulations governing savings and loan institutions stimulated apartment investment by easing credit terms. Tax regulations regarded apartments as businesses and permitted deductions for depreciation, sparking investment by silent partners in search of tax shelters. The extension of commercial strips and connecting traffic arteries, zoned to permit multi-unit dwellings, opened large land parcels to apartment construction. Along these connecting streets, building firms, utilizing the large-scale techniques perfected in the '40s, erected rows of

160. Tiki Hut apartments, 1964-65

as many as fifty apartment houses at a time. Financial incentive introduced equally monotonous Monopoly-board apartment houses as infill in older neighborhoods, replacing declining neighborhood stores and decaying Victorians.

As a mass-created, cost-efficient product, the average 1960s apartment building was a stucco box, maximizing space by packing as many dwelling units and parking spaces onto each lot as the building code and packaging ingenuity would permit. Four- to eight-unit, two-story structures usually featured open-corridor access along one wall, with parking cubicles and spaces at the back of the lot. Larger units were often built on the same plan, connected as an open square around a courtyard, with parking spaces sunk below grade along two or more sides. If coffee-shop entrepreneurs lured motorists off the street with eye-catching designs, apartment house developers could play the same game. The flat street-front surfaces of stucco boxes became graphic display boards where eye-catching patterns, glittering textures, suspended swag lamps, non-functioning trellises, or identifying names were posted to catch the apartment-seeker's eye.

161. View from freeway

Unsubdued flair, flamboyance, or what one apartment builder called "dramatic punch" was a commercial must to compete for the attention of potential renters. The same basic stucco cube, with an overstated A-frame and a concentrated planting at the entrance (ILLUSTRATION 160), went even further. It evoked images of luxury vacations, escapist movies, or a cheap motel in a tropical paradise. At any rate, in the commercial competition for apartment-seekers' attention, such visual dramatization proved the margin of entrepreneurial success. The 1960s left L.A. peppered with such garish images. Some called them "dingbat" apartments, others called them "kitsch". Out-of-town newspaper columnists sneered. Some Angelenos expressed embarrassment. Apartment building owners, however, contentedly continued to fill vacancies, collect rent and build even more structures with "punch" and "flair." The general public found them attractive and moved in.[28]

The 1960s spate of freeway construction reinforced automobile dependency and long commutes as a way of life for suburbanites. They have been blamed for the shallowness, lack of social responsibility, and the loss of community often remarked of L.A. culture by outside observers. From the isolation of his speeding vehicle, the freeway-traveler's perspective of his city fragmented into a succession of brief, long-shot glimpses. The elevation of freeways cut across suburbs enabled him to look down on rows of backyards, each with a pool — and a solitary person sunbathing beside it, a person programmed by advertising, movies and television, to believe the Los Angeles lifestyle was hedonistic bliss (ILLUSTRATION 161). Once beyond their own neighborhoods and on the freeways, Angelinos are too isolated by distance and speed to comprehend any neighborhood other than their own in any detail. Even on surface streets, the raucous signs and bizarre architecture of commercial enterprises out-shout the few pedestrians and the homeless for the attention of the motorist.[29]

In the 1970s, a growing number of Angelenos began to engage in a critical reappraisal of themselves and their relation to place. Articles analyzing L.A.'s good and bad points appeared with increasing frequency in the local press and in books. Local colleges introduced courses on Los Angeles history and cultural heritage. Concerned citizens formed organizations to preserve and

Is This the End of the Rainbow?

162. Hodges' Castle, 1974-78

restore historical landmarks, old houses, and murals. Civic-minded citizens lobbied and raised funds for new cultural monuments.[30] Why did this self-conscious re-evaluation of place, this readjustment of personal relationship with urban environment, take place when it did? There are several possible reasons. Nationwide, the moral confrontations of the Civil Rights movement and anti-war protests provoked critical introspection by society at large. The sorrow and disillusionment associated with political assassinations and scandals in government called for re-evaluations of personal meaning and morals. Rebellious youth sparked private as well as public struggles of conscience between professed values and pursued goals. About the same time, urban problems reached critical proportions. Issues such as traffic congestion, air pollution, crime, waste disposal, and race relations could no longer be ignored: it was time to find corrective programs. Maybe, too, the certainties of the Rosie and Joe generation were too simplistic for the generations that saw the horrors of wars, famines and "ethnic cleansing" every evening in their living rooms. Preceding waves of settlers had felt obliged to overlook or defend L.A.'s shortcomings because criticism of Los Angeles implied criticism of their own decision to locate there. By the 1970s, nearly one million Angelenos had been born there. They were not burdened by divided loyalties or nostalgia for other regions. Los Angeles was home. But, precisely because they had nowhere else with which to compare it, they could discuss its faults and commit themselves to correcting them. At any rate, a significant reassessment by Angelenos of themselves and of their city emerged in the mid-'60s and reached a crescendo in the mid-'70s and early '80s. This re-evaluation produced three forms of response recorded in housing form: revolt, reform, and reaffirmation.

Some houses have served as protest placards raised against the dehumanization of suburban sameness. A homeowner could so individualize his or her house that it stood out from the crowd as testimony to personal uniqueness. There is something rather heroic in a house like Hodges' Castle (ILLUSTRATION 162). The owner-built edifice began with a magnificent site, a knoll at the mouth of Malibu Canyon overlooking Malibu in one direction, the rugged mountains and creek ravine in the other. Without a fixed plan, the owner, a local physician, started in 1974 by building a one-bedroom apartment.

DREAMING ON

He added an upstairs unit in 1976 in what is now the guarded gatehouse (to the left, in the photograph). The main part of the castle went up in 1978. Then, he recounts, he descended for a view from the Malibu civic center below (the vantage point of the photograph). The castle, he thought, needed something more so he added the round tower on the right. The finished project contains many more rooms than its two occupants need or use. The frame construction, covered in false stone, is as much movie-set as it is a challenge to anonymity and suburban dullness. It has, in fact, appeared in a number of films and television episodes.[31]

The crisis of urban anomie, the anxious effort to resist homogeneity and, by implication, mediocrity, the

163. Gehry house, 1978

164. Detail of Gehry house

struggle to retain some tangible element of control over self and surroundings has contributed fame and a following to architect Frank O. Gehry. Eager to explore the unexpected, Gehry has created outrageous protests against regularity and rationalization. His own 1978 home (ILLUSTRATIONS 163 and 164), an enlarging encasement of a bungalow, was certainly "different," even exhibitionist.

Is This the End of the Rainbow?

Corrugated aluminum and chainlink fencing as external surface materials, a kitchen floored in asphalt street paving, and interior walls stripped down to framing and tarpaper, made startling protests against assembly line sameness. Sufficiently bizarre to attract widespread attention, Gehry's architectural protests are often lightened by whimsy, which may be the touch of grace that saves them and him from charges of insanity. Creative independence, uniqueness, insouciance, and surprise have brought Gehry numerous admirers, awards, and commissions.[32]

While individualized uniqueness in domestic architecture may be interpreted as a recent revolt against depersonalization and disorientation, in the longer view it continues a long-established Los Angeles pattern of individualistic dream images expressed in residential form. Angelenos had long tolerated bizarre houses, so it was a mark of a new outlook when a redecorated Beverly Hills mansion was vigorously protested by neighbors and excoriated by the local press. The 38-room Beaux Arts Italianate mansion built in 1917 for Beverly Hills developer Max Whittier (ILLUSTRATION 165), was purchased by an oil-rich Saudi Arabian sheik for his 23-year-old son in 1978. The younger sheik immediately initiated a $4 million redecorating project. The once-sedate white mansion was painted green; its brick chimneys were enlivened with blue and gold zigzag patterns; the fence-post urns sprouted large plastic flowers; the formerly chaste white statues of nude maidens were painted in full anatomical detail and coloration. The mansion was suddenly a traffic-stopper — literally — as tour buses, reporters, and amateur photographers gawked. The neighbors were outraged. The media engaged in satirical sallies. The sheik retreated to Saudi

DREAMING ON

Arabia. In 1980 thieves set the unoccupied house on fire. Beverly Hills residents were more relieved than sympathetic. The gutted structure was finally demolished in 1985, the property subdivided by new owners, and two new mansions — more compatible with nearby homes — planned. Over a decade later the lot remained empty, a mark of recession economics.[33]

The sheik's mistake had been one of timing. For nearly two centuries, waves of newcomers had churned the city's surface, exuding a youthfully vigorous image of incessant ferment. It was a culturally dynamic place where "anything goes." By the '60s and '70s, Los Angeles was coming to the end of its formative stage and entering a correctional phase. The sheik's plastic flowers and pornographic statuary, the false-stone castles, and exercises in corrugated chaos seemed to confirm the kitsch image of Los Angeles that newly self-conscious Angelenos strove to deny or diminish.

Recently, playwright Neil Simon defined L.A. as "paradise with a lobotomy." Chicago columnist Mike Royko explained to his readers why California "has such an abundance of flaky people": "The most popular theory is that, throughout our history, the nation's oddballs have headed West, looking for the land of their dippy dreams — and the oddest of the oddballs finally float down in California....You name it: If it babbles and its eyeballs are glazed, it probably comes from California."

Others favored such adjectives as vulgar, sleazy, uncultured, artificial, and most of all, plastic. Even friendly critics complained that Los Angeles lacked coherence and traditions, that it was marred by formidable environmental and social problems.

The sneers hit home. Los Angeles' cultural monuments were Disneyland, Forest Lawn Cemetery, and the Hollywood Wax Museum. Its streets were lined with giant hot dogs and movie-set houses. Tourism was a $4.6 billion business and it was this kind of thing the tourists came to see.[34] But, unnoticed, Los Angeles had been forming an intellectual and cultural elite, as its specialized economy attracted settlers to its cinematic arts, sciences and technology, and its educational establishments. By 1960 a cultural leadership had emerged from this element determined to improve the cultural tone of Los Angeles. In the next decade and a half Los Angeles professionalized its symphony orchestra, funded a Music Center, put the summer Hollywood Bowl symphony season on secure footing, and built two first-rate theaters, the Ahmanson and the Mark Taper Forum. The 1913 County Museum's mixed collection of art, bird eggs, and minerals was surpassed in 1965 by a new Los Angeles County Museum of Art opened on Wilshire Boulevard with major art works pre-committed to it by patrons and purchase funds. Other art museums joined the scene: UCLA's new gallery and art center in 1966, the Pasadena Museum of Art in 1969 (later renamed The Norton Simon), the expansion of the Huntington Library and Galleries, the J. Paul Getty museum in 1974.[35]

While the cultural reform activists erected monuments and elevated the level of the arts, civic leaders took up another reform cause. They sought to change the physical shape of the city, and with it, the shape of society. A Los Angeles City building height limit of 150 feet was rescinded in 1957. The limit had been partly to blame for the amorphous sprawl of the urban mass, particularly the dispersion of commercial activities that had prevented the formation of a focal metropolitan core. This phenomenon, in turn, has been blamed for the decay of the central city and the aging inner-city neighborhoods, the uneven availability of city services, and looming transportation problems.[36]

In an attempt to determine how Los Angeles urban forms and quality of life might be corrected and shaped for the future, the City Planning Department held a series of public meetings between 1964 and 1969 before presenting a set of long-range objectives and policy guidelines for channeling future public and private development. A 20-Year General Plan was adopted by the City Council in 1974. It called for the continuation of the low-density, single-family residence lifestyle demanded by most of the 70,000 citizens who had attended the public hearings. To rationalize continued urban impaction while protecting low-density living, the Plan advocated the development of 56 high-density centers or nodes. Ultimately, these centers should be largely traffic-free, as people come to rely on trams or pedestrian walkways to circulate among the concentration of stores, offices, entertainment centers, government and educational institutions, libraries, and restaurants. Planners hoped to combat the disorientation and isolation associated with unfocused suburban sprawl. Commercial and governmental services, localized in centers, would be more personal. Travel would be reduced to familiar patterns between residence and local center. To implement the Plan's vision, zoning and building codes were changed, permit issuance and school construction tied to the Plan, and so on. Although the realization of the Plan has been hampered, especially by inter-governmental obstacles, it is significant that the era of awakened concern, brought about such a comprehensive plan and that it was specifically dedicated to protecting the low-density housing forms characteristic of Los Angeles. Twenty years later, the hearing process was reopened to form a new General Plan for the next twenty years.[37]

One of the first and most spectacular high-density nuclei to emerge in the '70s was Bunker Hill. By the late '50s its once beautiful Victorian residences

166. Angelus Plaza, 1979

had become flophouses and firetraps. Between 1959 and 1964, an innovative corrective program was designed to simultaneously stimulate the local economy, revitalize the urban core, eliminate a slum, provide low-cost housing, all at little or no cost to the City and its taxpayers. An amendment to the state constitution permitted cities to create and endow a quasi-governmental redevelopment agency with the powers necessary to redevelop a defined slum area, including the power of eminent domain. It provided a novel source of redevelopment financing, the tax increment.

When the Los Angeles Community Redevelopment Agency (CRA) was authorized to redevelop Bunker Hill in 1959, the rundown area cost more in fire and police protection than the taxes it generated. The CRA acquired and cleared the area. It successfully attracted private investment, including the high-rise corporate headquarters of five banks and two major hotels. The 1959 tax assessment for the 25-block area (then a collection of dilapidated houses and rooming houses built between 1889 and 1919) was $24.5 million (in 1982 dollars). In 1982 the same 25-block district, filled with gleaming glass towers was assessed at $728.6 million. The difference between what would have been collected at the old assessment and what was collected at the new, known as increment, went to the CRA to reshape this and other designated areas by enticing private investment, constructing seed projects, creating public amenities, and providing a number of social services for residents.[38]

The government agencies, in partnership with the CRA, have turned to the construction of low-cost housing as a means of solving social problems and improving the urban quality of life. Angelus Plaza is a federally subsidized housing development for the elderly, partially financed by a CRA Housing Trust Fund. The four 16-story towers and a low-profile multi-purpose center were designed by Daniel L. Dworsky and Associates (ILLUSTRATION 166). Constructed of pre-formed concrete modules and innovatively bridging the Second Street tunnel, the complex has won prestigious architectural awards. It has also won applause as a model of civic concern for the human dimension. Medical, recreational, and shopping facilities are contained within the cluster. Age and

Is This the End of the Rainbow?

shared activities provide a sense of community. Though not without its critics, Angelus Plaza, at 1,093 units the largest federally-subsidized housing west of New York, represents the acme and showplace of the reform efforts of the '70s.[39]

The nadir, in housing terms, is told in the numbers of L.A.'s homeless. If houses tell of dreams and hopes, the sidewalk shelters seem to speak of hopelessness and despair. On the eve of the 1984 Olympics, L.A. was estimated to have 40,000 homeless living in cardboard boxes, under freeway overpasses, on the streets. In 1994, Los Angeles County streets were "home" to an estimated 43,000 to 77,000. Local government's chits for cheap hotels, the shelters set up by charities and churches, and the jails are insufficient to house them all. The city sets up temporary tent cities for them on ceremonial occasions like the Olympics and during winter cold snaps, then closes these down when the occasion is past. Private charities provide tarps and blankets out of which the lost Angelenos form makeshift dwellings. Angelenos tend to mourn an illusory past when L.A. had no such problems, but the city always had its darker side — its Sonoratown, its railroad house courts, its Depression-era shanty towns and its post-war chicken coop conversions. As the city grew and changed, those earlier expressions of meager lives made way for new streets and new buildings. The physical reminders that poverty existed in those times have disappeared, while the grand mansions remain. While history assumes a golden, nostalgic glow, unshadowed by any signs of poverty in the past, our understanding of the present is peopled by the homeless and the under-housed who impact the daily vision of anyone who slows down long enough to really look at the city. Like the residents of railroad camps and Hoovervilles, the transients of our era may have plans and hopes. They set up their shelters in regular rows that display tidiness (ILLUSTRATION 167), a proprietary sense of place, a form of community which L.A.'s earlier distressed people may also have shown — if anyone had thought to record them before they disappeared.

In an era of critical attention to the quality of urban life, there have been many in the mainstream who neither revolted nor felt called to reform. Recent

167. Transient shelters, 1991

domestic architecture reveals a third trend: a reaffirmation of connectedness to the place and its meaning. In an era of critical attention to the quality of urban life, there have been many who have expressed contentment. Since the 1970s, increasing numbers of Angelenos, native and newcomer alike, have re-examined their place with critically perceptive eyes, defined its features, and appreciated them as meaningful reference points.

Over the course of Los Angeles' past as recorded in its dwellings, certain themes have surfaced over and over, each recurrence somewhat time-altered as new arrivals discovered existing themes, redefined them for their own era's values, and re-expressed them in a new idiom. Recurrent themes allow us to measure the impact of changing times on the nature of settlers, and to contrast the shifting essence of the city one era against another. But it also illustrates the continuity across time and shared concepts of the ideal life.

Los Angeles is a city created from illusions. The illusions of each wave of newcomers were built into the structure of the city as houses, projecting the image of the city that attracted the succeeding wave. Before the turn of the century, Angelenos had experimented with fanciful images of exotica such as Moorish harem screens and castle turrets. In a search for a meaningful sense of place, literature and houses explored the link to Italy. Angelenos embroidered myths around the "Spanish" past to satisfy romantic dreams and to elevate a sense of place and meaning. They monumentalized the myth in Mission style homes. Bungalow dwellers found meaning in reference to place and climate by building for a simple life in a style that brought together the divergent ideals and beliefs of the progressives. But it was the 1920s that witnessed the great flowering of L.A. imagery. Whether the '20s builders chose revival styles for security, for pretense, or as personal expressions, the resulting Tudor, American Colonial, Islamic, Hansel and Gretel, Mayan, and castle houses were authenticated by film imagery in Hollywood's golden age. To movie-goers in the 1920s and '30s, a whole spectrum of images — from revival styles to fantasy, to various modern experiments, and especially to the Mediterranean Colonial mode — was affixed in housing to the Los Angeles landscape by links between the motion picture industry and the City of Angels. Myths had been created there, given film and architectural form, and then naturalized in the Los Angeles cityscape. The war-related population boom narrowed the acceptable images, patriotically favoring American-only myths. The Ranch style brought together the acceptable fragments of the '20s' spectrum in a standardized, mass-produced tract form. By the late '70s and '80s, a generation freed from visions restricted by global war began to study the dream-expressing houses of the past.

168. Northridge Estates,
1979

169. Neo-Hansel and Gretel,
1974

To Angelenos born during or since the Second World War, native to the place or brought here as children, the mixed variety of housing imagery seems natural. Born or raised in an urban kaleidoscope, they do not find it remarkable that a Tudor, a Cape Cod, and a Spanish Colonial should be sited together. Combating alienation, they seek absorption into an L.A. ethos, a sense of belonging. They select updated versions of images fixed in the past. In other words, Angelenos in the 1970s discovered that Los Angeles has architectural traditions of its own, not one or two styles, but a varied set of images to choose from. Phineas Banning, who came to Los Angeles in 1851, recorded the fulfillment of his dreams in a Greek Revival house like those he remembered from his youth in Delaware. Angelenos in the 1980s and '90s, looking for a tradition in house design that would draw childhood dreams together with adult accomplishments, could pick any style or mixture of styles from the smorgasbord of Los Angeles traditions and still feel the same sense of home that Banning's limited choice gave him. A house that stylistically expresses roots in the layers of Los Angeles illusions of reality paradoxically provides a tangible sense of permanence, of belonging, and of continuity vitally important in our ephemeral, depersonalized age. The recycling of styles from earlier periods is a measure of concurrence with previous settlers' definitions of the good life in L.A.

Tracts constructed in the remaining hilly corners of Los Angeles since the late 1970s have mixed Tudor, Mediterranean Colonial, and Hansel and

Gretel elements (ILLUSTRATION 168). Architects have been called upon to carry forward the fairytale fantasy forms of the 1920s. The board siding of the Ranch style has been applied to experimental forms(ILLUSTRATION 145). From fairytale to experiment, all are affirmations of established Los Angeles traditions. The variety and mixture are leading features of today's Los Angeles image.[40] Evocations of the Craftsman movement's attentions to texture and natural materials(ILLUSTRATIONS 169 and 170), of fantasy images revisited, and of the '20s predilection for fragmented volumes (ILLUSTRATION 171).

History is not static. New home construction, and with it, individualistic expression of dreams, fell off in the late '70s in favor of a new housing form, the condominium, introduced in 1966. Under a state condominium law, individuals who purchased units, even if located on an upper floor not attached to any real property, could hold title to the unit, while the land under the entire building would be jointly owned in undivided form by an association of the unit owners. Maximized land-use and shared facilities made "condos" nearly as inexpensive to build as apartments. Developers loved them. The rise of condominiums can be credited to problems in both the apartment and the single-residence markets. Investor interest in apartment construction and management fell off sharply in the late '70s due to rent control measures by local governments and a change in the tax code reducing the tax benefits of apartment investment. Apartment owners face rising maintenance costs, under the best of conditions, as buildings age. Condominium development quickly attracted investors who would realize profits from quick sale of units built on low-interest construction loans. The purchasers, not the developer's investors, would bear later maintenance

170. Stanton residence, 1980

171. Updated modern house, 1981

Is This the End of the Rainbow?

172. Carnaby Square condos,
1981

173. Marina Village condos,
1970s

174. Sea Colony condos,
1980

costs. Condo-conversion became popular with apartment owners who profitably discharged their obligations by converting their units to condos and offering them for sale. 700 of the 800 units in the Marina City development were converted to condos when a new purchaser took over in 1986.[41]

Changes in the single-residence market in the mid-seventies also contributed to the popularity of condominiums. The price of houses rose beyond the means of purchasers. As the available land within reasonable driving distance of workplaces shrunk, its desirability and price rose. The trend toward two-income families contributed to the home-price spiral. Foreign investors, affluent immigrants, and population pressure escalated prices further. Surges in mortgage interest rates occurred in 1977 and again in the mid-eighties, raising home prices and curtailing single-residence construction except at the luxury home level. The housing market in Southern California started to inflate at a notably higher rate than the national average in the mid-seventies. In 1988 the median-priced home in California was 70% higher than the national average. Wages, though higher than the national average, did not keep pace.[42] Meanwhile, condominiums offered other advantages over the detached dwelling. As increasing numbers of women joined the labor market, they found themselves barred from conventional home purchase by low earnings and lenders' policies. Independent women, first-time home purchasers, and the elderly turned to ownership of lower-priced residences in multi-unit condo developments as equity-building alternatives to apartments. While new tracts of moderate-income single-family residences are still being constructed on the distant fringes of the L.A. metropolis, in Palmdale, the Inland Empire, and Camarillo, but wage-earners may commute two hours each way to work, detracting from the quality of their lives. A close-in condominium, and especially its most attractive version, the garden condo, is a positive alternative to the

traditional suburban house.

Condos speak of Angeleno dreams as earlier housing forms did, but in a circumscribed manner. The eccentricities of individual owners are restricted by homeowner associations and contract stipulations: the external decorations and additions that in-dividualize look-alike residences and tell the passerby a bit about the particular dreamer inside are forbidden. However, the architectural features and style and the landscaping express occupants' tastes since a competitive condo market offers variety. Those styles that are not preferred by prospective purchasers do not sell well and are not repeated by market-savvy developers. In an era grown self-conscious about kitsch imagery, bright blue Hansel and Gretel condo units proved slow to sell (ILLUSTRATION 172). But buyers flocked to echoes of the California bungalow (ILLUSTRATION 173), the private facade and glass-opened rear vistas of the Streamline and International Modernists of the '30s (ILLUSTRATION 174), the familiar Spanish colonial (ILLUSTRATION 175), the Tudor (ILLUSTRATION 176), and the Cape Cod or American Colonial (ILLUSTRATION 177). Recycled versions of these styles confirm a long Los Angeles celebration of visual variety and make-believe mentality. They announce the rediscovery and renewed allegiance to the layered image of Los Angeles.[43]

175. Neo-Spanish condos, 1981

176. Neo-Tudor condos, 1982

177. Cape Cod condos, 1982

Irving Gill once wrote:

"Architecture, Victor Hugo [said], is the great book of the world, the principal expression of man.... [The] products of architecture are...the deposit left by a whole people,...the residue of successive evaporations of human society.... Each wave of time contributes its alluvium,...each individual brings his stone."[44]

EPILOGUE

178. Northridge Meadows apartments, January 17, 1994

EVERY RAINBOW IS SUPPOSED to have a pot of gold at its foot. We may spend a lifetime looking for the end of the rainbow, our spirits high as long as the mirage keeps hovering just ahead. In the final decade of the twentieth-century, Angelenos had to wonder if the rainbow had ended for good, if it had been nothing, after all, but an empty fantasy. A nationwide recession hit California hard. The end of the Cold War and America's new status as a debtor nation resulted in federal cutbacks in both military hardware and space missions. Federal deregulation of the airlines slashed the market for commercial aircraft. Local unemployment rose and lingered at about 9%. Progressive reformers in the 1910s, optimistically assuming that more democracy means better government, had amended the state constitution to add the initiative, referendum, and recall. In 1978, taxpayers, objecting to the rising costs of education and public service, welfare and future planning, had approved Proposition 13, an initiative measure that rolled back existing property taxes and shifted the burdens of the future to the people of the future. Increasingly, city, county, and state governments turned to taxes on business and growth as a way of balancing budgets. By the 1980s, employers were relocating to more hospitable states. The vacancy rates in the glass towers on Bunker Hill soared to a reputed 50%.[45] Bankruptcies and more vacancies followed. The CRA, politically controversial, was wracked by a succession of reorganizations, its effectiveness called into question.

Worse was to follow. News reports of widespread drug trafficking, gang violence, senseless drive-by shootings and other urban crimes escalated with the strained economy. Then on April 29, 1992 widescale civil disorder, quickly termed a "riot," erupted in Los Angeles, following a report of jury leniency in a case of Anglo policemen accused of beating a Black man in a widely televised case. At first glance, the 1992 disorder appeared to echo the Watts Riots of 1965. Over the next three days, a barrage of news coverage showed burning buildings and swarms of looters descending on others.

The next year, brush fires roared in Laguna Beach and Malibu, destroying hundreds of houses.

In 1994 a major earthquake centered in the San Fernando Valley jolted sleeping Angelenos awake. Chimneys and walls collapsed, second stories sagged, and household possessions turned into instant rubble. Hardest hit were the apartment houses and condos (ILLUSTRATION 178 and 179). Water and electricity were cut off.

SOMETIMES IT'S HARD TO SEE a thing clearly if we're too close to it. The focus is blurry but if we take a more careful second look...

Educators and activists have long been convinced that television is asocial and desensitizing. But the Black Angelenos who braved the 1992 violence at the intersection of Florence and Normandie to rescue a White beating victim, Reginald Denny, set out on their mission because they learned of his plight from TV. Community bonds among an urban population center of nearly nine million are no longer formed by personal contact but by electronic witnessing of each other's anger, pathos, nobility, and wrong-doing. The network news reports of the 1992 civil disorder were often shallow under the pressure of on-the-scene crisis reporting. But while their words spoke of race riots, and linked violence and looting to ethnic anger over the verdicts in the court case that sparked the outburst, their cameras captured looters of all races. The phrases "Black neighborhood" and "urban ghetto" did not match the cameras' views of burning stores in Hollywood and the Mid-Wilshire districts. In the visual accounts, victims were often small business owners, themselves hard-working, often poor and quite often recent immigrants with language and cultural barriers between themselves and their clientele. In the visual accounts, most of the 5,000 fires occurred in commercial structures, not in residences, and seemed to have loot and excitement as their primary motives. The visual stories were much more complex than the reporters' words. And the fact that so many conversations and discussions noted these discrepancies between visual and authoritatively spoken accounts may indicate a more sophisticated and critically perceptive television audience than critics assume.[46]

179. Apartment house, January 17, 1994

The relationship between Los Angeles and the automobile also demands refocused attention. In 1979-80 Los Angeles City Council studied over a hundred proposals for legislation to reduce smog. Since automobile exhaust accounted for two-thirds of the air pollution, it would have been natural to concentrate legislation on the automobile. But the council aides and Planning Department personnel devising the legislation assumed that Angelenos' cars were sacred and to tamper with them would be tantamount to political suicide. The resulting legislation concentrated instead on vents for paint shops, restrictions on the local sale of solvents, and the redesign of lawnmower engines. But there are signs that L.A. culture is not quite so blindly bound to the automobile. Thirty-six states now have more vehicles per capita than California. When the January 1994 earthquake closed down three freeways, including the nation's busiest, drivers took to surface streets and inched their way through a maze of side streets, for the most part exhibiting an unsuspected capacity for patience and politeness. Hastily erected train stations attracted commuters to mass transit who would never before have considered it.[47]

Even single-family housing will attract a different kind of buyer than the investor of previous generations. The insurance industry estimates only one-fifth of the region's houses carried earthquake coverage.[48] There has been a rush of "as is" real estate listings, sometimes at half the pre-earthquake price levels. The banks will assume abandoned properties after a temporary moratorium. Property values are expected to ratchet downward; recovery will take time. Condo-unit owners and apartment landlords scramble to find others with whom to share the liability for damages. Their headaches will affect future investment in such housing.

City building inspectors combed over 200,000 damaged structures after the earthquake. The patterns of damage that they recorded have led to new building codes. They have mandated deeper and sturdier footings for concrete block walls, new stronger chimneys, and plywood sheeting to add sheer strength to wood frame buildings. The new roofs are of concrete, tile, or composition material, mandated by the City in response to fires. The owner does not have the option of a new shake roof to replicate his Ranch style house's original appearance (ILLUSTRATION 180).[49] But when a damaged wall must be reconstructed, he has the choice of replacing the old stucco wall or redesigning it with new windows, a patio extension, a new doorway. An explosion of rebuilding, redesigning, and renovation, conscious decisions by owners about their tastes, their goals, their identities, and how to reflect those things in their houses, will affect the forms of domestic architecture into the future. This will be

180. Rebuilding, 1994

part of the vista that attracts the next wave of Angelenos.

After each disaster comes a re-assessment of life in Los Angeles: its tensions, its tenuous dependence on water, gasoline, electricity and freeways and its positive factors, its forward energies, its freedoms and possibilities, the things Angelenos like about their place and express in the process of remodeling, relocating, or replicating during the rebuilding period.

THE MAITRE D' IN LISBON had been through Los Angeles once. He had worked as a waiter in Vancouver for two years and then he had traveled with friends down the West Coast to the tip of Baja and returned to L.A. to catch his flight back to Portugal. His dream, he said, was to open a restaurant in Los Angeles. Why Los Angeles? Because people there were so casual, there was such an open feeling about the city, the weather, the beach. Crime? the homeless and high costs? of civil disturbance? fires? earthquakes? He shrugged unconcerned, and smiled.

The night clerk in the Philadelphia hotel with a magenta streak in her hair says she loves L.A.. She's been out there several times. Loves Melrose and the Venice Boardwalk. Sure, there's South Street in Philadelphia, but it's not the same as L.A.. She's an artist on the side. Makes jewelry. She thinks about moving to L.A. someday.

The workman's been on this job, replacing a quake-toppled concrete block wall, for three days. Jackhammered a two-foot deep trench required by the new City code. Carried enough blocks by wheelbarrow into this backyard for 125 feet of wall five feet high. Working every day like this, six days a week. He's looking to replace his old Chevy with a newer pick-up soon. His wife and kids have come up from a town near Guadalajara and they're sharing a place in North Hollywood with his brother's family. They hope to find an apartment of their own in Burbank, but vacant units are scarce since the earthquake. They want one with a yard where the kids can play.

The recent Ph.D. from Virginia who came out to interview for a position at a university reduced to tents and trailer modules by the earthquake says the damage is not so bad as the news reports made her believe. She's enthused about the opportunities for research at UCLA, USC, and the Huntington. She envisions a townhouse with a spare room where she can work at her computer. It must have a balcony. And she dreams of a patio where she and her husband can dine outdoors in the pleasant California evenings.

Los Angeles is a durable dream.[50]

LIST OF ILLUSTRATIONS

All photographs
by Carol Monteverde
except as noted:

Illustrations

NOTES

PREFACE

Quotation, McWilliams: Carey McWilliams, "Los Angeles Is an Event, Not a Mere City," Los Angeles Times, Nov. 24, 1976.

CHAPTER I Mystical Essence/Tangible Architectur-

(1) Mumford: Lewis Mumford, Sticks and Stones: A Study of American Architecture and Civilization. (NY: Dover Publications, Inc., 1924, 1955), 113.

(2) The 1990 population of Los Angeles City was 3,485,398, of which 74.9% were not born in California; about 1/2 of them were born in other states, 1/2 in foreign countries. Los Angeles County population was 8,863,164, of whom 74.5% were not California-born. Of these non-state-natives, 41% were born in other states, 44% were foreign born. (The discrepancy reflects those born in U.S. possessions, etc.) — U.S. Government. Department of Commerce. Bureau of the Census. 1990 Census of Population. Social and Economic Characteristics. Vol. 6: California. (Sept, 1993), 43, 1051.

(3) David Gebhard and Robert Winter, Los Angeles: An Architectural Guide. (Salt Lake City: Gibbs- Smith, 1994); Paul Gleye, The Architecture of Los Angeles. (Los Angeles: Rosebud Books, 1981); Charles Moore, Peter Becker, and Regula Campbell. The City Observed; Los Angeles: A Guide to Its Architecture and Landscapes. (N. Y.: Random, 1984).
An illustrated digest of the Los Angeles Cultural Heritage Commission's declared monuments has recently been published: Patrick McGrew and Robert Julian. Landmarks of Los Angeles. (N.Y.: Harry N. Abrams, Inc., Publishers, 1994.) Its iffy reliability is illustrated by the switched identities of the Pinney and Haskin residences (pp. 40 and 41) and the reversed photo of the Morgan (or Hale) residence (p. 46), but it contains attractive photographs.

(4) The average figure of 14.54 inches is found in: Warren A. Beck and Ynez D. Haase, Historical Atlas of California. (Norman, OK: University of Oklahoma Press, 1974), 5.
The figure is based on U.S. Weather Bureau figures. Rainfall for Los Angeles has been recorded since 1877. In 100 years it varied between a low of 4.85 inches (1960-61) and 38.18 inches (1883-84).

(5) For 1790 and 1800: Hubert Howe Bancroft, History of California, Volume I, 1542-1800. (N.Y.: McGraw-Hill Book Company, 1884, 1960), 460, 601, 661.
For 1820 estimate: J.M. Guinn, Historical and Biographical Record of Los Angeles and Vicinity... (Chicago: Chapman Publishing Company, 1901), 126.
Mexican Period: Hubert Howe Bancroft, History of California, Volume III, 1825-1840. (San Francisco: The History Company, Publishers, 1886), 632n, 633.
1850 Census: United States Census Office, The Seventh Census of the United States: 1850... (Washington, D.C.: Government Printing Office, 1853), cxi.
1860: United States Bureau of the Census, Population of the United States in 1860; Compiled from the Original Returns of the Eighth Census... (Washington, D.C.: Government Printing Office, 1864), 29.
1870: United States Census Office, The Statistics of the Population of the United States... (Ninth Census — Vol. I). (Washington, D.C.: Government Printing Office, 1872), 14, 90.
1890: Department of the Interior; Census Office, Report on Population of the United States at the Eleventh Census: 1890; Part I. (Washington, D.C.: Government Printing Office, 1894), 70.
1900-1910: Department of Commerce, Bureau of the Census, Thirteenth Census of the United States. Taken in the Year 1910; Volume I. Population 1910, General Report and Analysis. (Washington, D.C.: Government Printing Office, 1913), 82, 87.
1930: U.S. Department of Commerce, Bureau of the Census, Fifteenth Census of the United States: 1930. Abstract... (Washington, D.C.: Government Printing Office, 1933), 26.
1940: Sixteenth Census of the United States, 1940. Population, Volume I; Number of Inhabitants... (Washington, D.C.: Government Printing Office, 1942), 34.
1990: 1990 Census... (cited), 43, 1051.

(6) Our thesis is in direct conflict with architectural historian Harold Kirker's insistence on a theory of cultural conservatism, a theory unaltered for 20 years. Harold Kirker, "California Architecture and Its Relation to Contemporary Trends in Europe and Asia," California Historical Quarterly, Vol. LI, No. 4 (Winter 1972), pp. 289-305; Kirker, California's Architectural Frontier; Style and

Tradition in the Nineteenth Century. (Santa Barbara: Peregrine Smith, Inc., 1973). In her review of his most recent book, Anne Bloomfield reports Kirker's thesis and evidentiary bases exactly as they were two decades ago. — Anne Bloomfield, "In the Victorian Style." Review of Old Forms on a New Land: California Architecture in Perspective. (Niwot, CO: Roberts Rinehart Publishers, 1991), in California History 71 (Winter, 1992/93), 540-541.

CHAPTER II Simply Paradise: The Indians, to 1765

(1) We use the term "culturally extinct" in reference to the Gabrielinos after the 1860s. Through the mission system, intermarriage, and economic interaction with majority society an incalculable number of Indians took on the dress, culture, and language of Hispanic Californians. They were known by Spanish names. Culturally speaking, they were no longer Indians. In the 1850s Americans subjected the remaining Indians to a degrading labor system. In 1862-63 smallpox and measles epidemics swept through Los Angeles and, as McGroarty put it, "by the close of the year [1863] but few of the Indian population were left..." (John Steven McGroarty (editor), History of Los Angeles County, Volume I. (Chicago: The American Historical Society, Inc., 1923), p. 67.
Horace Bell, Reminiscences of a Ranger; or Early Times in Southern California. (Santa Barbara: Wallace Hebberd, 1927), pp. 34-36.)

(2) The Spanish displayed an enlightened spirit of inquiry about the nature and culture of the California Indians. Motivation tended to be utilitarian — potential as a work force, susceptibility to conversion, and ease of cultural transition. Franciscans Juan Crespi and Pedro Font and the soldier Pedro Fages made careful observations in their 18th-century accounts of exploration. The Franciscan priest at nearby Mission San Juan Capistrano from 1811 to 1826, Fray Geronimo Boscana, investigated the religious beliefs of the unconverted natives. A purely scientific expedition led by Alejandro Malaspina studied the natural features, including the human residents, of the Pacific Coast from 1789 to 1794. Despite the care with which the Spanish observations were made, value judgments reflected prejudices. For example, describing the Indians encountered in 1775 north of San Diego, Fages wrote that they had "homely features and ungainly figures; they are dirty, very slovenly, and withal evil-looking, suspicious, treacherous, and have scant friendship for the Spaniards." Travelling northward, his opinion improved grudgingly, when he met the Chumash Indians of Ventura. He found them to be "well built and of good disposition, very agile and alert, and ingenious to a degree." (Pedro Fages, A Historical, Political, and Natural Description of California by Pedro Fages, Soldier of Spain. (Herbert Ingram Priestly, trans.) (Berkeley: University of California Press, 1937), pp. 11, 21.

(3) The huge quantity of non-native water consumed in the City of Los Angeles alone, contributes to the basin's humidity via plants, soil, and direct evaporation. By the 1970s, Los Angeles was consuming over half a billion gallons of water a day, most of it piped into the region from the Owens, Colorado and Feather rivers. (Los Angeles Dept. of Water and Power, "Water for Los Angeles" (booklet), (Los Angeles, 1978).

(4) The 4,000 to 5,000 estimate of both Heizer and Kroeber has been revised upward to nearly double that figure by Sherburne Cook's not uncontroversial study, published in 1976, which places 310,000 Indians in California in 1769, of whom 20,000 were credited to the southern coastal mission belt. (Sherburne F. Cook, The Population of the California Indians, 1769-1970. (Berkeley: University of California Press, 1976), pp. 42-43.)

CHAPTER III Spanish Pueblo, 1781-1821

(1) There has long been a controversy among historians over the correct form of the pueblo's name. The question concerns the inclusion or exclusion of the words, "la reina" (the queen). The original plans for the establishment of the pueblo referred to it as "El pueblo de Nuestra Senora la Reina de los Angeles" — the Town of Our Lady, Queen of the Angels. The added words, "de la Porciuncula", referring to a Franciscan day of Indulgence, were part of the name of the Los Angeles River, but were not included in the town's title. (Raymund F. Wood, "Juan Crespi, The Man Who Named Los Angeles," Southern California Quarterly, Vol. LIII, No. 3 (Sept. 1971), pp. 213, 213.

(2) "The Best Advertised City...": A post-World War I slogan of the Los Angeles Chamber of Commerce and the All Year Club of Southern California, quoted in: Victoria Padilla, Southern California Gardens; An Illustrated History. (Berkeley: University of California Press, 1961), p. 91.

(3) Ordonez de Montalvo, Garci Rodriguez, Las sergas de Esplandian (c. 1510), cited by John and LaRee Caughey, California Heritage; an Anthology of History and Literature. (Itasca, Ill.: F.E. Peabody Publishers, 1962, 1971), pp. 49-50.

(4) 1769: The Spanish occupation of Alta California in 1769 was a well-planned sea and land operation led by Fray Junipero Serra and

Comandant Gaspar de Portola. Its inception, direction, and objectives must be credited to Jose de Galvez, whose instructions have been translated in: Maynard Geiger, OFM, (trans. and ed.), "Instructions Concerning the Occupation of California, 1769", Southern California Quarterly, Vol. XLVII, No. 2 (June 1965), pp. 209-218.

(5) There were very few Spanish land grants, even on this tenuous basis of land-use rather than true ownership. The Dominguez, Nieto, Verdugo, and Feliz grants were formal Spanish grants for soldiers' retirements. Less formal arrangements ranging from squatters' assumptions to unrecorded government awards were claimed by seven others. W.W. Robinson, Los Angeles from the Days of the Pueblo... (San Francisco: California Historical Society, 1959), pp. 23-27; ——, "The Spanish and Mexican Ranchos of San Fernando Valley," Southwest Museum Leaflets, No. 31 (Los Angeles: Southwest Museum, 1966), pp. 4-6; and Warren A. Beck and Ynez D. Haase, Historical Atlas of California. (Norman, Okla: University of Oklahoma Press, 1974), p. 24.

(6) Dissension between church and civil authorities appeared soon after the California frontier's establishment. Junipero Serra, the first head of the mission system, became embroiled in politicized disputes with each of three successive governors. N. Ray and Gladys Gilmore, Readings in California History. (N.Y.: Thomas Y. Crowell Company, 1966), pp. 37-56; Daniel J. Garr, "Power and Priorities: Church-State Boundary Disputes in Spanish California," California History, Vol. XVII, No. 4 (Winter 1978/79), pp. 364-375.

(7) Recent research on the details of the pueblo's founding refutes the glamorized accounts long accepted as the truth. Harry Kelsey, "A New Look at the Founding of Old Los Angeles," California Historical Quarterly, Vol. LV, No. 4 (Winter 1976/77), pp. 326-339. Education: An invalid soldier, Maximo Pina, taught school in Los Angeles in 1817 and 1818. This was the only formal educational endeavor in the pueblo in the years of Spanish administration. J.M. Guinn, Historical and Biographical Records of Los Angeles and Vicinity: Containing a Record of the City from Its Earliest Settlement as a Spanish Pueblo to the Closing Year of the Nineteenth Century. (Chicago: Chapman Publishing Company, 1901) p. 126.

(8) William Mason and Roberta K. Mason, "The Founding Forty-Four," Westways, Vol. 68, No. 7 (July 1976), pp. 20-23; and William Mason, "Tracking the Founders of Los Angeles," Los Angeles County Museum of Natural History Quarterly, Vol. 6, No. 1 (Summer 1967), pp. 26-30.

(9) Teodoro de Croix to Fernando de Rivera y Moncada, Arispe, December 27, 1779, cited by John and LaRee Caughey, Los Angeles: Biography of a City. (Berkeley, University of California Press, 1976), p. 67.

(10) Guinn, op. cit., p. 40.

(11) For 1790 and 1800: Bancroft: California, Vol. I. (cited) pp. 460, 601, 661. For 1820 estimate: Guinn, op. cit., p. 37.

CHAPTER IV From Mexican Pueblo to Bilingual Cowtown

(1) Mexican Land Grants: Beck and Haase, op. cit., p. 37.

(2) Four years after he arrived in Los Angeles, Don Coronel took over the public school system, "he having the necessary qualifications," in the estimation of the ayuntamiento (town council). A school had been established in 1827 and had met irregularly since, under a succession of teachers each of whom (with the one exception of Vicente Morago) had been found wanting in qualifications.Guinn, op. cit., pp. 115, 509.

(3) The first wood frame building in Los Angeles was the El Dorado Saloon and sometime Methodist Church. A prefabricated building shipped around the Horn, it was erected in 1851 or 1852 on the site later occupied by the Merced Theater. William Mason and Jeanne Duque, "Los Angeles Plaza, Living Symbol of Our Past," Terra, (Winter 1981), p. 17; J. Gregg Layne, "Annals of Los Angeles: Part II, From the American Conquest to the Civil War," California Historical Society Quarterly, XIII (Dec. 1934), p. 321.

(4) Hubert Howe Bancroft, op. cit., pp. 632 and 633.

(5) American observers opinions of Californio culture are drawn from a study of the followingsources: John Bidwell, A Journey to California, 1841; The First Emigrant Party to California by Wagon Train. The Journal of John Bidwell. (Berkeley: The Friends of the Bancroft library, 1964; originally published 1843). Edwin Bryant, What I Saw in California, Being the Journal of a Tour by the Emigrant Route and South Pass of the Rocky Mountains, Across the Continent of North America, the Great Desert Basin, and Through

California, in the Years 1846, 1847. (Santa Ana, Calif.: The Fine Arts Press, 1936; originally published 1848). Richard Henry Dana, Two Years Before the Mast. (New York: Bantam Books, 1959, 1963; originally published 1840). Thomas Jefferson Farnham, Travels in California with Map. (Oakland: Biobooks 1947; originally published 1840). John Charles Fremont (Allan Nevins, editor), Narratives of Exploration and Adventure. (N.Y.: Longmans, Green & Co., 1956; originally published 1844). Lansford W. Hastings, The Emigrants Guide to Oregon and California. (Princeton, N.J.: Princeton University Press, 1932; originally published 1845). Overton Johnson and William H. Winter, Route Across the Rocky Mountains, with a Description of Oregon and California, Their Geographical Features, Their Resources, Soil, Climate, Productions, &c, &c., by Overton Johnson and Wm. H. Winter, of the Emigration of 1843. (Lafayette, Ind.: J.B. Semans, Printer, 1846; originally published 1846.) James O. Pattie (Edited by Reuben Gold Thwaites), The Personal Narrative of James O. Pattie of Kentucky; During an Expedition from St. Louis, Through the Vast Regions Between that Place and the Pacific Ocean, and Thence Back Through the City of Mexico to Vera Cruz, During Journeyings of Six Years, Etc. Edited by Timothy Flint (1833). (Cleveland: The Arthur H. Clark Company, 1905; originally published 1833). Alfred Robinson, Life in California and A Historical Account of the Origin, Customs, and Traditions of the Indians of Alta California. (Oakland: Biobooks, 1947; originally published 1846). J. M. Shively, Route and Distances to Oregon and California, with a Description of Watering-Places, Crossings, Dangerous Indians, Etc., Etc. (Louisville, Ky.: Lost Cause Press, 1960; originally published 1846). Marius Duvall, A Navy Surgeon in California, 1846-1847; The Journal of Marius Duvall. (San Francisco: John Howell, 1957). Private diary. Chester S. Lyman (Edited by Frederick J. Teggart), Around the Horn to the Sandwich Islands and California, 1845-1850; Being a Personal Record Kept by Chester S. Lyman, Sometime Professor of Astronomy and Physics in Yale University. (New Haven, Conn.: Yale University Press, 1924). Private diary. Dale Morgan (editor), Overland in 1846; Diaries and Letters of The California-Oregon Trail. Vols. I & II. (Georgetown, Calif.: The Talisman Press, 1963). Private accounts.

(6) American writers castigated California's Mexican government as despotic, corrupt, cruel, with dishonest, and unintelligent officials. — Shively, op. cit., p. 14; Farnham, op. cit., p. 120; Hastings, op. cit., pp. 127-128, 152; Johnson, op. cit., pp. 88-90; and Bryant, op. cit., pp. 424, 434. All concluded that it would be not only justified, but a blessing, if the United States should take over the whole place. Criticism of differences in form of government thus served as a rationalization for conquest.

(7) The widespread weakness of the rancheros in arithmetic would facilitate advantageous figure-juggling by unscrupulous Yankees.

(8) Robinson, who had become a Californio by choice, marriage, citizenship, and property ownership (and, preconditionally, by conversion to Catholicism) wrote favorably. Robinson, op. cit., p. 47. But those others who discussed the subject betrayed the prejudice of an intolerant era. See Farnham, op. cit., p. 148; Lyman, op. cit., p. 247; and Hastings, op. cit., pp. 105, 114.

(9) The scientist, Chester Lyman, the explorer, Charles Fremont, and the Californio husband, Alfred Robinson, found race no obstacle. But Dana, op. cit., pp. 60-61; Bryant, op. cit., pp. 199, 433; Hastings, op. cit., p. 113; and Farnham, op. cit., pp. 101, 140; expressed blatant racism. Farnham was the least restrained in his description of "Los Espanioles del Alta California [sic], to wit, every Indian with a drop of Spanish blood under his filthy hide..." Ibid., p. 101.

(10) The noble bearing and manners of the Californios, even the least of them in their decline at the end of the 19th-century, were summarized by Dana's description in the 1830s: "A common bullock-driver, on horseback, delivering a message, seemed to speak like an ambassador at a royal audience. In fact, they sometimes appeared to me to be a people on whom a curse had fallen, and stripped them of everything but their pride, their manners, and their voices." Dana, op. cit., p. 61. The reliance on personal honor and oral contracts would be a major factor in the Californios' loss of land to Yankees.

(11) The low value on thrift and saving was a boon to merchants. Merchants increased sales by extending credit for advance orders. Debts which were so easy to contract were not always as easy to pay off. In the 1850s and '60s, land and cattle (the only collateral the rancheros owned) were attached for debts contracted in easier times. Out of friendship and trust in each other's word, many rancheros had guaranteed each other's loans, at the insistance of Yankee money-lenders who knew how to operate. Friends thus lost their lands, too.

(12) Quotation: Farnham, op. cit., pp. 61, 140. Dana, op. cit., pp. 36, 59, 63; Duvall, op. cit., p. 9; Bryant, op. cit., pp. 261, 315; Robinson, op. cit., pp. 84, 89; Bidwell, op. cit., p. 46; Hastings, op. cit., pp. 88, 132; and Johnson, op. cit., p. 89. All excoriate the Californios for their indolence.

(13) Perhaps the native courtesy, the low motive to material acquisition, and the open friendliness form the roots of the generosity to strangers described by Robinson, op. cit., pp. 227-229; Bryant, op. cit., p. 300; Hastings, op. cit., pp. 123, 125; Johnson, op. cit., p. 90; Bidwell, op. cit., p. 50; and Diary of Nicholas Carriger, 1846, contained in Morgan, op. cit., pp. 147, 149.

(14) Bryant, op. cit., p. 286; Robinson, op. cit., pp. 12-14; For examples of the racial reservations see Ibid., pp. 289-299; and Farnham, op. cit., p. 481.

(15) Dana remarked how rare glass windows were throughout the province in 1836. —Dana, op. cit., p. 63; But Hugo Reid, describing the Los Angeles house of Nathaniel Pryor in 1832, mentioned that its windows had both glass and grilles. —Susanna Bryant Dakin, A Scotch Paisano in Old Los Angeles: Hugo Reid's Life in California, 1832-1852, Derived from His Correspondence. (Berkeley: University of California Press, 1939), p. 9.

(16) Guinn quotes Leonardo Cota's recommendation that Angelenos be required by law to keep their houses plastered and whitewashed. The idea failed. No date is given for the episode. Guinn, op. cit., p. 65.

(17) Loretta Berner, Rancho Los Cerritos. (Ramona, Calif.: Acoma Books, 1975), passim.

(18) Kirker insisted that T. O. Larkin, the American consul in Monterey, be given credit for introducing two-story houses in California. —Kirker, California's Architectural Frontier, cited, pp. 13-14. But Vicente Sanchez had one — with a tiled roof besides — on the L.A. Plaza in the 1820s. —Mason and Duque, op. cit., p. 15. Kirker also draws the form from Larkin's New England roots. Later research gives substantial credit to Caribbean sources and the Southeastern U.S. experience with warm weather. —David Gebhard, "Some Additional Observations on California's Monterey Tradition," Journal of the Society of Architectural Historians, Vol. XLVI, No. 2 (June 1987), pp. 157-170.

(19) Reid's description of Pryor's house is contained in —Dakin, op. cit., p. 9. The features of his own house are in Ibid., p. 52.

(20) Nellie Van de Grift Sanchez, Spanish Arcadia. (San Francisco: Powell Publishing Co., 1929), p. 88.

(21) The Olivas Adobe near Ventura, is a fine existing example of the more typical exterior stairways.

(22) United States Census Office, The Seventh Census of the United States: 1850... (Washington, D.C.: Government Printing Office, 1853), p. cxi. United States Bureau of the Census, Population of the United States in 1860; Compiled from the Original Returns of the Eighth Census... (Washington, D.C.: Government Printing Office, 1864), p. 29. (Of the total of 4,366, 3,854 were listed as white, 66 as "free colored", and 446 as Indian.) For a discussion of the flaws in the early census figures for Los Angeles, based on computerized data analysis, see: Richard Griswold del Castillo, The Los Angeles Barrio, 1850-1890; A Social History. (Berkeley: University of California Press, 1979), p. 35.
Leonard Pitt, The Decline of the Californios; A Social History of the Spanish-Speaking Californians, 18461890. (Berkeley: University of California Press, 1966, 1971). See especially pp. 46-68. Bancroft, op. cit., pp. 700-701.

(23) George R. Stewart, The California Trail: An Epic with Many Heroes. (NY: McGraw-Hill Book Company, 1962), pp. 232, 296.

(24) Robert Glass Cleland, The Cattle on a Thousand Hills; Southern California, 1850-1880. (San Marino, Calif.: The Huntington Library, 1969), pp. 104, 106.

(25) Harris Newmark, Sixty Years in Southern California, 1853-1913 (Fourth Edition). (Los Angeles: Zeitlin & Ver Brugge, 1970), pp. 160-161.

(26) The decline of the cattle boom after 1855 is recorded in Cleland, op. cit., pp. 107-109.

(27) One historian reports that between 1848 and 1852, the Yuma ferry brought almost 25,000 Mexican immigrants into California from Sonora. —Griswold del Castillo, op. cit., p. 38.

(28) For the estimate of expelled Hispanic miners in 1850 see: Walton Bean, California; An Interpretive History. (NY: McGraw-Hill Book Company, 1968), p. 163.

(29) Bancroft estimated that women made up less than 8% of the non-Indian population of California in 1850. —Bancroft, op. cit., p. 699. Willaim B. Secrest, Joaquin, Bloody Bandit of the Mother Lode: The Story of Joaquin Murrieta. (Fresno: Saga-West Publishing Company, 1967), pp. 11-14; and Pitt, op. cit. pp. 76-84.

(30) "Nigger Alley" was a run-down section of adobe shacks extending eastward from the Plaza near the edge of the present Union Station, named for the dark skin of its early inhabitants, many of whom were Indians. In the 1850s it housed saloons, drifters, prostitution cribs, and Chinese. In 1871 it was the scene of a lynch mob which murdered 19 Chinese. Carolyn Strickler, "The Noose About Dave Brown," Westways, June 1977, p. 30; and J.M. Guinn, "The Story of a Plaza," Historical Society of Southern California, Annual Publications, IV, 247-256, quoted in Cleland, op. cit., pp. 70-74, 90-101; Pitt, op. cit., pp. 148-180; and Guinn, op. cit., pp. 131-138. Unfortunately, since all researchers rely on the notoriously creative memory of Horace Bell (Bell, op. cit., passim) and the hearsay-journalism ("We are told that....," "A gentleman of our acquaintance recalls...") of the Los Angeles Star, published 1851-1864, our evidence of exactly how flagrant criminal activity is unreliable. Robert Greenwood, The California Outlaw, Tiburcio Vasquez; Including the Rare Contemporary Account by George Beers, with Numerous Photographs and Excerpts from Contemporary Newspapers. (Los Gatos, Calif.: The Talisman Press, 1960); and Maj. Ben. C. Truman, Life, Adventures and Capture of Tiburcio Vasquez. The Great California Bandit and Murderer. (Los Angeles: Printed at Los Angeles Star Office, 1874).

(31) Griswold del Castillo, op. cit., pp. 42-56. Specific statistics provided in this work are controversial because no distinction is made between naturalized Mexican grantees like Stearns and Spanish-surnamed grantees, and the the later Sonoran land purchasers. Bare numbers also do not indicate cases of multiple heirs, subdivision sales, or sales with unclear titles. Cleland, op. cit., pp. 33-50, 111-123, analyzes mortgage rates, the injuries caused by tax rates, and the exacerbation of the squatter problem. Length of litigation was quantified by Bean, op. cit., p. 157. William Wolfskill's career and the details of his personal and business life involve the salvation and ruin of many old Californios. —Iris Higbie Wilson, William Wolfskill, 1798-1866; Frontier Trapper to California Ranchero. (Glendale: The Arthur H. Clark Company, 1965), passim. General reviews of the land issue are included in: Bean, op. cit., pp. 152-161; Andrew F. Rolle, California: A History (Third Edition). (Arlington Heights, Ill: AHM Publishing Corporation, 1978), pp. 275-283. The classic work, however, is: W.W. Robinson, Land in California; The Story of Mission Lands, Ranchos, Squatters, Mining Claims, Railroad Grants, Land Scrip, Homesteads. (Berkeley: University of California Press, 1948).

(32) John Steven McGroarty (editor), History of Los Angeles County, Vol. I. (Chicago: The American Historical Society, Inc., 1923), p. 67. For the effects on Sonoratown and the labor market, see: John W. Robinson, Los Angeles in Civil War Days, 1860-65. (Los Angeles: Dawson's Book Shop, 1977), pp. 113-114; Cleland, op. cit., pp. 80-81, 131-132.

(33) Quotation: Newmark, op. cit., pp. 257-258.

(34) Guinn, op. cit., p. 127-128; Newmark, op. cit., p. 309.

(35) Maymie Krythe, Port Admiral: Phineas Banning, 1830-1885. (San Francisco: California Historical Society, 1957). passim.

(36) The growth of the wine industry in Los Angeles is readily apparent in the quantities of wine produced: 1841: 24,000 gallons; 1850: 60,000; 1859: 250,000; 1875: 1,328,000. J. J. Warner, Benjamin Hayes, and J. P. Widney, An Historical Sketch of Los Angeles County, California; From the Spanish Occupancy, By the Founding of the Mission San Gabriel Archangel, September 8, 1771, to July 4, 1876. (Los Angeles: O. W. Smith, Publisher, 1876, 1936), pp. 113-114; Brian McGinty, "Uncovering L.A.'s Grapevine," Westways, December 1977, p. 23.

(37) Newmark, op. cit., pp. 285-286; and Wilson, op. cit., passim; and Warner, op. cit., pp. 76-77, 112-113. Rose's own harrowing description of the Indian attack forms Appendix IV of: Cleland, op. cit., pp. 264-273. Rose's ordeals paid off. By the 1880s he lived in palatial splendor on L.A.'s Bunker Hill. (William Pugsley and Roy W. Hankey, Bunker Hill, Last of the Lofty Mansions. (Corona del Mar, CA: Trans-Anglo Books, 1977), pp. 14-15.

(38) Lawrence Grow, Old House Plans; Two Centuries of American Domestic Architecture. (NY: Universe Books, 1978), pp. 24-27. A comparative illustration on page 27 was taken from Village and Farm Cottages by Henry W. Cleaveland, William Backus, and Samuel D. Backus. — Virginia and Lee McAlester, A Field Guide to American Houses. (N.Y.: Alfred A. Knopf, 1993), 194-200.

(39) Leonis Adobe Association, "Valley Landmark: The Leonis Adobe," (brochure). (Calabasas, undated). There were less than 18,000 sheep in California in 1850; by 1860 there were 1,000,000. (Cleland, op. cit., p. 139.)

(40) Ironically, the window of the Sanchez Adobe, reverses Leonis' efforts. Tomas Sanchez, the city sheriff in the 1860s, had married a descendent of the Verdugo family and constructed a house to look like those of the ranchero period — twenty years into the American period. His contemporary, Leonis, was trying to "fit in;" Sanchez was making a romantic "last stand."

CHAPTER V 1870s Promotionalism: The Railroad, Agriculture, and Health

(1) Frank M. Keffer, History of San Fernando Valley: In Two Parts, Narrative and Biographical. (Glendale: Stillman Printing Company, 1934), p. 47; and Newmark, op. cit., p. 381.

(2) Elizabeth I. Dixon (editor), "Early San Fernando: Memoirs of Catherine Hubbard Dace," Southern California Quarterly, Vol. XLIV, No. 3 (Sept. 1962), pp. 219-267.

(3) Remi Nadeau, City-Makers; The Men Who Transformed Los Angeles from Village to Metropolis during the First Great Boom, 1868-76. (Garden City, NJ: Doubleday & Co., Inc., 1948), pp. 11-13; and Cleland, op. cit., pp. 200-207, 173n.

(4) Cleland's figures are 8,700 for 1866 and 16,000 for 1869-70 (Ibid., p. 207). Nadeau shows a 50% increase, based on voting registration and school enrollment figures — which may have more to do with civic-mindedness and the arrival of more families with children than with population density.

(5) Warner, op. cit., p. 113; Cleland, op. cit., pp. 176-177; and Robert M. Fogelson, The Fragmented Metropolis; Los Angeles, 1850-1930. (Cambridge, Mass.: Harvard University Press, 1967), pp. 19-20.

(6) The Big Four, the capitalists behind the Central Pacific and Southern Pacific Railroads were Leland Stanford, Mark Hopkins, Collis P. Huntington, and Charles Crocker. In 1882 the railroad's land agent estimated that the Southern Pacific had been granted 10,445,227 acres of California land. Edna Monch Parker, "The Southern Pacific Railroad and Settlement in Southern California," Pacific Historical Review, Vol. VI, No. 2 (1937), pp. 103-119. In 1977 the Assistant Public Relations Manager of the Southern Pacific Transportation Company, Los Angeles, Richard Hall, claimed that the Southern Pacific was still the state's largest private landholder. (Address, October 1977 meeting of the Historical Society of Southern California.)

(7) The Big Four eventually established a monopoly over internal waterways, coastwise shipping, docking and warehouse facilities for the major Pacific ports, all rail lines, and major urban rail systems in California. This monopoly lasted, in some areas, into the 20th-century. — Oscar Lewis, The Big Four. (N.Y.: Alfred A. Knopf, Inc., 1938), and, in a fictional treatment, of — Frank Norris, The Octopus; A Story of California. (N.Y.: New American Library, 1900, 1964). Glenn S. Dumke, The Boom of the Eighties in Southern California. (San Marino: Huntington Library, 1963), pp. 17-22; and, Michael Magliari, "Populism, Steamboats, and the Octopus: Transportation Rates and Monopoly in California's Wheat Regions, 1890-1896," Pacific Historical Review, Vol. LVIII, No. 4 (Nov. 1989), pp. 449-469. Edward L. Lyman, "Outmaneuvering the Octopus; Atchison, Topeka and Santa Fe." California History 67 (June 1988), 94-107. A special issue of California History, Volume 70 (Sept. 1991), pinpoints several areas of conflict and contains a good bibliography: Blaine Peterson Lamb and Ellen Hatteman Schwartz, "The Paper Trail of the Iron Horse: The California State Railroad Museum Library." Ibid., 94-113. Public response to the S.P. is the subject of : William Deverell, Railroad Crossing; Californians and the Railroad, 1850-1910. (Berkeley: University of California Press, 1994)

(8) Railroad Role in Immigration: Parker, op. cit., p. 116 quotes Charles Crocker's Annual Report of 1882: "...the plan of the company for bringing immigrants from Europe at very low rates of fare, direct to such localities as they have previously decided upon, it is believed will soon result in settling the southern portion of the State with a thrifty population, and thus not only enhance the value of the company's lands, but, through the consequent increase of their productions largely augment the revenue of our road and add to the wealth and prosperity of the State."

(9) In Los Angeles, a hard political battle had to be fought before the pro-railroad element won. In November 1872 the city's voters promised $602,000 in bonds and in the stock of Banning's harbor line, as well as a choice site for a terminal. Remi Nadeau, Los Angeles from Mission to Modern City., (N.Y.: Longmans, Green and Co., 1960), p. 65.

(10) Railroad advertising took a number of different forms. One was descriptive accounts and guide books by hired authors. Charles Nordhoff, California for Health, Pleasure, and Residence: A Book for Travellers and Settlers. (N.Y.: Harper & Brothers, Publishers, 1873) and Major Ben Truman, Semi-Tropical California: It's Climate, Healthfulness, Productiveness, and Scenery... (San Francisco: A. L. Bancroft & Company, 1874). Pamphlets and press releases augmented these and the Southern Pacific hatched immigration societies such as the California Immigrant Office, 1869, to solicit settlement. — Parker, op. cit., p. 110...; Nadeau, City-Makers, (cited), p. 126.

(11) Ben C. Truman, Tourists' Illustrated Guide to the Celebrated Summer and Winter Resorts of California Adjacent to and upon the Lines of the Central and Southern Pacific Railroads. (San Francisco: H. S. Crocker & Co., Printers and Publishers, 1883), p. 223.

(12) Quotations: Nordhoff, op. cit., 1882 edition, pp. 102, 104. Real estate promoter Robert M. Widney printed a monthly Los Angeles sheet, the Real Estate Advertiser, beginning in 1870 for hotel distribution. Such early enterprisers are celebrated in —Nadeau, City-Makers (cited), pp. 13-14.

(13) W. McPherson, Homes in Los Angeles City and County, and Description Thereof, with Sketches of the Four Adjacent Counties. (Los Angeles: Mirror Book and Job Printing Establishment, 1873), pp. 21, 28, 32.

(14) Ludwig Louis Salvator, Los Angeles in the Sunny Seventies; A Flower from the Golden Land. (translated by Marguerite Eyer Wilbur.) (Los Angeles: Bruce McCallister/Jake Zeitlin, 1929), p. 113.

(15) Cultural Heritage Commission of the City of Pasadena, "The Treasures on Your Block, Area #2" (Pamphlet). (Pasadena, c. 1976, undated); and Salvator, op. cit., p. 45.

(16) San Gabriel Orange Grove Association: Dumke, op. cit., pp. 84-86; Guinn, op. cit., p. 188; Cleland, op. cit., pp. 210-211; Nadeau, City-Makers (cited), pp. 133-137.

(17) J. W. Wood, Pasadena, California, Historical and Personal; A Complete History of the Organization of the Indiana Colony. (Pasadena: J. W. Wood, 1917), pp. 59, 80-81, 89, 307.

(18) Nordhoff, op. cit., 1882 Edition, pp. 109, 150.

(19) "Abel Stearns' Ranchos" Ad: McPherson, op. cit., third and fourth pages, Advertisements Section.

(20) McPherson Quotation: Ibid., p. 70.

(21) Railroad Ticket Plans: Parker, op. cit., pp. 114-115.

(22) Quotation: Nordhoff, op. cit., 1882 Edition, p. 162.

(23) P. C. Remondino, M.D., The Mediterranean Shores of America. Southern California: Its Climatic, Physical, and Meteorological Conditions. (Philadelphia: The F. A. Davis Co., Publishers, 1892), p. v.

(24) Quoted in John E. Baur, The Health Seekers of Southern California, 1870-1900. (San Marino: The Huntington Library, 1959), p. 33.

(25) Nordhoff, op. cit., 1882 Edition, p. 78; and "Southern California: The Italy of America," undated pamphlet, pp. 1, 8; quoted in Baur, Health Seekers, (cited), p. 15.

(26) The doctor-patient ratio was abnormally high in Southern California cities throughout the last quarter of the century. Ibid., pp. 35-36, 80-81.

(27) Quotation: Los Angeles Express, Aug. 29, 1883; quoted in Ibid., p. 177n.

(28) This is Baur's most conservative estimate. Ibid., pp. 42, 80.

(29) Nordhoff, op. cit., 1882 edition, p. 104.

(30) William Henry Bishop, "Southern California, Part 3: From the Tehachapi Pass to the Mexican Frontier," reprinted from Harper's, 1883 in Skip Whitson (Compiler), Southern California 100 Years Ago: Vol. II, Albuquerque: Sun Publishing Company, 1976), p. 9.

(31) Judson A. Grenier (editor), Guide to Historic Places in Los Angeles County. (Dubuque: Kendall/Hunt Publishing Company, 1978),

p. 65; State of California, <u>California Inventory of Historic Resources</u>. (Sacramento: Dept. of Parks and Recreation, March 1976), p. 40.

(32) Wooden Houses: Salvator, <u>op. cit.</u>, p. 21.

(33) Guinn, <u>op. cit.</u>, p. 241; Salvator, <u>op. cit.</u>, p. 124.

(34) James, <u>op. cit.</u>, passim; Dixon, <u>op. cit.</u>, pp. 230-236; and Dumke, <u>op. cit.</u>, pp. 99-103.

(35) Victoria Padilla, <u>Southern California Gardens; An Illustrated History</u>. (Berkeley: University of California Press, 1961), p. 67. Los Angeles County Board of Education, <u>Historic Landmarks in Los Angeles County; A Descriptive Guide for Teachers</u> (Curriculum Supplement - Social Studies No. 5; Revised Edition), (Los Angeles: Office of County Superintendent of Schools, 1956), unnumbered page; and Gebhard and Winter, <u>op. cit.</u>, p. 351; and McWilliams, <u>Southern California...</u> (cited), p. 118. Santa Anita Rancho: In 1872 Harris Newmark paid $85,000 for the Santa Anita Rancho. He sold it to Baldwin in 1875 for $200,000. At Baldwin's death in 1909 his net worth was 20 million dollars. —Newmark, <u>op. cit.</u>, p. 474.

(36) Gingerbread Description: Smith, <u>op. cit.</u>, p. 8.

(37) Truman, <u>Tourists' Illustrated</u>...(cited), p. 222.

(38) Nadeau, <u>City-Makers</u>... (cited), p. 129; Salvator, <u>op. cit.</u>, p. 134.

(39) Ruth I. Mahood (editor), <u>California Mission Paintings by Edwin Deakin</u>. (Los Angeles: History Division, Los Angeles Museum of Natural History, Bulletin No. 3, 1966), in the introduction by Donald Cutter.

(40) Helen Hunt Jackson, <u>Glimpses of California and the Missions</u>. (Boston: Little, Brown & Company, 1883, 1919), p. 177.

(41) Mission Description: Bishop, <u>op. cit.</u>, p. 13.

(42) Helen Hunt Jackson, <u>Ramona</u>. (N.Y.: Grosset & Dunlap, 1884, 1912), p. 14.

(43) Richard Griswold del Castillo, "The del Valle Family and the Fantasy Heritage," <u>California History</u>, Vol. LIX, No. 1 (Spring 1980), p. 4.

CHAPTER VI The 1880s Boom: Victoriana Exoticized

(1) Charles Dudley Warner, <u>On Horseback: A Tour in Virginia, North Carolina, and Tennessee, with Notes of Travel in Mexico and California</u>. (Boston, 1889), p. 317, in Baur, <u>op. cit.</u>, p. 46.

(2) Rate Wars: Dumke, <u>op. cit.</u>, pp. 21-25.

(3) Theodore Strong Van Dyke, <u>Millionaires of a Day; An Inside History of the Great Southern California "Boom"</u>. (N.Y.: Fords, Howard & Hulbert, 1890), p. 45.

(4) <u>Ibid.</u>, p. 42; Guinn, <u>op. cit.</u>, p. 140.

(5) Van Dyke, <u>op. cit.</u>, p. 84.

(6) <u>Los Angeles Times</u>, Dec. 11, 1886, I-7.

(7) Quotation: Guinn, <u>op. cit.</u>, p. 140

(8) Dumke, <u>The Boom of the Eighties</u>... (cited), p. 80; and Los Angeles Conservancy, "Monrovia" (tour brochure), 1983.

(9) <u>Los Angeles Times</u>, Nov. 10, 1886, I-8.

Notes

(10) US Dept. of the Interior, Census Office, <u>Statistics of the Population of the United States at the Tenth Census</u>, (June 1, 1880)... (Washington, D.C.: Government Printing Office, 1883), p. 51. The 1890 census shows 101,454 for Los Angeles County after Orange County had been formed in 1889. Orange County's population in 1890 was 13,589. If we add the two counties we arrive at a total of 115,043. The L.A. County population of 33,381 in 1880 can then be compared with the 115,043 to indicate the decade's volume of growth. —United States Dept. of the Interior, Census Office, <u>Report on Population of the United States at the Eleventh Census, 1890,</u> <u>Part I.</u> (Washington, D.C.: Government Printing Office, 1895), pp. 70-71; Van Dyke, <u>op. cit.</u>, p. 42; Dumke, <u>The Boom of the</u> <u>Eighties...</u>, (cited), pp. 46, 49.

(11) <u>Los Angeles Times</u>, April 1888, quoted in "Boom! It was a Mania that Rivaled the Gold Rush," <u>Los Angeles Times</u>, Jan. 12, 1981, I-16.

(12) Dumke, The Boom of the Eighties...(cited), p. 270; 1890 Census (cited), p. 70.

(13) Construction Figures: Dumke, <u>op. cit.</u>, pp. 45, 52.

(14) For the stylistic adaptation of the English Queen Anne style in the United States, see Vincent J. Scully, Jr., <u>The Shingle Style and</u> <u>the Stick Style: Architectural Theory and Design from Downing to the Origins of Wright.</u> (Revised Edition). (New Haven, Conn.: Yale University Press, 1955, 1971), pp. 34-53. Features and variants is found in: McAlester and McAlester, <u>op. cit.</u>, 262-7.

(15) Horatio Alger, 1834-1899, wrote 135 novels on a poor-boy-makes-good format.

(16) Peggy Rinard, "Housing Development Rises that You Can't Move Into," <u>Los Angeles Times</u>, May 4, 1980, VIII-33.

(17) Cyma Corbels, Sanders House: Grenier, <u>op. cit.</u>, p. 70.

(18) David Gebhard, Harriette Von Breton, and Robert W. Winter, <u>Samuel and Joseph Cather Newsom: Victorian Architectural</u> <u>Imagery in California, 1878-1908</u>, (Santa Barbara: UCSB Art Museum, 1979), p. 15. The application of the terms "low art" and "lowbrow" to vernacular culture tends to obscure an exciting aspect of late 19th-century American culture: the dramatic socially broadening of access to culture. Lawrence W. Levine's significant study, <u>Highbrow/Lowbrow: The Emergence of Cultural Hierarchy in</u> <u>America.</u> (Cambridge, Mass.: Harvard University Press, 1989), made us all think afresh even if we disagree with some of his conclusions. For one thing, he also credits the elite as the moving force behind a two-track culture late in the 19th-century, without considering the power of the consumer to initiate budgetwise variations of wealthy models, or that these vernacular forms might have been satisfactory ends in themselves. Unlike the 1876 Mt. Pleasant house, the wooden middle-class Queen Anne of the 1880s were attractive structures on their own, and rarely attempted to replicate more expensive stone mansions.

(19) Charles Eastlake, shown houses such as these, rejected them as "bizarre and extravagant" perversions.; Kirker, <u>California's</u> <u>Architectural Frontier</u>,(cited), Plate 48, pp. 106-108 and City of Oakland, <u>Rehab Right: How to Rehabilitate Your Oakland House</u> <u>Without Sacrificing Architectural Assets.</u> (Oakland: City of Oakland, 1978), p. 12.

(20) Grenier, <u>op. cit.</u>, p. 70

(21) Andrew Jackson Downing, <u>Cottage Residences...</u>, (N.Y.: 1850), p. 51, in Scully, <u>op. cit.</u>, p. xliv.

(22) Samuel & Joseph C. Newsom, <u>Picturesque California Homes; A Volume of Forty Plates, Plans, Details and Specifications of</u> <u>Houses Costing from $700 to $15,000, and Adapted to Families Having Good Taste and Moderate Means. City and Country Homes.</u> (Los Angeles: Hennessey & Ingalls, Inc., 1884, 1978, passim; Samuel Newsom, <u>Some City and Suburban Homes.</u> (San Francisco, 1890), quoted in Gebhard, Von Breton, and Winter, <u>op. cit..</u>, p. 13.

(23) Mirano, <u>op. cit.</u>, No. 10; Grenier, <u>op. cit.</u>, p. 70; Gebhard, Von Breton, and Winters, <u>op. cit.</u>, pp. 76-77; and David Gebhard and Harriette Von Breton, <u>Architecture in California, 1868-1968.</u> (Exhibition Catalog) (Santa Barbara, the Art Galleries, UCSB, 1968), p. 10.

CHAPTER VII The 1890s: A Search for Meaning

(1) Charles Dwight Willard, <u>A History of the Chamber of Commerce of Los Angeles, California; From Its Foundation, September, 1888</u>

to the Year 1900. (Los Angeles: Kingsley-Barnes & Neuner Company, 1899), pp. 60, 66, 73.

(2) Los Angeles Chamber of Commerce: "Facts and Figures Concerning Southern California and Los Angeles City and County," (Los Angeles, 1904), p. 3. Ten thousand copies of this pamphlet were distributed. —Willard, op. cit., p. 76.

(3) Noteworthy examples of the books by doctors praising the healthfulness of the climate are: —Remondino, op. cit., and Lindley and Widney, op. cit., published in 1892 and 1888/1896, respectively.

(4) Baur, op. cit., pp. 47, 174-175.

(5) Wilson, op. cit., pp. 176-177.

(6) Willard, op. cit., pp. 88, 94; Los Angeles Chamber of Commerce, Southern California Resources, Progress and Prospects. (Pamphlet) (Los Angeles: A. Phillips & Co., Sept. 1891).

(7) Rolle, op. cit., pp. 323-326; Bean, op. cit., pp. 273-276. —Laurie Gordon and John Salkin, "'Eat Me and Grow Young!'; Orange Crate Art in the Golden State," California History, Vol. LVI, No. 1 (Spring 1977), pp. 52-71. —Josephine Kingsbury Jacobs, "Sunkist Advertising," Unpublished Ph.D. thesis, UCLA, 1966, quoted in Caughey and Caughey, op. cit., pp. 215-218.

(8) W.C. Patterson, quoted by Atcheson & Eshelman, Los Angeles Then and Now. (Souvenir book) (Los Angeles: Press Geo. Rice & Sons, Inc., 1897), p. 108.

(9) Limiting Factors to Industrialization: Willard, op. cit., pp. 172-178.

(10) Atcheson & Eshelman, op. cit.; Western Insurance News, Los Angeles, The Old and the New; Issued as a Supplement to the Western Insurance News. (Los Angeles: J. E. Scott, 1911); Los Angeles Chamber of Commerce, Facts and Figures…, (cited); Harry Ellington Brook, Los Angeles the Chicago of the Southwest. (Pamphlet) (Los Angeles Chamber of Commerce, 1904); Willard, op. cit., p. 143.

(11) Oil: Ibid., pp. 179-180, 298-299; Beck, op. cit., pp. 315-316.

(12) Southern Pacific Railroad's monthly, Sunset Magazine, in 1910 and reprinted in Western Insurance News, op. cit., pp. 81-94.

(13) Quotation: Anonymous, The Land of Sunshine, Fruit and Flowers (Souvenir Fold-out). (Columbus, Ohio: Ward Bros., 1898), unnumbered pages.

(14) Nurseries: Padilla, op. cit., pp. 58, 84.

(15) Although the 1989 Rose Parade celebrated the 100th anniversary of that event, the Los Angeles Times, 1-7, Jan. 2, 1890 reported on the event of the preceding day as the first Rose Parade.

(16) Edwin O. Palmer, History of Hollywood. (Hollywood: Edwin Ol Palmer, Publisher, 1938), p. 110.

(17) Ostrich Farm: James, op. cit., pp. 196-204.

(18) Anonymous, "A Country of Outings. I. — The Seaside," The Land of Sunshine; A Southern California Magazine, Vol. III, No. 2 (July 1895), pp. 92-96.

(19) George Wharton James, Travelers' Handbook to Southern California. (Pasadena: George Wharton James, 1904) pp. 205-219; Anonymous, "A Country of Outings. II. -Some Mountain Resorts," The Land of Sunshine; A Southern California Magazine, Vol. III, No. 3 (August 1895), pp. 144-145.

(20) The Mooers House was built as a speculative venture by building contractor, Frank Lorin Wright, the title listed in his wife's name. There was no record of its architect. However, in an 1896 advertising booklet put out by a furnace company I found a photograph

Notes

of a house attributed to architects Bradbeer & Ferris which is almost identical to the Mooers House. It was identified in the ad as the house of Charles Haddock, at 939 S. Olive, which is in the same neighborhood. —F.E. Browne, Comfortable Los Angeles Homes, and What People Say Who Live in Them. (Los Angeles: F.E. Browne, 1896), unnumbered page); Grenier, op. cit., p. 74; Mirano, op. cit., unnumbered; Mooers motives for purchasing the house apparently included the hope that it might entice his wife, whom he had abandoned 20 years before and who was in the process of divorcing him, to return. It didn't work. —Barbara Towers, "Mooers House: A Los Angeles Mansion and the Man Who Bought It," Southern California Quarterly, Vol. 66, (1984), pp. 221-234.

(22) Quotation: Dickinson, op. cit., unnumbered.

(23) This house was originally constructed 1899-1900 for Mr. and Mrs. Oliver P. Posey and sold to Doheny in 1901 for $120,000. A 1904 photograph (Los Angeles Chamber of Commerce, Los Angeles and Vicinity (Pamphlet). (Los Angeles, 1904), unnumbered pages) shows a view which looks quite as the house does today, cresting on the gables and all. The house was built of red brick covered with plaster. Following damage in the 1933 earthquake, half-timbering was replaced by steel — apparently without major restyling. — Cultural Heritage Board, City of Los Angeles, Fact Sheets on Historic-Cultural Monuments. (Los Angeles: Municipal Art Department, City of Los Angeles, 1974), p. 17; Mt. St. Mary's College Tour Notes, unpublished, Open House, 1978.

(24) Chateau in Wood: Grenier, op. cit., p. 74.

(25) Conservatory: Padilla, op. cit., pp. 103-105.

(26) This house on Alvarado Terrace was purchased from Calvin A. Boyle by Edward H. Barmore in 1908. "The Alvarado Terrace House Tour," (brochure), (Los Angeles Conservancy, 1982) — corrects references in Gebhard and Winter, op. cit., (1994) p. 202; and Grenier, op. cit., p. 76.

(27) E. Caswell Perry, "Leslie C. Brand," (unpublished manuscript), (Glendale, Brand Library, 1973).

(28) Quotation: Elizabeth Bacon Custer, "Memories of 'Our Italy'", The Land of Sunshine, Vol. III, No. 2 (July 1895), p. 52. Charles Dudley Warner, Our Italy. (NY: Harper Brothers, 1891).

(29) Newmark, op. cit., p. 592; Lynn Bowman, Los Angeles: Epic of a City. (Berkeley: Howell-North Books, 1974), p. 187.

(30) David Lindsey, "Venice of America," American History Illustrated, May 1980, p. 37, claims the Columbian Exposition was Kinney's primary inspiration source. But Tom Moran, the author of Fantasy by the Sea; A Visual History of the American Venice, in an address to the Southern California Historical Society, March 16, 1977, said the idea came to Kinney on shipboard after his escape from the war in Salonika.

(31) Tom Moran and Tom Sewell, Fantasy by the Sea; a Visual History of the American Venice. (Culver City: Peace Press, 1979, 1980), p. 19.

(32) The heavily-ornamented neo-classicism fostered by the Ecole des Beaux Arts in Paris and, especially as it devolved in the U.S. as a loosely applied stylistic term, "the Beaux Arts Style" did not represent a revival of any particular historic style. It rolled together the proportional standards set by Andrea Palladio, the ornamentation of the Loius XIV toXVI aristocracy, and borrowings from Jacobean, Moorish, Byzantine and Italian styles. William Peirce Randel, The Evolution of American Taste; The History of American Style from 1607 to the Present. (N.Y.: Crown Publishers, Inc., 1978), p. 127. Wayne Andrews, Architecture in America; A Photographic History from the Colonial Period to the Present. (N.Y.: Atheneum, 1960), pp. 102-103. —Randel, op. cit., p. 136.

(33) La Fiesta de Los Angeles remained an annual affair into the 1930s. —Newmark, op. cit., pp. 605-606.

(34) Turbese Lummis Fiske and Keith Lummis, Charles F. Lummis; The Man and His West. (Norman, Okla.: University of Oklahoma Press, 1975), p. 94. —Karen J. Weitze. California's Mission Revival (Santa Monica: Hennessey & Ingalls, 1984), 3-15.

(35) Weitze illustrates the calculated nature of Lummis' contributions to the mission myth with a Lummis quip: "'Plymouth Rock was a state of mind. So were the California Missions.'" —Ibid., 16. Five years after he took over Land of Sunshine the Chamber of Commerce boasted that it had a larger paid circulation than any other periodical printed west of Chicago. —Willard, op. cit., p. 291;

Weitze, op. cit., 74; —McWilliams, Southern California...(cited), pp. 78-79.

(36) Quotation: Lummis, Ibid., p. 88.

(37) The Santa Fe not only played a role in Landmark Club efforts, its stations in the Mission Revival style and cartooned Navajo children served as its logos for many years. Ibid., 89; Msgr. Francis J. Weber (Editor), The Mission in the Valley; A Documentary History of San Fernando, Rey de Espana. (Los Angeles: Archdiocese of Los Angeles, Chancery Archives, 1975), pp. 92-93.

(38) Kirker, California's Architectural Frontier, cited, p. 122, and Fiske, op. cit., p. 89, give a brief account of this campaign for a regional style. —Elmer Grey, "Architecture in Southern California," The Architectural Record, Vol. XVII, No. 1 (Jan. 1905), pp. 12-17; Weitze, op. cit., 44-128.

(39) One example of such an Hispanicized late-Victorian is the H. H. Wilcox house on Adams Boulevard. —Carroll Lachnit, "'Crazy House' Becoming a Gem Again," Los Angeles Times, March 14, 1980.

(40) Gebhard, Von Breton, and Winter, op. cit., pp. 30-31; Kirker, California's Architectural Frontier, cited, pp. 121-123; Weitze, op. cit., 19-43.

(41) Espandanas often went unpierced and un-belled, serving only as decoration and added height. There is a surmised link with Spanish-occupied Low Countries, where the stepped gable fronts were an old tradition. —Kurt Baer, Architecture of the California Missions. (Berkeley: University of California Press, 1958), pp. 32-33, 44-45.

(42) W. L. B. Jenney, "The Old California Missions and Their Influence on Modern Design," The Architect and Engineer of California., Vol. XI, No. 2 (Sept. 1906), pp. 27-28; J. J. Peatfield, "The California Exposition," The Californian, Vol. 5, Dec. 1893, quoted in Gebhard, Von Breton and Winters, op. cit., p. 31; Arthur Burnett Benton, "The California Mission and Its Influence Upon Pacific Coast Architecture," The Architect and Engineer of California, Vol. XXIV, No. 1 (Feb. 1911), 63, 71; Grey, op. cit., pp. 2-3.

(43) This house was built for City Councilman and real estate developer Pomeroy Powers in 1904 by architect Arthur L. Haley. It was located in the toney subdivision of Alvarado Terrace, in which Mr. Powers was one of the principals.

(44) The Erasmus Wilson residence, now part of the Mount Saint Mary College campus, was one of the fine homes built in the exclusive Chester Place subdivision which was laid out in 1895. The third floor is devoted to a large ballroom, with a birds-eye maple floor still beautiful today.

(45) A building permit dated 1913 marks the conversion of a single family residence into this multiple dwelling and adding two units to the south side of the existing two-story building. The Mission styling was presumably adopted at that time.

CHAPTER VIII Facing West

(1) Quotation: Lummis, "In the Lion's Den," Out West 15 (Jan. 1902), 60.

(2) One study found that the old middle-class — doctors, lawyers, and owners of small businesses — more than doubled between 1870 and 1910. But the new middle-class of white collar employees, clerks, technicians, and middle management, increased almost eightfold in the same period. — Frank Freidel. America in the Twentieth Century. (Fourth Edition). (N.Y.: Alfred A. Knopf, 1960, 1976), 20-21.

(3) Robert Winter. The California Bungalow. (Los Angeles: Hennessey & Ingalls, 1980), 49-51, must be credited with the definitive coverage of the bungalow living room as the "seat of male chauvinism."

(4) Walker, op. cit., 196, 201; Richard Hofstadter. The Age of Reform, From Bryan to F.D.R. (N.Y.: Vintage Books, 1955), 152, 189-190, 202-208.

(5) In the year 1900, $21 million worth of manufactured goods were produced in Los Angeles led by the following industries: iron items, glass, furniture, woolens, and processed foods. —Los Angeles County Museum, History Division. Los Angeles, 1900-1961 (Exhibition Catalog). (Los Angeles: 1961), 1.

(6) Paul Gleye. The Architecture of Los Angeles. (LA: Rosebud Books, 1981), 72-73.

(7) Ernest Marquez. Port Los Angeles; A Phenomenon of the Railroad Era. (San Marino: Golden West Books, 1975), 36-89; Charles Dwight Willard. The Free Harbor Contest at Los Angeles. (Los Angeles: 1899); Goerge E. Mowry, The California Progressives. (Chicago: Quadrangle Books, 1951), 39; Frederick L. Bird and Frances M. Ryan. The Recall of Public Officers; A Study of the Operation of the Recall in California. (N.Y.: The Macmillan Company, 1930); Tom Sitton. John Randolph Haynes; California Progressive. (Stanford: Stanford University Press, 1992); "Good Government Leaders Celebrate Victory at Mammoth Banquet; Champions of Civic Purity at Gathering," Los Angeles Evening Herald, Dec. 18, 1909, 6; Los Angeles County Museum. op. cit., 16.

(8) The city's water rights were secured in an 1895 court case, Vernon Irrigation Co. v. Los Angeles, and extended in Los Angeles v. Pomeroy and Hooker , (1899). — Remi A. Nadeau. The Water Seekers. (N.Y.: Doubleday and Company, 1950); Norris Hundley, Jr., The Great Thirst; Californians and Water, 1770s-1990s, (Berkeley: Universityof California Press, 1992), pp. 133-135; Los Angeles Department of Water and Power. "Water for Los Angeles," (pamphlet). (Los Angeles: 1978), 4; William Kahrl, "The Politics of California Water: Owens Valley and the Los Angeles Aqueduct, 1900-1927, Parts I and II," California Historical Quarterly 55 (Spring & Summer, 1976), 1-25, 98-120.

(9) Quotation: Gustav Stickley, "The Craftsman Idea," Craftsman Homes; Architecture and Furnishings of the American Arts and Crafts Movement. (N.Y.: Dover Publications, 1909, 1979), 197-198.

(10) Los Angeles County Museum, op. cit., 1. Department of the Interior; Census Office. Report on Population of the United States at the Eleventh Census; 1890; Part I. (Washington, D.C.: Government Printing Office, 1895), 70-71; Department of Commerce, Bureau of the Census. Thirteenth Census of the United States. Taken in the Year 1910; Volume I. Population 1910, General Report and Analysis. (Washington, D.C.: Government Printing Office, 1913), 82, 87, 104.

(11) A.W.N. Pugin. True Principles of Christian Architecture (1841) and Contrasts (1836; Thomas Carlyle. "Signs of the Times" (published in the Edinburgh Review in 1829) and Past and Present (1843)' John Ruskin. The Complete Works of John Ruskin (39 volumes edited by E. T. Cook and A. Wedderburn between 1843 and 1889, especially The Stones of Venice of 1853 and The Seven Lamps of Architecture of 1851; and Karl Marx. Economic and Philosophical manuscripts (1844) in Erich Fromm. Marx's Concept of Man. (N.Y.: Frederick Ungar Publishing Co., 1961, 1966).

(12) Quotation: William Morris, "The Lesser Arts," in G.D. H. Cole (editor). William Morris. (Centenary Edition) (Nonesuch Press, 1948), 496, Gilliam Naylor. The Arts and Crafts Movement; A Study of Its Sources, Ideals, and Influence on Design Theory. (Cambridge, Mass.: The M.I.T. Press, 1971), 108.

(13) Isabelle Anscome and Charlotte Gere. Arts & Crafts in Britain and America. (N.Y.: Rizzoli, 1978), 31, 37, 149150; Wendy Kaplan (Editor). 'The Art That Is Life': The Arts and Crafts Movement in America, 1875-1920. (Boston: Museum of Fine Arts, 1987), 57, 216-219; T. J. Jackson Lears. No Place of Grace: Antimodernism and the Transformation of American Culture, 1880-1920. (N.Y.: Pantheon Books, 1981), 61, 68.

(14) In its 16 years of publication, Stickley's magazine never exceeded an annual circulation figure of 22,500. — N. W. Ayer & Son's American Newspaper Annual and Directory..., [1905, 1910, 1915, 1916 editions] (Philadelphia: N W. Ayer & Son).

(15) Quotation: Stickley, "The Craftsman Idea," (cited), 195.

(16) Quotation: Ibid., 194.

(17) Quotation: Ibid., 203.

(18) Clifford Edward Clark, Jr. The American Family Home, 1800-1900. (Chapel Hill: The University of North Carolina Press, 1986), 131-192. Alan Gowans. The Comfortable House: North American Suburban Architecture, 1890-1930. (Cambridge, Mass.: The M.I.T. Press, 1986) pp. 41-65 provides a well-substantiated guide to the vernacularization of the bungalow in conscientiously categorized subtypes.

(19) Robert Schmutzler. Art Nouveau. (N.Y.: Harrn N. Abrams, 1977), 21-30, 129. Edward S. Morse. Japanese Homes and Their Surroundings. (Rutland, Vt.: Charles E. Tuttle Company, 1887, 1972), and Ralph N. Cram. Impressions of Japanese Architecture and

the Allied Arts. (N.Y.: The Baker & Taylor Co., 1905). Greene & Greene Collection, Huntington Library, San Marino, California. Tatami proportions, see Morse, op. cit., 118, 122-123.

(20) One book which brought the aesthetics of the tea ceremony to American attention was Kakuzo Okakura, The Book of Tea. (N.Y.: Dover Publ., 1906, 1964).

(21) Winter, The California Bungalow (cited), 19-23.

(22) A. W. Smith, Quotation: Smith, op. cit., 31; Anonymous, "The Bungalow at Its Best," (, in The Architectural Record 20 (Oct. 1906), 296-305); "The California Bungalow; A Style of Architecture Which Expresses the Individuality and Freedom Characteristic of Our Western Coast," The Craftsman, 13 (Oct. 1907), 68-80).

(23) The symbiosis between Native American arts and the Craftsman movement are exemplified by Anonymous, "New Hopi Architecture on the Old Mesa Land: From Notes by Ethel Rose," The Craftsman 30 (July 1916), 374-382 and Ernest Batchelder, The Principles of Design (Second Edition) (Chicago: The Inland Printer Company, 1906), Frank McNitt, Richard Wetherill: Anasazi. (Revised Edition) (Albuquerque: The University of new Mexico Press, 1957, 1966), and U. S. Hollister, The Navajo and His Blanket, 1903, and George Wharton James, Indian Blankets and Their Makers, 1920. Lummis' excitement is evident in the letter he wrote home the day he arrived in Lima: "And such ruins as there are all around here! And such ground plans and such treasures! Wonderful pottery, and wonderful cloths, and mummies, and idols, and gold and silver, and everything! I shall be just wild when I get into it...." — Davis Dutton, "For My Eve, Tu Fiel Carlos," Westways (Nov. 1978), 30; Fiske, op. cit., 99; Anscombe and Gere, op. cit., 209-210.

(24) Quotation: Anonymous, "Some California Houses that Show an Interesting Use of the Popular and Adaptable Cobblestone," The Craftsman 13 (Nov. 1907), 192.

(25) Randell L. Makinson, Greene & Greene: Architecture as a Fine Art. (Salt Lake City: Peregrine Smith, Inc., 1977), 27; Makinson, Greene & Greene; Furniture and Related Designs. (Santa Barbara: Peregrine Smith, Inc., 1979), 10. The Arts and Crafts links of Louis B. Easton and Elbert Hubbard, of Ernest Batchelder and George Wharton James are treated in: Anonymous, "House Lives On?" Pasadena Heritage 3 (Spring 1979), 1; Anderson, Moore & Winter, op. cit., 23, 60; Anscombe & Gere, op. cit., 210.

(26) Quotation: Anonymous, "The California Bungalow, A Style of Architecture...", (cited), 68.

(27) Elmer Grey, Quotation: In Ibid., 73. Randell L. Makinson, "Greene and Greene: The Gamble House," The Prairie School Review 5 (1968), 7.

(28) Esther McCoy, Five California Architects. (Los Angeles: Hennessey & Ingalls, 1960, 1987), 108-109; Makinson, Greene & Greene; Architecture...(cited), 70-72.

(29) Quotation: Charles Greene, letter to Mrs. James A. Garfield, 1904, quoted in Ibid., 92.

(30) Reyner Banham, Introduction to Makinson, Greene & Greene; Architecture as a Fine Art, cited, p. 14; Banham, Los Angeles; The Architecture of Four Ecologies. (N.Y.: Penguin, 1971, 1976), 69-72.

(31) "The Japanese Print as a Reformer: Its Power to Influence Home Decoration," The Craftsman 30 (May 1916), 131.

(32) Joseph S. O'Flaherty, Those Powerful Years; The South Coast and Los Angeles, 1887-1917. (Hicksville, N.Y.: Exposition Press, 1978), 305; Quotation: Willard, op. cit., 201.

(33) Morse, op. cit., 84-87; Janann Strand, A Greene & Greene Guide. (Pasadena; Janann Strand, 1974), 70.

(34) McCoy, op. cit., 125; the almost three-dimensional relief Batchelder tiles of the ballroom exterior are Romanesque in subject and style and the windowed wall has an enclosed grilled balconet a la Granada.

(35) Quotation: Batchelder, op. cit., 21, 34.

(36) Quotation: Una Nixson Hopkins, "The Development of Domestic Architecture on the Pacific Coast," The Craftsman 13 (Jan. 1908), 457.

(37) Spencer Crump, Ride the Big Red Cars; How Trolleys Helped Build Southern California. (Glendale, CA: Trans-Anglo Books, 1970), en toto. Additional references include: Steven L. Easlon, The Los Angeles Railway Through the Years. (Sherman Oaks, CA: Darwin Publications, 1973; Fogelson, op. cit., 85-92; William F. King, The Vintage Years, Our Valley Before 1945. (San Bernardino, CA: Mt. San Antonio College Community Services, 1975), Chapter IX; and Sam Bass Warner, Jr., The Urban Wilderness; A History of the American City. (NY: Harper & Row, Publishers, 1972), 135-137.

(38) Western Insurance News (cited), 96.

(39) Working blueprints for bungalows were available for prices from $5 to $25. — City of Oakland, Planning Department, op. cit., 28; Katherine Cole Stevenson and H. Ward Jandl. Houses by Mail: A Guide to Houses from Sears, Roebuck and Company. (Washington, D.C.: Preservation Press, 1986).

(40) Lot Size, Cost, and Credit Terms: Ibid., p. 28.

(41) Quotation: Ernest Ingold, "Home-Building and the Southland," Out West 1 (Mar. 1911), 235, 237-238.

(42) Winter, The California Bungalow, (cited), 60.

(43) Harry Ellington Brook, "Los Angeles, California: The City and County," (23rd Edition, pamphlet) (Los Angeles Chamber of Commerce, Aug. 1910), 58; James W. Abbott, "Among Cities Los Angeles Is the World's Greatest Wonder. Why?" (pamphlet) (Los Angeles: The Cadmus Press, 1914), 14-15.

(44) Los Angeles County Museum, op. cit., 4; Gerald T. White, Formative Years in the Far West; A History of Standard Oil Company of California and Predecessors Through 1919. (N.Y.: Appleton-Century-Crofts, 1962), 464-466.

(45) Quotation: Harrison Gray Otis, in Western Insurance News (cited), 81.

(46) Under "Principle Port Exports" all entries are direct agricultural or mining products or their by-products. There was no mention at all of either aircraft or motion pictures.— Los Angeles Chamber of Commerce, L. A. Today, May 1, 1916. (pamphlet), 11.

(47) In the between-census-year of 1924 the estimated population was recapped as follows: "At the end of 1910, population = 319,198; At the end of 1920, population = 576,673; At the end of 1924, population = 1,275,000 (estimated)" — "L.A. Crowding for Fourth Place," Southern California Business (Jan. 1924), 11. The 1920 and 1924 figures were ballooned by a number of annexations to the city, especially the acquisition of most of the San Fernando Valley in 1915.

(48) Gerald T. White, op. cit., 134-135, 152-153; Rolle, op. cit., 432; J. Paul Getty, My Life and Fortunes. (N.Y.: Duell, Sloan and Pearce, 1963), 62, 78.

(49) "Did You Know These Things?", Southern California Business 2 (Apr. 1923), 36; Los Angeles Chamber of Commerce, L. A. County; Facts and Figures, 1925. (Los Angeles, 1925), 16. Increased gasoline consumption: E.C. Noel, "Oil Industry Offers Surprises," Southern California Business 2 (Jan. 1924), 38: During the year 1922 California produced a daily average of 1,899,974 gallons of gasoline, with a daily consuption of 1,763,807 gallons. During the first ten months of [1923] there was a daily consumption of 3,335,714 gallons.

(50)Irvin Ashkenazy, "Birdmen over Dominguez Hill," Westways, (Jan. 1975), 14-17.

(51) "Aviation Giant Donald Douglas Is Dead at 88," Los Angeles Times. (Feb. 3, 1981), I-1; Beck, op. cit.; Bill Bradley, (compiler), Commercial Los Angeles, 1925-1947. (Glendale, CA: Interurban Press, 1981), unnumbered text page for photo #151; Frank Freidel, America in the Twentieth Century (4th edition), (NY: Alfred A. Knopf, 1976), 106; "Aircraft Pioneer Jack Northrop Dies at Age 85," Los Angeles Times. (Feb. 20, 1981), I-1; Kindelberger: Bowman, op. cit., 289; and Los Angeles County Museum of Natural History, op. cit., 45; W.D. Longyear, "Take Airplanes for Instance," Southern California Business 8 (Aug. 1929), 10-11; and A.W. Poole, "Where

the Aviation Industry Centers," Southern California Business 8 (May 1929), 9.

(52) Building permit dated 5-27-1913. Original owner, N.T. Dennis. The finished structure measured 35 by 41 feet.

(53) Clay Lancaster, The Japanese Influence in America. (N.Y.: Walton H. Rawls, 1963), 90, 96, 127.

(54) A list of 35 leading manufactures of L.A. in 1923, and their relative worth is in L. A. County: Facts and Figures, 1925 (cited), 11.

(55) "Movies Go West," California Historical Courier 29 (July 1977), 7; Kevin Brownlow, Hollywood: The Pioneers. (N.Y.: Alfred A. Knopf, 1979), 28, 46; Gilbert Seldes, An Hour with the Movies and the Talkies. (Philadelphia: J. B. Lippincott Company, 1929), 33-34.

(56) O'Flaherty, op. cit., 271. By 1922 the Chamber of Commerce had moved up its claim: "There are [only] eleven days in the year without sunshine," it boasted on the inside front cover of a pamphlet of that year. But on page 14 the writer hedged: "...the sun shines over three hundred days in the year." — Los Angeles Chamber of Commerce, "Los Angeles Today; October, 1922." (pamphlet) (Los Angeles: Neuner Corporation, 1922).

(57) Marc Wanamaker, "Before Hollywood was Hollywood," Los Angeles Times Supplement (Aug. 31, 1980), 62; E. O. Palmer, History of Hollywood, Volume II: Biographical. (Hollywood: Arthur H. Cawston, 1937), 117; Donald J. Newman, "The Town on the Range Where Westerns Grew Up," Los Angeles Times Calendar (Feb. 1, 1981), 24.

(58) Brownlow, op. cit., 54-57; Wanamaker, op. cit., 62.

(59) Ibid., 62; Palmer, Volume II (cited), 117, 241; and John D. Weaver, Los Angeles: The Enormous Village: 1781-1981. (Santa Barbara: Capra Press, 1980), 71; Marc Wanamaker, "Thomas H. Ince, Father of the Western," (Unpublished course material, UCLA Extension; Marc Wanamaker, instructor) (May 6, 1981), 1. Inceville was on a Pacific Electric freight line until 1931. — Marquez, op. cit., 113-116.

(60) Quoting C.B. DeMille in: [Virginia Pearson], Film Flashes; The Wit and Humor of a Nation in Pictures. (N.Y.: Leslie-Judge Company, 1916), unnumbered page; Lloyd C. Gardner and William L. O'Neill, Looking Backward; A Reintroduction to American History. (N.Y.: McGraw-Hill Book Company, 1974), 298.

(61) Lewis Jacobs, "Film as Big Business," in Barbara H. Solomon (editor), Ain't We Got Fun; Essays, Lyrics, and Stories of the Twenties. (N.Y.: New American Library, 1980), 195; Anthony Slide and Edward Wagenknecht, Fifty Great American Silent Films, 1912-1920; A Pictorial Survey. (N.Y.: Dover Publ., Inc, 1980), 29; Max Vorspan and Lloyd P. Gartner, History of the Jews of Los Angeles. (San Marino: The Huntington Library, 1970), 132.

CHAPTER IX Revivalism: Insecurity and Pretense

(1) 100% Americanism: John Higham, Strangers in the Land; Patterns of American Nativism, 1860-1925. (NY: Atheneum, 1971), pp. 198-199, 204-205.

(2) Michael Goldman, "The Liberty Style," Portfolio, Vol. III, No. 6 (Nov/Dec 1981), p. 93; Anscombe and Gere, op. cit., pp. 189-191.

(3) President Wilson's unkind characterization of Harding as "bungalow-minded" (quoted in Winter, op. cit., p. 13) and the fact that Sinclair Lewis' paradigm of mediocrity, George Babbitt, was at home in a bungalow are two random examples of the bungalow put-down.

(4) Brown, op. cit., pp. 38-40, 83, — the number of building permits in Los Angeles for 1913 for private residences was 16,442; for 1914-1918 it was below 10,000 each year, reaching a low of 6,381 in 1918; in 1919 the number rose to 13,344. According to his sampling, bungalows as a building type were prominent through 1919, after which they quickly dwindled.

(5) This home was apparently built as a rental investment. The city directory shows the first occupants to be a Mr. and Mrs. Charles Andrews, Mr. Andrews being identified occupationally with the Jones Book Store in Los Angeles. —Glendale City Directory, 1927.

(6) A flu epidemic and a coal shortage closed theaters in the winter of 1919. Market testing in the spring quickly settled on the new

formulae.James E. Bowen, "Bright Future Ahead of Photoplays," <u>Southern California Business</u>, Vol. I, No. 8 (Sept. 1922), p. 46; Maurice Bardeche and Robert Brasillach, <u>The History of Motion Pictures</u> (translated by Iris Barry). (N.Y.: W. W. Norton & Company, Inc. and the MOMA, 1938), p. 199; Quotation: Psychoanalyst Barbara Low, quoted in Seldes, op. cit., p. 62.

(7) Quotation: <u>Ibid.</u>, p. 113. —David Naylor, <u>American Picture Palaces; The Architecture of Fantasy.</u> (N.Y.: Van Nostrand Reinhold Company, 1981).

(8) Arthur S. Link and Stanley Coben, <u>The Democratic Heritage: A History of the United States. Vol. 2: Since 1865.</u> (Waltham, Mass.: Ginn and Company, 1971), p. 446; Weekly Attendance: Leuchtenburg, op. cit., p. 196.

(9) Anonymous, <u>Film Flashes; The Wit and Humor of a Nation in Pictures.</u> (N.Y.: Leslie-Judge Company, 1916), unnumbered pages.

(10) Bardeche and Brasillach, op. cit., p. 200; King Vidor, "Hollywood, 1915: Reminiscence of a Simple Time," <u>Los Angeles Times Supplement</u>, August 31, 1980, p. 28; Drama Academies: <u>Los Angeles Times</u>, August 20, 1922, III-43-44; Cowboys: Diana Serra Cary, "Head 'em Off at the Pass," <u>Westways</u>, Oct. 1977, pp. 30, 34-35; Beauty Contests: del Zoppo, op. cit., p. 32; <u>Merton of the Movies</u> by Marc Connelly and George S. Kaufman opened Nov. 13, 1922 at the Cort Theater. —Wayne Warga, "Marc Connelly at l.86: Laurels Unrested," <u>Los Angeles Times Calendar</u>, April 17, 1977, p. 52.

(11) Quotations: Guy W. Finney, <u>The Great Los Angeles Bubble.</u> (Los Angeles: Guy W. Finney, 1929), pp. 18-19, 13.

(12) Writers like H. L. Mencken, Sinclair Lewis, and Duncan Aikman are always mentioned in this context, but the anti-rural bias underlay much of the other writing of the period, too. The role of literature in forming the new cultural attitudes is to be found in: — William E. Leuchtenburg, <u>The Perils of Prosperity, 1914-32.</u> (Chicago: The University of Chicago Press, 1958), pp. 154-157, 172-173, 225-226. "All is deadly, dumb and democratic.... [T]he ill repute of the city may arise from the disappointment of the expectant tourist who, having read of the... delinquencies ['the alleged immoralities of the moving picture kings and queens' being chief among them], hopes to find the place... reeking with wine and the hootcheekootchee. He arrives to discover a population of Iowa farmers and sun-burned old maids in an endless chain of cafeterias, movie palaces and state picnics. He... declares that the city of the angels is just as dull as the traditional kingdom of heaven." —Paul Jordan-Smith, "Los Angeles: Ballyhooers in Heaven," in Duncan Aikman (editor). <u>The Taming of the Frontier.</u> (N.Y.: Minton, Balch & Company, 1925), pp. 273, 279.

(13) Leuchtenburg, <u>Perils</u> (cited), pp. 179-180; Anonymous, "An Auto for All," <u>IronAge</u>, Vol. 217, No. 15 (April 12, 1976), p. 201; Quotation: Frederick Lewis Allen, <u>The Big Change: America Transforms Itself, 1900-1950,</u> (N.Y.: Bantam Books, 1961), p. 110.

(14) Richard R. Mathison, <u>Three Cars in Every Garage; A Motorist's History of the Automobile and the Automobile Club in Southern California.</u> (Garden City, N.Y.: Doubleday & Company, Inc., 1968), chapters 1-8; Los Angeles Chamber of Commerce, "Los Angeles Today; May 1, 1916," (pamphlet) (Los Angeles: The Neuner Company, 1916), p. 31; 1925: Los Angeles Chamber of Commerce, <u>Facts and Figures, 1925</u> (cited), p. 17; C.T. Boyd, "Auto Registration Hits New Mark," <u>Southern California Business</u>, Vol. III, No. 3 (April 1924), p. 17; Ashleigh Brilliant, "Some Aspects of Mass Motorization in Southern California, 1919-1929," <u>Southern California Quarterly</u>, Vol. XLVII, No. 2 (June 1965), p. 191.

(15) Quotation: Anonymous, "Over 600,000 Motorists Will Come," <u>Southern California Business</u>, Vol. III, No. 3 (Apr. 1924), p. 14; Mayor of Los Angeles in his annual message of 1921 reported that "nearly 7,000 people were registered at the Elysian Park Auto Camp," —Laurance L. Hill, <u>La Reina: Los Angeles in Three Centuries. Fourth Edition.</u> (Los Angeles: Security-First National Bank of LA, 1931), p. 167.

(16) Anonymous, "From All Quarters They Come to Us," <u>Southern California Business</u>, Vol. II, No. 1 (Feb. 1923), p. 21; Anon., "Over 600,000 Motorists...(cited), p. 14; Anon., "The Way the Tourists Come In," <u>Ibid.</u>, Vol. III, No. 12 (Jan. 1925), p. 26; Anon., "New Peak-Load of Tourists Coming," <u>Ibid.</u>, Vol. II, No. 10 (Nov. 1923), p. 26.

(17) W. W. Robinson, "The Southern California Real Estate Boom of the Twenties," <u>The Quarterly — Historical Society of Southern California.</u> Vol. XXIV, No. 1 (Mar. 1942), p. 25; and Jacqueline R. Kasun, <u>Some Social Aspects of Business Cycles in the Los Angeles Area, 1920-1950.</u> (Los Angeles: The Haynes Foundation, 1954), p. 10. Population Figures from 1920 to 1930 for the City range from 576,673 to 1,238,048 and County from 936,455 to 2,218,492. Anon., "Pocket Book Los Angeles," <u>Southern California Business</u>, Vol. IX, No. 12 (Dec. 1930), p. 36; Anon., "March of Events," <u>Ibid.</u>, Vol. II, No. 12 (Jan. 1924), p. 34; U.S. Dept. of Commerce, Bureau of

the Census, Fifteenth Census of the United States (Washington D.C.: Govt. Printing Office, 1933), pp. 26, 52. A chart of the value of building activity in several other towns in Los Angeles County, contained in —Anonymous, "Southern California in the Lead," Southern California Business, Vol. III, No. 1 (Feb. 1924), p. 30 shows the leap in values from 1922 to 1923.

(18) Quotation: Hill, op. cit., p. 171.

(19) Quotation: Union Pacific Railroad Company, California. (Omaha, Neb.: General Passenger Agent, Union Pacific System, 1927) [Tourist Brochure], pp. 20, 34.

(20) C. T. Boyd, "Building Charts Tell Graphic Story," Southern California Business, Vol. III, No. 1 (Feb. 1924), p. 19; Anon., "March of Events... 1930", (cited), p. 40; Anon., "Pocket Book Los Angeles, 1930" (cited), p. 36.

(21) Los Angeles Times, Feb. 5, 1922, V-5.

(22) Brentwood Ad: Los Angeles Times, Aug. 20, 1922, V-3; Girard Ad: Los Angeles Times, June 23, 1923, I-4.

(23) Los Angeles Times, Aug. 1, 1920, V-7.

(24) A 1920 ad for a six-unit rental investment of 3 and 4-room apartments being built on South Figueroa priced at $26,000 promised an income of $350 per month, all furnished with new furniture, hardwood floors, built-in beds, and six garages. —Los Angeles Times, Aug. 22, 1920, V-5.

(25) Los Angeles Times, Aug. 20, 1922, V-4.

(26) Los Angeles Times, Aug. 20, 1922, V-2.

(27) Los Angeles Times, June 17, 1923, V-3.

(28) Palos Verdes Estates, stunt flying: Los Angeles Times, June 17, 1923, I-4; Whitley Ad: Los Angeles Times, June 24, 1923, V-5.

(29) In 1920 the leading states of origin were Illinois, New York, Ohio, Pennsylvania and Iowa in that order. By 1930 it had shifted to Missouri, Texas, and Iowa, followed by Oklahoma, Kansas, Colorado, New York, Pennsylvania and Iowa in order. Fogelson, op. cit., pp. 80-81; and Eshref Shevsky and Marilyn Williams, The Social Areas of Los Angeles: Analysis and Typology. (Berkeley: Univeristy of California Press, 1949), pp. 22-23; Anon., "Where the 850,000 Residents of Los Angeles Came From," Southern California Business, Vol. II, No.4 (May 1923), p. 16; Classified Headings: Los Angeles Chamber of Commerce, Some Facts & Figures...1925 (cited), pp. 359-371.

(30) Ralph Hancock, The Forest Lawn Story. (Los Angeles: Academy Publishers, 1955), passim; Jessica Mitford, The American Way of Death. (N.Y.: Simon and Schuster, Inc., 1963, quoted in Gilmore & Gilmore, op. cit., pp. 371-374; and "Forest Lawn: Where One Never, Never Says 'Cemetery,'" Los Angeles Times. Mar. 6, 1983, VI-1,6; Barbara Rubin, Robert Carlton, and Arnold Rubin, L.A. in Installments: Forest Lawn. (Santa Monica: Westside Publications, 1979).

(31) Aimee Semple McPherson, The Story of My Life. (Hollywood: International Correspondents, 1951); Lately Thomas, Storming Heaven; The Lives and Turmoils of Minnie Kennedy and Aimee Semple McPherson. (N.Y.: Ballantine Books, 1970). Bruce Henstell, Sunshine and Wealth; Los Angeles in the Twenties and Thirties. (San Francisco: Chronicle Books, 1984), pp. 94-97; and David L. Clark, "Miracles for a Dime; From Chautauqua Tent to Radio Station with Sister Aimee," California History, Vol. LVII, No. 4 (Winter 1978/79), pp. 354-363. Glenn Chesney Quiett, They Built the West; An Epic of Rails and Cities. (N.Y.: D. Appleton-Century Company, 1934), pp. 311-312. Beck and Williams, op. cit., pp. 386-388; Cary McWilliams, "Aimee Semple McPherson: Sunshine in my Soul," 1949, excerpted in Gilmore & Gilmore, op. cit., pp. 287-292; and McWilliams, Southern California... (cited), pp. 259-262. I must thank the many older students in my Humanities course, The Cultural Heritage of Los Angeles, at Los Angeles Valley College, over the years, who have shared their memories of visits to Angelus Temple in Sister Aimee's heyday. Harry Carr, Los Angeles, City of Dreams. (N.Y.: D. Appleton-Century, 1935), p. 336, encapsulated the colorful preacher in these words: "Aimee is the high-pressure salesman of salvation."

(32) Illustration 79: The owner-builder was Earl Le Moine. At the time the building permit was taken out he resided at 825 S. Vermont — not far from the building site — he was listing himself as a building contractor, and he had moved a few blocks to a more prestigious address on South Plymouth Boulevard. Did he build the castle as a speculative venture? or did he built it for himself only to have someone persuade him to sell for enough profit to enable him to move up to Plymouth Boulevard and launch him on a new career as a building contractor? or did he built it, move in, and then find it so unliveable he moved out within the year?

(33) A 1923 article defending the wildly imaginative buildings going up in L.A. explained: "The "architecture" of the sets has become a very important factor and each studio now maintains a staff of highly trained architects. Here, for once, the designer, relieved of all scruples against overstepping the [traditional architectural canons], has an unprecedented opportunity to exercise his ingenuity ad infinitum. The result, however, good or bad, is a mere fabrication of an idea — maximum display at a minimum cost and built relatively but for a day. The people behold an endless and ever-changing panorama of the fantasies of a designer's brain. A miniature Bagdad arises in their midst, only to be replaced by a representation of Monte Carlo, and this, in turn, may be followed by a feudal castle with all adjuncts. As a matter of psychology, some of the people are bound to react accordingly; and one may feel assured that, as prospective clients, they will indeed tax the imagination of their architects." —Prentice Duell, "The New Era of California Architecture: Los Angeles," The Western Architect, Vol. XXXII, No. 8 (Aug. 1923), p. 88. David Gebhard is of the opposite opinion: that sets did not inspire L.A. architecture but that sets were inspired by the real-life buildings to be seen around L.A. This is a difficult premise to maintain since movies with cute period sets predated the period revivals of the 1920s. —Gebhard & Von Breton, L.A. in the Thirties (cited), pp. 109-110.

(34) One Tudor style mansion was publicized by successive sets of movie-famous occupants. 649 West Adams was Theda Bara's home at her popularity peak (1915-18), then sold to Fatty Arbuckle, who lived in it until scandal wrecked his career. Director Raoul Walsh and his actress wife, Miriam Cooper, lived in it next, followed by producer Joe Schenck and his famous wife, Norma Talmadge. — Charles Lockwood, Dream Palaces; Hollywood at Home. (N.Y.: Viking Press, 1981), p. 49, 67.

(35) Pickfair began as a rustic hunting lodge, purchased by Douglas Fairbanks a month before his 1919 marriage to Mary Pickford. He had it remodeled and enlarged into a 5-bedroom home. Its exterior was embellished by Tudor half-timbering, but the whole was painted a dignified monochrome — atypical of the times. As the couple's entertainment grew lavish, the house became inadequate. In 1932 architect Wallace Neff was enlisted to expand the house and change its style to the bland Regency style popular in the '30s. —Ibid., pp. 93, 100-101; Charles Lockwood and Jeff Hyland, The Estates of Beverly Hills. (Beverly Hills: Margrant Publishing Company, 1984), p. 44; Alson Clark, Wallace Neff; Architect of California's Golden Age. (Santa Barbara: Capra Press, 1986), pp. 97-99.

(36) Illustration 83: The permit was taken out on March 10 and the final inspection took place July 20, 1926. The brick facing and a second chimney were added by the same builder in 1935. The same owner-contractor was simultaneously building the house in Illustration 94 next door.

(37) Villa de Leon was designed by architect Kenneth MacDonald, Jr. in 1927. Local historians Helen Lutjiens and Katherine LaHue, in A Sketch Book of Pacific Palisades, California. (Santa Monica: Phyllis Genovese, 1975), p. 28, state that it was built for a wool merchant named Leon Kauffman. But the cornerstone of the house gives the owner's name as Fran Kauffman. The ram's head motif appearing in the reliefs over the windows and again in the wrought iron gates may be the origin of the story that wool was the source of Kauffman's money.

(38) Quotation: Gwendolyn Wright, Building the Dream; A Social History of Housing in America. (N.Y.: Pantheon Books, 1981), p. 210.

(39) Who's Who in Los Angeles County, 1932-33. (Los Angeles: Charles J. Lang, Publisher, 1933), p. 67; Lenora King Berry, Southwest Blue Book; A Society Directory of Names, Addresses, Telephone Numbers, Names of Clubs and Their Offices, 1931-32. (Los Angeles: Lenora King Berry, November 1931), unnumbered pages.

(40) Jesse E. Smith, longtime Ford dealer in Glendale, maintained a home on North Central Avenue. Merrie Land was occupied by William and Flora Parris for a number of years beginning in 1924. —Glendale City Directory (1922-1931 issues), (Glendale: Glendale Directory Company, 1922-1931).

(41) Except for chimney placement, the house is almost identical to the MacPheadris-Warner house in Portsmouth, New Hampshire, circa 1716.

(42) Gebhard & Winter, A Guide...(cited), estimate 1925 for this four-unit apartment complex (originally 5 units). The original building permits have been lost — only permits for interior alterations and exterior sandblasting, dated 1973 and 1958, can be located. It may have been coincidental, but 1924 saw the release of a Douglas Fairbanks hit, The Thief of Baghdad, with elaborate Islamic sets. The tall, attention-drawing sets had been erected in Culver City and remained there for over a decade. —Lockwood, op. cit., p. 156; Brownlow, op. cit., pp. 165, 167.

(43) Architect Robert Stacy-Judd made a specialty of revival styles patterned on the pre-Columbian Southwestern and Mezo-American cultures. For years he crusaded for an "All-American Architectural Style" as an inspiration to patriotism and cultural eminence. — Robert B. Stacy-Judd, "Some Local Examples of Mayan Adaptations," The Architect and Engineer, Vol. 116, No. 2 (Feb. 1934), pp. 21, 30. The Home Builder; California Homes & Gardens. [Los Angeles; Vol. IV, No. 7 (July 1926), includes American Indian forms as one style choice.—Anonymous, "New Hopi Architecture on the Old Mesa Land: From Notes by Ethel Rose," The Craftsman, Vol. XXX, No. 4 (July 1916), pp. 374-382.

(44) The owner was Fran Kauffman, but what her stage name was, if, indeed, she got so far as to have one, in not known.

(45) Quotation: Edmund Wilson, The American Jitters; A Year of the Slump. (Freeport, N.Y.: Books for Libraries Press, Inc. reprint, 1932, 1968), pp. 226, 228.

CHAPTER X Los Angeles Finds Its Own Style

(1) Thomas P. Gates, "Palos Verdes Estates: The City Beautiful," SAH/SCC Review (Issue 2, 1984), p. 6; Augusta Fink, Time and the Terraced Land, (Berkeley: Howell-North Books, 1966), pp. 111-112.

(2) The house was built in 1906 for banker H.M. Gorham. Gorham was the nephew and cousin of Sen. John Jones and Roy Jones, developers of Santa Monica. In the next decade, Gorham commissioned the house seen in Illustration 97 for his mother-in-law, Mrs. E. N. Halliday. The Gorham house cost $16,000 to build. It was made of poured, reinforced concrete, a material that Irving Gill also experimented with. — "Adelaide Drive House Tour" (5 Nov. 1989) (walking guide), (Los Angeles Conservancy and the Adelaide Drive Residents Association).

(3) Of the many historic accounts of early California written in the 1920s-1940s some were intensely polemicized at the expense of historical accuracy. For example, George Wharton James, The Old Franciscan Missions of California. Second Edition. (Boston: Little, Brown, and Company, 1925), Charles Francis Saunders, A Little Book of California Missions. (N.Y.: Robert M. McBride & Company, 1925), Hill, op. cit. pp. 11-12.

(4) See the inside cover ads in the May and July 1923 issues, and the January 1924 issue of Southern California Business for Hellman Bank, and for a W.P. Jeffries Company, Engragers and Printers. The Los Angeles Central Library was completed in 1926. It contains two sets of murals on California History, by Dean Cornwall and Albert Herter. Business buildings also commissioned murals for their lobbies in the 1920s on romanticized local history themes such as in the Title Guarantee Building at 5th and Hill — a 1929 mural by Hugo Ballin on the Treaty of Cahuenga signed in 1847.

(5) Quotations: Mrs. Christine Sterling, Olvera Street: Its History and Restoration. (Los Angeles: The Old Mission Printing Shop, Church of Our Lady Queen of the Angels, 1933), 6-7, 9.

(6) Quotation: James H. Collins, "A One-Woman Revolution," Southern California Business 9 (June 1930), 15.

(7) Ed Ainsworth, Enchanted Pueblo; Story of the Rise of the Modern Metropolis around the Plaza de Los Angeles. (Los Angeles: Bank of America, undated but after 1958), 48; Carey McWilliams found this dichotomy of terms continuing from 1848 to the onset of Mexican-American activism in the 1940s, but in my memory, the divergent labels persisted in the Los Angeles community until the more assertive 1960s Chicano activism. — Carey McWilliams, "A Play on History," Westways (May 1979), 18-19.

(8) After the 1971 earthquake, the San Fernando Mission had to be reconstructed. The results received much public criticism because the walls were smooth, the recopied Indian-painted wall decorations were bright-hued, and the church smelled like new paint and plaster. With some exasperation, the docents would point out that that was how it was when it was first built in 1797; the musty odors, faded decoration, and falling plaster were not experienced by those who lived there.

(9) Quotation: "Casa de Adobe Handbook,", (Los Angeles: Southwest Museum, 1973), 8. It is only fair to point out that the Museum has since exerted efforts to improve the authenticity of the Casa.

(10) Mission Style, Commercial Application: Weitze, op. cit., 84-111.

(11) Carleton Monroe Winslow, Clarence S. Stein, & Bertram Grosvenor Goodhue, The Architecture and the Gardens of the San Diego Exposition. (San Francisco: Paul Elder and Company, Publishers, 1916), 15.

(12) Goodhue had collaborated in the writing of a book on the subject (The Spanish Colonial Architecture of Mexico, by Sylvester Baxter, published in 1902), and having won a reputation as an expert, designed the Pro-Cathedral in Havana, and the Washington Hotel at Colon. — C. Matlack Price, "The Panama-California Exposition, San Diego, California. Bertram G. Goodhue and the Renaissance of Spanish-Colonial Architecture," The Architectural Record 37 3 (Mar. 1915), 140. The building-by-building description of the San Diego Exposition in Winslow, Stein, & Goodhue, op. cit., 28-148, listed the source for each. This was a means of authenticating their work to the public, and overcoming any criticism.

(13) The Million Dollar Theater, 307 S. Broadway, L.A. (Albert C. Martin, architect); 1918 also the chain of Ralphs and Roberts markets, and St. Vincent's church (Albert C. Martin), 1923-25.

(14) Illustration 97: Although the Davis brothers may have designed the Halliday residence in 1919, the building permit is dated March 14, 1923. The house has approximately 6,000 square feet, including a butler's pantry, guest accommodations, a maid's room, and chauffeur's quarters. Subsequent owners have relayed the information that Mrs. Halliday entertained a great deal.

(15) Rexford Newcomb: The Spanish House for America; Its Design, Furnishing, and Garden. (Philadelphia: J.B. Lippincott Company, 1927), 51.

(16) Gill, "The Home of the Future..." (cited), 142, 148-151; David Gebhard, "Irving Gill," in: Anderson, Moore, & Winter, op. cit., 112-119.

(17) Walter S. Davis, Henry Davis, H. Scott Gerity, and Loyall F. Watson, California Garden City Homes: A Book of Stock Plans. (Los Angeles: Garden City Company of California, 1915), quoted without page number in Stefanos Polyzoides, Roger Sherwood, James Tice, and Julius Shulman, Courtyard Housing in Los Angeles; A Typological Analysis. (Berkeley: University of California Press, 1982), 102. The authors of the latter book cite a large number of the 1915 to 1931 direct-observation and plan-book publications on the architecture of Spain, Mexico and the Mediterranean.

(18) Prentice Duell, "The New Era of California Architecture," The Western Architect 32 (Aug. 1923), Plates 1-16, feature works by Marston and Van Pelt; Johnson, Kaufmann and Coate; Carleton M. Winslow; Pierpont and Walter S. Davis; and the firms of Walker and Eisen; and Elmer Grey. Garrett Van Pelt, Old Architecture of Southern Mexico. (Cleveland: J. H. Jansen, 1926). Reginald D. Johnson, "Development of Architectural Styles in California," The Architect and Engineer 87 (Oct. 1926), 108-109; "Trend of Architecture in California Residences," Pacific Coast Architect 31 (Feb. 1927), 75-79. Alson Clark, "The 'Californian' Architecture of Gordon B. Kaufmann," Society of Architectural Historians, Southern California Chapter Review 1 (Summer 1982), 3.

(19) The house in Illustration 99, according to its building permit, was estimated at $15,000. Its original owner was Birger Tinglof. The Byers house, seen in Illustrations 100 and 104 was built in 1922 and featured in a Los Angeles Times article, "Couple See Their Home as Labor of Love" (Nov. 17, 1985) and in the article by Reginald Johnson previously cited (Pacific Coast Architect, Feb. 1927), 79. I have been in the El Greco house in Toledo, and I don't find a close resemblance between it and the portions of the Byers house illustrated. Gebhard & Winter, op. cit., 52.

(20) Illustration 101: The current owner believes this house was constructed in 1923. Glendale building permits date back to 1922 and there is nothing in file before a 1929 addition. If the owner's account of reutilized bunkhouse foundations is correct, the July 17, 1929 permit for a rear residence ("rear", relative to the Sanchez Adobe) may be the original building permit. It showed Mary D. and Anna S. Jones as owners. The Glendale City Directories do not reflect residency for this address until 1931, when it lists Mary Davis Jones and Anna Susan Jones. Paul Robinson Hunter and Walter L. Reichardt, (editors), Residential Architecture in Southern California. ([Los Angeles]: Southern California Chapter, The American Institute of Architects, 1939), 27-39; and Kirker, op. cit., 12-22.

(21) Wallace Neff: "Wallace Neff", Pasadena Heritage 6 (Spring 1982), 7; "Wallace Neff, Architect for Famous Homes, Dies," Los Angeles Times (10 June 1982); and notes, Wallace Neff Homes Tour, Pasadena Heritage (Nelson Carnes, docent), 16 May 1981. (p. 374). Paul Robinson Hunter and Walter L. Reichardt (editors), Residential Architecture in Southern California. ([Los Angeles]: Southern California Chapter, The American Institute of Architects, 1939), 7; and David Gebhard and Harriette Von Breton, Architecture in California, 1868-1968. Exhibition Catalogue. (Santa Barbara: The Art Galleries, U.C.S.B., 1968), 19.

(22) Hill, op. cit., (1931 edition), 165; Taylor, op. cit., 36; and John Robert Dunkle, The Tourist Industry of Southern California; A Study in Economic and Cultural Geography. (UCLA Thesis for M.A. in Geography, June 1950), 82-84, 87-88, 91-93, 103, 116-118.

(23) Quotation: "Pilgrimage Play Attracts Tourists to Los Angeles," Southern California Business 1 (July 1922), 42.

(24) Palmer, op. cit. 211-213, 218, 220, 237-239. The Pilgrimage Play was produced by Mrs. Christine Wetherill Stevenson at what is now called the John Anson Ford Theater from 1920 to 1923. After her death, the property and play rights were willed to the Los Angeles Times publisher, Harry Chandler, and his associates. Chandler had succeeded his father-in-law, Harrison Gray Otis, as head of the powerful newspaper on the latter's death in 1917.

(25) Quotation: Howard S. Nichols. "Los Angeles County, California" (pamphlet) (Los Angeles Chamber of Commerce, 1925), 7.

(26) California. (Omaha, Neb.: General Passenger Agent, Union Pacific System, 1927), 6, 8, 18; Kevin Starr, "The Sporting Life," California History, (Special Edition) 63 (Winter 1984), 26-31; Bruce Henstell, Sunshine and Wealth; Los Angeles in the Twenties and Thirties. (San Francisco: Chronicle Books, 1984), 117-129; Kennedy Ellsworth, "Give the Summer Tourist a Chance to Play," Southern California Business 8 (July 1929), 18-19, 38, 47.

(27) William May Garland, "Just What We May Expect in 1932," Southern California Business 9 (Nov. 1930), 10-11; and "Mixing Games and Business Profitably," Southern California Business 3 (Dec. 1924), 15, 35; 1932 Olympics: Paul Zimmerman: "1932: Out of Adversity, a Proud Heritage," Los Angeles Times, Home Magazine, (25 July 1982), 10; Zimmerman, "L.A.'s Xth Olympiad", Westways (Aug. 1976), 54-57,78; "L.A.'s '32 Olympics — Bright Days Amid Dark Times," and "Olympic Village Concept Began in L.A.", Los Angeles Times (21 May 1978), II-1, and "Athletes' Village A Novelty when L.A. Hosted '32 Games", Los Angeles Times (9 Oct. 1977), II-1.

(28) Tom Zimmerman's "Paradise Promoted; Boosterism and the Los Angeles Chamber of Commerce," California History 64 (Winter 1985), 22-33.

(29) The planting preferences of Spanish Colonial landscapists and home-owners is described in Padilla, op. cit., 92 and Taylor, op. cit., 23.

(30) Rexford Newcomb, The Spanish House for America... (1927),(cited), pp. 13-32, 79-140; R.W. Sexton, Spanish Influence on American Architecture and Decoration. (N.Y.: Brentano's, Inc., 1927), pp. 10-14. Polyzoides, et al, op. cit., 20-29.

(31) Lockwood, op. cit., passim; Brendan Gill, The Dream Come True; Great Houses of Los Angeles. (N.Y.: Lippincott & Crowell, Publishers, 1980), passim; Luitjens & LaHue, op. cit., 25-27;, and the following articles from the Los Angeles Times: "Mansion Undergoes Restoration" (8 Apr. 1984), "The Villa: Home for Hollywood Greats" (29 Mar. 1981), "Many Estates Being Eaten Away" (4 Oct. 1981), "Laughlin Park: Here Film Pioneers Felt Right at Home" (4 May 1986).

(32) Quotation: Mary Pickford Fairbanks, "Spanish Architecture Ideal for the California Home," The Architect and Engineer 87 (Dec. 1926), 117-118.

(33) Whitley Park Ad: Los Angeles Times (24 June 1923), V-5.

(34) Castellamare, Miramare, and the Los Angeles Times Demonstration Home: Lutjiens & LaHue, op. cit., 22, 24, 36; "A House with L.A. in Mind," Los Angeles Times (5 May 1985), VIII-21. In 1943 this same house was purchased by the refugee-author Lion Feuchtwanger, and it became the center of the international circle of literary and intellectual figures who resided in the L.A. area.

(35) Illustration 78: This is one of the houses described in the Wilshire Highland Square ad, a tract in the Hancock Park area. It was

built for a Mrs. Alice M. Dearden by Hart Brothers Construction Company in 1929. The building permit, in the space for architect, shows "Builders Plan Service". The projected cost of the house and a detached, 3-car garage was $12,000.

(36) Illustrations 106 and 107: Gillette Regent Square, in Santa Monica, took out the building permit for the house in Illustration 107 on September 13, 1924. The projected cost was $4,500. The purchaser was listed as Frank E. Bivens. Almost seven years later, on April 1, 1931, a private contractor, John W. Spellman, took out the building permit for the house across the street, Illustration 106. The permit showed the tract as Gillette Regent Square, indicating that the developer had sold an empty lot, but was, perhaps, no longer in the building business. The purchasers were Mr. & Mrs. Henry Dixon. The projected cost of this smaller house was $6,000.

(37) Illustration 108: Paul Edgar Murphy, "Native Architecture in Southern California," American Mercury, (April 1928), quoted in David Gebhard, "Tile, Stucco Walls and Arches: The Spanish Tradition in the Popular American House," in Charles W. Moore, Kathryn Smith, & Peter Becker (editors), Home Sweet Home; American Domestic Vernacular Architecture (Los Angeles: Craft and Folk Art Museum, 1983), 104. The brighter colors and the use of the word "jazzed" or "elephant's foot" stucco patterning was hotly debated by contemporary purists. Sexton, op. cit., 32, 127, 153, Newcomb, op. cit., 33, 45-46.

(38) Illustration 109: This Pasadena court was built in 1927. The designer was Clarence Hudson Burrell, and the contractor was Burrell & Co. Builders, Inc. The view shows the manager-owner's end unit and, on the left, one of the units on the left-hand row, as well as a portion of the central garden.

(39) Illustration 110: In the depths of the Depression, the hard-pressed building industry attempted to persuade wealthy individuals to invest in building apartments. In a full page ad in the Los Angeles Times (1 Feb. 1933), I-5, written in news format, the headline caught the eye of property owners, such as the owner of the Hollywood lot who was persuaded to build the castle-style apartments seen in Illustration 81:"PROPERTY OWNERS ENTER 1933 WITH RENEWED HOPE Vacant Lots Turned into Dollars Through New Plan." The copy explained how Security Finance Co. could turn your vacant lot into an income source by building an apartment house on it. It pointed to more than twenty completed in 1932. A second article followed, pointing out the lack of income from vacant property, and arguing: "[T]here has been no normal building for four years, which means there is an actual shortage of new modern places to rent. Of course, there are many places now unrented, but most of these were built...wholly unmindful of the fact that ...people demand plenty of light and air." The writer claimed to know of cases where there were as many as 30 applicants for one unit, and it pictured three Spanish-colonial style apartment houses. However, the building permit for this Glendale apartment house (Illustration 110) records the risk of the Depression era. The permit was taken out on December 6, 1935. The proposed valuation was $12,500. The owner was listed as Emanuel Woolman. But by the final inspection date, March 30, 1936, ownership had changed hands. The new owner was L.R. Webb who owned a fashionable department store in Glendale.

CHAPTER XI Daring Originals

(1) Walter Gropius indirectly defined modern architecture "not so much a ready-made dogma ...but an attitude towards the problems of our generation which is unbiased, original and elastic." —Walter Gropius, Architectural Record, May 1937, quoted in Leonardo Benevolo, History of Modern Architecture. Vol. Two: The Modern Movement. (Cambridge, Mass.: The M.I.T. Press, 1960, 1971), 652. For the identifying features of modernism see Ibid., 428-433; Walter Gropius, The New Architecture and the Bauhaus. (London: Faber and Faber Limited, 1935), 8-9,19-20, 27-29,31-33, 44; Jurgen Joedicke, A History of Modern Architecture. (N.Y.: Frederick A. Praeger, 1959), 49-50, 74; Nikolaus Pevsner, The Sources of Modern Architecture and Design. (N.Y.: Oxford University Press, 1968), 1, 113, 123-125: and Vincent Scully, Jr, Modern Architecture:The Architecture of Democracy. (N.Y.: George Braziller, 1965), 15, 26-27, 40-42.

(2) Aline Barnsdall's 1916 group, called Players Producing Company, included Norman Bel Geddes as scenic designer, Richard Ordynski as artistic director, and Kira Markham as an actress. — Kathryn Smith, "Frank Lloyd Wright, Hollyhock House, and Olive Hill, 1914-1924," Journal of The Society of Architectural Historians 38 (Mar. 1979), 15-22, 29, 31.

(3) Cited in Albert Bush-Brown, "Louis H. Sullivan, Architect." in Global Architecture: Louis H. Sullivan... (Tokyo: A.D.A. Edita, 1979), unnumbered pages; Burchard and Bush-Brown, op. cit., 204, 245-259; Pevsner, op. cit., 38.

(4) Esther McCoy, Five California Architects, (cited), 59-99; David Gebhard, "Irving Gill", in Anderson, Moore, & Winter, op. cit., 112-118; Bruce Kamerling, Irving Gill; The Artist as Architect. (San Diego: The San Diego Historical Society, 1979); Mary Mix Foley, The American House, (N.Y.: Harper & Row, Publishers, 1980), 245-246; and David P. Handlin, op. cit., 295-299.

(5) Irving J. Gill, "The Home of the Future: The New Architecture of the West: Small Homes for a Great Country: by Irving J. Gill: Number Four." The Craftsman 30 (May 1916), 141-142.

(6) Ibid., 147-8.

(7) Frank Lloyd Wright, "In the Cause of Architecture," The Architectural Record 23 (Mar. 1908), quoted in Frederick Gutheim (Editor). In the Cause of Architecture: Frank Lloyd Wright; Essays by Frank Lloyd Wright for Architectural Record, 1908-1952, with a Symposium on Architecture with and without Wright by Eight Who Knew Him... (N.Y.: Architectural Record, a McGraw-Hill Publication), 1975), 53-61; Lancaster, op. cit., 84-89; and Roth, op. cit., 208; Frank Lloyd Wright, "Organic Architecture," The Architects' Journal, (Aug. 1936), quoted in Frank Lloyd Wright. Frank Lloyd Wright, Selected Writings, 1894-1940. (Frederick Gutheim, editor). (N.Y.: Duell, Sloan and Pearce, 1941), 179.
FLW's psychological depths are thoughtfully plumbed by Robert C. Twombly, Frank Lloyd Wright: His Life and His Architecture. (N.Y.: John Wiley & Sons, 1979), 121-173; and in Norris Kelly Smith, Frank Lloyd Wright: A Study in Architectural Content. (Englewood Cliffs, N.J.: Prentice-Hall, Inc., 1966), 96-111.

(8) Kathryn Smith, op. cit., 19-21, 29; and Twombly, op. cit., 196-198; Norris Kelly Smith, op. cit., 110-111.

(9) "America must possess her own art. By virtue of his most ancient profession, the prerogative of the architect is leadership. Therefore it is to be hoped that in the Maya art he will visualise the opportunity to create and establish an ALL-AMERICAN ARCHITECTURAL STYLE." Robert Stacy-Judd, "Some Local Examples of Mayan Adaptations," The Architect and Engineer 116 (Feb. 1934), 21-30.

(10) David Gebhard and Harriette Von Breton, Lloyd Wright, Architect; 20th Century Architecture in an Organic Exhibition. Exhibition Catalogue, University of California, Santa Barbara Art Galleries, November 23 to December 22, 1971. (Santa Barbara: The Regents, University of California, 1971), 31-32.

(11) The mansarded roof line harks to Palenque, the plain lower facade contrasted to the ornate frieze of stylized hollyhocks is directly related to Puuc architecture as found at Uxmal, etc.; the canted walls of the interior hallways relate to the corbelled arches and tunnels typical to Classic Mayan structures everywhere; the repeated geometric pattern of the bas-relief frieze is akin to the Puuc and Chichen Itza relief mosaics composed of pre-formed pieces; the hollyhock finials especially intrusive to the view from the rooftop terraces are reminiscent of the false temple decorations in the Rio Bec style; and the colonnaded courtyard is directly related to the temples and courtyards at Chichen Itza. Richard E.W. Adams, Prehistoric Mesoamerica. (Boston: Little, Brown and Company, 1977), Michael D. Coe, The Maya. (Third Edition) (N.Y.: Thames and Hudson, Inc., 1980), Joyce Kelly, The Complete Visitor's Guide to Mesoamerican Ruins. (Norman, OK.: University of Oklahoma Press, 1982), and Tatiana Proskouriakoff, An Album of Maya Architecture. (Norman, OK.: University of Oklahoma Press, 1946, 1983).

(12) Hollyhock House Style Choice: Kathryn Smith, op. cit., 20.

(13) Many of the commercial buildings in this style are illustrated in Ave Pildas, Art Deco Los Angeles. (N.Y.: Harper & Row Publishers, 1977); descriptions of the style characteristics as applied to architecture are in John J.-G. Blumenson, Identifying American Architecture: A Pictorial Guide to Styles and Terms, 1600-1945. (Nashville, TN: American Association for State and Local History, 1977), 76-77; and Gebhard and Winter, A Guide... (cited), 25-26, 701-703; the best discussion is in Paul Gleye, The Architecture of Los Angeles, (L.A.: Rosebud Books, 1981), 120-129; Bevis Hillier, The World of Art Deco, (Exhibition Catalog, The Minneapolis Institute of Arts, July-Sept. 1971) (N.Y.: E.P. Dutton, 1971), 26-32.

(14) Lloyd Wright (1890-1978) was the oldest of Frank Lloyd Wright's six children. He was 19 when his father wrecked the family. In 1910 he followed his father to Europe, where he assisted him in the drawings for the European portfolio publications. When his father no longer needed or wished for his services or presence he returned to the United States. He went to San Diego where Gill was planning for the 1915 Panama California International Exhibition. He worked briefly in Gill's office as a draftsman, followed by a period as co-owner of a landscaping firm. —Gebhard and Von Breton, Lloyd Wright (cited), 5-23. Resettled in Los Angeles by 1916, he became part of Aline Barnsdall's social circle. FLW was in Japan working on the Imperial Hotel so Lloyd, conveniently in Hollywood, was given the job of construction supervisor for Hollyhock House. It was not long before trouble developed between the client and the absent architect. In 1920 FLW ordered Rudolph Schindler to replace Lloyd. Although he worked on other Southern California projects of FLW's from time to time, Lloyd never became the "right hand man" of his father. That he spent a lifetime explaining away the apparent rejections by his parent indicates that they mattered a great deal to him.

(15) Dennis Sharp, <u>Modern Architecture and Expressionism</u>. (N.Y.: George Braziller, 1966), defines Architectural Expressionism as a posthumous label referring to intense and seemingly irrational experiments, utopianistic, free, plastic, unconventional — visionary, fantastic, dreamlike.

(16) Andrew Rolle, <u>Los Angeles: From Pueblo to City of the Future</u>. (San Francisco: Boyd & Fraser Publishing Company, 1981), 63-64; Brownlow, op. cit., 240-262), <u>Los Angeles Times</u>: (26 Nov. 1981), V-1, (12 Apr. 1981), Cal.-3, (23 Mar. 1980) Cal.-33, (7 Sept. 1980), Cal.-3, (18 Nov. 1982) V-2, (14 July 1982) Cal.-2, (15 May 1983) Books-1, (6 Feb. 1983) Cal.-43, (3 Mar. 1981) Books, (4 Sept. 1983) VII-1; (30 Nov. 1981) VI-2, (21 Dec. 1982) I-1, (14 Feb. 1977) IV-4, and (27 Apr. 1983); <u>Newsweek</u> (1 Dec. 1980) 97. Books about the heavy migration from Europe beginning in the early 1930s are: Jarrell C. Jackman and Carla M. Borden (editors), <u>The Muses Flee Hitler: Cultural Transfer and Adaptation 1930-1945</u> (Smithsonian, 1983); Anthony Heilbut, <u>Exiled in Paradise: German Refugee Artists and Intellectuals in America, From the 1930s to the Present</u> (Viking, 1983); and John Russell Taylor, <u>Strangers in Paradise</u>, (Holt, Rinehart & Winston, 1983).

(17) Esther McCoy comments on Schindler. "...it was necessary in the twenties to teach the client something about the new architecture. Schindler compared his role in this regard to that of Mrs. Galka Scheyer who came to Los Angeles in 1921 to exhibit and stimulate interest in works by Klee, Kandinsky, Feininger and Jawlensky. Both he and Mrs. Scheyer, Schindler wrote, were `dispelling popular prejudice.'" (in the introduction by Esther McCoy to R.M.Schindler, <u>R.M.Schindler: An Exhibition of the Architecture of R.M. Schindler (1887-1953)</u>. (Catalog) (Berkeley: The Regents of the University of California, 1967), p. 9.

(18) Jurgen Joedicke, <u>A History of Modern Architecture</u>. (N.Y.: Frederick A. Praeger, 1959), 48-50; Esther McCoy, in the Introduction to R.M. Schindler, op. cit., 6-7; R.M. Schindler, "Space Architecture," <u>California Arts & Architecture</u> 47 (Jan. 1935), 17-20.

(19) David Gebhard's, <u>Schindler</u>. (Santa Barbara: Peregrine Smith, Inc., 1980); John Dreyfuss, "Paper Chase: Springing Architecture Loose," <u>Los Angeles Times</u> (28 Oct. 1981), VI-1.

(20) "Our present scheme of social life in which we drudge behind the scenes most of the time in order to present an `impressive' face for a few moments of company is outworn....Our house will lose its front-and-back-door aspect. It will cease being a group of dens, some larger ones for social effect, and a few smaller ones (bedrooms) in which to herd the family. Each individual will want a private room to gain a background for his life....A work-and-play room, together with the garden, will satisfy the group needs....A simplified cooking will become part of a group play, instead of being the deadly routine for a lonely slave." R.M. Schindler writing in Philip Lovell's column, "Care of the Body," <u>Los Angeles Times</u> (2 May 1926), Sunday Magazine, 27.

(21) The unusual social arrangement of the occupants was apparently satisfactory: the Chases and the Schindlers lived together until 1925, when the Chases moved out and the Neutras moved in. The Neutras stayed until 1929. The Schindlers separated in the late '20s, but the two continued to live in the different wings of the same house for over two and decades more.

(22) David Gebhard, "R.M. Schindler and The Modern Movement, 1910-1953", in <u>Schindler-Catalog</u>, (cited), 20.

(23) Dr. Phillip Lovell, "Care of the Body," <u>Los Angeles Times</u> (14 Mar. 1926), Sunday Magazine, 24. The intertwining of the name architects and the chain of commissions is well illustrated in the case of Lovell. Aline Barnsdall set up an experimental school on Olive Hill, attended by her daughter and other children. The school was run by her friend Mrs. Leah Lovell. Mrs. Lovell's sister and brother-in-law, were the Samuel Freemans, for whom Frank Lloyd Wright built one of his knit-block houses. Miss Barnsdall herself had Schindler design a Palos Verdes home for her (never built), and the Lovells had him build their beach house in Newport Beach. For their town house, the Lovells turned to Schindler's partner, Richard Neutra. — Kathryn Smith, op. cit., 29.

(24) R.M. Schindler in Lovell, op. cit., (all are in Sunday Magazine section): (14 Mar. 1926), 24-25; (21 Mar. 1926), 25; (4 Apr. 1926), 25; (11 Apr. 1926), 30; (18 Apr. 1926), 27; and (2 May 1926), 27.

(25) McCoy, <u>Five California Architects</u>, (cited), 153; and R.M. Schindler, "A Residence in Los Angeles, California," <u>The Architectural Record</u> 65 (Jan. 1929), 8.

(26) McCoy, <u>Five California...</u> (cited), 157-163; and Friends of the Schindler House, "R.M.Schindler House, A National Historic Landmark," bulletin, undated.

(27) Thomas S. Hines, Richard Neutra and the Search for Modern Architecture; A Biography and History. (N.Y.: Oxford University Press, 1982), 22-55. The correspondence between Schindler and Neutra is published in its entirety in Esther McCoy, Two Journeys: Vienna to Los Angeles. (Santa Monica, California: Arts and Architecture Press, 1979).

(28) Hines has pointed out how many of the acknowledged masterpieces of Modern Architecture were built in the period between 1926-1930 in Europe. In the U.S., Hines avers, there were only three significant works: the Philadelphia Savings Fund Society Building (1929-32; Howe & Lescaze); the Lovell Beach House (Newport Beach, R.M. Schindler, 1926); and the Lovell Health House (Los Angeles, Richard Neutra, 1928-29). — Hines, op. cit., 69.

(29) Quotation: Richard Neutra, Mystery and Realities of the Site. (Scarsdale, N.Y.: Morgan & Morgan, Publishers, 1951), 41.

(30) Quotation: Hines, op. cit., 78.

(31) Le Corbusier quoted in Benevolo, op. cit., 444-445; Gropius, in his 1935 book, The New Architecture and the Bauhaus (translated by P. Morton Shand) (London: Faber and Faber Limited), 27-29, 31-44.

(32) Hines, op. cit., 89.

(33) Richard Neutra, Amerika: Die Stilbildung Des Neuen Bauens in Den Vereinigten Staaten ["America: The Stylistic Development of New Building in the United States."] (Vienna: Schroll, 1930), discussed in Ibid., 91; Gregory Ain, "The V.D.L. Research House", California Arts & Architecture 47 (Jan. 1935), 27.

(34) The exhibit went on to tour a number of American cities. The Los Angeles County Museum refused to show it, so it was staged at the new Bullocks Wilshire department store, a paragon of Art Deco stylishness. — Hines, op. cit., 104.

(35) Quotation: Editorial, California Arts & Architecture 47 (Jan. 1935), 11.

(36) The Edwards house was Ain's first completed project. Information on the cost, architect's fee, and owner's occupation were provided by the current owner, Dr. Theodore Lindauer. He has restored the house, from a truly wretched state at the time of his purchase, to pristine condition applauded by the aging architect who was invited to inspect the results. Esther McCoy, The Second Generation. (Salt Lake City: Gibbs M. Smith, Inc., 1984), 83; David Gebhard, Harriette Von Breton, and Lauren Weiss: The Architecture of Gregory Ain; The Play Between the Rational and High Art. , Exhibition Catalog, University of California Santa Barbara, 1980. (Berkeley: The Regents of the University of California, 1980); and — Esther McCoy, "Gregory Ain's Social Housing"...(cited).

(37) Donald J. Bush, The Streamlined Decade. (N.Y.: George Braziller, 1975), 1-2, 6-9, 99-101.

(38) When something of a recession occurred in 1927 marketing firms sought to stimulate purchasing by repackaging their products to appear "new" and "improved". Designers already experienced at simultaneously exciting consumers, selling products, and minding budgets became the first practitioners of the new field of industrial design. One of the pioneers was Norman Bel Geddes, who had come to Hollywood as a set designer in Aline Barnsdall's theatrical company. In the motion picture industry, he had found himself in a highly technical and experimental business in which there was a constant demand for inventions to solve problems as they arose. In the film industry, Bel Geddes established a high-tech reputation for his lighting and sound innovations. In 1927 he set up his own industrial design business with pioneering designs in transportation and kitchen appliances. — Bush, op. cit., 18.
Richard Neutra had been hired by a bus company to restyle the shells to a more streamlined look in 1931. — Hines, op. cit., 99-101. Henry Dreyfuss, another theatrical designer turned industrial designer, used the word "cleanlining." — Ibid., 19. Industrial designer Raymond Loewy's restyled radio cabinet increased its sales by a factor of seven. —Raymond Loewy, Industrial Design. (Woodstock, N.Y.: The Overlook Press, 1979), 98. See also Bush, op. cit., 16-21. Jeffrey L. Meikle, Twentieth Century Limited; Industrial Design in America, 1925-1939. (Philadelphia: Temple University Press, 1979), 4, 39, 153-154; and Elisabeth Kendall Thompson, Houses of the West. (N.Y.: McGraw-Hill Book Company, 1979), viii-ix.

(39) Diana Williams Hlava, "Streamline Moderne: Cruise into L.A.'s Past," Los Angeles Times (17 Apr. 1983), VIII- ; and Robert Winter, "The Architecture of the City Eclectic," California History 60 (Spring 1981), 73.

(40) Illustration 125: The building permit for the Ulm house was issued on January 19, 1937 for a two story house valued at $7,500. It

has been attributed to William Kesling, a designer/contractor who had worked for Schindler previously, but who had been indicted in December 1936 for misappropriating materials. He is known to have continued working, illegally, after his license was revoked. Whoever designed the house was a highly original thinker: each of the rooms is an unconventional shape. In fact, only one room has four rightangle corners.

Illustration 126: This small Santa Monica house was built for a T.G. Hamilton by contractor William A. Stanley. The building permit, dated September 23, 1941, estimates the value of the proposed work at $4,450.

(41) The intent of the International Style was always zealously serious. By its frequent allusion to ocean liners or airplanes, the Streamline Moderne is on the verge of joining the programmatic architecture of giant ice cream cones, bowler hats, and the Coca-Cola Bottling Co., a prime local example of commercial Streamline Moderne in which a factory was made to look like an ocean liner. Located at 1334 S. Central, a cluster of ordinary buildings was remodelled in 1936 by Robert Derrah, an architect with a background in the motion picture industry, into its present nautical form. Tours are occasionally arranged and the interior is an even greater tour de force than the exterior.

(42) David Gebhard, 4/16/83 lecture at Woodbury University, sponsored by L.A. Conservancy; (cited); Bush, op. cit., 150-153; and Winter, "The Architecture of the City Eclectic" (cited), 73; Gebhard finds three reasons to explain why Streamline Moderne was more prolifically expressed in L.A. than elsewhere: (1) There were three local industries which continued relatively healthy: motion pictures, oil, and aircraft-defense industries. Building did not suffer as badly as it did in many cities. (2) The climate had permitted the use of quick and cheap wood-frame and stucco construction not so practical in other regions, making it inexpensive to create almost any image. Movie sets had shown the limitless possibilities of these materials. (3) Films had legitimized futuristic images. Mr. Gebhard points out that this legitimization was not just for L.A., but for the nation of movie-goers. — Gebhard, 4/16/83 lecture...(cited.)

It must be added, however, that, as with other images projected from Hollywood to the rest of the nation, it was associated with the Hollywood source by movie-viewers and added to their concept of what LA was. Movie industry insiders legitimized this style for the local image by building Streamline Moderne homes which were seen in fan magazines and on tours past the homes of the stars. A case in point is the house built in 1931 by Cedric Gibbons (who was then head set designer at MGM Studios) for himself and his wife, screen star Dolores del Rio. See also Los Angeles Times, Home Magazine, (11 Apr. 1982) 19.

(43) Quotation: Russell Hitchcock, "An Eastern Critic Looks at Western Architecture," California Arts and Architecture 57 (Dec. 1940), 41.

CHAPTER XII Ordinary Dreams

(1) Hitchcock, op.cit., 41. See quotation Ch. 11 note (43).

(2) Of the five industrial urban centers, Chicago, Detroit, New York, Philadelphia, and Los Angeles, LA had the highest percentage of one-family detached residences.In 1940, even after a depression decade of apartment building, 52.3% of the dwelling units in Los Angeles were one-family detached residences, while contemporaneously industrializing Detroit reckoned 41.1%, and Chicago, New York, and Philadelphia respectively figured 15.9%, 10.1%, and 8.4%. The precise breakdown for Los Angeles was: 52.3% one-family detached; 13.2% one-family attached and two-family; 9.2% three- and four-family; 1.5% attached to business; 6.3% five- to nine-family; 5.5% ten- to nineteen-family; and 11.5% twenty family and larger. Earl Hanson & Paul Beckett, Los Angeles: Its People and Its Homes, (Los Angeles: The Haynes Foundation, 1944) p. 16; Fogelson, op. cit., pp. 144-145. The average value of an owner-occupied dwelling unit in 1940 in New York was $6,110; it was $4,126 in Chicago, $3,865 in Philadelphia, $4,189 in Detroit, and $4,625 in Los Angeles. (Ibid., p. 13.) Of course, there was a wide variation in value from one section of the Los Angeles Basin to another. With the exception of Beverly Hills, Palos Verdes and San Marino (all over $10,000 average value), houses in other L.A. communities ranged from $2,787 to $5,842. Earl Hanson, Los Angeles County Population and Housing Data; Statistical Data from the 1940 Census. (Los Angeles: The Haynes Foundation, 1944), p. 17.

(3) Gleye, op. cit., pp. 97-98. Mr. Gleye conclusively discredits the common myth that L. A.'s height restrictions were designed as an earthquake safety measure. He emphasizes the "commitment to maintain an appropriate scale for the city" as the major consideration, along with structural safety. There may have been other motives, as well. The three outside experts appointed to work with city officials on the study committee were John S. Morrow, president of the Pacific Board of Fire Underwriters, John C. Austin, a young architect who would become prominent in the 1920s, '30s, and '40s, and architect John Parkinson. Morrow could be expected to approve measures which would reduce fire loss, which equates with claims payoffs. Austin made valuable contacts among City officials which may have influenced his selection as one of the architects of the 1926-28 City Hall a decade later. It was a good opportunity for a young

architect to win attention among the businessmen in the community who had an interest in following the committee's deliberations. John Parkinson was a vocal defendent of steel-frame construction who expressed such confidence in the new technique that he might have been expected to speak out in opposition to height limitations. During his service on the committee he was overseeing construction of the tallest building in the city (the 12-story Braly Building at the southeast corner of Fourth and Spring). In the 25 years following the imposition of height restrictions, John Parkinson designed 21 buildings on Spring Street, as well as many other important commercial landmarks. The limited office space in 150-foot high buildings required the construction of a great many more commercial edifaces in Los Angeles than would have been the case if there had been no height restrictions. Could there have been a conscious or subconscious motive of multiplying architectural commissions to follow the completion of the attention-getting Braly Block?

(4) Sam Bass Warner, Jr. The Urban Wilderness; A History of the American City. (N.Y.: Harper & Row, Publishers, 1972), p. 29; Mel Scott, Metropolitan Los Angeles: One Community. (Los Angeles: The Haynes Foundation, 1949), p. 86; and Warner, op. cit., p. 31.

(5) An excellent source for information on specific industries in Los Angeles in the '20s and '30s is the magazine, Southern California Business, published monthly by the L.A. Chamber of Commerce. There are wide discrepancies in the figures for L.A.'s manufactured product value, depending on the motives and statistical corrections of the contemporaries who reported them. Max Vorspan and Lloyd P. Gartner, History of the Jews of Los Angeles. (San Marino: The Huntington Library, 1970), p. 126, gives the value of the city's product as $278,000,000 for 1920, $757,000,000 for 1930; the county's product value as $418,000,000 for 1920 and $1,319,000,000 for 1930. Jacqueline Rorabeck Kasun. Some Social Aspects of Business Cycles in the Los Angeles Area, 1920-1950. (Los Angeles: The Haynes Foundation, 1954.), p. 9. Los Angeles County increased its quantity of manufactured output by 134% between 1919 and 1927, according to U.S. Census figures quoted by Shannon Crandall, "Industrial Los Angeles County," Southern California Business, (Vol. VIII, No. 5) June 1929, p. 11. The Chamber of Commerce habitually gave more dramatic, inconsistent figures. Its literature, when uncorrected by Census figures, claimed a manufactured product value of $15,134,000 in 1900, $109,458,000 in 1915, $788,652,885 in 1920, $1,151,643,537 by 1923, and estimated $1,300,000,000 for 1927.("March of Events in Figures," Southern California Business, (Vol. VIII, No. 1) Feb. 1929, p. 40. The figures are consistent with earlier years' quotations. But in its pamphlet of the same year, (Los Angeles Chamber of Commerce, "Los Angeles County, California" (Pamphlet), (Los Angeles: L. A. C. of C., 1929), p. 51), its figures are quoted from the Census: a 1927 manufacturing output worth $980,334,000 with a Census estimate of $1,096,000,000 for 1929, with 104,000 on the payroll in some 4,200 manufactories. Total employment increased from 266,000 workers in 1920 to 724,000 in 1930, according to Vorspan & Gartner: op. cit., p. 126. The portion of those employed persons in factory jobs were 92,000 in 1927, according to census figures and were estimated at 104,000 for 1929. (Los Angeles Chamber of Commerce, "Los Angeles County...1929" cited, p. 51.)

(6) Fourteenth Census, (cited), pp. 64, 151; Fifteenth Census, (cited), pp. 26, 52

(7) One study recorded the percentage of dwelling units existing in 1940 which had been built before 1900, between 1900 and 1919, between 1920 and 1930, and in the decade preceding the study. Hanson, op. cit., p. 16. Another study found that of the stock of dwelling units existing in 1940 in the five major industrial cities in the U.S., those in Los Angeles were the newest; some two-thirds had been constructed since 1920. Hanson & Beckett, op. cit., pp. 14-15. Gleye, op. cit., pp. 71-73, has turned attention to sub-standard housing during the 1910s. He cites a 1913 study which found 630 housing courts sheltering an estimated 10,000 people — which indicates, of course, that some of them had to be grossly overcrowded. Most of these were concentrated in Sonoratown.

(8) Marc A. Weiss, The Rise of the Community Builders; The American Real Estate Industry and Urban Land Planning. (N.Y.: Columbia University Press, 1987), presents a detailed study of the process of developer predetermination of class, and of the relationship of financial institutions to the process. See also: Gwendolyn Wright, op. cit., p. 201.

(9) Quotation: Quiett, op. cit., p. 313.

(10) In 1922 a three to five room "cottage" in the industrial section, with bath, could be expected to cost $40 to $75 per month, while a five or six room "comfortable bungalow" with bath and electric lights, in a good location within 30 minutes (by Model T) of the business center, might cost between $50 and $100 per month. Indicative of the rate of inflation, the 1916 version of the same pamphlet title had estimated $12 to $20 for the former and $18 to $22 for the latter. (Los Angeles Chamber of Commerce, "Los Angeles Today; October, 1922" (pamphlet) (Los Angeles: Neuner Corporation, 1922) p.29.); and same citation, 1916 edition, p. 30.

(11) Frank J. Taylor, California: Land of Homes, (Los Angeles: Powell Publishing Company, 1929) pp. 59-60.

(12) Quotations: Los Angeles Times, Part V, p. 4, June 24, 1923.

(13) Quotation: Taylor, op. cit., p.60.

(14) There were only 102 Blacks in Los Angeles according to the 1880 census. This had swelled to 1,258 by the 1890 census, to 2,131 in 1900, and 7,599 in 1910. By that latter year, Blacks represented 10.7% of the U.S. population, only 0.9% of California's population, but 2.4% of the Los Angeles City residents. Not only did Los Angeles serve as the focal center of Black migration in the state of California; there were four times as many Blacks here as in any other city in the American West. Octavia B. Vivian. Story of the Negro in Los Angeles County. (San Francisco: R and E Research Associates, 1970; reprint of report originally published by Federal Writers' Project of the Works Progress Administration, 1936), p. 5; and Lawrence Brooks de Graaf. Negro Migration to Los Angeles, 1930 to 1950. Ph.D. Dissertation, University of California, Los Angeles, 1962, (Reprint: San Francisco: R and E Research Associates, 1974), p. 9

(15) The one instance of labor recruitment of Blacks occurred in 1903. During the construction of a Southern Pacific inter-urban railway in Los Angeles, the laborers, who were mostly Mexican, struck for higher wages. The railroad broke the strike by hiring Japanese and Blacks, some 1,400 of the latter. (Lawrence B. De Graaf, "The City of Black Angels: Emergence of the Los Angeles Ghetto, 1890-1930," Pacific Historical Review, Vol. XXXIX, No. 3 (Aug. 1970), pp. 330-331.)

(16) De Graaf, Negro Migration..., (cited), p. 16.

(17) William M. Mason and James Anderson, "The Los Angeles Black Community, 1781-1940," Bulletin No. 5, Los Angeles County Museum of Natural History, History Division, 1969, p. 44; Vivian, op. cit., pp. 5-6; The town of Watts, southwest of Los Angeles proper, had been incorporated in 1907. At the time, it was a semi-rural community of small homes. Its householders commuted to jobs in L.A. by the Pacific Electric interurban. Interestingly, the key role in its transformation around 1910 was played by one of the young progressive idealists who had been instrumental in the political reform of Los Angeles, Marshall Stimson. In his autobiography, Stimson recalled: "Around 1910 I noticed that Negroes were coming into the city and found it hard to get settled. I bought a large tract of land south of Watts and [subdivided it]. I placed a Negro agent in charge and announced it was a tract restricted to Negroes. I interested several of the finest Negro preachers to call attention to their members of this opportunity to acquire a home...."
The area was soon nicknamed "Mudtown". (Marshall Stimson, Fun, Fights and Fiestas in Old Los Angeles, a privately published autobiography edited by Gordon Stimson in 1966; quoted in: MaryEllen Bell Ray, The City of Watts, California: 1907 to 1926. (Los Angeles: Rising Publishing, 1985), p. 15.)

(18) Quotation: De Graaf, "City of Black Angels...", (cited), p. 340.

(19) De Graaf, Negro Migration..., (cited), pp. 20; 79-80.

(20) De Graaf, "City of Black Angels...", (cited), p. 351; Paul Bullock, "Watts: Before the Riot," in Roger Daniels and Spencer C. Olin, Jr. Racism in California; A Reader in the History of Oppression. (N.Y.: The Macmillan Company, 1972), pp. 285-288; and "McCone Commission Report," quoted in Ibid., p. 291.

(21) G. Bromley Oxnam, The Mexican in Los Angeles; Los Angeles City Survey. (Interchurch World Movement of North America, 1920. Reprint by R and E Research Associates, San Francisco,). Carey McWilliams, North from Mexico; The Spanish-Speaking People of the United States. (N.Y.: Greenwood Press, Publishers, 1948, 1968), and Ray, op. cit., p. 15.

(22) McWilliams, North... (cited), pp. 174, 215. Census ambivalence as to the definition of race or national origin or linguistic identification makes it difficult to determine numbers of Mexicans and their descendents with any accuracy. There are no consistent statistics about border-crossings, either. McWilliams used the following figures for the statewide number of Mexican aliens present: 1900: 8,086, 1910: 33,694, 1920: 88,881, 1930: 368,013, Ibid., p. 163. 1940 Census: Hanson & Beckett, op. cit., p. 12.
A limited poll taken in 1923 of Mexican immigrant Angelenos attending night school found 50.77% expected to return to Mexico to live. [Evangeline Hymer, A Study of the Social Attitudes of Adult Mexican Immigrants in Los Angeles and Vicinity (1923). (Thesis, University of Southern California, 1923). (Reprinted, R and E Research Associates, San Francisco, 1971), p. 14.

(23) The 1913 and 1916 studies were cited by Oxnam (1920). He reported that in 1916 there were 1202 such courts in Los Angeles and Mexicans were the main residents. In 298 of these courts, Mexicans were the sole occupants. Oxnam, op. cit., p. 6-7; McWilliams, North... (cited), p. 223 and DeGraaf, "Black Angels," (cited), p. 339.

(24) Boyle Heights and the harbor area were original cluster points for settlers from Greece, Serbia, and Armenia in the pre-World War I decade. The 1912 outbreak of war in Serbia, the 1915 Turkish massacre of Armenians, the 1917 revolution in Russia, and the losses suffered by various minorities throughout Eastern Europe during the War, impelled thousands to seek new lives among their earlier established compatriots in Los Angeles. (Richard G. Lillard, Eden in Jeopardy; Man's Prodigal Meddling with his Environment: The Southern California Experience. (N.Y.: Alfred A. Knopf, 1966), p. 37; Dr. Charles A. Frazee, "The Orthodox and Eastern Churches," in Msgr. Francis J. Weber (editor). The Religious Heritage of Southern California. (L. A.: Interreligious Council of Southern California, 1976), pp. 4954; and de Graaf, "Black Angels..." (cited), pp. 350-351.)

Between 1900 and 1917 Jewish organizations assisted resettlement in U.S. cities. In Los Angeles, New York garment workers were promised jobs with Cohn-Goldwater & Company, contributing to the rapid growth of the local garment industry. Local Jewish organizations sponsored groups of Russian Jews fleeing the pogroms of the early 20th-century. Later between 1933 and 1942 some 1,500 to 2,000 families fleeing Nazi persecution in Western Europe made new homes in Los Angeles. (Vorspan and Gartner, op. cit., pp. 109-116, 144-145, 196-199, 205-206; Reva Clar, The Jews of Los Angeles; Urban Pioneers. (pamphlet) (L.A.: The Southern California Jewish Historical Society, 1977); and The Council on Jewish Life, op. cit., pp. 79.)

Assisted immigration had helped swell the Jewish minority in Los Angeles from an estimated 2,500 in 1900 to some 18,000 to 20,000 by 1920. Occupations among the city's Jewish inhabitants were 40% white collar, 22% managers and proprietors, and 5% professionals, with only 33% serving in the more traditional immigrant trades. By 1940, only 24% were in the last category and 11.2% were professionals. A major factor for the upward mobility is that in the 1920 Boom, the bulk of Jewish newcomers were acculturated American Jews of German ancestry, largely indistinguishable from other American middle-class arrivals. By 1930, an estimated 70,000 Jews were included in the Los Angeles population. They were not relegated to a ghetto neighborhood. (Vorspan and Gartner, op. cit.,; and The Council on Jewish Life, Jewish Los Angeles, A Guide. (The Jewish Federation-Council of Greater Los Angeles, 1976,) p.8.

(25) Quotation: John Steinbeck, The Grapes of Wrath, (N.Y.: Penguin Books, 1976 (1939), p. 98.

(26) In 1935 the Federal Resettlement Agency inaugurated a program to build minimal standard housing in government managed camps. By 1940 there were 15 permanent camps in existence or under construction, plus 3 mobile camps, two collective farm experiments, and 16 part-time cooperative farming experiments statewide. Camps improved the lot of some, but by no means all, the migrant workers in the state. Walter J. Stein, California and the Dust Bowl Migration. (Westport, Conn.: Greenwood Press, Inc., 1973), pp. 37, 40, 45-55, 147-152, 156-160, 167, 179-180; John Anson Ford, Thirty Explosive Years in Los Angeles County. (San Marino,CA: The Huntington Library, 1961), pp. 8, 12.

(27) James H. Collins, "They ALWAYS Do" (Editorial), Southern California Business 8 (Dec. 1929), 22. In the next issue, the Chamber President reassured his business readers that the preliminary results of a survey of industry, trade, and finances in the Southwest "are 90% encouraging". — "The President's Page" (Editorial), Southern California Business 9 (Feb. 1930), 7; Philip B. Kennedy, "'Build Now...Quickly!' Says the Banker," Southern California Business 9 (May 1930), 12-12, 38-39; Duncan Aikman, "California Sunshine," The Nation 132 (11 Apr. 1931), 450; and Robert Gottlieb and Irene Wolt, Thinking Big; The Story of the Los Angeles Times, Its Publishers and Their Influence on Southern California. (N.Y.: G.P. Putnam's Sons, 1977), 205.

(28) Quote: John C. Porter, Mayor of Los Angeles,Aikman, op. cit., 448. Aimee Semple MacPherson's Angelus Temple made food and clothing available 24 hours a day. The Angelus Temple commissary served one and a half million free meals during the Depression. Sister Aimee maintained charge accounts at department stores and often sent the indigent in on a cold day to purchase sweaters etc. The police frequently sent homeless families to the temple for lack of official channels for help. — Student reminiscences and David L. Clark, "Miracles for a Dime: From Chautauqua Tent to Radio Station with Sister Aimee," California History 57 (Winter 1978/79), 354-363.

(29) David L. Clark, Los Angeles: A City Apart. Woodland Hills, CA: Windsor Publications, Inc., 1981), 125; Stephen Longstreet, All Star Cast; An Anecdotal History of Los Angeles. (N.Y.: Thomas Y. Crowell Company, 1977), 203; Los Angeles Times (28 Oct. 1979); and Bean, op. cit., 410.

(30) Sinclair's defeat was due mainly to the opposition's claim that if Sinclair were elected, half the unemployed in the nation would pour into California for the jobs and welfare promised by E.P.I.C. The movie industry took up the anti-Sinclair cause, faked newsreels were distributed to theaters showing hordes of studio extras made up as bums and revolutionaries flocking into California under Sinclair's standards. The Republican victor, Frank Merriam, won with 1,138,000 votes to 879,000 for Sinclair and 302,000 for a third candidate. — Fay M. Blake & H. Morton Newman, "Upton Sinclair's EPIC Campaign," California History 63 (Fall 1984), 305-312; Cleland, op. cit., 222-227; and Gottlieb & Wolt, op. cit., 205-212.

(31) The Plan called for pensions to be paid by a revolving fund fed by a 2% tax on business transactions. The pensioner was required to

spend the entire $200 within the month — which was supposed to re-energize the economy. It proposed to spend $24 million per year on pensions for 9% of the population at a time when the total national income was $40 million — clearly not a workable solution.— Leuchtenberg, Franklin D. Roosevelt...(cited)., 103-105.

(32) Workers of the Writers' Program of the Works Projects Administration in Southern California, Los Angeles, A Guide to the City and its Environs. (N.Y.: Hastings House, Publishers, 1941), p. 58; and David L. Clark, Los Angeles: A City Apart. (cited), p. 126. Besides the grassroots co-op movement, there were a number of other stop-gap innovations. (Los Angeles Times, Feb. 3, 1933, II, 16.)

(33) Shevsky & Williams, op. cit., 47-48; McWilliams,Southern California... (cited), 166-171. L.A.'s out-of-state critics rarely failed to include Iowa Picnics in their sneers as a prime example of the low-brow cultural climate they depicted here.A good example is to be found in Duncan Aikman (editor), The Taming of the Frontier. (N.Y.: Minton, Balch & Company, 1925), 279.

(34) Paul Kagan, New World Utopias; A Photographic History of the Search for Community. (N.Y.: Penguin Books, 1975), 48-75. Photographs credited to Warrington's daughter, show this building under construction and complete. It was originally credited with psychical properties. See also: McWilliams, Southern California... (cited), 252-256; Palmer, op. cit., 210-218.

(35) Quotations: Duncan Aikman (editor), op. cit., 285, 290.

(36) W.W. Robinson and Lawrence Clark Powell, The Malibu; I. Rancho Topanga Malibu Sequit: An Historical Approach; II. Personal Considerations: Essays. (Los Angeles: The Ward Ritchie Press, 1958), 27-38; "For Years, May Rindge Held State at Bay" in the Los Angeles Times (13 July 1980); Los Angeles Times (28 Nov. 1982), VII-1, 18-20; and Ibid. (22 July 1984), Calendar Section, 5-9.

(37) Mason & Anderson, op. cit., 45; Vorspan & Gartner, op. cit., 205-206.

(38) Bessie Averne McClenahan. The Changing Urban Neighborhood; From Neighbor to Nigh-Dweller; A Sociological Study. Los Angeles: University of Southern California, 1929, pp. 17, 33, 46, 48, 73, 84, 90-91.

(39) Quotation: Ibid., 90. 1948 Court Case: Shelly v. Kramer, [334 U.S. 72], cited in de Graaf, Negro... (cited), 203.

(40) David L. Clark. Los Angeles: A City Apart. (Woodland Hills, Calif.: Windsor Publications, Inc., 1981), 170. The incorporated town of Watts was a predominantly-white, semi-agricultural suburb prior to World War I for workers who commuted by streetcar into Los Angeles. After the war, the low real estate prices of the area attracted a sizeable number of Black purchasers and renters. As late as 1936, the attraction could be comprehended through a look at the houses in the area:
"The physical aspects of many Negro homes in this ...section,...are very pleasing. Ten percent of the approximately 2,000 Negro population, own or are yet buying bungalows created from the Spanish and American California type, [which] are equipped in the modern interior fashion. As is to be expected, especially since the recent financial slump, for every two modern homes constructed there are five in the district in wretched appearance, sheltering over-crowded family units. Rents range from $10 to $20 monthly; a few of the dwellers derive sustenance from truck gardens in their front and back yards." — Vivian, op. cit., 29.
At the time of the Watts Riots in 1965, one-third of the houses in Watts were owned by their occupants. — "The McCone Commission Report," quoted in Daniels & Olin, op. cit., 291. One of the immediate contributing factors to the Watts riots involved housing discrimination. During the nationwide civil rights fervor in November 1964, three-fourths of California's voters had passed a statewide ballot initiative measure, repealing the state's fairhousing law clearly violating the 14th Amendment to the U.S. Constitution.

(41) Leonard Leader, "When L.A. Blocked the Borders", Los Angeles Times (2 Feb. 1986), II-4; Robert Mayer, "Closing the Borders — 1936" from Robert Mayer (editor), Los Angeles, A Chronological & Documentary History, 1542-1976. (Dobbs Ferry, N.Y.: Oceana Publications, Inc., 1978.), 125-126; Stein, op. cit., 73-75; Ford, op. cit., 13-14; and Gottlieb & Wolt, op. cit., 220.

(42) The 1930 census found 167,024 persons identified as Mexicans in the county. In 1940, of those California residents born in Mexico, only 4% had arrived before 1900; over 40% had arrived in 1920 or later. — Shevsky & Williams, op. cit., 20; Abraham Hoffman, "Stimulus to Repatriation: 1931 Federal Deportation Drive and the Los Angeles Mexican Community," Pacific Historical Review 42 (May 1973), 205-218; McWilliams, North from Mexico... (cited), 195; and Stein, op. cit., 36-37.

(43) Official figures showed 16.9% unemployed in Los Angeles in January 1931, but an insurance company's study showed 20.9%. (Vorspan and Gartner, op. cit., p. 123).

(44) America House: Ford, op. cit., p. 13.

(45) Housing Surplus: Kasun, op. cit., pp. 56-57.

(46) Quotation: Time-Life Books, This Fabulous Century; Volume IV. 1930-1940. (N.Y.: Time-Life Books, 1969), p. 244.

(47) Gwendolyn Wright, op. cit., pp. 225-229; and William E. Leuchtenburg, Franklin D. Roosevelt and the New Deal, 1932-1940, (N.Y.: Harper & Row, Publishers, Torchbook Edition, 1963), pp. 135-136.

(48) Eugene Weston, Jr. "Ramona Gardens Housing Project," California Arts and Architecture, Vol. 57 (Dec. 1940), pp. 34-35.

(49) National Housing Agency, Federal Public Housing Authority, Public Housing Design; A Review of Experience in Low-Rent Housing. (Wash. D.C.: United States Government Printing Office, June 1946); Quotation: Gwendolyn Wright, op. cit., p. 218; This book has a good section on the problems built into government housing, pp. 217-239, as does Warner, op. cit., pp. 238-240.

(50) Federal Standards and Site Planning: National Housing Agency..., op. cit.,, p. 23.

(51) Esther McCoy, "Gregory Ain's Social Housing," Arts & Architecture, Vol.1 (New Series), No. 2 (Winter 1981), p. 66.

(52) David Gebhard and Harriette Von Breton, L.A. in the Thirties, 1931-1941, (Santa Barbara: Peregrine Smith, Inc., 1975), p. 107; and Richard Pommer, "The Architecture of Urban Housing in the United States during the Early 1930s," Journal of the Society of Architectural Historians, Vol. XXXVII, No. 4 (Dec. 1978), pp. 262-264.

CHAPTER XIII Rosie and Joe and a House in L.A, 1939-1960

(1) Los Angeles Times (3 Sept. 1939), II-2.

(2) Department of Commerce, Bureau of the Census, Sixteenth Census of the United States, 1940. Population, Volume I: Number of Inhabitants... (Washington, D.C.: Government Printing Office, 1942), 122; ——, A Report of the Seventeenth Decennial Census of the United States; Census of Population: 1950. Volume I. Number of Inhabitants. (1952), 5-12; ——, The Eighteenth Decennial Census of the United States; Census of Population: 1960. Volume I, Characteristics of the Population. (1962), 1, 51.

(3) Frank J. Taylor & Lawton Wright, Democracy's Air Arsenal, (NY: Duell, Sloan and Pearce, 1947), 23; Kotkin & Grabowicz, op. cit., 39; "City of the Angels", Fortune 23 (Mar. 1941), 91.

(4) Jackson Mayers. Burbank History. (Burbank: James W. Anderson, 1975), 99-102; Los Angeles Chamber of Commerce, "Los Angeles: From Ciudad to Metropolis..." (Pamphlet), (15 Oct. 1948, unnumbered pages; Taylor & Wright, op cit., 33-43; Arlene Elliott, "The Rise of Aeronautics in California, 1849-1940", Southern California Quarterly 52 (Mar. 1970), 17; "City of the Angels," (cited), 90.

(5) Security-First...(cited), 22 (1 Feb. 1943) and 21 (1 Sept. 1942); "Did You Know These Things?" Southern California Business 2 (Apr. 1923), 36; Los Angeles Chamber of Commerce, L.A. County; Facts and Figures, 1925. (Los Angeles Chamber of Commerce, 1925), 16; E.C. Noel, "Oil Industry Offers Surprises," Southern California Business 2 (Jan. 1924), 38; Welty & Taylor, op. cit., 200-201, 206, 217; "The Standard Story...Four Wells to Five Continents," (pamphlet) (Standard Oil Company of California, 1977); Warren A. Beck & David A. Williams, California; A History of the Golden State. (Garden City, NY: Doubleday & Company, Inc., 1972), 418; Mel Scott, Metropolitan Los Angeles: One Community. (Los Angeles: The Haynes Foundation, 1949), 40.

(6) Otto Friedrich, City of Nets; A Portrait of Hollywood in the 1940's. (Cambridge, MA: Harper & Row, Publishers, 1986), 23-24; Los Angeles Times (2 Sept. 1939), II-7; Joel Kotkin & Paul Grabowicz, California, Inc. (NY: Rawson, Wade Publishers, Inc., 1982), 113-115; Lewis Jacobs, "Film as Big Business," in Solomon, op. cit., 201-202; "Motion Pictures Up-and-Up," Southern California Business 16 (Jan. 1937), 9; and "Hollywood's Retail Market," Southern California Business 16 (Feb. 1937), 26; Robert Glass Cleland, California in Our Time, (1900-1940). (NY: Alfred A. Knopf, 1947), 273-275; Security-First...(cited) 22 (4 Nov. 1943). One indication of the slow recovery from the Depression is the increase from 23,000 to 31,000 studio employees between 1935 and 1939. — Southern California Business 16 (Jan. 1937); Numbers differ from source to source. Cleland claims a 1939 production cost of $216 million, Friedrich claims $170 million, for example. — Cleland, op. cit., 275.

(7) Security-First... (cited) 21 (1 Oct. 1942); 21 (1 Dec. 1942); 22 (2 Jan. 1943); and (18 Feb. 1946), 4. See also, Dunkle, op. cit., 81-86; Shevky & Williams, op. cit., 25-27; Cleland, op. cit., 255; Mayers, op. cit., 115.

(8) 1942 domestic box office receipts were estimated at $1,300,000,000, credited to increased attendance and to higher ticket prices. — Security-First... (cited) 21 (3 Aug. 1942).

(9) Kasun, op. cit., 55-56; Wright, op. cit., 241; Joseph B. Mason, History of Housing in the U.S., 1930-1980. (Houston: Gulf Publishing Company, 1982), 10, 30-32; Dolores Hayden, Redesigning the American Dream: The Future of Housing, Work, and Family Life. (NY: W.W. Norton & Company, 1984), 34.

(10) The Los Angeles Chamber of Commerce formed a Construction Industries Committee to explore ways of exploiting the new housing opportunities. — "A Report on Small Dwellings," and "Introducing the `Package House`," Southern California Business 16 (May 1937), 11, and (June 1937), 15. Pasadena formed a Better Housing Bureau in 1935 to promote cost-cutting innovations by means of design competitions and displays. — "Historic Model Home," Pasadena Heritage 8 (Spring 1984), 4-5.

(11) L.A. City building permit dated 3/17/1939; contractor: Krandell Mtg. & Investment Co.
Originally the house had a shingle roof. The styling is discussed in: Wright, op. cit., 242; Gebhard & von Breton, op. cit., 108.

(12) L.A. City Building Permit, 8/7/40. The contractor was F.H. Dolan. The five room house on the left measured 38 by 30 feet and was valued at $2900. There was also a detached single-car garage, although many houses in this tract had double garages. See also, Mason, op. cit., 37.

(13) Kasun, op. cit., 55-57; Security-First... (cited), 21 (2 Jan. 1942), 3; 22 (4 Nov. 1943), 3-4. Housing surveys in 1939 and 1940 listed up to 106,000 substandard dwelling units in Los Angeles County, mostly for inadequate plumbing, or need of repair. Scott, op. cit., 100; "City of Angels", (cited), 91.

(14) The original Park La Brea units were such an investment bonanza, due to the continued local housing shortage, that a multi-story phase was added in 1948. The cluster of new high-rise apartments had no previous counterpart in Los Angeles. They were modern and efficient but there was little of the local cultural tone about them. They were more closely related to the urban housing plans of such European Modernists as Le Corbusier (La Ville Radieuse) and Richard Neutra (Rush City Reformed). The original appellation was, "Parklabrea". Gebhard and Von Breton, op. cit., 108; "Parklabrea Apartments," Architect and Engineer 156 (Feb. 1944), 20.

(15) Wartime Controls: Security-First... (cited), 21 (1 July 1942), 2; (3 Aug. 1942), 1; (1 Dec. 1942), 1; 22 (12 July 1943), 2.

(16) "Aliso Village, Los Angeles," Architecture and Engineering 152 (Jan. 1943), 14; "The Housing Authority of the City of Los Angeles Presents a Solution," California Arts & Architecture 60 (May 1943), 50, 63; Fred'k W. Jones, "Millions for War Housing," Architecture and Engineer 154 (July 1943), 17; National Housing Agency, Federal Public Housing Authority, Public Housing Design: A Review of Experience in Low-Rent Housing. (Washington, D.C.: United States Government Printing Office, June 1946), 23; Wright, op. cit., 218; Sam Bass Warner, Jr, The Urban Wilderness; A History of the American City. (NY: Harper & Row, Publishers, 1972), 238-240; Harrison Stephens, "Los Angeles Completes 5 Lanham Act Projects," Architect and Engineer 154 (Sept. 1943), 15-16, 18; SecurityFirst... (cited), 21 (3 Aug. 1942). 1.

(17) Duration housing, such as Banning Homes and Wilmington Hall, was constructed near the shipyards: temporary structures for childless working couples and single men. But the shipyards hired few women, whereas up to 75% of the jobs in aircraft plants were open to them. No temporary housing, however, was set up for them near the aircraft plants. And neither single women nor women with children whose husbands were military inductees were accommodated in the permanent housing projects in Los Angeles.

(18) "Northrop's green plant...on a field that was farmland a year ago", the Vultee plant across the street from an orange grove, the Douglas-Long Beach plant "its buildings spreading like huge dominoes across a flat." Only one called attention to itself: "The arching roof of Douglas's parent factory stands high above a skyline of homes at Santa Monica...." —City of the Angels," (cited), 9293.

(19) Leila J. Rupp, Mobilizing Women for War; German and American Propaganda, 1939-1945. (Princeton: Princeton University Press, 1978), 139.

(20) Security-First...(cited), 22 (4 May 1943); Ibid. 21, (1 Oct. 1942); Ibid. 22 (4 Nov. 1943); Taylor & Wright, op. cit., 107119; Mayers, op. cit., 119; Hedda Hopper's column, Los Angeles Times (3 Aug. 1943), I-10. The large numbers of female workers is somewhat misleading. A large proportion of women worked only part time. Many changed jobs or moved, following husbands in military service. Women fluctuated in and out of the job market, and much of the time they were employed was devoted to training or retraining. — D'Ann Mae Campbell, "Wives, Workers and Womanhood: America During World War II." (Ph.D. Dissertation, University of North Carolina, 1979), 31-32.

(21) U.S. Government, Office of War Information, Bureau of Intelligence, "Women and the War; Special Intelligence Report," Aug. 19, 1942; ———, Magazine Section, "War Jobs for Women" (pamphlet), Nov. 1942; Rupp, op. cit., 140-150; Campbell, op. cit., 92-95.

(22) Rupp, op. cit., 143; U.S. Government, Office of War Information, "War Jobs for Women," (cited). In the peak war year, 1943, there were only 25,000 WAACs (Women's Auxiliary Army Corps).

(23) Rupp, op. cit., 150-161; SecurityFirst...(cited), 21 (1 Oct. 1942) and (1 July 1942); "Women Warworkers Quit Plants in Droves," Los Angeles Times (17 Dec. 1945), I-1.

(24) Issei is the term for foreign-born immigrant Japanese who, by U.S. laws still operative in the 1940s, were classed as "aliens ineligible for citizenship;" Nisei is the term for second-generation, American-born, and thus natural-born American citizens; Kibei were Nisei who had been sent to Japan for their educations. Partly because the Japanese educational system was intensely nationalistic, they were particularly suspect. Under the relocation program, they were isolated as maximum-security cases, often separated from their families. Many of the Kibei chose repatriation to Japan, at least for the duration of the war.

(25) Four of the best accounts are: Bill Hosokawa, Nisei; The Quiet Americans. (NY: William Morrow and Company, Inc., 1969), 207-256; Roger Daniels, Concentration Camps USA: Japanese Americans and World War II. (NY: Holt, Rinehart and Winston, Inc., 1971), 22-41; Harry H.L. Kitano, Japanese Americans; The Evolution of a Subculture. (Englewood Cliffs, NJ: Prentice-Hall, Inc., 1969), 22-32; and Robert A. Wilson & Bill Hosokawa. East to America: A History of the Japanese in the United States. (NY: William Morrow and Company, Inc., 1980). For further insight into local aspects: Bruce T. Torrence, Hollywood: The First 100 Years. (Hollywood: The Hollywood Chamber of Commerce & Fiske Enterprises, 1979), 181; Anthony Turhollow, A History of the Los Angeles District, U.S. Army Corps of Engineers, 1898-1965. (L.A.: U.S. Army Engineer District, 1975), 281. Even the removal of the Japanese did not automatically reduce the antagonism against them, as witness the editorial response of the Los Angeles Times to the 1943 suggestion that the internees be released to federally-supervised work projects: its furious opposition was voiced in an April 17, 1943 editorial: "Bleeding Hearts Discuss the Jap Problem" (I-4).

(26) A 1941 study found that of the 6000 employees of Vultee Aircraft none were Black. Douglas Aircraft had ten Black employees out of a total of 33,000, and these were relegated to menial work. Lockheed-Vega and the shipyards had only slightly better hiring records, and the unions were largely closed to Blacks, as well. A campaign organized by Black women in the summer of 1942 met with some success. The changing labor market was an even more effective catalyst to integration. — Neil A. Wynn, The Afro-American and the Second World War. (NY: Holmes & Meier Publishers, 1975), 39-42, 61; de Graaf, "Negro Migration..."(cited), 103-120, 179-203; Beck & Williams, op. cit., 423-425; Kasun, op. cit., 13-17; Rodney Steiner, Los Angeles , The Centrifugal City. (Dubuque, Iowa: Kendall/Hunt Publishing Company, 1981), 63-64; Wright, op. cit., 218; "Homes for 500 Will Be Built in Watts Area," Los Angeles Times (10 Aug. 1943), I-3. Restrictive covenants were only outlawed in May, 1948, by the U.S. Supreme Court case, Shelley vs. Kraemer. — See Weaver, "The Laboratory..."(cited), 74.

(27) McWilliams, North from Mexico (cited), 227274; Wayne Moquin & Charles Van Doren, A Documentary History of the Mexican Americans. (NY: Praeger Publishers, 1971), 294-314; Hoffman, "Stimulus to Repatriation..." (cited), 205-218; Rios-Bustamente & Castillo, op. cit., 144-162; Beck & Williams, op. cit., 419.

(28) Mathison, op. cit., 197; Security-First (cited) 21 (2 Mar. 1942); Dave Packwood, "A Second Chance for Tires," Westways 34 (Feb. 1942), 8-9; ———,"A Tire Rationing Board at Work," Westways 34 (Mar. 1942), 6-7; James H. Collins, "Let's Take Stock of Motors," Southern California Business 15 (June 1936), 8-9; Time-Life Books: This Fabulous Century; Volume V: 1940-1950. (NY: Time-Life Books, 1969), 164; Howard, op. cit., A.: 72; Crump, op. cit., 201; Security-First...(cited) 21 (2 Nov. 1942) and (5 Mar. 1943).

(29) William Myers. Iron Men and Copper Wires; A Centennial History of the Southern California Edison Company. (Glendale: Trans-Anglo Books, 1983), 194-195; William K. Baxter, "Blackouts and Your Driving," Westways 34 (Jan. 1942), 7; Welty & Taylor,

Notes

op. cit., 220; Time-Life Books, op.cit., 203; "'42 Air Raid That Wasn't Set Off Guns, Confusion," Los Angeles Times (25 Feb. 1979); Weaver, Los Angeles: The Enormous Village (cited), 130-132. The anti-aircraft barrage was blamed for a precipitous drop in retail sales for the next couple of days. — Security-First...(cited) 1 (2 Mar. 1942). I. Magnin opened a registration desk to sign up volunteers for the Aircraft Warning Service. "Volunteer Now...," read its ads, "Win your wings; defend our coast; protect your home; do your part..." Los Angeles Times (2 Aug. 1943), I-2. Robert Clark, "Magicians in Khaki", Westways 36 (Feb. 1944), 10-11; Will Connell, "Think Before You Shoot," Westways 34 (Apr. 1942), 11-12.

(30) Bill Bradley, The Last of the Great Stations; 40 Years of the Los Angeles Union Passenger Terminal. (L.A.: Interurbans Publications, 1979), 8-21, 84-95; Howard, op. cit., 56, 68; Harold Lloyd's 1923 movie, Safety Last.

(31) Between Dec. 7, 1941 and April 1, 1946, Fort MacArthur alone inducted 750,000 soldiers. 38,000 marines at a time were stationed at Camp Pendleton with a high point population of 86,000. One study estimates 7 million passed through L.A., but this appears to be the total of all five West Coast ports. Even a fifth of this number represented an enormous military presence. Kotkin & Grabowicz, op. cit., 38; Charles J. Sullivan, Army Posts and Towns; The Baedeker of the Army. (Fourth Edition) (L.A.: Haynes Corporation, Publishers, 1942), passim; Nancy Langley, "Maritime Catalina," Westways 36 (Jul. 1944), 6-7; "M.F.", "Men Who Man the Ships," Westways 34 (Jun. 1942), 12-13; Beck & Haase, op. cit., 86-88; Turhollow, op. cit., 16. Information on Fort MacArthur per telephone conversation Jan. 29, 1987 with officer on duty at the Center for Military History, 20 Massachusetts Avenue NW, Washington D.C., (202) 272-0320; Robert M. Witty & Neil Morgan, Marines of the Margarita: The Story of Camp Pendleton and the Leathernecks Who Train on a Famous California Rancho. (San Diego: Frye & Smith, Ltd., 1970), 71, 90. Pass and A.W.O.L. information was based on personal reminiscences by Ernest Jacobs, Lester Baker, John Davis, and Gene Monteverde. Other than being placed on report — a blot on one's record which would prolong one's military stint — little disciplinary action was taken, in my informers' memory — especially if the unit was about to be shipped overseas anyway.

(32) The six categories were: direct accounts of war issues; a second, showing the Nature of the Enemy (negatively, of course); a third, showing the British, Russians, etc. in a positive light in order to boost the united allied cause; a fourth, to urge increased production and contribution to the war effort; a fifth, to show the American Way of Life in a positive light; and the sixth, on the soldier or sailor's experience. Under the circumstances of relocation, of course, the Japanese roles had to be played by Chinese or by Anglos — Colin Shindler, Hollywood Goes to War; Films and American Society, 1939-1952. (London: Routledge & Kegan Paul, 1979), 37-41, 70-71. Security-First...(cited), 21, No. 8. Friedrich, op. cit., 111, 129-130, 210-211. Franklin Fearing, Evaluation of Motion Pictures as a Medium of Instruction and Communication: An Investigation of the Effects of Two Motion Pictures Produced by Army Air Forces First Motion Picture Unit. (Los Angeles: 22 July 1944) (typed manuscript; author was Professor of Psychology, University of California, Los Angeles. The study was ordered by the Commanding Officer, First Motion Picture Unit, Army Air Forces.).

(33) U.S. Department of the Army, Army Talk: Orientation Fact Sheets (weekly publication) (Washington, D.C.: U.S. Government Printing Office, 1944), No. 29: "Know and Have Faith in America and Its Future: Soldiers of Production."

(34) Los Angeles Times (18 Apr. 1943), I-1; Friedrich, op. cit., 105; Mathison, op. cit., 195; Wynn, op. cit., 27; Daily News Morgue, UCLA Special Collections, #27032, December 1941. Among the stars who went to war were Robert Montgomery, Tyrone Power, William Holden, and Jimmy Stewart, baseball star Hank Greenberg and the entire football team of Loyola University. Black servicemen could identify with popular boxer Joe Louis.

(35) Torrence, op. cit., 194-195, 201-203; Friedrich, op. cit., 108, 158-160; Joe Kennelley & Roy Hankey, Sunset Boulevard, America's Dream Street. (Burbank: Darwin Publications, 1981), 74; "Hedda Hopper Puts on Show at Canteen," Los Angeles Times (9 Aug. 1943), I-9; Witty & Morgan, op. cit., 118-119; Friedrich, op. cit.,; "War Half Over But Entertaining Just Begun," Hollywood Sun; Hollywood Studio Union News. (16 May 1945), 3; "Amateur Actors Tour Hospitals," in Ibid., (16 May 1945), 7; Letter to the Editor, in Ibid., (23 May 1945), 2.

(36) Torrence, op. cit., 180; Witty & Morgan, op. cit., 82, 118-119. Studio trucks and drivers were pressed into service to transport army troops and equipment. Studio fire departments served military bases. The Marine Camouflage School was set up on a back lot at 20th Century Fox so that the skills of Hollywood's scenarists could be tapped.

(37) "Angelus Temple Program, Mar. 28, 1943"; "World's Spiritual Plunge Likened to Diving Plane," Los Angeles Times, (9 Aug. 1943), II-8. The 20,000 seat Bowl, laboring under wartime conditions of dimouts, gas rationing, a wartime federal excise tax on tickets, and Army regulations limiting audience size to 5,000 (raised to 10,000 in 1943), still managed to give away 10,000 free tickets each

season to servicemen in uniform. — Grace G. Koopal, Miracle of Music. (Hollywood: Charles E. Toberman, 1972), 180-184; "War Loan Pageant Held at Pershing Square," Los Angeles Times, (16 Apr. 1943), II-1; "Screen and Stage: Bleachers Set for Event," Los Angeles Times, (12 Aug. 1943), I-14; "Reception Awaits Stars," Los Angeles Times, (21 Dec. 1943), I-6.

(38) Howard, op. cit., 63; Zelda Cini and Bob Crane, Hollywood, Land and Legend. (Westport, CT: Arlington House, 1980), 131-136; Rex Stewart, "Days and Nights When the Music Wouldn't Stop," Los Angeles Magazine 11 (Sept. 1966), 69; Historical Society of Long Beach, The Pike on the Silverstrand. (Long Beach, 1982), 60-67; U.S. Govt., Office of War Information Report (cited), 14. (Curfew hours on most bases were 11:00 or 11:30 p.m., enforced by bed checks.) Ivan Light, "From Vice District to Tourist Attraction: The Moral Career of American Chinatowns, 1880-1940," Pacific Historical Review 43 (Aug. 1974), 391.

(39) Mauricio Mazon, "Social Upheaval in World War II: `ZootSuiters' and Servicemen in Los Angeles, 1943." Ph.D. Dissertation, UCLA, 1976, 162-167; Tom Moran & Tom Sewell, Fantasy by the Sea; A Visual History of the American Venice. (Culver City: Peace Press, 1980), 83-85; Ralph H. Turner and Samuel J. Surace, "Zoot-Suiters and Mexicans," in Daniels & Olin, op. cit., 210-219; Weaver, op. cit., 136-137; McWilliams, op. cit., 238-258; McWilliams, "The Zoot-Suit Riots," The New Republic 108, 24 (14 June 1943), 317-320.

(40) For the U.S. as a whole, the rate of marriages per 1000 single women increased from 69 in the 1930s to 92 in the 1940s. In 1940, 48% of all women between the ages of 14 and 34 were married; by 1946 the percentage was 59. — Campbell, op. cit., 33. Conversations with Beverly Hall, Gladys Denman, Hilda Harte.

(41) "Give Them a Lift!", Westways 34 (Jan. 1942), 1011; Hedda Hopper's column and "Role Music Has in War Recounted," Los Angeles Times, (16 Apr. 1943), I-15 & II-7; "War Spurs Clubdom Growth," and "Soldiers, Sailors, Marines — Free!", Los Angeles Times, (17 Apr. 1943), I-6 and II-8; "Servicemen and Homeless Will be Christmas Guests," and "Southland Hospitality Awaiting Servicemen," Los Angeles Times, (19 Dec. 1943), II-1 and II-2; "Half Million Servicemen Get Red Cross Greeting," Los Angeles Times, (17 Dec. 1945), II-1.

(42) Taylor & Wright, op. cit., 175; miscellaneous articles, Los Angeles Times, (17-20 Dec.), I-1, 2.

(43) The number of persons employed in manufacturing in Los Angeles County in August 1939 had been 185,000; at the peak of the war effort, in August 1943, there were 650,000 manufacturing employees. By December 1945 the number was down to 330,000. However, this was still 80% higher than the prewar figure. —Security-First... (cited), 25 (3 Jan. 1946), 1-2; and Ibid., 24 (Sept. 18, 1945), 1. Women were 32 to 33 % of the industrial workers in L.A. from August 1943 through April 1945. There is not even a figure available for the 1930s, since women had no statistically perceptible place in factories at that time. -Ibid., (18 Mar. 1946), 3.

(44) One example of special interest influence on the planning process in this period is the maneuvering of business interests successful in obtaining passage of the 1948 California statute authorizing the creation of Community Development Agencies. Martin J. Schiesl, "City Planning and the Federal Government in World War II; The Los Angeles Experience." California History 59 (Summer 1980), 127-143; Simon Eisner, "What Do You Mean — Planning?" California Arts & Architecture 60 (May 1943), 26, 46. Los Angeles, City of. The City of Los Angeles; The First 100 Years, 1850-1950. (1949), 16-78.

(45) Security-First...(cited), (Oct. 1947), 4, and (Apr. 1947), 4; Crump, op. cit., 189; Bradley, op. cit., 23; "Los Angeles: Forgotten Sun," Newsweek 27 (23 Dec. 1946); Marvin Brienes, "Smog Comes to Los Angeles," Southern California Quarterly 58 (Winter 1976), 515-532.

(46) Taylor & Wright, op. cit., 169-175; "PostWar Planning Now," Architect and Engineer 156 (May 1944), 37-38, "Post-War Outlook for Building Industry," Architect and Engineer 156 (June 1944), 4748; Security-First...(cited) 25 (3 Jan. 1946); Ibid.,(18 May 1946); "Aviation Giant Donald Douglas is Dead at 88," Los Angeles Times, (4 July 1949), 8; Kotkin, op. cit., 38; Nash, op. cit., 325-326; James L. Clayton, "The Impact of the Cold War on the Economies of California and Utah,1946-1965," Pacific Historical Review 36 (Nov. 1967), 453-457; "Kaiser Builds Steel Plant and Hospital," Architect and Engineer 154 (Aug. 1943); R.R. Shoemaker, "Impressive Construction Program at Port of Long Beach, Calif.," The American City 60 (Apr. 1945), 97; Turhollow, op. cit., 54; "Lockheed Builds Nation's Largest Cafeteria," Architect and Engineer 156 (Feb. 1944), 16-17; Scott, op. cit., 40; Security-First...(cited), 25 (3 Jan. 1946), 2; Ibid., 25 (5 Sept. 1946); Ibid., (Dec. 1946), 2; Ibid., 27 (15 Jan. 1948), 2, and (June 1948), 1-2, and 27 (Nov. 1948), 2; and 27 (Sept 17, 1948).

(47) Ad for USS Building Steels, back cover, Architect and Engineer 154 (Aug 1943).

(48) Los Angeles Times, (18 Dec. 1945), I-1 & I-3; (19 Dec. 1945), I-3; (20 Dec. 1945), I-2; Security First...(cited), 27, No. 4, and 25 (5 Sept. 1946), 1; D'Ann Campbell, "Was the West Different? Values and Attitudes of Young Women in 1943," Pacific Historical Review 47 (Aug. 1978), 455-456; quotation from a Ladies Home Journal poll, June 1944, in Rupp, op. cit., 161.

(49) Wright, op. cit., 242-243; Schiesl, op. cit., 138; Mayers, op. cit., 126; Los Angeles Times, (21 Apr. 1946), II-3; (20 Dec. 1945), I-2; (22 Apr. 1946), II-1.

(50) Michael Goodman, "The Post-War House Beautiful," Architect and Engineer 156 (Jan. 1944), 22-23, 34.

(51) The first prize went to a design by Eero Saarinen and Oliver Lundquist of Washington, D.C.; the second to I.M. Pei and E.H. Duhart, of Cambridge, Massachusetts; and the third to Raphael S. Soriano, of Los Angeles. John Entenza, "Competition: "Designs for Postwar Living," California Arts & Architecture 60 (Mar.-Apr. 1943), 34, 35, inside back cover, "Designs for Postwar Living; Notes to the Contestants," Ibid., 60 (May 1943), 26, 45; "Announcement: The Case Study House Program," Arts & Architecture 62 (Jan. 1945), 36-39; Introduction, and "Case Study House Number 11," Ibid., 63 (July 1946), 44-45, 46-55; "Case Study House #2," Ibid, 63 (Nov. 1946), 36-38; Esther McCoy, Case Study Houses, 1945-1962. (Second Edition). (L.A.: Hennessey & Ingalls, Inc., 1977), 1-19; Nancy C. Langley, "Modern Architecture Explained," and "Case Study House Program, Part II," Los Angeles Times, Home Magazine, (5 May 1946); Gleye, op. cit., 145-146. A comprehensive anthology on the Case Study program is: Elizabeth A. T. Smith (editor). Blueprints for Modern Living: History and Legacy of the Case Study Houses. (Los Angeles: The Museum of Contemporary Art; and Cambridge, Mass.: The MIT Press, 1990).

(52) Michael O'Brien, "Mar Vista's Modern Landmark," Los Angeles Conservancy 9 (May/June 1987), 12; Gebhard, Von Breton, & Weiss, op. cit., 17-18; McCoy, The Second Generation (cited), 82, 96, 118-130; conversations with Kathleen Wickham.

(53) Richard Neutra, "Planning Postwar Fabrication," California Arts & Architecture 60 (May 1943), 22-25; R.M. Schindler, "Prefabrication Vocabulary,", Ibid., 60 (June 1943), 25-27; advertisement for San Pedro Lumber Company featuring prefab design by Neutra, Ibid., 60 (Feb. 1943), 9; "America's Ideal Postwar Home for the Average Family," Architect and Engineer 162 (Sept. 1945), 21; McCoy, The Second Generation (cited), 114-118; "Post-War Outlook for Building Industry," Architect and Engineer 156 (June 1944), 47; "Barkers and Homasote and Prefabrication," California Arts and Architecture 60 (Nov. 1943), 34-35; "Materials for Design, 1947", Progressive Architecture/Pencil Points 28 (Jan. 1947), 42-43.

(54) Ads in Los Angeles Times, (21 Apr. 1946), II-1; (5 May 1946), II-3; (12 May 1946); Paul R. Williams, The Small Home of Tomorrow. (Hollywood: Murray & Gee, Incorporated, 1945), 4041; Los Angeles Times, (21 Apr. 1946), II-1; Paul Oppermann, review of: The Community Builders' Handbook. (Prepared by the Community Builders' Council of the Urban Land Institute, Washington, D.C., 1947), in Journal of the American Institute of Planners 14 (Winter 1948), 37. See also: Vernon B. McClurg, A Catalog of Small Homes of California, Volume I. (Hollywood: Murray & Gee, Inc., 1945); ——, Small Homes of California, Volume No. 2. (1946); Sunset Magazine, Sunset Homes for Western Living. (San Francisco: Lane Publishing Co., 1946); John P. Dean and Simon Breines, The Book of Small Houses. (NY: Crown Publishers, 1946); and William J. Hennessey, (Editor), America's Best Small Houses. (NY: The Viking Press, 1949). The competitions and publicity on the part of the popular press is described in Wright, op. cit., 253; and Joseph B. Mason, History of Housing in the U.S., 1930-1980. (Houston: Gulf Publishing Company, 1982), 51-52.

(55) Security-First...(cited), (Oct. 1946), 2-4; (3 Jan. 1946), 4; Los Angeles Times, (18 Apr. 1946), II-1; and (21 Apr. 1946), I-1; Security-First...(cited), (11 Feb. 1947), 1-2; (3 June 1946), 24; (15 July 1946), 2; (Jan. 1947), 2-3; (June 1947), 2; (Nov. 1947), 2-3; (16 Dec. 1947), 2; (17 Sept. 1948), 1-3; (16 Aug. 1948), 1. As the material shortage ended, building activity broke new records. In the July-September quarter of 1948, 22,950 family dwelling units were completed in Los Angeles County. —Security-First...(cited), (14 Oct. 1948), 1.

(56) Illustration 139: Apartment house at 26th Street and Montana Avenue, Brentwood. Building permit dated 1952.

(57) Kaiser Services, Kaiser Today; Forty Years of Progress. (Oakland, 1954), unnumbered pages; Bradley, Commercial Los Angeles, 1925-1947 (cited), closing pages (unnumbered); Evelyn De Wolfe, "Little Boxes of 'Ticky-Tack'," Los Angeles Times, (26 May 1985), VIII-7.

(58) Scott, op. cit., 100; Mason, op. cit., 53.

(59) Illustration 142: Ranch Style, Northridge. Estimated late 1950s. No original building permit on file. 1976 permit to add a 12x15' bedroom shows the original structure as a single story dwelling with attached garage, measuring 28x72'.

(60) Builder Cliff May has often been credited with fathering the form. The general forms of the style appeared in a house he built near San Diego in 1931, and in 1938 he built a house for himself in Los Angeles in the full-blown Ranch style. But William W. Wurster had built a house with similar characteristics with a board and batten exterior in Northern California in 1927. The typology of the "Ranch style" or "Western house" — a typical ranch style — is shown in Architectural Forum, The Book of Small Houses, (NY: Simon and Schuster, Inc., 1936), 170; Williams, op. cit., 22-23; Gebhard & Winter, op. cit., 705; David Gebhard, et al., A Guide to Architecture in San Francisco & Northern California. (Second Edition) (Santa Barbara: Peregrine Smith, Inc., 1976), 474; Cliff May, Cliff May. The California Ranch House. (Oral History, Marlene L. Laskey, interviewer) (Oral History Project, UCLA) (Regents of the University of California, 1984), 5, 23, 8687, 103; Esther McCoy and Evelyn Hitchcock, "The Ranch House,"in Moore, Smith, & Becker, op. cit., 88-89; Paul Robinson Hunter and Walter L. Reichardt (editors), Residential Architecture in Southern California. (L.A.: Southern California Chapter, The American Institute of Architects, 1939), 27; Sunset Magazine, op. cit., 15; Robert Winter, The California Bungalow. (L.A.: Hennessey & Ingalls, Inc, 1980), 55-57; Mary Mix Foley, The American House. (NY: Harper Colophon Books, 1980), 259; Gebhard & Von Breton, Architecture in California (cited), 20-21.

(61) George N. Fenin and William K. Everson, The Western; From Silents to Cinerama. (NY: Bonanza Books, 1962), 145-281; Stan Chambers, "L.A. Television: The Early Days," Los Angeles 1781-1981 (Advertising Supplement to the Los Angeles Times), (31 Aug. 1980), 40-42,51. William R. Brown, Imagemaker: Will Rogers and the American Dream. (Columbia, MO: University of Missouri Press, 1970) and Bryan B. Sterling and Frances N. Sterling, A Will Rogers Treasury: Reflections and Observations. (NY: Crown Publishers, 1982).

(62) "Bird of Paradise Was a Hen in Colony Founder's Eden", Los Angeles Times, (29 Nov. 1985), II-8, 10; "Horse Ranch Sale to Mark Era's End," Ibid, (13 May 1985), II-6; "Noted Ranch Property at Tarzana Sold," Ibid., I-6, Aug. 5, 1943; Robert Gottlieb and Irene Wolt, Thinking Big: The Story of the Los Angeles Times, Its Publishers and Their Influence on Southern California. (NY: G.P. Putnam's Sons, 1977), pp. 127145; Frank M. Keffer, History of San Fernando Valley; In Two Parts, Narrative and Biographical. (Glendale: Stillman Printing Company, 1934), pp. 100101; Rodney Steiner, Los Angeles, The Centrifugal City. (Dubuque, Iowa: Kendall/Hunt Publishers, 1981), pp. 143-148.

(63) Security First National Bank, Research Department, The Growth and Economic Stature of the San Fernando Valley, 1960. (Los Angeles, Sept. 1960). To avoid sentimentality, it should be pointed out that citrus trees' bearing life for market-quality fruit is about 50 years. Environmental concerns obliged citrus growers to replace the smudge-pots which they had employed to ward off freeze damage, with wind equipment. Grove owners who sold out just before their 1910s trees would have declined also avoided the costly conversion to wind generators. The agricultural era was doomed, with or without housing tracts. Still, there is a certain irony to the replacement of real ranches with phony ones.

(64) May, op. cit., 5, 23, 86-87, 103. For example of magazine coverage, see "California's New Best Seller," House & Home 4 (July 1953), 93-98.

(65) Advertisement for the "Amestoy Park" development, Walter H. Leimert Co. in Los Angeles Times, (18 July 1948), I-12. See also, "Fortitude Is Leimerts' Watchword," Los Angeles Times, (9 Nov. 1986), VIII-1.

(66) Two recent analyses of the permutations of the stucco box are: Kirk E. Peterson, "Eclectic Stucco;" and John Beach and John Chase, "The Stucco Box;" — both in Moore, Smith, & Becker, op. cit., 112-129. Gebhard & Von Bretton, Lloyd Wright... (cited), 64, 92; Gleye, op. cit., 143; Hines, op. cit., 199; Gebhard, Schindler (cited), 175. Gebhard goes so far as to assert the woody works of these modernist masters as "the prototype" of the mass-produced Ranch style house.

(67) Los Angeles Times, (12 May 1946), III-1; and (22 June 1947), III-2; L. Morgan Yost, Edward I. Fickett, and Joseph Eichler, "The Architects' New Frontier — the Volume-built House," House & Home 4 (July 1953), 92-94; Advertisement, Los Angeles Times, (18 July 1948), I-12.

CHAPTER XIV Is This the End of the Rainbow?

(1) Art Seidenbaum, "Looking Into the Mirror of Playful L.A.," Los Angeles Times editorial, (25 Oct. 1976); Nelson & Clark, op. cit., 1, 60; "Red White & Blue Tours," Better Homes and Gardens, (Nov. 1976), 201; John Grimond, "The 'Economist' Survey of Los Angeles," Los Angeles Magazine. (May 1982), 181; Christopher Rand, Los Angeles, The Ultimate City. (NY: Oxford University Press, 1967), 3.

(2) While the California bungalow of the 1900s and 10s had received national attention in such magazines in its day, it had shared the pages with other Craftsman styles. And the shingle-sheathed California version never proliferated in the rest of the country like the Ranch style house did.

(3) The process of housing taking over the hills, both by "mountain cropping" and stilt-suspension is the subject for several sighs in Banham, op cit., 103-109.

(4) Quotation: McCoy, Second Generation, (cited), xii.

(5) Beck & Williams, op. cit., 428-440; Rand, op. cit., 68-100; Kotkin & Grabowicz, op. cit., 9, 17-19, 40-41; Grimond, op. cit., 198; Security Pacific National Bank. The Sixty Mile Circle; The Economy of the Greater Los Angeles Area. Los Angeles: May 1981, 9.)

(6) A direct correlation between census figures, technical skills, and the growth of defense and electronics industries has been established by: James L. Clayton, "The Impact of the Cold War on the Economies of California and Utah, 1946-1965," Pacific Historical Review 36 (Nov. 1967), 449-473. In 1980 California received one-fourth of all the prime contracts awarded by the Dept. of Defense and 44% of those awarded by the National Aeronautics and Space Administration (NASA), most of these to Southern California. — Grimond, op. cit., 198; John L. Chapman, Incredible Los Angeles. (NY: Harper & Row, Publishers, 1967), 122; Kotkin, op. cit., 40; Mayers, op. cit., 150-151; Grimond, op. cit., 204; Security Pacific..., op. cit., 3. Revisiting the Military-Industrial Complex", occupied all of Part VI, Los Angeles Times, 10 July 1983.

(7) The Malin Residence ("Chemosphere") is an octagon 60 feet across, mounted on a service stem 5 feet in diameter, 30 feet high. Lautner had come to Los Angeles from an apprenticeship under Frank Lloyd Wright to supervise Wright's 1939 Sturgis House in Brentwood. While the lapped horizontal forms seen in the base of the "Chemosphere" are an apparent legacy of Lautner's contact with Wright's Usonian period, the rest of the concept is light-years' removed from Wright's designs. Lautner went on to produce even more stunning residences in Malibu and Mexico. David Gebhard and Susan King, A View of California Architecture: 1960-1976. Exhibition Catalog, San Francisco Museum of Modern Art, 1977, 1976.), 7, 57; "John Lautner," Society of Architectural Historians Southern California Chapter Newsletter 4 (Feb. 1980), 3; Sam Hall Kaplan, "Lautner Still Ahead of His Time," Los Angeles Times, (14 Sept. 1986), VIII-2.

(8): Illustration 152: The Strick house is located in the Santa Monica Canyon area. It was built in 1964-65. —Interview with Anne Strick, 4/16/79. Her term to describe the feeling produced by the living room was "swashing".

(9): Illustration 153: The 1956 building permit for this Santa Monica house do not indicate an architect. The contractor was Frank Bivens, the owners Mr. and Mrs. Lawrence Babcock.

(10) The March 10, 1933 Long Beach quake registered 6.3 on the Richter Scale. The Feb. 9, 1971 Sylmar-San Fernando quake was 6.5 and the Oct. 1, 1987 Whittier Narrows, 5.9. The Jan. 17, 1994 Northridge quake hit 6.8. The 1870s travelogue writer who said earthquakes usually occur in August was wrong.

(11) Illustration 154: The original building permit for this house was taken out by Siegfried Heymann in 1966. The plans were changed and the permit renewed several times and the house completed as amended in 1969. There are three stories in this 3,300 square foot dwelling. The similarity to Schindler's work extends to the upper story cube, an echo of Schindler's "sleeping baskets." Compare Illustration 154 with 117.

(12) Eichler Homes, Inc. was a pioneer in open housing, that is, selling homes within its tracts without regard to race or ethnicity. Approximately one-tenth of the Balboa Highland homes were originally sold to Blacks — all of them successful professionals able to afford the tract's higher-than-average prices. That this policy caused few problems was attributed, in part, to the uniqueness of the

houses which, in turn, "attracted buyers who saw themselves as more liberal and more cosmopolitan than those who lived in conventional homes." — Ned Eichler, The Merchant Builders. (Cambridge, MA: The MIT Press, 1982), 93, 270. Esther McCoy, A. Quincy Jones: A Tribute. Exhibition Catalogue. (California State University Dominguez Hills, 1980), 6-8; Alan Hess, "The Eichler Homes," Arts & Architecture. 3 (Vol. 3, 1984), 38-41; Patricia Ward Biederman, "Community Is Credited with Integration of Valley Housing," Los Angeles Times, (23 June 1985), II-8, 13-15.

(13) Los Angeles County Museum, History Division. op. cit., 41-43.; Carla C. Sobala (compiler). Los Angeles...Today. (ULI 1975 Fall Meeting Project Brochure) (Washington, D.C.: ULI-the Urban Land Institute, 1975), 88-90; "Marina Rent Hike Rejected," Los Angeles Times, (21 Apr. 1988), II-2.
Born in England, 1928; educated at the School of Architecture, University of Sydney, Australia, Anthony J. Lumsden worked in offices of Eero Saarinen in the 1950s, of Kevin Roche-John Dinkeloo & Associates in the early 1960s. He joined DMJM in L.A. in 1964. Marina City, Marina del Rey was constructed in 1972-1975. — Gebhard & King, op. cit., 57-58.

(14) Illustration 157: Architects Rebecca L. Binder and James G. Stafford received a 1985 Honor Award from the American Institute of Architecture for this 1982 four-unit townhouse, Pacific Townhomes. It is only one example of a significant current trend of in-fill residential designs in progress in the Los Angeles area in the innovative and functionally-oriented modernism sometimes labelled "the Machine Aesthetic". — "L.A. Breakthroughs," Sunset, (Mar. 1986), 95-105; "Winner of 1985 Honor Award of American Institute of Architects Designed by Rebecca L. Binder and James G. Stafford". —L.A. Times, (16 June 1985); John Chase, "Typecasting Style," Arts & Architecture, Vol. 1 (New Series)3 (Aug. 1982), 51-53.

(15) Los Angeles County and City Commissions on Human Relations. McCone Revisited: A Focus on Solutions to Continuing Problems in South Central Los Angeles. (Report on Public Hearing, January 1985)

(16) Francine F. Rabinovitz, "Minorities in Suburbs: The Los Angeles Experience," Working Paper No. 31. Joint Center for Urban Studies of M.I.T. and Harvard, March 1975., 9.

(17) Built in 1942 and extended in 1954, Estrada Courts Housing Project is operated by the City of Los Angeles. Located at Olympic Boulevard and Lorena Street, it is on the edge of East Los Angeles.

(18) The term "Chicano" is a slang term for a person of Mexican descent, once used as a casual term among Mexicans and as a disrespectful term by outsiders. In the 1960s era of ethnic activism, it was adopted as a proud and defiant badge of minority identity. The term is still used, but less frequently than its depoliticized equivalent, "Mexican American." Currently, the terms "Latino" and "Hispanic" are finding preference because it is inclusive of other large minorities with common cultural, but not national, roots: Cubans, Guatemalans, Puerto Ricans, Salvadorans, etc., and even Brazilians. In a 1983 poll, the Los Angeles Times asked L.A. residents of Mexican descent what they called themselves and what they wished to be called by others. The results: Mexicano 25% (preferred by foreign-born), Mexican-American 23% (preferred by American-born), Latino 18%, Hispanic 14%, Chicano 4% (Those preferring this label tended to be American-born, college educated, and under 30.) Frank Sotomayor, "'A Box Full of Ethnic Labels,'" Los Angeles Times, (25 July 1983), I-3.

(19) "Mi Abuelita" (1970) by former high-school art teacher Judy Baca in what was then known as Lincoln Park, now Plaza de la Raza. Ms. Baca also directed the mural "The Great Wall of Los Angeles," a 2,000 foot mural in Van Nuys begun in 1976 devoted to the minority experience in California history created by talented interracial high school artists. — Eva Sperling Cockcroft and Holly Barnet-Sanchez, Signs from the Heart: California Chicano Murals. (Venice, CA.: Social and Public Art Resource Center, 1990), 26-29, 76-82. John and Joe Gonzalez, "The Birth of Our Art", at the GOEZ Art Gallery, 3757 E. First Street, East Los Angeles, 1969. — Lorraine Panicacci, "TELACU Award Honors GOEZ Art Gallery," Belevedere Citizen, (1 Jan. 1976). "The Torn Wall", City Terrace: Alan Weisman, "Born in East L.A.", Los Angeles Times Magazine, (27 Mar. 1988), 13-14; Max Benavidez and Kate Vozoff, Speaking engagement on Chicano Murals, P.A.C.E. program, Harbor College, 23 Oct. 1983; Victor Valle, "Chicano Art: An Emerging Generation," Los Angeles Times, (7 Aug. 1983), Cal.-4-6.

(20) Indirectly, the Mexican muralist movement inspired the WPA mural program that graced the interior walls of public buildings across the United States during the Depression. Directly, the movement touched L.A. in the 1930s when both Orozco and Siquieros created murals for private commissions in the area. One of these, "America Tropicale" by Siqueiros on a wall in Olvera Street, caused an uproar because it depicted a mestizo Mexican crucified on a double cross under an American eagle. Such a provocative message was more than local merchants could tolerate. It was whitewashed. Another of Siquieros' murals, of similar polemical passion,

was bricked over. Orozco's safer subject, a depiction of Prometheus, has survived at Pomona College. Nancy Dustin Wall Moure, Painting and Sculpture in Los Angeles, 1900-1945. Exhibition Catalog. (Los Angeles County Museum of Art, 1980), n. 37; Shifra M. Goldman, "Siqueiros and Three Early Murals in Los Angeles," Art Journal 33 (Summer 1974), 321-327; film, "America Tropicale," edited by Shifra Goldman, produced by KCET; Suzanne Muchnic, "Orozco's `Prometheus' Centerpiece for Fiesta," Los Angeles Times, (11 Sept. 1984).

(21) Raul A. Lopez, "Art History, Relevance, and the Barrio," Art Journal 33 (Summer 1974), 333; Marcos Breton, "Murals: Symbols of Pride or Violence to East L.A. Gangs?" Los Angeles Times,(27 Oct. 1986), V-1; Barbara Baird, "Street Art — for Its Own Sake or as Statement," Los Angeles Times, (6 Feb. 1983); Richard Romo, East Los Angeles; History of a Barrio. (Austin, TX: University of Texas Press, 1983), 171; Louis Richard Negrete, A Symbolic Interactionism Perspective on the Emerging Chicano Movement Ideology in East Los Angeles, 1968-1972. Ph.D. Dissertation in Sociology. United States International University, San Diego, CA, 1976, 238246, 269; David Kahn, "Chicano Street Murals: People's Art in the East Los Angeles Barrio," Aztlan, International Journal of Chicano Students. 6 (Spring 1975), 117-121. The most readable study is: Cockcroft and BarnetSanchez, op. cit.. A catalog-guide is available, as well: Robin J. Dunitz, Street Gallery; Guide to 1000 Los Angeles Murals. (Los Angeles: RJD Enterprises, 1993).

(22) "Innocence" by Norma Montoya, 1973, is at the Estrada Courts Housing Project, 3201 Olympic Blvd. U.S. Government, Office of Housing and Urban Development, "Horizons on Display; The Murals of Estrada Courts," (Pamphlet), 1975; "Street Art Explosion in Los Angeles," Sunset. (April 1973), 110-112; Lorraine Panicacci, "A Brief Description of 40 GOEZ Murals," (Booklet) (Los Angeles: GOEZ Art Studios & Gallery, 1976); "An Indigenous Art," (Editorial), Los Angeles Times, (5 May 1976); George Beronius, "The Murals of East Los Angeles," Los Angeles Times, (April 14, 1976), Home Magazine, 10-17, 22-23; Daniel Lopez, a resident of La Estrada and a painter in the local mural group known as "Muralistics", who served as a guide for my class tours in 1976, 1977, and 1979.

(23) Estrada Court is the location of only a fraction of the more than 300 Chicano murals of the 1970s. Two other housing projects, Ramona Gardens and Maravilla, are also important sites. First Street, Soto Street, and Whittier Boulevard offer other concentrations. By 1983 it was estimated that about 30% of L.A.'s Hispanic minority rank in the middle class. Upward mobility has been expressed in the real estate market as formerly Anglo suburbs are being converted into middle-class communities of hispanic homeowners. Not surprisingly, a trend toward political conservatism has accompanied this centrifugal movement. "Upwardly Mobile Latinos Shift Their Political Views," Los Angeles Times (26 Dec. 1987), II-1. "Breaking Down the Barrios," Newsweek, (4 Sept. 1978), 85; Richard A. Garcia, "Do Zoot Suiters Deserve Hoorays?," Editorial, Los Angeles Times, (27 Aug. 1978), V6; Sylvie Drake, "'Zoot Suit': Tailor-Made as L.A. Theater," Los Angeles Times, (27 Aug. 1978), Cal-54; Sylvie Drake, "'Zoot Suit' at the Taper," Los Angeles Times, (18 Aug. 1978), IV-1; William Overend, "The '43 Zoot Suit Riots Reexamined," Los Angeles Times, (10 May 1978), IV-1; Dan Sullivan, "Putting the Boomp into 'Zoot Suit'," Los Angeles Times, (16 Apr. 1978), Cal-1.
As for muralist successes, Willie Herron was featured in a show at UCLA's Wight Gallery in 1990; Gronk had a show at the Los Angeles County Museum of Art in 1994, among others.
Quoting Bill Davis, Housing Project Manager at Estrada Courts, telephone conversations 2/1/88 and 2/4/88.

(24) In the 1990 census, two of every five residents of Los Angeles County was Hispanic. Two-thirds of the kindergartners in L.A.'s schools are Hispanic. The numbers are subject to great inaccuracies. There may have been as many as 1.1 million undocumented aliens in Los Angeles County at the time of the 1980 census many of whom feared to identify themselves. At any rate, the census found a decline of non-Hispanic whites from 57% of the L.A. City population to 48% between the 1970 census and the 1980 census. In 1983 they were estimated at 3.8 million of L.A. County's 7.9 million people, while Hispanics number 2 million, of whom 1.6 million share Mexican origins. Hispanics are expected to constitute more than half the population of both the City and the County before the year 2000. —"The New Ellis Island,'" (cited), 19; "County Reports on Tax Impact of Illegal Aliens," Los Angeles Times, (25 Dec. 1985); "L.A. Now a Minority City, 1980 Census Data Shows," Los Angeles Times, (6 Apr. 1981), I-1; Frank Sotomayor, "Latinos: Diverse Group Tied by Ethnicity," Los Angeles Times, (25 July 1983), I-1. In the 1990 census, Los Angeles City recorded 1,841,182 "white" residents (52.8%). But the number who count themselves in the new designation of "white not of hispanic origin" is only 1,299,604, or 38.3% of the population. Those who count themselves in the new category, "hispanic origin of any race" number 1,391,411, or 39.9%. — 1990 Census, General Population Characteristics... (cited), 1011.

(25) My parents' 1952 purchase in Santa Monica sold 21 years later for 13 times their purchase price. Inflated dollars account for some of this apparent gain. Gerald Nash, op. cit., 324-327; Rodney Steiner, Los Angeles, The Centrifugal City. (Dubuque, IA: Kendall-Hunt Publishing Company, 1981), 77-88; and Grimond, op. cit., 195-200. Wright,op. cit., 256; Dolores Hayden. Redesigning the American Dream: The Future of Housing, Work, and Family Life. (NY: W.W. Norton & Company, 1984), 18, 34-37, 40-42, 50, 56-57, 98, 107;

Warner, op. cit., 31-33, 143144, 147-148, 233-240; Hayden, op. cit., 34-37; Mason, op. cit., 53-65, 9798, 136-138; Wright, op. cit., 256; and Martin Mayer, op. cit., 5, 16, 6264; 207-245, 340, 356.

(26) Mumford is quoted in V. Barrett Price, "The Ultimate Western City," in South Dakota Review. Los Angeles As West. (Special Edition of the South Dakota Review) 19 (Spring/Summer, 1981), 2526. Architectural historian Reyner Banham, who loved to love the worst of L.A., admitted the monotony of its tract flatlands, which he termed "The Plains of Id." — Banham, op. cit., 161. Geographers Nelson and Clark recognized the prevalence of the image — and wrote a volume to contradict it: Nelson & Clark, op. cit., 21-28. Urban planners confirmed demographic homogeneity. — Burns & Harman, op. cit., 68. Others looked for historical explanations: "Los Angeles: Forgotten Sun," Newsweek, 27 (23 Dec. 1946), 2627; and Brienes, op. cit., 515-532; Steiner, op. cit., 14-15, 143-151. Citizens held panel discussions to evaluate their sameness. — Bill Boyarsky, "San Fernando Valley: A Refuge No More," Los Angeles Times, (20 Feb. 1983), IV-1.

(27) This pattern is regarded as a contributory factor to suburban anomie by — John Pastier, "Utopia, Suburbia, Atopia," Arts & Architecture. 2 (New Series; 1984), 64-67, 90. One might also argue that the strips, with their forest of signs and their flamboyant building forms, are what provide the sense of spacial orientation to local residents — reference points that prevent anomie. Los Angeles Department of City Planning, The Visual Environment of Los Angeles. (Los Angeles, April 1971), 28-31, 55, 60-61; and Preston, op. cit., 10-13. Jack Smith, Jack Smith's L.A.. (NY: McGraw-Hill Book Company, 1980), 56; Sam Hall Kaplan, L.A. Lost & Found; An Architectural History of Los Angeles. (NY: Crown Publishers, Inc., 1987), 144-145, 148; Banham, op. cit., 113-124, 137-139; Alan Hess, "California Coffee Shops," Arts & Architecture. 2 (New Series; 1984), 42-50; Los Angeles Department of City Planning, op. cit., 58-59.

(28) 90.4% of the housing built near Lockheed Aircraft in Burbank in the 1960s were apartments. —Mayers, op. cit., 173-174. Eichler, op. cit., 134-137. John Beach and John Chase, "The Stucco Box," in Moore, Smith, & Becker, op. cit., 118-123; David Gebhard, "L.A., The Stucco Box," Art in America. 58 (May-June 1970), 130-133; Banham, op. cit., 174-177; Kaplan, op. cit., 42, 145. L.A. City planners' suggestions for correction of tasteless and monotonous apartment houses were published in Los Angeles Department of City Planning, op. cit., 50-53.

(29) In 1967, more than 100,000 back-yard pools had been constructed in Greater Los Angeles, and this figure was growing at a rate of about a thousand a month. — Chapman, op. cit., 37; Kotkin & Grabowicz, op. cit., 14; Warner, op. cit., 120, 143-144; Pastier, op. cit., 64-66; Fogelson, op. cit., 194-196, 273-274; Grimond, op. cit., 210; Department of City Planning, op. cit., 66; Banham, op. cit., 213-215; 217-221.

(30) The Los Angeles City Municipal Arts Department created a Cultural Heritage Board in 1962 to designate and protect worthy sites and structures. A number of citizen groups formed in the '70s: Pasadena Heritage in 1976, the Los Angeles Conservancy in 1978. Los Angeles City Cultural Heritage Board, Municipal Art Department. Fact Sheets on Historic-Cultural Monuments, 1979; Patrick McGrew and Robert Julian, Landmarks of Los Angeles. (N.Y.: Harry N. Abrams, Inc., 1994).
Two examples of the revisionist trend in historiography are: Walton Bean. California, An Interpretative History, (NY: McGraw-Hill Book Company, 1968), and Leonard Pitt, California Controversies; Major Issues in the History of the State. (Glenview, IL: Scott, Foresman and Company, 1968).
Penepole Pollard and I initiated a course in the Humanities Department at Los Angeles Valley College titled "The Cultural Heritage of Los Angeles" in the Spring 1976 semester.

(31) Interview with Tom and Pat Hodges, 30 June 1983. See also: Paul Dean, "On Mountaintop in Malibu, One Man's Home is Literally a Castle," Los Angeles Times,(27 Feb. 1981), V-1; Suzanne Schlosberg, "Keeper of the Castle," Los Angeles Times, (18 June 1988); Mary Ann Beach Harrel, " The Vernacular Castle," in Moore, Smith, & Becker, op. cit., 72-75; and Gill, op. cit., 134-135. Gill's book, along with: Charles Jencks, Daydream Houses of Los Angeles. (NY: Rizzoli, 1978), and Michelle Bekey, "Beverly Hills," American Preservation, 3 (JanFeb 1980), 47-58, present pictorial lampoons of such eccentric residences of recent vintage. Doug Smith, "Duplications of Grandeur," Los Angeles Times, (3 Aug. 1986), II-4.

(32) Michael Webb, "A Man Who Made Architecture an Art of the Unexpected," Smithsonian. (April 1987), 48-59; Gleye, op. cit., 165-166; Elizabeth McMillian and Leslie Heumann, "New Venice," Society of Architectural Historians, Southern California Chapter Newsletter 5 (Apr. 1981), 3; Gebhard & King, op. cit., 54-55; "Architect of the Year: Frank Gehry," Arts & Architecture 1 (Fall 1981), 28-29; "Trendy Projects Win Most AIA Awards," Los Angeles Times,(13 Oct. 1985), VIII-1; "Gehry: Quite the Man About Town," Los Angeles Times, (21 Feb. 1988), VIII-2. Henry N. Cobb, The Architecture of Frank Gehry. (NY: Rizzoli, 1987).

(33) This photograph was taken in 1979, at the height of the controversy. Basten, op. cit., 27, 50; "Sunset Sheiks," Newsweek, (10 July 1978), 12; "Sheik's Nude Statues No Longer Cavort," "Unblushing Statues Back on Pedestals," "Is the Sheikh's Mansion in Beverly Hills for Sale?", "Fire at Sheik's Mansion Evokes Little Sympathy," "Sheik's Mansion Will Be Demolished," in Los Angeles Times, (14 July 1978, 15 July 1978, 4 Feb. 1979, 3 Jan. 1980, and 12 May 1985, respectively).

(34) Roselle M. Lewis, "An Ammunition Belt for Defenders of the City of Angels," Los Angeles Times Home Magazine (24 June 1979), 3; Mike Rokyo, "Should America Fence Off California?", Los Angeles Times, (23 Apr. 1979), II-11; Chapman, op. cit., 41; Edward Thorp, The Other Hollywood. (London: Michael Joseph, 1970); Lawrence Dietz, "Michelangelo Meets McDonald's: The Los Angeles Cultural Map," New West, Vol. 1, No. 15 (Nov. 8, 1976), pp. 50-55; Alan Cartnal, California Crazy. (Boston: Houghton Mifflin Company, 1981).

(35) James W. Toland (editor), The Music Center Story: A Decade of Achievement, 1964-1974. (L.A.: The Music Center Foundation, 1974); Bruce Henstell, "Chords and Discords," Westways, Sept. 1977, 28-31, 75; Patricia Bowie, "From Spanish Guitar to Pioneer Banjo to Symphonic Strings: A Cultural Transformation in Southern California," and Marian G. Cannon, "His Music Left an Echo: A Biography of Harley Hamilton, 1861-1933," both in The Californians. 1 (May/June 1983), 20-30 and 31-34; "65 and Still Growing," Terra. 16 (Winter 1978), 21-24; Grimond, op. cit., 182, 187; Nelson & Clark, op. cit., 61. "Art Goes to the Bank, Earns Interest," Los Angeles Times, (21 July 1978), IV-1; "CBS Gives $2.1 Million to 12 L.A. Groups," Los Angeles Times, (22 Sept. 1978), II-2; "Arco Opens Exhibit Center," Los Angeles Times, (3 May 1976), IV-1; "ARCO to Close Its Art Gallery," Los Angeles Times, (27 June 1984), VI-1; "On the Passing of ARCO's Center for Visual Art," Los Angeles Times, (1 Aug. 1984), VI-1. Grimond, op. cit., 204-208; "Museum Mania Grips the Globe; L.A. at Center," Los Angeles Times, (23 May 1987), I-1; "It's a Given: L.A. Has Earned the Respect of Collectors," Los Angeles Times, (10 July 1983), Calendar-78; "State of the Arts," Los Angeles Times, (15 May 1983), Calendar: 3-11, 44, 51, 59-61, 86-87, 96; "Los Angeles" The Fizz that Was — and Is," Los Angeles Times, (29 May 1983), Cal: 4-29; "Los Angeles: Redesigned for the Arts," Los Angeles Times, (10 Oct. 1987); Hunter Drohojowska, "LACMA Expands," and Michael Sorkin, "Critique," in Arts & Architecture 2 (New Series, 1983), 26-28 and 29-30; "The Scrutable Joe Price and His Museum," Los Angeles Times, (23 Dec. 1984), Cal. 83,85; "The County Museum of Art — at 20, Almost Grown Up," Los Angeles Times, (31 Mar. 1985), Cal:3-4; "A Museum Goes Mod," Los Angeles Times, (18 Nov. 1986), Cal: 4-7; "Museum Facade and Art Function: New Babylon Meets Wilshire Boulevard," Los Angeles Times, (15 Nov. 1987), V-3; "Battle for the Masterpieces," Los Angeles Times Magazine,, (22 May 1988), 8-19; "The Simon Caches in on Treasures," Los Angeles Times, (29 Jan. 1984), Cal:84-85; "Shrewd Move," Los Angeles Times, (1 Mar. 1987), Cal-4; "A New Look at Huntington," Los Angeles Times, (30 Sept. 1981), V-1; Michael Olmert, "Truth and Beauty Are Still in Flower at the Huntington," Smithsonian, (Feb. 1982), 64-72; "New Gallery Colonizes the Huntington," Los Angeles Times, (8 July 1984), Cal-3; "The Huntington's Glorious Restoration," Los Angeles Times, (28 Sept. 1986), Cal:6-7; "2 Visions of Hope: Modern Art Museum(s) and Bunker Hill," Los Angeles Times, (2 Sept. 1979), Cal:1,81; "Temporary Contemporary: Its Time Is Now," Los Angeles Times, (20 Nov. 1983), Cal:5-7; John Pastier, "MOCA Builds," Arts & Architecture 2 (New Series, 1983), 3135; Wayne Warga, "Something Special for February," Westways. (Feb. 1984), 67; "Panza Purchase Shifts Balance Toward MOCA," Los Angeles Times, (11 Mar. 1984), Cal:92-93; "Bigger is Better at Contemporary Museum," Los Angeles Times, (15 Mar. 1984); "MOCA: A Downtown Oasis in a Former Wasteland," Los Angeles Times, (25 Aug. 1985), Cal:92; "A Heavenly Addition to City of Angels," Los Angeles Times, (30 Nov. 1986), Cal:4-5.

(36) Nelson & Clark, op. cit., 21-24. The downtown redevelopment projects have given downtown a new focus.

(37) Los Angeles City Planning Department, "Information Paper,"(pamphlet), 1972; ——,"Concept Los Angeles; The Concept of the Los Angeles General Plan," 1974; ——, 'History of Los Angeles, 1781-2001" (Centers Implementation Program Information Document), March 1983; ——, Keeping the Good Life: Can We Protect Our Lifestyle in the FAce of Growth and Change?" (brochure), March 1983; ——, The Visual Environment of Los Angeles, (cited), pp. 28-33.
Between 1979 and 1983 my students and I heard informative, persuasive, and impassioned presentations on this subject by Jon Perica, Gurdon Miller, and Peter Lynch of the Los Angeles City Planning Department. Los Angeles is not a solid spot on the map, but one riddled with holes representing autonomous cities and unincorporated areas. Its shape was politically determined — its long tentacle reaching to the harbor, in particular. Any comprehensive planning involves multiple agencies of government. In order to widen a boulevard the cooperation and coordination of the other cities through which it extends is necessary. Air pollution regulations cannot be handled independently by one city government or another within the Greater L.A. Basin. Super-agencies, such as the Southern California Air Quality Management District have been created as an umbrella. Still, in order to get action on a specific measure, it must get each of 70 local government bodies to pass ordinances. One of the most obvious obstacles to the implementation of the General Plan is its dependence on public transportation and extensions of the freeway network. At its inception, this did not seem impossible, since federal funds were available. Since that time, the Reagan Administrations, first at the state and then the federal level, have cut hopes.

A bond issue for a pilot transit system, the Downtown People Mover, though strenuously promoted by the Los Angeles Times, failed at the polls. The shared power of several governmental agencies has produced many examples of the "push-me-pull-you" syndrome. The General Plan adopted by Los Angeles County's Department of Regional Planning in 1970 was so aggressively pro-growth that concerned citizens went to court. "New Master Plan for County Unveiled," Los Angeles Times, (30 Jan. 1978), II-1. In 1994, City officials were scrambling to set up public hearings for a replacement General Plan since the current one expires in 1998. Another reform that restricts growth is the requirement imposed by the State of California in 1972, for Environmental Impact Reports (EIRs), evaluating the potential harm of a project to wildlife habitats, archeological artifacts, air quality, water, and the flavor and density of the existing neighborhood. EIRs are costly and time-consuming and a recognized factor in the high cost of homes in Southern California, they restrain development and illustrate the reform zeal that surfaced in the late '60s-early '70s period. — Steiner, op. cit., 196-197; and Los Angeles Department of Planning, "Information Paper," (cited), 6.

(38) Proposals for slum clearance on Bunker Hill were voiced during World War II, as part of the advanced planning for the war's end. — Dan Cherrier and Miles Swanson, "Bunker Hill: Rehabilitation of a Blighted Area," California Arts and Architecture 60 (July 1943), 32-34. The City of Los Angeles had set up the CRA in 1948, for the purpose of conducting such a project. The amendment to the State Constitution which permitted tax increment financing, and thus made possible the kind of comprehensive redevelopment the CRA contemplated, was passed in 1955. Federal funds were subsequently acquired for the project. The final plan was adopted by City Council in 1959. Eminent domain procedures began on Bunker Hill that year but a series of legal objections and appeals held up new building projects until 1964. U.S. Supreme Court action in that year cleared the way for the dynamic building program that is now in its final stage of completion. —Community Redevelopment Agency of Los Angeles, "Bunker Hill Urban Renewal Project: History and Program for Completion," (Report prepared for the Bunker Hill Biennial Review), Feb. 24, 1982, 1-3.

(39) "Bunker Hill Housing Plan Gets Go-Ahead," Los Angeles Times, (1 Sept. 1977), II-1; "Financing OK'd for Elderly Housing Project," Los Angeles Times, (2 Jan. 1979); "U.S. Project Changes Face of Bunker Hill," Los Angeles Times, (20 Feb. 1979), II-1; "Housing Blossoms in Arid Downtown," Los Angeles Times, (26 July 1983). Angelus Plaza won a design award from the Los Angeles Chapter of the American Institute of Architects and the top award in the high-rise category in a nationwide competition for concrete buildings. — "Design Winner," Los Angeles Times, (20 Mar. 1983), VI-20; "Dworsky Firm Big Winner in Los Angeles AIA Awards," Los Angeles Times, (30 Oct. 1983), VIII-1.

(40) Newspaper advertisements for tract openings from the late 1970s into the '80s (when condominiums and tracts in distant counties took their place) often showed peculiar combinations of historical style references — almost like the 1880s. For example, a Kaufman & Broad ad in the Los Angeles Times, (21 Apr. 1985), VIII-3, shows a model with Tudor half-timbering, Palladian windows, and peaked dormers — with a Spanish tile roof. The nine models were labelled, "The California Series."

(41) Eichler, op. cit., 135-143; Mason, op. cit., 117-118, 134; Steiner, op. cit., 57. In a 1981 survey of the merchant builders operating in Southern California, the Los Angeles Times found that of 15,503 dwelling units constructed that year, 7,751, or 50%, were single-family units, 1,629 (10.5%) were apartment units, and the remaining 6,123 (35.5%) were condo units. — "Worst 12 Months in 36 Years," Los Angeles Times, (21 Mar. 1982), VII-1. Mayer, op. cit., 340, 348-349; "Snyder Co. Buys Marina City Club," Los Angeles Times, (10 Aug. 1986); An ad for the Marina City condos two years later priced one to three bedroom units from $188,000 to $479,000, penthouses from $758,800 to $916,300. — Los Angeles Times, (17 July 1988), VIII-3.

(42) "Housing Affordability Takes a Fall," Los Angeles Times, (12 June 1988), VIII-1; Mayer, op. cit., 356; "Housing Forecast: 1988 Starts Down, but Far from Out," Los Angeles Times, (17 Jan. 1988), VIII-1; "The Affordability Gap," Los Angeles Times, (15 May 1988), VIII-1; a chart comparing Southern California home prices to the national level is shown in Los Angeles Times, (22 Nov. 1981), VII-4; See also, "'Feeding Frenzy' Engulfs Southland Home Market," Los Angeles Times, (17 June 1988), I-1; "Dream to Own Still Going Strong," Los Angeles Times, (14 July 1985); "Housing Industry Will Never Be the Same Again, Experts Say," Los Angeles Times, (18 July 1982), IV-1; Chuck Halloran, "L.A. - The Third Century City," The UCLA Monthly 11 (May-June, 1981), 2; Grebler, op. cit., 200.

(43) Illustration 172: "Carnaby Square," 10140/10150 Reseda Blvd., Northridge. This 1981 project, originally painted a garish blue, with cream trim, was slow to fill. An active sales promotion lasted two years. Illustrations 174: "Sea Colony," Notice the similarity to the Streamline Moderne on the front: the ship railings and portholes, blank visage toward the street. Like Gregory Ain's Edwards House (Illustrations 122-124), which shares these streetside features, the back opens up to sunshine and privacy. Although this is a very large complex, bordering the public beach, each balcony-terrace is private. Billed as luxury condos, the original purchase price, in 1980 dollars, was: 2 bedrooms from $290,000, penthouses from $410,000. (ad, Los Angeles Times, (28 Sept. 1980), IX-33) Permission to build at

Notes

the beach site was obtained from the California Coastal Commission on the proviso that a certain number of units would be offered at low or moderate cost. —<u>Society of Architectural Historians, Southern California Chapter Newsletter</u> 5 (Apr. 1981), 4.

(44) Quotation: Irving Gill, "The Home of the Future: The New Architecture of the West: Small Homes for a Great Country: by Irving J. Gill: Number Four," <u>The Craftsman</u> 30 (May 1916), 140.

(45) An air conditioning serviceman, chatty clerical workers at lunch, and half-empty parking structures during working hours (1993 and 1994) testify to low occupancy. The frequent changes in management and ownership of the downtown towers also indicate the economic instability.

(46) Television coverage is central to my thesis, here, but the material I reviewed for the Civil Disorder is in my collection of <u>Los Angeles Times</u> coverage daily from 30 April 1992 through 12 May 1992 and review of 22 May 1922, and <u>Newsweek</u> (11 May 1992). The material I reviewed for the Northridge Earthquake is in my collection of <u>Los Angeles Times</u> daily issues from 18 Jan. 1994 through 23 Jan. 1994. An estimated 3.7 million viewers saw the beating of Reginal Denny in 1992. The October 1992 fires drew a 3.5 million local TV audience. A recap of high viewer moments is included in: "Simpson Chase, Capture Draw High TV Ratings," <u>Los Angeles Times</u>, (21 June 1994), F-2.

(47) I was serving as an intern to a City Council office at the time, and assigned to this program. The proposals were voted by Council in July 1980. But the E.P.A. enforcement mechanism was subsequently dismantled under the Reagan administration, and the whole program unevenly instituted at the local level. "We're No More Car Crazy Than the Folks Down the Road," <u>Los Angeles Times</u>, (20 June 1994), B-1.

(48) No one seems to know what percentage of the damaged structures were or weren't insured. The 20th Century Insurance Company, the largest auto insurer in the region, has announced a withdrawal from homeowners insurance. Since its rates were approximately 40% lower than leading competitors, its removal is expected to result in a spurt of new rate increases from the remaining insurers.

(49) Number of building inspections from Los Angeles City Department of Building and Safety, 28 June 1994. "Valley: Hidden Homeless," <u>Los Angeles Times</u>, 5 July 1994, B4; "A Hard Fall from Grace," <u>Los Angeles Times</u>, 7 October 1994, E4.

(50) Conversations July 1993, April 1994, May 1994, and March 1994, respectively. The image of a rainbow touching earth in the southern portion of a map of California accompanies a human interest article on the dreams of recent arrivals to Los Angeles: "An Illusion Too Real to Fade," <u>Los Angeles Times</u>, (20 June 1994), A-1. Migration from other states into California in 1993 was the lowest since the beginning of World War II, according to a recent news article. Los Angeles County only added 71,800 in 1993. — "Population Growth at New Low," <u>Los Angeles Times</u>, (18 May 1994), A-3.

INDEX

DESIGN AND TYPOGRAPHY BY Mike Fink x height

PRINTING AND IMAGING BY Navigator Press

LOS ANGELES: *The End of the Rainbow* was set in **Truesdell**,
designed by Fredric Goudy in 1931, and **Metro**, designed by
W.A. Dwiggins in 1932. Monotype's new PostScript version
of **Truesdell** was digitized by Steve Matteson in 1993
from letterpress proofs of 16-point fonts which reside at the
ROCHESTER INSTITUTE OF TECHNOLOGY.